Ancient Maritime Loan Contracts

LAW AND SOCIETY IN THE ANCIENT WORLD

The study of law in ancient societies has a distinguished tradition in both Anglo-American and continental scholarship. Many of our fundamental ideas about ancient society were built on research into legal sources. These traditions continue to provide a foundation for newer approaches to law and society. More recent scholarship draws on a range of methodologies to analyze legal practices, including critical legal studies, sociology of law, economics, and literary criticism.

This series, distinguished by its emphasis on interdisciplinary approaches to law and society, seeks out innovative approaches to ancient legal studies that bring new perspectives to legal topics as well as to broader questions concerning the impact of law on commercial, political, and cultural practices in the ancient world.

Recent Titles in the Series

Ancient Maritime Loan Contracts
Peter Candy

The Reputation of the Roman Merchant
Jane Sancinito

The Discovery of the Fact
Clifford Ando and William P. Sullivan, Editors

Law and Transaction Costs in the Ancient Economy
Dennis P. Kehoe, David M. Ratzan, and Uri Yiftach, Editors

The Law of Ancient Athens
David D. Phillips

Ancient Maritime Loan Contracts

Peter Candy

University of Michigan Press

Ann Arbor

Published in the United States of America by the
University of Michigan Press
Printed and bound by CPI Group (UK) Ltd, Croydon, CR0 4YY

First published January 2025

A CIP catalog record for this book is available from the British Library.

Library of Congress Cataloging-in-Publication Data

Names: Candy, Peter (Peter Frank), author. | Michigan Publishing (University of Michigan), publisher.
Title: Ancient maritime loan contracts / Peter Candy.
Other titles: Law and society in the ancient world.
Description: Ann Arbor [Michigan] : University of Michigan Press, 2025. | Series: Law and Society in the Ancient World | Includes bibliographical references (pages 207–226) and indexes. | Texts in English, transcriptions of papyri in Ancient Greek.
Identifiers: LCCN 2024031903 (print) | LCCN 2024031904 (ebook) | ISBN 9780472133550 (hardcover) | ISBN 9780472221905 (ebook)
Subjects: LCSH: Contracts, Maritime (Greek law) | Contracts, Maritime (Roman law) | Law, Ancient. | Mediterranean Region—Commerce—History.
Classification: LCC KL4316 .C36 2025 (print) | LCC KL4316 (ebook) | DDC 343.3809/6—dc23/eng/20240805
LC record available at https://lccn.loc.gov/2024031903
LC ebook record available at https://lccn.loc.gov/2024031904

DOI: https://doi.org/10.3998/mpub.12705344

This book will be made open access within three years of publication thanks to Path to Open, a program developed in partnership between JSTOR, the American Council of Learned Societies (ACLS), University of Michigan Press, and The University of North Carolina Press to bring about equitable access and impact for the entire scholarly community, including authors, researchers, libraries, and university presses around the world. Learn more at https://about.jstor.org/path-to-open/

Cover illustration: A restored fresco from the "House of the Orchard," Pompeii. Courtesy of the Ministry of Culture, Archaeological Park of Pompeii, Italy.

To my parents

Mental frameworks are also prisons of the *longue durée.*
—Fernand Braudel

Contents

Abbreviations

Citations of ancient texts are done in accordance with standard scholarly conventions. All abbreviated references to authors from classical antiquity and their works follow the conventions in the *Oxford Classical Dictionary* (4th ed.) and the Liddell-Scott-Jones *Greek-English Lexicon* (9th ed.). All abbreviated references to papyri and epigraphic sources follow the conventions in those disciplines.

AIUK	Attic Inscriptions in UK Collections
AJA	*American Journal of Archaeology*
AUPA	*Annali del Seminario Giuridico della Università di Palermo*
Bas	Basilica (ed. H. J. Scheltema–N. van der Wal)
Bas Schol	Basilicorum Scholia (ed. H. J. Scheltema–D. Holwerda)
BASP	*Bulletin of the American Society of Papyrologists*
BICS	*Bulletin of the Institute of Classical Studies*
BIDR	*Bullettino dell'Istituto di diritto romano*
C	Codex of Justinian
Camodeca, *TPS*	Camodeca, G. *Tabulae Pompeianae Sulpiciorum (TPSulp.): Edizione critica dell'archivio puteolano dei Sulpicii*. 2 vols. (Rome: Quasar, 1999)
Carey	Carey, C. *Lysiae orationes cum fragmentis* (Oxford: Oxford University Press, 2007)
CCGG	*Cahiers du Centre Gustave Glotz*
CIL	Mommsen, Th., et al., eds., *Corpus Inscriptionum Latinarum*, 17 vols. (Berlin: BBAW, 1863–)
CTh	Code of Theodosius
D	Digest of Justinian
DDbDP	Duke Databank of Documentary Papyri
Dike	*Dike: Rivista di storia del diritto greco ed ellenistico*
G	Institutes of Gaius

GRBS	*Greek, Roman, and Byzantine Studies*
Historia	*Historia: Zeitschrift für Alte Geschichte*
HRP	Babusiaux, U., C. Baldus, W. Ernst, F.-S. Meissel, J. Platschek, and T. Rüfner, eds. *Handbuch des Römischen Privatrechts*. 3 vols. (Tübingen: Mohr Siebeck, 2023)
IG II^2	Kirchner, J., ed. *Inscriptiones Graecae: Vol. II et III. Inscriptiones Atticae Euclidis anno posteriores. Editio altera* (Berlin: De Gruyter, 1913–40)
ILS	Dessau, H., ed. *Inscriptiones latinae selectae*, 3 vols. (Berlin: Apud Weidmannos, 1892–1916)
Index	*Index: Quaderni camerti di studi romanistici*
J. Inst	Institutes of Justinian
IVRA	*IVRA: Rivista internazionale di diritto romano e antico*
JAH	*Journal of Ancient History*
JHS	*Journal of Hellenic Studies*
JJP	*Journal of Juristic Papyrology*
JRS	*Journal of Roman Studies*
Kaser, *RP*	Kaser, M. *Das römische Privatrecht*. 2 vols. (Munich: C.H. Beck, 1971)
Kaser, *RZ*	Kaser, M. *Das römische Zivilprozessrecht*. 2nd ed., rev. K. Hackl (Munich: C.H. Beck, 1996)
Labeo	*Labeo: Rassegna di diritto romano*
Lenel, *EP*^{3}	Lenel, O. *Das Edictum perpetuum: Ein Versuch zu dessen Wiederherstellung*, 3rd ed. (Leipzig: Tauchnitz, 1927)
Lenel, *Pal*	Lenel, O. *Palingenesia Iuris Civilis*, 2 vols. (Leipzig: Tauchnitz, 1889)
LSJ	Liddell, H. G., and R. Scott, *A Greek-English Lexicon*, 9th ed., rev. H. S. Jones with the assistance of R. MacKenzie, with revised supplement (Oxford: Oxford University Press, 1996)
Nov	Novels of Justinian
Polis	*Polis: Journal for Ancient Greek and Roman Political Thought*
PS	Pauli Sententiae
RDN	*Rivista di diritto della navigazione*
RIDA	*Revue internationale des droits de l'Antiquité*
RHD	*Revue historique de droit français et étranger*
SDHI	*Studia et documenta historiae et iuris*
TAPhA	*Transactions and Proceedings of the American Philological Association*

TH	*Tabula(e) Herculanensis(es)*
TP	*Tabula(e) Pompeiana(e) (= TPN/ TPSulp)*
TPN	*Tabula(e) Pompeiana(e) Nova(e) (= TP/ TPSulp)*
TPSulp	*Tabula(e) Pompeiana(e) Sulpiciorum (= TP/ TPN)*
TvR	*Tijdschrift voor Rechtsgeschiedenis*
Tyche	*Tyche: Beiträge zur Alten Geschichte, Papyrologie und Epigraphik*
Wolf, *TPN*	Wolf, J. G. *Neue Rechtsurkunden aus Pompeji: Tabulae Pompeianae Novae* (Darmstadt: WBG, 2010)
ZPE	*Zeitschrift für Papyrologie und Epigraphik*
ZRG RA	*Zeitschrift der Savigny-Stiftung für Rechtsgeschichte. Romanistische Abteilung*

Preface

Maritime loan contracts, or *nautikai syngraphai*, were documents recording the terms of agreement on which a creditor lent a sum of money to a merchant or carrier to finance the purchase of a cargo for a trading expedition overseas. The unique and distinguishing feature of the contract was the inclusion of a clause by which the debtor's obligation to repay the principal with interest was made conditional upon the safe arrival of the ship at its final destination (the so-called condition *salva nave*). In this sense the transaction combined the loan with an element of insurance. They were the lifeblood of *emporía*, the long-distance trade in commodities that flourished in the Mediterranean and Black Seas, probably from about the eighth century BCE. They were also among the first private agreements to be committed to writing *in extenso*; and from at least the late fifth century BCE—our earliest evidence for the institution—they were highly standardized in their terms, containing boilerplate clauses in a tried-and-tested construction. Maritime loan contracts were a familiar feature of maritime trade in the Mediterranean world from at least the late fifth century BCE through to the late Middle Ages (the best part of 2,000 years), when they were eventually superseded by the contract of marine insurance.[1] This study is dedicated to the first millennium of their existence, that is, from their inception to the time of Justinian (sixth century CE).

My motivations for writing this book are twofold. The first is to provide a holistic account of the history of maritime loan contracts and their various lives both at the heart of the ancient economic system and as objects of dispute, interpretation, and analysis in the legal systems of both classical Athens and Rome. The main challenge in this respect is that the evidence for maritime loan con-

1. See S. Lohsse, "Vom Seedarlehen zur Versicherung in der mittelalterlichen Rechtswissenschaft," *ZRG RA* 133 (2016): 372–99; also, Phillip Hellwege and Guido Rossi, "Maritime Risk Management. Marine Insurance, General Average, Sea Loan," in *Maritime Risk Management: Essays on the History of Marine Insurance, General Average and Sea Loan*, ed. Phillip Hellwege and Guido Rossi (Berlin: Duncker & Humblot, 2021), 9–16.

tracts during the period is fragmentary, diverse, and thinly distributed. We have only very limited opportunities to study them directly. Though no complete original contract has survived, we have the (main) terms of two such documents by report. We also have two original documents that might represent part of a maritime loan contract—but their identification is uncertain. Otherwise, we are compelled to approach them only indirectly: through the speeches of the Attic orators (fourth century BCE); the writings of the Roman jurists (first century BCE—early third century CE); imperial constitutions (third—sixth century CE); and through references to maritime loan contracts in connected loan documentation (interspersed second century BCE—second century CE). Unsurprisingly, the fragmentation of the evidence is reflected in the state of the literature, which is broadly divided between studies into the commercial documents,[2] their appearance in the Athenian orations,[3] and their treatment in Roman law.[4] One of the aims of this study is to produce a holistic account that shows their significance in both an economic and legal context.

The second motivation is to use maritime loan contracts as a means of studying more closely the relationship between law and commerce in the ancient world. In the ancient Mediterranean, long-distance trade was conducted using standard form contracts that governed the relationship between merchants and financiers (maritime loan contracts), merchants and carriers (contracts of affreightment), and merchants and warehousemen (storage contracts). These standard forms comprised the structural underpinnings of seaborne trade, showing a remarkable degree of continuity for over two millennia. In this sense, they were creatures of the *longue durée* since they represented the response of traders to their environment and the exigencies of carriage by sea. These long durational aspects are picked up in the first and second chapters, which address the commercial documents and their place in the economic system, respectively.

In the remaining chapters, attention turns to the response of individual legal cultures to maritime loan contracts, and the interaction between international commercial practice and legal institutions in those special contexts. In this respect, the evidence confines us to classical Athens and Rome; though but for the chance of survival, we might equally have been able to examine the

2. E.g., Federico De Romanis, *The Indo-Roman Pepper Trade and the Muziris Papyrus* (Oxford: Oxford University Press, 2020).

3. E.g., Stephan Schuster, *Das Seedarlehen in den Gerichtsreden des Demosthenes: Mit einem Ausblick auf die weitere historische Entwicklung des Rechtsinstitutes: dáneion nautikón, fenus nauticum und Bodmerei* (Berlin: Duncker und Humblot, 2005).

4. E.g., Ivano Pontoriero, *Il prestito marittimo in diritto romano* (Bologna: Bononia University Press, 2011)

responses of other cultures, including other Hellenic *poleis* (e.g., Rhodes, Syracuse), the Punic cities (e.g., Carthage), and Egypt under the Ptolemies. Chapter 3 therefore examines the continuity of commercial practice with dispute resolution at classical Athens and Rome; chapter 4 the responses of each of those legal cultures to the common problems of interpretation thrown up by maritime loan contracts; and chapter 5 the Graeco-Roman mental framework that governed their understanding of finance, with its implications for the treatment of maritime loan contracts in Roman law from the perspective of the regulation of interest rates. Appendix I contains an excursus on the specific problem of the enforcement of maritime loan contracts in Roman law, which informs the analysis in the second part of chapter 3.

A few brief remarks on translations and transliteration. I have generally endeavored to provide my own translation of the texts. Where I have used translations by other scholars, this has been noted. Editions of the Greek and Latin documents that I have translated in the first chapter may be found in appendix II. For texts that I have translated, but which do not appear in appendix II, interested readers will need to consult the authoritative scholarly editions. With regard to transliteration, I have preferred to take a literal approach, to preserve the contrast between the Greek and Roman material. I transliterate the Greek diphthong epsilon-iota as *-ei-* (not *-i-*); *-e-* stands for epsilon (ε), *-ē-* for eta (η); *-o-* stands for omicron (ο), *-ō-* for omega (ω).

I would like to thank Professor Paul du Plessis, Professor John Cairns, and the readers at the University of Michigan Press for their generosity in reading the manuscript and for providing me with the benefit of their knowledge and criticism. I am also grateful to the Executive Committee, the series editors, and the copyediting and production team at the University of Michigan Press; and most especially to Ellen Bauerle, Senior Acquiring Editor for Classical Studies, for their support in publishing this book. I would also like to record my gratitude to Augusto Aquila, for his assistance in the preparation of the manuscript. Naturally, I am solely responsible for any errors that remain. I owe special thanks to my late uncle, Roy Bishop, for allowing me the use of his home at Craobh Haven, Argyll, as a place to think and write; and to Lee Roy and Mark Gillanders for encouraging me in the completion of this project. To all these and to the countless others who have supported me in my work, I am grateful.

Peter Candy
Cambridge
March 2024

Ancient Maritime Loan Contracts

CHAPTER ONE

Maritime Loan Contracts

Evidence for the Contents of Maritime Loan Contracts

We have four documents that may represent the contents of a maritime loan contract from the ancient period. Only two of these can almost certainly be linked to a genuine *nautikē syngraphē*: the first, a contract produced in the fourth-century-BCE oration *Against Lakritos* (Dem. 35.10–13); and the second, the main clauses of an agreement that provided the basis for a legal discussion by the second-century Roman jurist Q. Cervidius Scaevola (D.45.1.122.1). Another document (SB III 7169), the (copy of a) loan contract connected with the financing of an expedition from Alexandria to (probably) the Punt that was concluded at Ptolemaic Alexandria during the first half of the second century BCE, might be a maritime loan contract, but is too lacunose to determine. Quite likely the recto of the so-called Muziris papyrus (SB XVIII 13167, second century CE), which records terms related to a trading expedition between Alexandria and the Malabar coast, has preserved the latter half of a maritime loan contract; but again the identification of the document is uncertain. These fragments are complemented by a range of other documentary sources, several of which belonged to more extensive dossiers that sometimes cross-refer to maritime loan contracts. Together, these documents form the basis for a study into the structure of *nautikai syngraphai*, their typical clauses, and how the standard terms hung together as a whole.

Dem. 35.10–13[1]

The earliest of the extant contracts and the only one to be transmitted in a complete form consists of a document introduced into an oration delivered by Androklēs of Sphettos *Against Lakritos* in the late 350s or early 340s BCE.

1. See appendix II, no. 1.

Though the authorship of the oration, which is traditionally attributed to Demosthenes, is uncertain, there is little doubt that the speech is a genuine fourth-century production and that the documents adduced as evidence by the speaker are authentic.[2] I give the contract in translation followed by a summary of its terms:

> [10] Androklēs of Sphettos and Nausikratēs of Karystos lent to Artemōn and Apollodōros, both of Phaselis, 3,000 drachmae in silver for a voyage from Athens to Mendē or Skionē, and from there to Bosporos—or if they so choose, for a voyage to the left parts of the Black Sea as far as the Borysthenes—and thence back to Athens, on interest at the rate of two hundred and twenty-five drachmae on the thousand; but, if they should sail out from the Black Sea to Hieron after the rising of Arktouros, at three hundred on the thousand, on the security of three thousand jars of Mendean wine, which shall be conveyed from Mendē or Skionē in the twenty-oared ship of which Hyblesios is owner. [11] They give these goods as security, owing no money upon them to any other person, nor will they make any additional loan upon this security; and they agree to bring back to Athens in the same vessel all the goods put on board in the Black Sea as a return cargo; and, if the goods are brought safe to Athens, the borrowers are to pay to the lenders the money due in accordance with the agreement within twenty days after they shall have arrived at Athens, without deduction except for such jettison as those sailing in the ship may have made by common agreement, and anything they may pay to enemies; but without deduction for any other loss. And until such time as they shall themselves have paid the money due in accordance with the contract they shall admit the creditors control over the goods offered as security, which must not be liable to any (other) seizure. [12] And, if they shall not pay it within the time agreed upon, it shall be lawful for the lenders to pledge the goods or even to sell them for such price as they can get; and if the proceeds fall short of the sum which the lenders should receive in accordance with the contract, it shall be law-

2. The *communis opinio* is that the document reported in the speech is authentic: Schuster, *Das Seedarlehen*, 131 (with earlier literature); also, Douglas M. MacDowell, *Demosthenes, Speeches 27–38* (Austin: University of Texas Press, 2004), 15 and 131; Alain Bresson, *L'économie de la Grèce des cités (fin VIe-Ier siècle a. C.)*, vol. 2 (Paris: A. Colin, 2008), 67. For the procedure concerning the production of documents during the hearing of a case, Mirko Canevaro, *The Documents in the Attic Orators: Laws and Decrees in the Public Speeches of the Demosthenic Corpus* (Oxford: Oxford University Press, 2013), 1–2.

ful for the lenders, whether severally or jointly, to collect the amount by proceeding against Artemōn and Apollodōros, and against all their property whether on land or sea, wheresoever they [the debtors] may be, precisely as if judgment had been rendered against them and they had defaulted in payment. [13] And, if they do not enter the Black Sea, but remain in the Hellespont ten days after the rising of the Dog Star and disembark their goods at a port where the Athenians have no right of reprisals, and from thence complete their voyage to Athens, let them pay the interest written into the contract the year before. And if the vessel in which the goods shall be conveyed suffers aught beyond repair, but the security is saved, let whatever is saved be the joint property of the lenders. And regarding these matters nothing shall have greater legal authority than (this) contract.

Witnesses: Phormiōn of Piraeus, Kephisodotos of Boeotia, Helidoros of Pithos.

Androklēs, of Sphettos, a deme in Attica, and his 'friend' Nausikratēs, of Karystos, a *polis* in the south of Euboea, had lent to Artemon and Apollodōros, both from Phaselis on the south coast of Lykia in Asia Minor, 3,000 drachmae (half a talent) for a maritime venture from Athens to the Black Sea coast and back again. According to the written agreement, the borrowers were obliged to travel first to either Mendē or Skionē, both towns on the westernmost promontory of Chalkidikē in central Macedonia, where they were to acquire a consignment of Mendean wine, which they would then ship either to the Cimmerian Bosporos (a kingdom centered at Pantikapaion, located at the eastern end of the Crimean Peninsula overlooking the Kerch Strait) or to a destination on the west coast of the Black Sea as far as the modern Dneiper.[3] Once there, they were to sell the wine and use the proceeds to purchase a new cargo (probably grain) for transport back to Athens. The same vessel—an *eikosoros* owned by Hyblesios (literally a twenty-oared ship, but by the fourth century BCE a merchant vessel)—was to be chartered for both the outward and return voyages.

In return for the use of the money, Artemōn and Apollodōros agreed to pay a fixed yield of 22.5 percent of the sum lent, which would rise to 30 percent if they failed to depart the Black Sea by the autumnal equinox (c. 19

3. Routes tracing the west coast seem generally to have been preferred, traffic along the east coast being more susceptible to piracy: Sergey Saprykin, "The Pontic Proxenies and the Sea Routes of the Ancient Greeks in the Euxine," *International Journal of Maritime History* 26, no. 2 (2014): 353–63.

September—i.e., after the close of the traditional sailing season, after which time the increased likelihood of adverse sailing conditions heightened the creditor's risk). Conversely, if the borrowers had not advanced farther than the Dardanelles by "ten days after the rising of the dog-star" (ἐπὶ κυνι, i.e., late July, after which there would not have been enough time to complete the intended journey without exposing the ship to an intolerable degree of risk), they were to put in at a port at which the property of Athenian citizens was not subject to seizure,[4] purchase a countercargo, and then to return, paying the same yield as if the enterprise had come off as originally intended.[5]

If the goods were brought safe to Athens, the borrowers were obliged to repay both capital and yield within twenty days of their arrival, less any money that had been paid as ransom to pirates or toward contribution for jettison (ἐντελὲς πλὴν ἐκβολῆς) made with the consent of all those on board (οἵ σύμπλοι). This, however, was subject to the qualification that if the ship went down but some of the merchandise was saved, the surviving goods were to become the shared property of the parties. Security was taken over the outward and return cargoes, to which the creditors were to be given access on the borrowers' arrival at Athens pending satisfaction of the debt. If the debt remained unpaid after twenty days, the creditors were entitled to dispose of the secured merchandise (τὰ ὑποκείμενα), or else to use it to raise money by pledging it as security, and to recover any shortfall from the debtors' personal property. The contract also contained a so-called *praxis* (enforcement) clause, containing a standard "καθάπερ ἐκ δίκης" formula purporting to empower the creditors to enforce their rights (including the right to seize the debtors' personal property) as if a court of law had already passed judgment in their favor. Finally, the parties agreed that nothing should have greater legal authority (i.e., should be treated as *kyriōteron*) than the terms of the *syngraphē*.

D.45.1.122.1 (Scaev. 28 dig.*)*[6]

Some of the terms of a second maritime loan contract are reported in a text authored by the Roman jurist Q. Cervidius Scaevola in about the middle of the second century CE:

4. For *sylai*, the right of 'reprisal,' see, further, Pascal Arnaud, "Ancient Sailing-Routes and Trade Patterns: The Impact of Human Factors," in *Maritime Archaeology and Ancient Trade in the Mediterranean*, ed. Damian Robinson and Andrew I. Wilson (Oxford: Oxford Centre for Maritime Archaeology, 2011), 64–65.

5. For this reading, see MacDowell, *Demosthenes*, 136 n. 25.

6. See appendix II, no. 2.

> Callimachus took from Stichus, slave of Seius, a money loan on maritime terms (*nautica*) in the province of Syria for a sea voyage from Berytus to Brentesium. It was lent for the full two hundred days of sailing under pledge and hypothec over the goods purchased at Berytus to be transported to Brentesium and over those that would be bought at Brentesium for carriage by ship to Berytus. And it was agreed between them, that after Callimachus had arrived at Brentesium he himself would depart for Syria before what would then be the next *ides* of September with other goods having been purchased and loaded onto a vessel, or, if by the aforementioned date he had not replenished the merchandise nor sailed out from that *civitas*, that he would return the whole sum as if he had completed the voyage without interruption and pay all the costs of those escorting the money so that they might take it to Rome. And this is what Callimachus promised in faith to Stichus, slave of Lucius Titius, would be properly given and done in response to his question . . .[7]

Scaevola reports that a merchant called Callimachus, likely a peregrine, took a loan of *pecunia nautica* from Stichus, the slave of Seius (later referred to as Lucius Titius), for a maximum term of two hundred days.[8] Under the terms of the agreement Callimachus was bound to purchase goods at Berytus (modern Beirut), the port of departure, and to transport them to Brentesium (modern Brindisi), where he would sell them. Eros, a fellow slave of Stichus, was to accompany him on the journey, and the revenue from the sale of the original cargo would be used to acquire new merchandise. Callimachus would then ship the goods back to Berytus where, once sold, he could repay the sum he had borrowed out of the proceeds. If, however, Callimachus failed to depart Brentesium with a fresh cargo before 13 September, he was bound to make repayment to Eros and pay all costs for the money to be carried to Rome. Security was taken over both the outward and return cargoes by

7. For a full translation, see below, 139–40.

8. The trip ought not to have taken more than three weeks' sailing time each way: Adriaan J. B. Sirks, "Sailing in the Off-Season with Reduced Financial Risk," in *Speculum Iuris: Roman Law as a Reflection of Social and Economic Life in Antiquity*, ed. Jean-Jacques Aubert and Adriaan J. B. Sirks (Ann Arbor: University of Michigan Press, 2002), 142–43. Cf. the earlier view that 200 days was the time required for the completion of the enterprise: Richard Duncan-Jones, *Structure and Scale in the Roman Economy* (Cambridge: Cambridge University Press, 1990), 21; Christoph Krampe, "Der Seedarlehensstreit des Callimachus—D. 45,1,122,1 Scaevola 28 digestorum," in *Collatio iuris Romani: Études dédiées à Hans Ankum à l'occasion de son 65e anniversaire*, ed. Robert Feenstra et al. (Amsterdam: Gieben, 1995), 221–22.

means of pledge and hypothec.[9] Once the terms had been agreed, they were made binding by way of stipulation and recorded in a *cautio*.

The text does not repeat the loan documentation in its original form but represents (probably accurately) the terms of an agreement that were relevant to Scaevola for the purpose of responding to a legal question. The spelling of Brentesium (a transliteration of Βρεντέσιον, for Brundisium) indicates that the jurist had in front of him an original *nautikē syngraphē* composed in Greek.[10] Several other replies preserved in Scaevola's *digesta* also show that he was interested in discussing the interpretation of Greek materials (contracts, wills, and so forth) from the perspective of Roman law.[11] Possibly the *syngraphē* was originally accompanied by a Latin chirograph, since both the introductory phrase "*Callimachus mutuam pecuniam nauticam accepit*" and the concluding stipulatory language would appear to reproduce the technical formulations used in standard acknowledgments of debt. It is perhaps impossible to know whether Scaevola had been asked to respond in a real case or was using the document as the basis upon which to ask an abstract legal question (i.e., about the interpretation of penalty clauses, see chapter 4). Probably the case has been confected;[12] though it is striking that the legal question at the heart of the response was

9. *Pignus* and *hypotheca* likely carry the same meaning here: Ulrich von Lübtow, "Das Seedarlehen des Callimachus," in *Festschrift für Max Kaser zum 70. Geburtstag*, ed. Dieter Medicus and Hans H. Seiler (Munich: C.H. Beck, 1976), 338. According to Éva Jakab, the arrangement "must have been a contractual pledge without possession based on a Greek model": Éva Jakab, "Loans and Securities: Tracing Maritime Trade in the Archive of the Sulpicii," in *Roman Law and Maritime Commerce*, ed. Peter Candy and Emilia Mataix Ferrándiz (Edinburgh: Edinburgh University Press, 2022), 144 and 166 n. 75. See, also, Dietmar Schanbacher, "Zu Ursprung und Entwicklung des römischen Pfandrechts," *ZRG RA* 123 (2006): 54–55.

10. Fritz Pringsheim, *Der Kauf mit fremdem Geld: Studien über die Bedeutung der Preiszahlung für den Eigentumserwerb nach griechischem und römischem Recht* (Leipzig: Veit, 1916), 147; Arnaldo Biscardi, *Actio pecuniae traiecticiae: Contributo alla dottrina delle clausole penali*, 2nd ed. (Turin: Giappichelli, 1974), 200; Fernando Reinoso Barbero, "El foenus nauticum de Calímaco," in *Scritti in onore di Arnaldo Biscardi*, ed. Franco Pastori, vol. 5 (Milan: Istituto Editoriale Cisalpino, La Goliardica, 1984), 309; G. Purpura, "Ricerche in tema di prestito marittimo," *AUPA* 39 (1987): 213 (= "Ricerche in tema di prestito marittimo," in *Studi romanistici in tema di diritto commerciale marittimo* [Soveria Mannelli: Rubbettino, 1996], 117); Krampe, "Der Seedarlehensstreit," 214; Schuster, *Das Seedarlehen*, 177.

11. D.44.7.61 pr. (Scaev. 28 *dig.*): Lenel, *Pal*, 2:265–66. See, also, D.17.1.60.4 (Scaev. 1 *resp.*); D.20.1.34.1 (Scaev. 27 *dig.*); D.26.7.47 pr. (Scaev. 2 *resp.*); D.31.88.15 (Scaev. 3 *resp.*); D.32.37.5, 6 (Scaev. 18 *dig.*); D.32.39.1 (Scaev. 20 *dig.*); D.32.101 pr. (Scaev. 16 *dig.*); D.33.4.14 (Scaev. 15 *dig.*); D.33.8.23.2 (Scaev. 15 *dig.*); D.34.1.16.1 (Scaev. 18 *dig.*); D.34.4.30.1, 3 (Scaev. 20 *dig.*); D.40.4.60 (Scaev. 24 *dig.*); D.40.5.41.4 (Scaev. 4 *resp.*); and D.50.9.6 (Scaev. 1 *dig.*).

12. Similarly, Jean Rougé, *Recherches sur l'organisation du commerce maritime en Méditerranée sous l'Empire romain* (Paris: S.E.V.P.E.N., 1966), 350; Geoffrey E. M. De Ste Croix, "Ancient Greek and Roman Maritime Loans," in *Debits, Credits, Finance and Profits*, ed. Harold C. Edey and Basil S. Yamey (London: Sweet & Maxwell, 1974), 55; Arnaud, "Ancient Sailing-Routes," 69; Dominic Rathbone, "Maritime Loans," in *The Oxford Classical Dictionary*, 4th ed., ed. S. Hornblower, A. Spawforth, and E. Eidinow (Oxford: Oxford University Press, 2012). Cf., e.g., Mario Talamanca, "I clienti di Q. Cervidio Scevola," *BIDR* 42 (2000): 542–43.

litigated at Athens in the speech *Against Phormiōn*, and similar cases must also have arisen during the Roman period. There is, too, the intriguing possibility that this particular oration might have been familiar to Scaevola, the speeches of several Attic orators (including Demosthenes) appearing on the syllabus in Roman schools of rhetoric.

SB III 7169[13]

A third document that may preserve the contents of a maritime loan contract consists in an acknowledgment of debt likely made at Ptolemaic Alexandria about the first half of the second century BCE:[14]

> [5]]6. Archippos gave as a loan to Demetrios . . .
>
> Archippos son of Eudemos . . . aged . . . with a scar on the left-hand side of his forehead, gave a loan to Demetrios . . . aged . . . with a scar on his face in the middle of his forehead and to Hipparchos son of Hipparchos . . . half-bald, broad-faced, with a scar on his forehead and to D . . . son of [?] of the *epigone* (i.e., descendants of foreign military settlers), aged . . . [10] chin (beardless?—Wilcken) and to S . . . chos son of Lysimachos of Lacedaemonia . . . aged . . .-five, with a scar on the right-hand side of his face and to Tr . . . os son of Tre . . . of Massalia . . . trim, broad-faced, with a scar on his left hand to the aforementioned five associates (*synploi*) through Gnaeus . . . ['without interest'—Wilcken] for the duration of one year from the present month. Those who have taken the loan will repay the debt to the lender . . . If they then return to the Egyptian territory from the Arōmatophoros land after the time limit has elapsed, in the same way . . . [15] from that day in which they will arrive in the territory, within [50, 70, 80, or 90—De Romanis] days . . . If instead they do not repay within the time-limit they will pay at the same time the debt with a penalty of half (*hemiolion*) and interest of two drachmas per mina each month beyond the expiration of the time-limit according to the royal decree (*diagramma*). Guarantors for payment . . . of Thessalonica, leader of the foreign military company, aged . . .-seven, blonde, slim, with curly hair and a scar . . . and . . . son of . . .]tos of Elea, of the royal guards . . . of second choice, forty years of age . . . on

13. = P. Berol. 5883 + 5853. See appendix II, no. 3.

14. Ulrich Wilcken, "Punt-Fahrten in der Ptolemäerzeit," *Zeitschrift für ägyptische Sprache und Altertumskunde* 60 (1925): 86–102.

the right [hand?] and Kintos . . . son of]nis of Massalia of those [who sail on the outer sea?] . . . , forty, very large, blonde, . . . [20] on the left [hand?] and Demetrios son of Apollonios of Carthage, of those who sail on the outer sea, thirty . . . with a monobrow, mute(?), and Kintos son of Kintos . . . mercenary,[15] forty . . . and Archippos shall have a right of execution against the borrowers and the guarantors from all their assets (present and future) exactly as if judgment had been passed. It is imposed upon . . . the above-written Demetrios and Hipparchos . . . the aforementioned *arōmata* . . . where eventually the unloading of the *arōmata* takes place . . . for the things that belong to those from the same voyage . . . [25] the articles that will be sold by Archippos (?—cf. Wilhelm) . . . so as to be unloaded in (or on) the Egyptian territory . . . of the weight of the arrived *arōmata* (?) . . . If they do not abide by the terms of the agreement (?)[16] . . .

Archippos, son of Eudemos, gave a loan to five *synploi*, or associates, for a journey to the Arōmatophoros, probably on the Horn of Africa.[17] The loan was given "through Cnaeus" (διὰ Γναίου, l.12), whose name and role within the transaction indicate that he may have been a banker (or some other kind of intermediary) of Italian extraction.[18] Of the five associates, two can be identified by name (Demetrios and Hipparchos); and a further two by their place of origin (a Lacedemonian, son of Lysimachos, and a Massiliote). All that can be said about the fifth is that his name began with the letter "D . . ." (l. 9). Later

15. I.e., *taktomisthos*, a member of a class of soldiers in the Ptolemaic army ('with a fixed wage') of uncertain type: see, generally, Sandra Scheuble, "Bemerkungen zu den μισθοφόροι und τακτόμισθοι im ptolemäischen Ägypten," in ". . . *vor dem Papyrus sind alle gleich!" Papyrologische Beiträge zu Ehren von Bärbel Kramer (P. Kramer) = ArchPF*, ed. R. Eberhard (Berlin: De Gruyter, 2009), 213–22; also, Christelle Fischer-Bovet, *Army and Society in Ptolemaic Egypt* (Cambridge: Cambridge University Press, 2014), 119.

16. "ἐὰν δὲ μὴ{ἐὰν δὲ μὴ} ἐπιθῶσιν, καθ[ὼς πρόκειται]." This lacunose clause is difficult to reconstruct. Purpura translates, "Se non . . . carichino come è stabilito" ("If not, let them load as it is established . . ."): Purpura, "Ricerche," 248–49. The key to understanding the clause is the verb '*epitheō*,' which literally means "to run upon, at, or after:" LSJ, s.v. 'ἐπιθέω.' A fairly literal translation of the whole phrase would be, "If they do not proceed, according to how it has been determined . . ." The best model is perhaps the penal condition reported verbatim from a maritime loan contract at Dem. 56.38, which imposed a penalty for violation of the agreement. If this clause was intended to achieve a similar result, then a less literal interpretation might be "If they do not abide by the terms of the agreement . . ."

17. Arabia has also been suggested. For discussion, see Matthew A. Cobb, *Rome and the Indian Ocean Trade from Augustus to the Early Third Century CE* (Leiden: Brill, 2018), 32; Steven E. Sidebotham, *Berenike and the Ancient Maritime Spice Route* (Los Angeles: University of California Press, 2011), 34.

18. Raymond Bogaert, "Banquiers, courtiers et prêts maritimes à Athènes et à Alexandrie," *Chronique d'Égypte* 40 (1965): 146–54; also, Pierre Jouguet, "Dédicace grecque de Médamoud," *Bulletin de l'Institut français d'archéologie orientale* 31 (1931): 22 and 25.

in the document (ll. 22–26), a series of undertakings to do with the use of the vessel seem only to bind Demetrios and Hipparchos, which suggests that they at least were *nauklēroi* (merchant-carriers). Archippos does not appear to have taken security over the cargo or ship: instead, three Ptolemaic army officers—a Thessalonican, an Elean, and a third with a Celtic name—stood surety for the loan, together with two merchants ("those who sail on the outer sea")—a Massiliote and a Carthaginian (ll. 17–21).[19] The international character of the transaction is a consequence of the parties' military associations, several of whom appear to have been serving as mercenaries in the Ptolemaic armies.

The five associates had a year to complete the enterprise, after which they would be liable to pay a penalty (ἡμιόλιον, *hēmiolion*) equal to one-and-a-half times the amount of the debt (i.e., a 50 percent uplift) in addition to interest at the legal limit of 2 percent per month (24 percent p.a.) (l.16).[20] Archippos however conceded that, if the traders were delayed, they would still be allowed a grace period of either 50, 70, 80, or 90 days to transship the goods from the Red Sea coast up the Nile to Alexandria before overtime interest began to run.[21] Near to the end of the document, there is a *praxis*-clause containing a standard "καθάπερ ἐκ δίκης" formula (l. 22). Whether Archippos shouldered the risk for the loan, at least while the goods were under sail, cannot be ascertained: though there is no explicit evidence for the inclusion of a condition *salva nave*, the document is so lacunose that it yields no information on this point.[22]

What was the structure of the transaction between Archippos and the five associates? Wilcken's original conjecture was that the *synploi* referred to in the papyrus might have entered into a partnership with each other and also into a profit-sharing arrangement with their creditor.[23] The basis for the conjecture

19. Michael I. Rostovtzeff, "Foreign Commerce of Ptolemaic Egypt," *Journal of Economic and Business History* 4, no. 4 (1932): 756; Peter M. Fraser, *Ptolemaic Alexandria*, vol. 2 (Oxford: Clarendon Press, 1972), 275 n. 216. On the military personnel, Louis Robert, *Études épigraphiques et philologiques* (Paris: Champion, 1938), 206; also, Hans Hauben, "'Ceux qui naviguent sur la mer extérieure' ("SB" III 7169)," *ZPE* 59 (1985): 135–36.

20. Wilcken, "Punt-Fahrten in der Ptolemäerzeit," *Zeitschrift für ägyptische Sprache und Altertumskunde* 60 (1925), 95–96; Bogaert, "Banquiers," 148. See, also, Naphtali Lewis, "The Meaning of Σὺν Ἡμιολίᾳ and Kindred Expressions in Loan Contracts," *TAPhA* 76 (1945): 126. Cf. De Romanis, who points out that the one-year term ought to be understood as corresponding to the expected duration of a single expedition to the Punt and back: De Romanis, *Pepper Trade*, 165–66.

21. Federico De Romanis, "Time to Repay a Maritime Loan: A Note on SB III 7169 and SB XVIII 13167 Recto," *Sileno: Rivista semestrale di studi classici e cristiani fondata da quintino cataudella* 40 (2014): 76.

22. Also urging caution, Gerhard Thür, "Hypotheken-Urkunde eines Seedarlehens für eine Reise nach Muziris und Apographe für die Tetarte in Alexandria: (zu P. Vindob. G. 40.822)," *Tyche* 2 (1987): 243; Claire Préaux, *L'économie royale des Lagides* (Brussels: Éditions de la Fondation Égyptologique Reine Élisabeth, 1939), 364; Bogaert, "Banquiers," 149–51.

23. Wilcken, "Punt-Fahrten," 93 n. 1, and 100; Vincenzo Arangio-Ruiz, *Lineamenti del sistema contrattuale nel diritto dei papiri* (Milan: Vita e pensiero, 1928), 85.

are the letters ']κα' at the beginning of l. 13, which Wilcken reconstructed as '[ἄτο]κα.'[24] On a literal translation, this would suggest that the money was given ἄτοκος (*atokos*), that is, 'without a yield.'[25] Wilcken then fell back upon a suggestion made by Lipsius, that profit-sharing (on a participatory model) may have been an alternative means by which lenders demanded a return in a maritime context.[26]

Since Wilcken's original publication, however, several studies into the use of the word *atokos* in loan contracts in the papyri have shown that it can carry several possible meanings. According to Pestman, it is common in the papyri to find loans in which the stated sum was intended to represent the total amount that the debtor was obliged to repay (i.e., the sum of the capital and a fixed yield combined).[27] From here, Pestman identified three possibilities: (1) that the borrower simply received a gratuitous loan; (2) that he received the sum stated, but owed the yield in some other form (e.g., as a *quid pro quo*); or (3) that he received less than the sum stated since the yield was already included in the amount represented as the principal.[28]

Assuming Wilken's reconstruction is correct, and that Archippos was not lending gratuitously, the loan could have been structured in one of two ways. The first possibility is that the yield was owed as a *quid pro quo*. This would not only capture Wilcken's original conjecture, but also a later hypothesis advanced by Wilhelm, who offered a new reading of the clauses in ll. 22–26. In Wilcken's original publication, the editor took l. 25 to refer to obligations binding on Demetrios and Hipparchos to perform libations on their return to Egypt to which Archippos would make a contribution.[29] Wilhelm preferred instead to understand "τὰ παρασταθησόμενα ὑπὸ τοῦ Ἀρ[χίππου" as referring to articles supplied by the creditor and entrusted for transport and sale to the traders receiving the loan.[30] The words that follow—"ὥστε ἀποχαταστῆσαι εἰς τὴν χώραν"—would also fit the description of goods shipped from the

24. Wilcken, "Punt-Fahrten," 100; also, Paul M. Meyer, "Juristischer Papyrusbericht IV," *ZRG RA* 46 (1926): 330; Jouguet, "Dédicace grecque," 22.

25. On the meaning of *tokos* within the context of Greek financial terminology, see below, 154–55.

26. Wilcken, "Punt-Fahrten," 100; Justus H. Lipsius, *Das attische Recht und Rechtsverfahren* (Leipzig: O. R. Reisland, 1905), 723. If Wilcken's conjecture is right, this would make the structure of the contract similar to one regulated by the Code of Hammurabi (i.e., a credit-partnership arrangement, in which the creditor participated in the profits).

27. Pieter W. Pestman, "Loans Bearing No Interest?," *JJP* 16–17 (1971): 24.

28. Pestman, "Loans Bearing No Interest?," 24–26.

29. Wilcken, "Punt-Fahrten," 99.

30. Adolf Wilhelm, "Papyrus Tebtunis 33," *JRS* 27 (1937): 148–49; also, Sidebotham, *Berenike*, 34.

Arōmatophoros to the χώρα, that is, Egypt. If, then, all the clauses in ll. 22–26 were governed by the verb ἐπιτιθέναι, l. 25 could be restored "ἐπιθεῖναι δὲ χα] ὶ τὰ παρασταθησόμενα ὑπὸ τοῦ Ἀρ[χίππου." The meaning of the verb, a *hapax*, would therefore be something like "to put a load upon another load or upon a ship," obliging the two *nauklēroi* to transport Archippos' merchandise on their vessel and imposing a fine on them should they fail. The *atokos* character of the loan might therefore indicate that the yield was replaced by a share of the profits (Wilcken) or (partly) demanded in the form of services to be performed by the borrowers (Wilhelm), or both.

The second possibility is simply that the document records a straightforward acknowledgment of debt that included both principal and yield.[31] In a fourth-century Karanis document from the Michigan collection, for example, the loan is stated to be ἄτοκος in the body of the contract, though the docket (perhaps the lender's copy) gives an amount of the principal as a third less.[32] If this is right, then the loan was structured according to the third of Pestman's configurations and did not necessarily contain any provisions by which the yield was demanded as a *quid pro quo*.

Each of these (hypothetical) reconstructions is within the technical meaning of the word *atokos*. Both are possible: Wilcken's conjecture is no more likely, at least on its face, than either of the explanations put forward by Wilhelm and (more especially) Thür. On the other hand, the significant differences between the structure of the arrangement documented in this papyrus and the other surviving maritime loan contracts from the classical period, particularly with reference to the personal nature of the guarantees and the absence of any evidence for a condition *salva nave* (notwithstanding the lacunae), make it possible that the agreement was not structured according to the orthodox pattern of a maritime loan contract in the Attic style.[33] The conclusion must therefore be that, owing in a large part to the fragmentary state of the document, it is not possible to say whether the yield demanded by the creditor was intended to consist of a predetermined sum or a share of the profits.

31. Thür, "Hypotheken-Urkunde," 243.

32. P. Mich. Inv. 1410: on which, John C. Shelton, "Two Contracts of Loan from the Michigan Papyrus Collection," *JJP* 18 (1974): 158–60; also, Roger S. Bagnall, "Price in 'Sales on Delivery,'" *GRBS* 18 (1977): 95.

33. See, also, Kasper G. Evers, *Worlds Apart Trading Together: The Organisation of Long-Distance Trade between Rome and India in Antiquity* (Oxford: Archaeopress, 2016), 99.

SB XVIII 13167 (the 'Muziris papyrus')[34]

The surviving columns on the recto of the so-called Muziris papyrus (second century CE) likely also provide an insight into the structure of maritime loan contracts in the context of the Indian Ocean trade.[35]

Recto.ii

. . . your other agents or managers and having weighed
I will . . . to . . . cameleer . . . for the shipment of the . . . to Koptos
and I will bring [sc. the cargo] through the desert with vigilance and precaution
up to the public customs warehouses in Koptos and I will
put [sc. the cargo] under the power and seal of yourself or your administrators
or whoever of them is there up to the loading [sc. of the cargo] on the river and I will load
at the required time in a safe river ship and I will convey [sc. the cargo] downstream up to the
customs warehouse of the quarter-tax in Alexandria and likewise
I will put [sc. the cargo] under your or your people's power and seal for
all the expenses from [= met with] the loan from now until the payment of the quarter-tax—the
costs of the desert transports, the river freights and the other due outlays—
so that, if, on the occurrence of the time established for the repayment in the loan contracts for
Muziris, I do not properly pay the aforesaid loan in my name,
then you and your agents or managers shall have the choice and complete
power, if you choose, to carry out execution
without notification or summons and to get possession and own the aforesaid

34. = P. Vindob. G 40822. See appendix II, no. 4. Translation by De Romanis, *Pepper Trade*, 15–16. Cf., e.g., the translations by Lionel Casson, "New Light on Maritime Loans: P. Vindob G 40822," *ZPE* 84 (1990): 200; and Dominic Rathbone, "The 'Muziris' Papyrus (SB XVIII 13167): Financing Roman Trade with India," *Bulletin de la Société archéologique d'Alexandrie* 46 (2000): 40.

35. On Rome's trade with India, see Gary K. Young, *Rome's Eastern Trade: International Commerce and Imperial Policy, 31 BC-AD 305* (London: Routledge, 2001); Sidebotham, *Berenike*; Evers, *Worlds Apart*; Cobb, *Rome and the Indian Ocean Trade*.

security and levy the quarter-tax and transfer the three parts that will
remain to whomever you choose and sell and re-hypothecate
and cede to another, if you choose, and handle the security
whichever way you want and buy for yourself at the then
current price and subtract [sc. its value] and reckon the future
proceeds from the goods
for the payment in full of the loan, with the benefit of assumption
regarding the proceeds
being on you and your agents or managers, and us being absolutely
free from
misrepresentation; the shortfall or surplus with respect to the capital
will be on me, the borrower and mort-

The Muziris papyrus, first published in 1985, provides a window into the enormous trade flows that extended from the Indian subcontinent to the western Mediterranean via Egypt at the height of the Roman Empire.[36] The papyrus contains the incomplete fragments of two texts on its recto and verso, respectively. In a single column on the recto is a section near to the end of a contract relating to a loan that was used to fund a venture between Alexandria and Muziris, a trading port in southwest India on the Malabar coast. On the verso is part of a valuation of the cargo of the ship *Hermapollon*, probably in connection with the same expedition. The total value of the goods listed, which included malabathrum, tortoiseshell, black pepper, Gangetic nard, ivory tusks, and *schidai*,[37] amounted to 1,151 t. 5,852 dr., or HS 6,911,852:[38] as Rathbone notes, more than enough to purchase a premium estate in Italy at the time.[39] Since the valuation was made after deduction of the 25 percent customs levy raised on goods entering the empire at the frontier (the *tetartē*), the value of the merchandise before tax was proportionately greater: HS 9,215,803.

36. H. Harrauer and P. J. Sijpesteijn, "Ein neues Dokument zu Roms Indienhandel. P. Vindob. G 40822," *Anzeiger der philosophisch-historischen Klasse / Österreichische Akademie der Wissenschaften* 122 (1985): 124–55. Recently the object of a book-length treatment by De Romanis, *Pepper Trade*.

37. For a breakdown of the cargo, De Romanis, 250, table 10.6 and fig. 10.5; on quantities, cf. Federico Morelli, "Dal Mar Rosso ad Alessandria: il «verso» (ma anche il «recto») del «papiro di Muziris» (SB XVIII 13167)," *Tyche* 26 (2011): 221–26.

38. Accepting the reading of Morelli, 214; followed by Federico De Romanis, "Playing Sudoku on the Verso of the 'Muziris Papyrus,'" *Journal of Ancient Indian History* 27 (2012): 75–101; Andrew I. Wilson, "Red Sea Trade and the State," in *Across the Ocean: Nine Essays on Indo-Mediterranean Trade*, ed. Federico De Romanis and Marco Maiuro (Leiden: Brill, 2015), 23.

39. Although Rathbone's comparison with the value of real property in Italy during the same period is based upon the original reading of 1,154 t. 2,852 dr. in the *editio princeps*, the observation stands: Rathbone, "The 'Muziris' Papyrus," 49.

The surviving part of the recto consists of all but the very left-hand edge of the second of two columns of writing.[40] What remains is therefore only the second half of what was originally the record of a longer agreement between a merchant (the 'I' of the text) and financier (the 'you'), neither of whom are identified. Broadly speaking, the text in the surviving column, which begins *in medias res*, takes up two themes. The first half (recto.ii.1–12) dealt with the provisions governing the transport of the goods from the Red Sea coast to Alexandria via Koptos: the merchant was obliged to hire the creditor's own cameleer (or to use a camel driver hired by the lender's agents) for the journey across the desert; to provide for the protection of the merchandise; and to store it at the tax-receiving warehouse in Koptos, where it was to be kept under the financier's seal.[41] Further, he was to charter a safe boat to carry the goods down the Nile; to store them in the tax-receiving warehouse at Alexandria, again under the financier's seal; and to pay the quarter-tax (*tetartē*) and all other expenses incurred to that point. The second half of the column (recto.ii.12–26) provided for the lender's rights in security. If the debtor failed to repay on time, it was agreed that the creditor should be able to take possession and full title to the goods immediately and without legal process, pay the quarter-tax, and to deal with the property as his own. He could then raise money on the goods, either by selling them or using them as collateral to secure another loan; and after subtracting the yield and principal for himself, he was obliged to hand over any surplus, but equally entitled to sue the debtor personally if the money came up short. Alternatively, the lender could elect to purchase the cargo from the merchant at prevailing prices (i.e., an option to buy).

The nature of the document preserved on the papyrus recto has proved controversial.[42] The interpretations are variously that the recto contains details of a maritime loan contract (*Seedarlehensvertrag*) drawn up at Muziris between a merchant and a *nauklēros*, the latter taking the loan and giving his ship as security (Harrauer and Sijpesteijn); the latter part of a supplementary agreement concluded at the Red Sea port between a merchant and financier for the overland leg of the journey to Alexandria (Casson);[43] part of a more extensive loan dossier drawn up at Alexandria between a merchant and financier, that included a (maritime) loan contract (now lost), and a security document

40. For hypothetical reconstructions of the document's missing columns, see De Romanis, *Pepper Trade*, 24, fig. 0.2.

41. See, also, P. Cair. Zen. I 59010, in which provision is made at l. 23 for the hiring of camels.

42. For a thorough review of the historiography, Evers, *Worlds Apart*, 101–4.

43. Lionel Casson, "New Light on Maritime Loans: P. Vindob. G 19792," in *Studies in Roman Law in Memory of A. Arthur Schiller*, ed. Roger S. Bagnall and William V. Harris (Leiden: Brill, 1986), 11–17; Casson, "New Light" (1990), 195–206.

(*Sicherungsurkunde*), a portion of which has been preserved on the papyrus recto (Thür);[44] part of a "master contract" between a merchant and financier containing standard operational terms, which was supplementary to a brief loan contract that set out the specific details of the agreement (Rathbone);[45] a second loan contract between a merchant and financier, drawn up at the Red Sea port, to record the terms of a new financing agreement (Morelli);[46] and most recently, the latter part of a maritime loan contract in its own right (De Romanis).[47]

Before De Romanis, most scholars had accepted that the reference at recto. ii.12–13 to a deadline for repayment in "the loan contracts for Muziris" indicated the existence of a separate document containing the main terms of agreement. The papyrus recto would then be part of a document that was secondary or supplementary to this original contract. According to De Romanis, however, previous interpretations assume that the deadline for repayment, which is not otherwise evident, must have been specified elsewhere as a calendric date. But commercial trading expeditions venturing south and east from the ports on the Red Sea coast were governed by long-established customary deadlines that were aligned with the sailing season and the monsoon winds.[48] In addition, the use of the preposition ἐν with the plural δα[νείου σ]υνγραφαῖς (i.e., "the contracts for (a voyage to) Muziris") indicates that the repayment deadline was established in relation to a category of contracts rather than several copies of specific contracts. De Romanis therefore argues that the clause at recto.ii.12–13 was intended to refer to the traditional date for repayment that was customary for the repayment of commercial loans bankrolling the trade between Alexandria and Muziris.[49] If this is right, then the grounds for supposing that the main heads of agreement were contained in a separate document would be removed.

De Romanis' argument that the papyrus recto preserves the latter half of the *nautikē syngraphē* concluded by the merchant and financier for the return enterprise Alexandria–Muziris–Alexandria is compelling.[50] The central considerations are as follows. First, the entire first column of the papyrus recto—that

44. See, generally, Thür, "Hypotheken-Urkunde;" also, in response to Casson, Thür, "Zum Seedarlehen κατὰ Μουζεῖριν. P. Vindob. G 40822," *Tyche* 3 (1988): 229–33. Followed by Jakab, "Loans and Securities," 149 and 168 n. 114.

45. Rathbone, "The 'Muziris' Papyrus," 41.

46. Morelli, "Dal Mar Rosso," 205.

47. De Romanis, *Pepper Trade*, 169.

48. See, e.g., Plin. *HN* 6.104: on which, De Romanis, "Time to Repay," 80–81; De Romanis, *Pepper Trade*, 168–69.

49. De Romanis, "Time to Repay," 82–83; De Romanis, *Pepper Trade*, 169.

50. See, also, Rathbone, "The 'Muziris' Papyrus," 41; De Romanis, "Time to Repay," 82–83; De Romanis, *Pepper Trade*, 4; Evers, *Worlds Apart*, 107.

is, 26 lines of c. 44–55 letters each—is missing.[51] Since the surviving second column commences with terms governing the merchant's conduct at the Red Sea port, whatever terms made up the first column must have dealt with more than the actions to be taken following the ship's arrival.[52] This is supported by the use of ἑτέρων at recto.ii.1, which implies that other agents or representatives of the lender who were not the same as those active at the Red Sea port had already taken some action before the ship arrived.[53] Together with Thür's arguments showing the likelihood that the enterprise was structured as a return trip,[54] the most obvious explanation is therefore that the missing first column consisted of the terms of the maritime loan contract from the point of departure to arrival at the Red Sea port, leading into the second column, which set out the (largely standard) terms addressing the final leg of the journey to Alexandria.

Second, I do not think that it matters which restoration one prefers at recto. ii.10 ('λοι[ποῦ' or the paleographically preferable 'πλο[ίου'): even if one accepts the restorations proposed by Casson or Morelli (i.e., "with all the payments [out of my own pocket] from now until payment of the quarter-tax"), the lack of mention of any expenses connected to the sea voyage does not show that the present document was only concerned with arrangements following the ship's arrival at the Red Sea port. Both the agreements produced in the speech *Against Lakritos* and drawn up at Ptolemaic Alexandria for the expedition to the Punt (SB III 7169) make no provision for which of the parties should bear the costs: most likely on the assumption that these were to be paid by the borrower. If recto.i governed the maritime part of the venture (i.e., Alexandria–Muziris–Red Sea port), then I agree with Thür and Rathbone that the most natural reading of recto.ii.10–13 is that the merchant undertook to pay all the expenses "from now" (i.e., the time at which the document was signed, probably at Alexandria) to the payment of the *tetartē* (i.e., at Alexandria on the return), including (but not limited to) those costs connected with the overland leg of the journey from the Red Sea port to the final destination (which were additional to the ordinary expenses incurred in connection with the main body of the maritime loan contract).

Third, it remains to explain the reference to the "date for repayment speci-

51. De Romanis, *Pepper Trade*, 170.

52. De Romanis, "Time to Repay," 79.

53. De Romanis, 79–80; also, Harrauer and Sijpesteijn, "Ein neues Dokument," 136; though cf. Rathbone, "The 'Muziris' Papyrus," 42.

54. These are (1) that "ἄλλα" at recto.ii.2 refers to the return journey, its counterpart, lost in the preceding lines, referring to the outbound trip; (2) the plural "ναύλων" at recto.ii.11 indicates journeys in both directions; (3) the restored plural "φο[ρέτρων]" at recto.ii.10–11 covers the same; and (4) that the expression "*kata Mouzirin*" could mean "for (a voyage concerning) Muziris," not "at Muziris" (as Casson had originally suggested).

fied in the loan contracts *kata Mouzirin*" at recto.ii.12–13. Thür's reading (which opens the possibility that the loan was given, e.g., at Alexandria) and Rathbone's observation, that the account at verso.ii.27 specifies that it deals with the return cargo (*ekpepleukoton*),[55] makes it likely that transaction was for a return rather than a single trip (transactions of the latter type also generally being more opportunistic in character).[56] As for the clause itself, I am persuaded by De Romanis that the phrase was intended to establish a customary repayment deadline that would have been instantly recognizable to anyone involved in the trade between Alexandria and Muziris.[57] Probably, like so many other clauses in maritime loan contracts, this was a standard formulation established by long use, included in the recto.ii boilerplate as a standard term. If this is right, that the standard terms in recto.ii were preceded in recto.i by the bespoke terms of the maritime loan contract, then this missing portion would have set out the individual details concerning, for example, the identity of the parties, the sums involved, the route, specific penalty clauses, and so forth. In this regard the structure of the maritime loan contract for Muziris bears similarities to eighteenth-century French marine insurance contracts, which typically consisted of a first half setting out the individual terms of agreement (e.g., the parties' names, the sums, the route) followed by a boilerplate in the second half, which was anonymized for repeatability. The two halves were then sometimes separated with a distinctive tear, enabling the parties to each retain a portion of the original that could be rematched later.

All this provides a basis upon which to reconstruct what are likely to have been the basic structural elements of the transaction. Probably the Muziris papyrus recto originally consisted of a *nautikē syngraphē* concluded between a merchant and financier for a return expedition Alexandria–Muziris–Alexandria (recto.i), appended to a standard set of terms for the overland leg of the journey Red Sea coast–Alexandria (recto.ii). The enterprise likely followed the ordinary contractual pattern of a return maritime loan contract for the route Alexandria–Muziris–Alexandria. Though we lack the names of the parties, the sums involved (an initial investment, by Rathbone's estimation, of perhaps 1–2 million dr. for the purchase of the outbound cargo) indicate that the creditor must have been a wealthy member of the Alexandrian or Italian mercantile elite.[58] *Peripl. M.*

55. Rathbone, "The 'Muziris' Papyrus," 42.

56. Cf. Casson, "New Light" (1990), 206.

57. De Romanis, *Pepper Trade*, 169; cf. Jakab, "Loans and Securities," 149 and 168 n. 115.

58. For an estimate of the size of the original loan, Dominic Rathbone, "The Financing of Maritime Commerce in the Roman Empire I-II AD," in *Credito e moneta nel mondo romano: Atti degli Incontri capresi di storia dell'economia antica (Capri 12–14 ottobre 2000)*, ed. Elio Lo Cascio (Bari: Edipuglia, 2003), 221. On the participation of the elites, see Evers, *Worlds Apart*, 91–97.

Rubr. 56 shows that a variety of different Egyptian products found a market in the Malabar ports, such as patterned linen, crude glass, and metals such as gold. As for the yield, Thür has argued that the absence of any mention of interest at recto.ii.22–23 indicates that it was capitalized (i.e., given *atokos*, 'without interest'), which would be consistent with other maritime transactions from the same period.[59] Though we lack the information to know whether repayment of the loan was conditional upon the safe arrival of the ship at its destination (i.e., subject to a condition *salva nave*), the whole context of the transaction suggests that this must have been the case.[60] If, as De Romanis argues, recto.i was concerned with the maritime part of the expedition, then it will most likely have specified a (customary) time limit for repayment (referred to at recto.ii.12–13). Possibly the contract even made provision (like the Callimachus contract) for departure from the Malabar coast by the ides of January, failure to abide by which would give rise to negative consequences for the debtor. As both Casson and Thür noticed, security was over the goods acquired with the loan proceeds (not, as the original editors suggested, the ship).[61] The apparent lack of a penalty for failure to repay can be explained by the inclusion of an option to purchase on default (recto.ii.21–22): perhaps (as Rathbone has suggested) it was always anticipated that the lender would acquire the cargo from the merchant on his return to Alexandria.[62] Finally, as De Romanis notes, it is possible that the contract also allowed the borrower two or three months' grace to transport the goods overland from the Red Sea Coast to Alexandria (in the same manner as the concession made to the five *synploi* in SB III 7169), in the missing recto.iii.[63]

The Structure of Maritime Loan Contracts

These four documents provide an essential starting point for identifying the basic features and typical construction of maritime loan contracts during the ancient period.

Single and Return Voyages

The sources distinguish between two basic structures: maritime loan contracts supporting either a return (ἀμφοτερόπλουν, *amphoteroploun*) or a single

59. For example, the Callimachus loan and the loan given by Keler and Charēs. See Thür, "Hypotheken-Urkunde," 242–43; though cf. Rathbone, "The 'Muziris' Papyrus," 42.
60. Cf. Evers, *Worlds Apart*, 104.
61. Casson, "New Light" (1986), 76; Thür, "Hypotheken-Urkunde," 241.
62. Rathbone, "The 'Muziris' Papyrus," 43.
63. De Romanis, *Pepper Trade*, 169.

(ἑτερόπλουν, *heteroploun*) voyage.[64] Loans given for a return voyage were the norm, particularly when the creditor was a moneylender whose business was portside. In the speeches of the Attic orators, all the disputes arising from maritime loan contracts concerned loans given on these terms: on two occasions for journeys Athens–Bosporos–Athens;[65] one for a round-trip Athens–Egypt–Athens;[66] and another Athens–Syracuse–Athens.[67] However this is hardly surprising for trips originating at Athens, where grain laws prohibited the lending of money on any ventures that did not involve the import of grain to Piraeus.[68] A passage in the speech *Against Phormiōn* implies that it was also possible for the parties to negotiate a clause permitting the debtor to discharge the debt at the outport, converting the expedition from *amphoteroploun* to *heteroploun*.[69] In the later evidence, most of the documented transactions were probably *amphoteroploun*: certainly the journey in the Ptolemaic contract from a port on the Red Sea Coast to the Arōmatophoros and thence to Alexandria; Callimachus' route Berytus–Brentesium–Berytus;[70] and probably also the journey Red Sea coast–Muziris–Alexandria anticipated by the Muziris papyrus.

By contrast, loans given for single journeys appear normally to have been extended by merchants and *nauklēroi* who were travelling on the same vessel as their debtor. According to Androklēs, one of the excuses provided by Lakritos for the failure of his brother to repay the loan is that he and his associate lent 100 Cyzicene staters from the proceeds of the sale of the outward cargo at Bosporos to another Phaselite who had since traveled on to Chios.[71] In the oration *Against Phormiōn*, Chrysippos complains that his debtor was more concerned with paying off Theodoros and the vessel's *nauklēros*, both of whom were traveling on the same ship and whose loans were for the outward voyage only, than observing the terms of his agreement with him.[72] According to Demon's version of events in the oration *Against Zēnothemis* the creditors who had been deceived into making loans to Zēnothemis and the *nauklēros* Hēgestratos for

64. The words *amphoteroploun* and *heteroploun* (and the corresponding plurals) never appear as substantives referring to the journey itself (for which we would expect masculines, not neuters), but only as modifiers, for example, of a stated journey (*argyrion*), loan (*daneion*), or sum of money lent (*chrēmata*).

65. Dem. 34.6, 23 and 25; 35.10. In the speech *Against Lakritos*, Androklēs also alleges that Apollodōrus breached the contract by borrowing money on the same security (i.e., both the outward and return cargoes) from an Aratos of Halikarnassos: Dem. 35.21–23.

66. Dem. 56.27, 36 and 45.

67. Such is the implication of Dem. 32.20.

68. Cf. the creditors' refusal in the speech *Against Dionysodōros* to break the grain laws by contracting for a voyage Athens–Egypt–Athens/Rhodes: Dem. 56.5.

69. Dem. 34.31–32.

70. Near to the end of the oration *Against Lakritos*, Androklēs uses the same apparently standard formulation "from Athens to Pontus and back again from Pontus to Athens": Dem. 35.53.

71. Dem. 35.36.

72. Dem. 34.8 and 22.

the single trip between Syracuse and Athens traveled with the pair and later made common cause with the former against Demon and his partner (following Hēgestratos' untimely demise).[73] Only one transaction in the Roman evidence can definitely be identified as *heteroploun*: namely, the loan given by Aurelia Juliana to an unnamed debtor for a voyage from the port of Salona to an unspecified destination in Africa.[74]

Taken together, the relationship between loans given for return and single trips seems therefore to have been that once the core financing for a return journey had been obtained from lenders in port, the viability of the expedition gave rise to opportunities for those on board to make incidental loans to their fellow travelers for one or other legs of the voyage.[75] The reasons for the preference of professional lenders for the *amphoteroploun* structure are obvious: they conducted their business in port, and the most profitable enterprises were those in which the capital remained productive for the whole time it remained exposed to the sea-risk. If conditions were right, it was also possible for lenders to agree to finance repeat journeys within the same season, achieving a multiplier effect as consecutive cargoes were bought and sold.[76] Single loans were attractive for similar reasons: once the viability of the expedition had been confirmed, it made sense for all those making the voyage to put spare capital to work; and it provided the additional opportunity for travelers to exchange currencies through the medium of the purchase and sale of merchandise.[77]

---

73. The implication of Dem. 32.12.

74. The maritime loan contracts referred to in two documents related to expeditions along the Levantine coast may have been *heteroploun*, but we do not know the details: P. Cair. Zen. I 59010 (third century BCE) and SB XIV 11850 (second century CE). According to Paoli, Nov. 106 shows that lending for single voyages had fallen into desuetude by the time of Justinian: Ugo E. Paoli, *Studi di diritto attico* (Firenze: Bemporad & Figlio, 1930), 29 n. 1. However, it must be remembered that the *emporoi* and *nauklēroi* called to give evidence in that case were asked to speak to the customs surrounding their relationships with professional moneylenders, whose loans were almost always given for return journeys.

75. This is consistent with the conclusion of Paoli, *Studi di diritto attico*, 28.

76. Nov. 106. See, also, the oration *Against Dionysodōros* (Dem. 56.30), in which lenders are described putting the same money to work "two or three times" between Rhodes and Egypt during the course of the sailing season.

77. Paoli, *Studi di diritto*, 33–34. For merchants as money changers, see Pl. *Politicus Prm.* 289c. Touchstones (*coticula*) have also been recovered from shipwreck sites: Antoinette Hesnard et al., "L'épave romaine Grand Ribaud D (Hyères, Var)," *Archaeonautica* 8 (1988): 92. See, also, Plin. *HN.* 33.126: on which, Jean Andreau, *Banking and Business in the Roman World*, trans. Janet Lloyd (Cambridge: Cambridge University Press, 1999), 146. The relative scarcity of finds of coins among shipwreck assemblages shows how reluctant maritime traders were to expose hard currency to the perils of the sea: William V. Harris, "A Strange Fact about Shipboard Coin Hoards Throws Light on the Roman Empire's Financial System," *Athenaeum* 107 (2019): 150–55.

Principal

In its standard configuration a creditor who lent on maritime terms transferred a sum of money to the debtor for the purchase of a cargo on condition that he would only be obliged to discharge the debt if the ship arrived safely at its destination. In the Athenian evidence, the amounts of the principals advanced range between 800 and 4,500 drachmae with a median of between 2,000 and 3,000 drachmae: that is, about the value of a respectable townhouse in Athens at the time.[78] The only definite figure for a principal advanced during the Roman period comes from the loan made by Keler and Charēs (SB XIV 11850), which at seven talents was enough to buy about 150 tons (500 *artabas*) of wheat at prevailing prices.[79] Though the sum of the original loan attested to by the Muziris papyrus is nowhere mentioned in the surviving portion of the document, the valuation of the cargo on the verso, which amounted to almost HS 7 million after deduction of the quarter-tax, suggests an initial investment of perhaps HS 1–2 million.[80] In both contexts, the amounts in question serve to underline Rathbone's point that cargoes were frequently more expensive and valuable than the ships that carried them:[81] in the case of the Muziris loan, the value of the cargo was almost thirty times the projected cost of building the 300-ton ship in which it was probably transported and worth more than a large and productive villa-estate near Rome.[82]

Maritime Yield

Loans given subject to a condition *salva nave*, and therefore on the basis of a *nautikē syngraphē*, produced a so-called maritime yield (*tokos nautikos*, *faenus nauticum*). The yield was 'maritime' because of the uncertainty of the duration of the voyage, which meant that it was not susceptible to denomination by time.[83] It followed that the lender could turn a substantial profit, especially if the

78. 800 dr. in Dem. 50.17; 2,000 dr. + 1,000 dr. + 4,500 dr. in Dem. 34.6; 3,000 dr. in Dem. 56.6; 3,000 dr. + 1,100 dr. + 100 Cyzicene staters (= c. 2,800 dr.; see Dem. 34.23 for the conversion rate) in Dem. 35.8, 23, 36; 4,000 dr. in Dem 52.20. Probably the 7,000 dr. in Dem. 27.11 represents the sum of more than one loan. See, generally, De Ste Croix, "Maritime Loans," 44. For the price of Athenian townhouses cf. Dem. 27.10 and 31.1: Schuster, *Das Seedarlehen*, 55.

79. For the equivalence, Rathbone, "Financing," 218.

80. Rathbone, "Financing," 221. See below, 62–63.

81. Rathbone, "Financing," 211.

82. SB XVIII 13167. According to Pliny the Younger, an estate at Tifernum Tiberinum was worth about HS 5 million in 100 CE: Plin. *Ep*. 3.19.7.

83. For this characterization, see chapter 5 below.

whole enterprise came off quickly, in which case the yield when expressed as an annual rate (once the duration of the voyage was known) could well exceed 100 percent. Rates were variable and depended upon many factors: the maximum term of the loan, the anticipated duration of the voyage, the dangerousness of the route, whether the loan was configured on a one-way or return basis, and so forth. Normally, lenders and borrowers were accustomed to dealing in conventional gradations, such that we find references in the sources to fixed yields of one-tenth (*tokos epidekatos*), one-eighth (*tokos epogdoos*), one-sixth (*tokos efektos*), one-fifth (*tokos epipemptos*), and one-third (*tokos epitritos*).[84] In Aristotle's *Rhetoric*, the comparison of Moeroklēs, a contemporary of Demosthenes and self-proclaimed lender at rates of one tenth (*epidekatōn tokōn*) with the "man [who] played the villain at 33⅓ percent (*epitritōn*)" suggests that these rates represent the outer limits of the range.[85] In Xenophon's *Poroi*, meanwhile, it is proposed that if citizens were to contribute money toward a capital fund for the construction of accommodation near to Piraeus for use by *emporoi* (merchants) and *nauklēroi*, on terms that each investor would receive a return equivalent to three obols per day, then a person who contributed ten *minae* would see an annual return of nearly one fifth—"just like maritime rates" (ναυτικὸν σχεδὸν ἐπίπεμπτον).[86]

This figure, a fifth-part, is broadly consistent with the yields demanded on return loans in the orations preserved in the Demosthenic corpus: Phormiōn received his loan of 2,000 dr. from Chrysippos and his partner for a voyage between Athens and Bosporos on condition that he repay 2,600 dr. (i.e., a yield of 30 percent);[87] Artemōn and Apollodōros received 3,000 dr. from Androklēs and Nausikratēs for the same on condition that they pay interest at a rate of 225 dr. on the thousand (i.e., a yield of 22.5 percent).[88] In the latter contract, the parties agreed on an adjustable rate, which would rise to 300 dr. on the thousand (i.e., one-third) if the borrowers failed to commence their return journey from the Black Sea before the rising of Arktouros (c. 19 September), with the increase accounting for the additional risk associated with navigation beyond the end of the traditional sailing season. The same contract contains a yet more specific term, which states that if the debtors had not entered the Euxine by ten days after the rising of the Dog Star, they were not to proceed but rather to

84. For a summary of the rates attested to in the Greek evidence, Karl G. Billeter, *Geschichte des Zinsfusses im griechisch-römischen Altertum bis auf Justinian* (Leipzig: Teubner, 1898), 40.

85. Arist. *Rh.* 1411a16–18: on which, Paul Millett, *Lending and Borrowing in Ancient Athens* (Cambridge: Cambridge University Press, 1991), 91.

86. Xen. *Por.* 3.9.

87. Dem. 34.23.

88. Dem. 35.10.

remain in the Hellespont, unload their goods at a safe port, acquire a counter-cargo, and return to Athens. If they did all this, interest would be charged at the same rate as "the previous year;" that is, the original and lower rate of 225 dr. on the thousand, since the turning of the legal year was at midsummer and therefore just before the beginning of the dog days in late July.[89] The terms of the loan taken by Callimachus were similar, but not identical: in that agreement, the stipulation that Callimachus should repay the whole amount of the loan to Eros, the supercargo, at Brentesium if he failed to depart from Apulia before the ides of September, would have been a more severe imposition on the debtor, who was paying *amphoteroploun* rates despite having taken the profit from the sale of only one cargo.

As to be expected, the rates that could be demanded on loans given for voyages of short duration were significantly lower.[90] The sources indicate that for voyages of no more than several days (perhaps in each direction) it was customary to demand a yield of one-eighth (i.e., 12.5 percent of the principal). In Nov. 106, for example, the *emporoi* and *nauklēroi* called by the praetorian prefect to give evidence attest to one-eighth as the customary yield on purely financial loans. The same figure appears again in the context of a maritime loan contract concluded for a short single journey from Sestos to Athens in the fourth century BCE;[91] maritime loan contracts connected to voyages along the Egyptian and Levantine coasts during the third century BCE and the second century CE;[92] and in a joke about a loan given to a *nauklēros* recorded in the *philogelos* (a collection compiled in the fourth or fifth century CE):[93]

> A smart aleck (*scholastikos*), a lender by trade, demanded that a *nauklēros* who was his debtor bring him a funerary urn for him and for his two eight-year-old sons, funerary urns just right for them.

Interpreting the quip presents some difficulties. A *scholastikos* who had lent money to a *nauklēros* demanded in return a cinerary urn for himself and one

89. See August Böckh, *The Public Economy of the Athenians*, trans. Anthony Lamb (London: Sampson Low, 1857), 191.

90. See, generally, Paoli, *Studi di diritto*, 64–68.

91. Dem. 50.17. This loan, however, should not be regarded as typical since it was taken by the trierarch Apollodōrus for the purpose of paying the crew's wages.

92. P. Cair. Zen. I 59010 (third century BCE), for which see Campbell C. Edgar, *Catalogue général des antiquités égyptiennes du Musée du Caire* (Le Caire Impr. de l'Institut français d'archéologie orientale, 1925), 17–19; also, Purpura, "Ricerche," 251–52. For SB XIV 11850 (second century CE), see below, 26–27.

93. *Philogelos* 50: "Σχολαστικὸς δανειστὴς ναυκλήρῳ χρεώστῃ ἐνετέλλετο σοφὸν αὐτῷ κομίσαι καὶ δύο παιδικὰς τοῖς ὀκταέτεσι παιδίοις αὐτοῦ, δικαίου μέτρου ὡς εἰς αὔξησιν."

for each of his two eight-year-old children. The use of the past tense indicates that the debt had become due, which suggests that the urns were demanded in lieu of a financial return.[94] The adult-sized urn therefore represented the principal and the children's urns the yield. The ages of the children are not coincidental: their smaller urns were intended to represent the customary yield of one-eighth on a maritime loan.[95] The joke probably consists in a play on the idea of growth: just as a maritime yield was conceived as having grown out of the principal (i.e., τόκος, *faenus*), but was fixed in proportion to the sum lent, so too the children were their father's offspring, though their funerary urns were fixed in proportion to their age. In any case, the simple point is that the ages of the children add to the evidence that a yield of one-eighth appears to have been customary in loans given on maritime terms, or at least those given in connection with voyages of a relatively short duration. If the loan was given for a single trip, it is likely that even lower rates could be expected: in Diphilos' comedy *The Painter*, a fragment of which is preserved by Athenaeos (second century CE), a cook describes the fortunes of a shipmaster who has sailed into Piraeus from Byzantium "in three days, without a scratch; who is pleased that he has made a profit of ten or twelve percent; who talks about his freight and passage money and boasts of his interest-producing capital."[96] The low rate must surely account for the advantages to the creditor of direct supervision of the borrower, the associated potential for currency exchange, and the fact that he was already making the journey in any case.

Methods by Which the Yield Was Demanded

A novel issued by Justinian in 540 CE shows that there were two ways by which creditors were accustomed to demand the yield on a maritime loan.[97] Two moneylenders—Petros and Eulogētos—had petitioned Justinian's praetorian prefect, John the Cappadocian, about disputes that had arisen with merchants (*emporoi*) and carriers (*nauklēroi*) over the customs surrounding maritime lending. Their request, which was communicated by John to Justinian, was for the prevailing usages to be clarified by imperial decree. Justinian therefore

---

94. Anna Tarwacka, *European Legal Culture through the Prism of Jokes: The Example of the Philogelos* (Wrocław: Europe of Nations and Freedom, 2018), 99–100.

95. Cf. Jean Rougé, "Le Philogélôs et la navigation," *Journal des Savants* 1–2 (1987): 11–12.

96. Ath. 7.292b: on which, Böckh, *Public Economy*, 187; cf. Billeter, *Geschichte*, 35; also, De Ste Croix, "Maritime Loans," 52, who thinks that the profit was derived from the captain's trading activity and not from lending.

97. Nov. 106.

instructed John to convene a conference of *nauklēroi* so that they could testify to the "ancient custom" (*antiqua consuetudo*) under oath. His report was as follows:

> . . . The evidence they gave, with the extra backing of an oath, was that such loans were of various kinds. Should the lenders have so chosen, they would load one modius of wheat or barley aboard the ship for each coin of whatever sum they lent, without making any payment on it to the public tax-collectors; as far as they were concerned, the vessels would sail tax-free, and they would have that as profit on what they had lent. Additionally, they would receive interest at just one gold piece in ten, with the risk of the venture being the regard of the lenders themselves. However, should the lenders not choose that method, they would receive interest at one-eighth on each coin. This would not be counted as due on any definite date, but only on the ship's safe return; and under that arrangement, it might happen that the time extended up to even a year, should the ship have spent so long away that the year had actually come to an end, or even been exceeded—whereas, if she had returned sooner, and the time only lasted a month or two, they still had the benefit of the three carats [i.e., one-eighth of a 24-carat solidus] whether the elapsed time was as short as that, or whether the loan had remained with the borrower for longer. Just the same thing applied if the traders chose to make another consecutive voyage, so that the form of the loan was fixed for one shipment at a time: it depended on the agreement reached between the parties whether it should stay the same, or be altered. However, if they should have come back, on the ship's safe return, when she could not sail again because of the season, a time-limit was given to the borrowers by the lenders of just twenty days, during which no demand for interest on what was owing could be made until sale of the shipment had taken place. Should the debt remain outstanding for longer than that, the nature of the loan changed at once and became a terrestrial one, as the lenders no longer had the worry over the perils of sea-going, and interest of two-thirds of one per cent was payable to the owners of the capital. That is what they all said, giving their evidence on oath; and that is the information you gave us, for us to put our decision into legislation . . . [98]

98. Translation by David J. D. Miller and Peter Sarris, eds., *The Novels of Justinian: A Complete Annotated English Translation*, vol. 2 (Cambridge: Cambridge University Press, 2018), 697–700.

The *nauklēroi* testified that maritime credit transactions could be structured in a number of different ways. In one method, the creditor assumed the risk and required the borrower to carry and pay duties on one *modius* of grain or barley per *solidus* lent, in addition to paying one *aureus* for each ten *modii* received. In another method, the creditor simply demanded a yield equivalent to an eighth part of the capital, not calculated with reference to a definite due date, but owing instead on the ship's safe return. According to the *nauklēroi*, there were therefore (at least) two ways of demanding the yield: the first involving the combination of a financial yield with a *quid pro quo* (i.e., the service of carrying and paying tax on the goods); the second expressed solely in financial terms.

Yields Expressed Solely in Financial Terms

A papyrus from second-century-CE Roman Egypt provides an insight into some of the lending techniques employed by lenders making purely financial loans:

> SB XIV 11850[99]
>
> From: the [. . . ? bank] of Marcus Claudius Sabinus;
> To: Zōilos son of Zōigas and Kallimēdēs son of Diogenēs, from [Aska]lōn;
> (dated) Mecheir 19, year 12 of Emperor Caesar Titus Aelius Hadrianus Antoninus Augustus Pius:
>
> By order of Gaius Longinus Keler and Tiberius Claudius Charēs, to you with Sōstratos and Sōsos, both sons of Diopeithēs, from Askalōn, co-owners together with you of the vessel named 'Antinoos Philosarapis Sōzōn,' and joint sureties for discharge (of) a maritime loan according to a maritime loan contract, of which the copy left on land is with me, the banker, on (the security of) your own(?) aforesaid vessel and [all] its gear [and the] last freight, so that the four of you have 7 tal. 5,160 dr. of

99. = SB VI 9571; P. Vindob. G 19792. See appendix II, no. 5. First published and translated by Lionel Casson, "New Light on Maritime Loans," in *Symbolae Raphaeli Taubenschlag dedicatae*, ed. Isabella Bieżuńska-Małowist and Henryk Kupiszewski, vol. 2 (Warsaw: Ossolineum, 1956), 89–93. For alternative translations, see, e.g., Gilbert Charles-Picard and Jean Rougé, *Textes et documents relatifs à la vie économique et sociale dans l'empire romain, 31 avant J.-C.—225 après J.-C. Collection Regards sur l'histoire* (Paris: Société d'Edition d'Enseignement Supérieur, 1969), no. LXII; Rathbone, "Financing," 217–18.

> silver, with the 7 tal. which you had by hand, the remaining [5,]160 dr., without prejudice to one of them, Gaius Longinus Keler, as regards the other [. . dr.] which [Kallimedes] son of Diogenes owes him [—-] yie[ld] tal. [—-.

SB XIV 11850 is a banker's receipt that contains a reference to a *nautikē syngraphē* and refers to some of its clauses.[100] The papyrus, which comes from the Fayyum (probably the village of Karanis), is dated to 13 February, 149 CE (just ahead of the sailing season) and belonged to the archive of a bank run by a certain M. Claudius Sabinus.[101] In the document, two creditors—C. Longinus Keler and Ti. Claudius Charēs—are described as having ordered a payment of the balance on a maritime loan to four borrowers from Askalōn in Palestine. The four borrowers—Zōilos, Kallimēdēs, and two brothers, Sōstratos and Sōzōn—were co-owners (*synnauklēroi*) of a light merchant vessel (*akatos*) bearing the name *Antinoos Philosarapis Sōzōn*.[102] Zoilos and Kallimēdēs received the funds (probably from Sabinus' bank in Alexandria) and the four borrowers jointly guaranteed repayment.[103]

The document states that the money paid over by the bank was advanced as a "maritime loan, in accordance with a maritime (loan) contract." A copy of the agreement was left on land with the bank, and security taken over the ship, its gear, and the "last freight."[104] The total amount of the loan is given as 7 talents and 5,160 drachmas (i.e., 47,160 drachmas, enough to buy c. 150 tons of wheat in the province at the time).[105] Seven talents is recorded as already having been paid out in cash. A figure—]60 or]160—is then given below, and it is reasonable to assume (with Biscardi) that it records the receipt by the borrowers of the remaining 5,160 dr.[106] The document ends with a statement that the rights of one of the lenders, Keler, were not to be diminished in relation to other debts owed to him by one of the borrowers, Kallimēdēs. There is, at the end of the

100. Seidl argued that the loan recorded in the papyrus was one for which two shipmasters had made their *exercitores* liable on the basis of the *actio exercitoria*: Erwin Seidl, "Review of Symbolae Raphaeli Taubenschlag dedicatae, 2 (=Eos, 48/2 [1956]), Ossolineum, Vratislaviae-Varsaviae," *SDHI* 23 (1957): 360; Seidl, "Juristische Papyruskunde," *SDHI* 24 (1958): 439.

101. For Karanis, Rathbone, "Financing," 217.

102. On *akatos*-type vessels and the ship's name, Casson, "New Light" (1986), 13; Casson, *Ships and Seamanship in the Ancient World* (Baltimore: Johns Hopkins University Press, 1995), 159–60.

103. According to Rathbone, SB III 6291 (= P. Freib. II 8) shows that Sabinus' bank was located in Alexandria: Rathbone, "Financing," 218.

104. For the security aspect, see below, 41.

105. Rathbone, "Financing," 218.

106. Biscardi, *Actio*, 205.

fragment, an unmistakable reference to a "yield" (τοκ[), though I agree with Casson that whatever was said here was likely connected to the arrangement between Keler and Kallimēdēs discussed immediately above.[107]

Rathbone's prosopographical research into the background of the actors identified in the papyrus sheds light upon the context of the loan.[108] The *tria nomina* of both the banker (Sabinus) and lenders (Keler and Charēs) indicate that they were Roman citizens, and possibly (in the case of the lenders) Romanized Greeks. Sabinus looks to have run a bank that served the Romanized Egyptian elite, and Keler (probably also Charēs) appears to have been involved variously in landowning, tax-collecting, state supply contracts, and lending.[109] All things considered, the lenders likely anticipated that any dispute would ultimately end up in front of the prefect of the province, which is precisely what happened in 142 when the adjudication of a lawsuit in which Keler was involved was delegated by the magistrate to the prefect of the (Alexandrian) fleet.[110] Roman law was therefore a relevant consideration.

How was the loan structured from a financial perspective? Some scholars have taken the document at face value and supposed that the 5,160 dr. was the second installment payable on a loan totaling 47,160 dr.[111] This is certainly possible: the language used is similar to that in other loan documents in which the money was paid in installments.[112] The oddly specific figure has led to speculation about what the sum was for. Jones suggests that the original loan may have amounted to 8 t., the 7 t. and 5,160 representing this sum less a handling fee charged by the bank.[113] A better explanation, however, has been offered by Thür, who argues that the actual sum of the loan was 7 t. (i.e., 42,000 dr.), and the 5,160 dr.—roughly 12 percent of the principal—was the amount to be owed by the borrowers as the yield.[114]

Thür's interpretation is also consistent with the second loan structure reported by the *nauklēroi* in Nov. 106 (i.e., of a yield expressed solely in financial

107. Casson, "New Light" (1986), 14.

108. Rathbone, "Financing," 218–20.

109. Rathbone, 219.

110. Gerhard Thür, "Arnaldo Biscardi e il diritto greco: (riflessioni sul prestito marittimo SB VI 9571)," *Dike* 3 (2000): 185. For the case in 142 CE, P. Stras. IV 281: on which, Rathbone, "Financing," 219.

111. E.g., Casson, "New Light" (1986), 14; Rathbone, "Financing," 218; David F. Jones, *The Bankers of Puteoli: Finance, Trade and Industry in the Roman World* (Stroud: Tempus, 2006), 183.

112. Herbert C. Youtie, "Notes on Papyri," *TAPhA* 91 (1960): 260–63.

113. Jones, *The Bankers of Puteoli*, 183.

114. Thür conjectures that a bank charge of 120 dr. would explain the difference between the lower amount of 12 percent of the principal (i.e., 5,040 dr.) and the higher sum of 5,160 documented here: Thür, "Arnaldo Biscardi," 283; also, Éva Jakab and Ulrich Manthe, "Recht in der römischen Antike," in *Rechtskulturen der Antike*, ed. Ulrich Manthe (Munich: C.H. Beck, 2003), 280.

terms). Several other points of alignment lend further support. First, we know that the loan was given subject to a maritime loan contract (*nautikē syngraphē*) and must therefore have been productive of a maritime yield, conventionally expressed as a fixed proportion of the principal. Whereas Thür reckoned that the 5,160 dr. amounted to c. 12 percent of the principal, in fact the figure is closer to 12.5 percent, or one-eighth, which is the same proportion that the *nauklēroi* in Nov. 106 claimed was the customary yield.[115] If, as is possible, the loan given here was for the short three-day trip (without stops) from Alexandria to Askalōn, then a yield of one-eighth would be consistent with the other short voyages attested in the evidence for which a similar yield was demanded. All this counts in favor of the view that the 5,160 dr. recorded in SB XIV 11850 was therefore intended to represent the yield demanded by the lender and was calculated as a fixed proportion of the sum lent.

The question that arises is, if the 5,160 dr. represents the yield, why does the document appear to show the borrowers receiving it from the lenders? The most plausible explanation is that the loan was given *atokos*, just like the loan given to the five *synploi* at Ptolemaic Alexandria by Archippos. On Thür's analysis, this meant that the debtor had received less than the sum stated since the yield was already included in the amount represented as the principal. Significantly, the same hypothesis (i.e., capitalization of the yield) has been relied upon by a number of scholars to explain the absence of due dates and stipulations for interest in the loan documents preserved in the archive of the Sulpicii, which relate to business transacted in the port of Puteoli during the middle part of the first century CE. In this connection, two possible techniques have been advanced: (1) that the lender deducted interest in advance from the sum paid out to the debtor, so that the amount of the principal was effectively overstated;[116] and (2) that after the lender had counted out the principal to the borrower, a portion was immediately and voluntarily paid back in the name of 'future interest.'[117] In practical terms, these latter two explanations are quite similar: both involved stating the whole amount of the debt as a lump sum with a view to creating a single obligation for the debtor to repay. When taken together with the argument that the 5,160 drachmas in SB XIV 11850 represent

115. 12.5 percent of 42,000 is 5,250: i.e., 90 dr. more than the sum of 5,160 attested here.

116. See Plut. *De vitando* 5; also, [Ps.-]Asc. *Verr.* 1.36.91: on which, Lucio Bove, *Documenti di operazioni finanziarie dall'archivio dei Sulpici: Tabulae Pompeianae di Murécine* (Naples: Liguori, 1984), 41–42 and 47–48; Giuseppe Camodeca, *L'archivio puteolano dei Sulpicii* (Naples: Università Napoli Federico II, 1992), 174–77; also, Camodeca, *TPS*, 2:134; and Peter Gröschler, "Die Konzeption des Mutuum cum Stipulatione," *TvR* 74 (2006): 267–69.

117. Koenraad Verboven, "The Sulpicii from Puteoli and Usury in the Early Roman Empire," *TvR* 71 (2003): 17–19.

the yield of one-eighth on a maritime loan of seven talents, the document was likely intended as an acknowledgment by the borrowers of the total amount of the debt, which was engineered by stating the yield as having been received, when in fact they had either not received it at all or already paid the yield up-front as 'future interest.'

On the evidence presented thus far, it is not possible to say which of these two methods—overstatement of the principal or the payment of 'future interest'—was used in the transaction documented by SB XIV 11850. There are, however, slight indications in the juristic texts that the technique of demanding 'future interest' was sometimes relied upon by maritime lenders. According to Florentinus, a lender who accepted interest in advance appeared tacitly to have agreed that he would not seek the capital during the period for which the interest was paid.[118] Ulpian agreed, adding that if the creditor brought a claim during the intervening period the borrower would be able to repel it using the *exceptio doli*.[119] Both opinions proceed from the idea that since *usura* was conceived as the creditor's reward for furnishing the borrower with the use (*usus*) of the money, he ought only to be able to recover the capital once the funds had been at the debtor's disposal for a period of time commensurate to the amount of the interest paid.[120]

The technique also features in the 28th book of the *digesta* of Q. Cervidius Scaevola, in the fragment immediately preceding the text reporting the terms of Callimachus' loan contract:[121]

> [pr.] A borrower who had taken a loan at Rome (*qui Romae mutuam pecuniam acceperat*) promised by stipulation to pay it back in a distant province three months later. After a few days he testified before the creditor that he was prepared to repay the money in Rome, having deducted that sum which he had given to the creditor in the name of interest. The question was, since he offered the whole sum for which he was bound by stipulation, whether it could still be sought at the time and place where performance was promised? Scaevola replied that the stipulator was able to sue at the place where performance was promised on the appointed day.
>
> [1] Callimachus took from Stichus, slave of Seius, a money loan on maritime terms (*mutuam pecuniam nauticam accepit*) in the province of Syria for a sea voyage from Berytus to Brentesium . . .

118. D.2.14.57 pr. (Flor. 8 *inst.*).

119. D.44.4.2.6 (Ulp. 76 *ad ed.*): ". . . *si creditor usuras in futurum acceperit* . . ." The possibility that interest could be paid in advance was also countenanced by Justinian: C.4.32.28.1 (Iust., 529).

120. See, e.g., D.36.1.60(58).6 (Pap. 9 *resp.*); also, D.22.1.16.1 (Paul. 1 *decr.*). Ambrose put the issue with chiastic brevity in *de Tobia*, 5: "*usum requirit, ut adquirit usuram*."

121. D.45.1.122 pr.–1 (Scaev. 28 *dig.*).

The structure of the loan described in the *principium* is analogous to those discussed by Florentinus and Ulpian: a borrower, who took a loan in Rome and promised to repay it in a distant province three months later, changed his mind after only a few days and attempted to tender repayment in Rome, but only of the sum that remained following deduction of the amount he had already paid to the creditor in the name of interest (*detracta ea summa, quam creditori suo usurarum nomine dederat*).[122] The question was whether the creditor was still entitled to sue on the stipulation at the promised place and time, notwithstanding that the borrower was apparently offering to satisfy the whole debt (*in integrum summam*). Both Mommsen (*nec integram*) and Cohn (*non integram*) suggested emending *in integrum summam* to resolve the fact that the borrower appeared to be offering less in Rome than he would have owed in the distant province.[123] The emendation is unnecessary: when the borrower tendered early repayment, he had not yet had use of the funds, which made it arguable that the money paid upfront "in the name of interest" ought still to be conceived as a part of the principal that he was bound to repay under the stipulation. The question was therefore whether, in offering to repay the loan early, less the money already handed over in the name of interest, this would fulfill the promise and discharge the obligation. Scaevola's reply was that it would not: the borrower could be held to his promise to perform at a certain time and place, a further consequence of which was that, having had the use of the money for three months, he was obliged to pay the whole sum for which he was bound, without being able to deduct the money he had paid upfront.[124]

The passage continues into the fragment reporting the contents of the mari-

122. Alice Cherchi, *Ricerche sulle 'usurae' convenzionali nel diritto romano classico* (Naples: Jovene, 2012), 29–34; also, Camodeca, *L'archivio puteolano*, 175–76; Camodeca, *TPS*, 2:133–34; Camodeca, "La prassi giuridica municipale: Il problema dell'effettività del diritto romano," in *Gli statuti municipali*, ed. Luigi Capogrossi Colognesi and Emilio Gabba (Pavia: IUSS Press, 2006), 541; cf. Peter Gröschler, *Die Tabellae-Urkunden aus den pompejanischen und herkulanensischen Urkundenfunden* (Berlin: Duncker & Humblot, 1997), 158–59; Gröschler, "Darlehensvalutierung und Darlehenszins in den Urkunden aus dem Archiv der Sulpizier," in *Festschrift für Rolf Knütel zum 70. Geburtstag*, ed. Holger Altmeppen, Ingo Reichard, and Martin J. Schermaier (Heidelberg: C.F. Müller, 2009), 392–94; Gröschler, "Il 'mutuum cum stipulatione' e il problema degli interessi," in *Quaderni lupiensi di storia e diritto*, ed. Francesca Lamberti (Lecce: Edizioni del Grifo, 2009), 120–22.

123. Max Cohn, *Die sogenannte actio de eo quod certo loco: Eine Untersuchung aus dem römischen Recht* (Berlin: Weidmann, 1877), 98.

124. This is consistent with Ulpian's decision in D.13.4.9 (Ulp. 47 *ad Sab.*) that a person who had stipulated performance in a certain place was entitled to refuse it elsewhere. If the person who owed the money failed to perform in the agreed place, the plaintiff could rely upon the praetorian *actio de eo quod certo loco*, which empowered the judge to increase the sum due to reflect the plaintiff's *interesse* in performance at that place. This would be relevant if, for example, the plaintiff had lent *pecunia traiecticia* to the borrower on terms that it be repaid elsewhere. If the borrower failed to repay at the place specified, so that the plaintiff incurred a loss (e.g., because he was forced to default on a debt, so that a penalty became due, or his goods were sold as security), he would have the action to increase the obligation of the borrower in order to recover: D.13.4.2.8 (Ulp. 27 *ad ed.*).

time loan contract entered into by Callimachus. Focusing upon the structure of the loan, several features indicate that the yield was capitalized in the manner that I suggested for the loan to Zōilos and Kallimēdēs (SB XIV 11850). First, given that Scaevola apparently had access to the *cautio*, the absence of an interest clause in the otherwise detailed description of the terms of the contract indicates that the obligation to pay the yield was documented elsewhere. If, as was typical in maritime loan contracts, the lender demanded the yield as a fixed sum, then it was likely expressed as part of the total acknowledgment of debt in the chirograph.[125] This explains why Scaevola was limited to stating that the loan was "*nautica*" (i.e., given for a fixed yield and with an uncertain due date), since it was impossible to ascertain the portion of the acknowledged debt that represented the yield. Second, certain stylistic features suggest a continuity between the arrangement described in the *principium* and the loan to Callimachus. In the *principium*, the borrower received his money as a *mutuum*—"*qui Romae mutuam pecuniam acceperat*"—and then immediately repaid a portion of it to the lender. In the next passage, Callimachus received his loan on the same basis—"*Callimachus mutuam pecuniam nauticam accepit*"—the only difference being that the money was understood to be "*nautica*." This stylistic continuity suggests, if only lightly, that the loan not only involved the capitalization of the yield, but perhaps also the payment of future interest (as in the *principium*). Third, and finally, the condition that required Callimachus to leave Brentesium with a new cargo before 13 September makes sense in light of this structure. If he failed to leave by this date, he was obliged to pay everything he owed to Eros at Brentesium, as if the voyage had come to an end without interruption. Since Callimachus owed a fixed sum, this meant an equivalent amount to that originally transferred by the lender, notwithstanding the merchant's voluntary payment of a portion of the proceeds upfront. The condition was therefore penal in substance:[126] since the yield had been paid in advance and negotiated in the context of a round trip during which two lots of cargo were intended to be bought and sold, repayment of an *amphoteroploun* yield at the outport would have required Callimachus to find the difference without having profited from the sale of goods on his return to Berytus.

Interlinked Contracts

Interlinked contracts are agreements in which "the two parties trade in at least two markets on the condition that the terms of all such trades are jointly deter-

125. Drawing the same conclusion, Gröschler, *Die Tabellae-Urkunden*, 161 n. 46.
126. Biscardi, *Actio*, 79; Pontoriero, *Il prestito marittimo*, 146.

mined . . . Loosely speaking, there is a 'package' or 'bundled' deal, in which each element in the deal is connected to every other in an essential way."[127] In the context of long-distance trade, one option available to merchants and carriers was to interlink the two standard form contracts at the heart of the enterprise: that is, a maritime loan contract with a contract of affreightment. The only firm evidence for this phenomenon is furnished by Nov. 106, in which creditors bargained for the carriage of their goods in combination with a reduced financial yield on the capital advanced as a loan.[128] Though the evidence is late, there are good reasons to believe that the same technique was practiced during earlier periods: the *nauklēroi* were asked to attest to the ancient customs, several of which find correspondence in the classical documentation (e.g., the customary yield of one-eighth, the twenty-day grace period).[129] Notwithstanding that the novel has no direct corroboration in the rest of the evidence from the Roman period, there are a handful of documents that can be interpreted in a manner that is consistent with the first of the loan structures reported by the Constantinopolitan *nauklēroi*.

TPSulp. 78[130]

On the 3rd of the ides of April under the consulate of M. Aquila Iulianus and P. Nonius Asprenas at Dikaearcheïa, I, Menelaos, son of Irēnaos, from Keramos, hereby acknowledge that I have received from Primus, slave of Publius Attius Severus, the sum of 1,000 *denarii* according to the duly signed document of affreightment we have concluded. I will repay willingly the money that I have taken out according to the agreement that I have made with him. And I have set as surety for the payment of the above-mentioned 1,000 *denarii*, Marcus Barbatius Keler.

I, Quintus Aelius Romanus, have written on behalf and in the presence of Marcus Barbatius Keler at his request and by his mandate, because he says that he does not know his letters, that he [Keler] guarantees the above-mentioned 1,000 *denarii* to Primus, slave of Publius Attius Severus, on behalf of Menelaos, son of Irēnaos, from Keramos—as

127. Clive Bell, "Credit Markets and Interlinked Transactions," in *Handbook of Development Economics*, ed. Hollis Chenery and T. N. Srinivasan, vol. 1 (Amsterdam: Elsevier, 1988), 797. See also Debraj Ray, *Development Economics* (Princeton: Princeton University Press, 1998), 561–72.

128. For a more developed version of this argument, Peter Candy, "Credit for Carriage: TPSulp. 78 and P. Oxy. XLV 3250," in *Roman Law and Maritime Commerce*, ed. Peter Candy and Emilia Mataix Ferrándiz (Edinburgh: Edinburgh University Press, 2022), 171–86.

129. Similarly, Purpura, "Ricerche," 327.

130. = *TP* 13; *TPN* 68. See appendix II, no. 6. For alternative translations (into German), see Éva Jakab, "Vectura pro mutua: Überlegungen zu TP 13 und Ulp. D. 19, 2, 15, 61," *ZRG RA* 117 (2000): 245 n. 2; Wolf, *TPN*, 103–4.

has been written above. (Three seals of Menelaos, Q. Aelius Romanus, and M. Barbatius Keler.)

TPSulp. 78 consists of a diptych of wax tablets made up of two *chirographa* dated 11 April, 38 CE, discovered in 1959 at a site near to Pompeii among a collection of over 100 *tabulae* kept by a financial business that was operated by the Sulpicii during the middle part of the first century CE.[131] The first chirograph, which was written in Greek, contained declarations made by an individual called Menelaos, son of Irēnaos, who hailed from Keramos in Karia (Asia Minor). In the document Menelaos declared: first (p.1, ll. 5–9), that he had received 1,000 *denarii* (= HS 4,000) from a certain Primus, slave of P. Attius Severus, "arising from a sealed contract of affreightment" ("ἐκ ναυλωτικῆς ἐκσφραγισμένης"); second (p.1, ll. 10–12), that he would willingly repay the money "according to" the document of affreightment concluded between them; and third (p. 1, l. 12—p. 2, l. 3), that a certain M. Barbatius Keler would stand as surety in his stead. The second chirograph, which was composed in Latin, contained a declaration made by a certain Q. Aelius Romanus that, because Keler was illiterate, he was acting on his behalf, and that the latter agreed to guarantee Menelaos' repayment of the money.

There are a wide variety of views on the transaction that lay behind the documentation. The transfer of the 1,000 *d.* from Primus to Menelaos has been understood variously as money handed over for transport to an agent overseas (Wolf);[132] a maritime loan (Ankum—though he later abandoned this position in favor of Wolf's);[133] a '*Versicherungsdarlehen*,' or 'insurance loan' (Gofas);[134]

131. The Sulpicii were well-connected businessmen who specialized as credit-intermediaries and financiers for long-distance traders: Koenraad Verboven, "Capital Markets and Financial Entrepreneurs in the Roman World," in *Capital, Investment, and Innovation in the Roman World*, ed. Paul Erdkamp, Koenraad Verboven, and Arjan Zuiderhoek (Oxford: Oxford University Press, 2020), 394–95. The presence of two *chirographa* in the same document is unusual, but not unique: Camodeca, *TPS*, 2:178; also, Joseph G. Wolf, "Aus dem neuen pompejanischen Urkundenfund: Die 'naulotike' des Menelaos—Seedarlehen oder Seefrachtvertrag?," in *Iuris vincula: Studi in onore di Mario Talamanca* (Naples: Jovene, 2001), 426.

132. Joseph G. Wolf, "Aus dem neuen pompejanischen Urkundenfund. Der Seefrachtvertrag des Menelaos," *Freiburger Universitätsblätter* 65 (1979): 34.

133. Johan A. Ankum, "Tabula Pompeiana 13: ein Seefrachtvertrag oder ein Seedarlehen?," *IVRA* 29 (1978): 168–69; Ankum, "Minima de Tabula Pompeiana 13," *Cahiers d'histoire. Navires et commerces de la Méditerranée antique. Homage à Jean Rougé* 33 (1988): 282; Ankum, "Observations sur le prêt maritime romain, sujet cher à Henryk Kupiszewski," in *Le droit romain et le monde contemporain: Melanges à la mémoire de Henryk Kupiszewski*, ed. Witold Wołodkiewicz and Maria Zabłocka (Warsaw: Université de Varsovie, 1996), 67–68. Cf. Ankum, "Noch einmal: die Naulootike des Menelaos in TP 13 (=TPSulp. 78)—Ein Seedarlehen oder ein Seefrachtvertrag?," in *Roman Law as Formative of Modern Legal Systems: Studies in Honour of Wieslaw Litewski*, ed. Janusz Sondel, P. Ścislicki, and Jaroslaw Reszczynski (Krakow: Jagiellonian University Press, 2003), 454.

134. Dimitri C. Gofas, "Encore une fois sur la Tabula Pompeiana 13 (essai d'une interprétation nouvelle)," in *Symposion 1993. Vorträge zur griechischen und hellenistischen Rechtsgeschichte (Graz-Andritz, 12–16 September 1993)*, ed. Gerhard Thür (Cologne and Vienna: Böhlau, 1994), 251–66.

an '*aestimationsabrede*,' or cargo valuation (Thür);[135] money advanced to pay *portoria* and other fees (Jones, Rathbone);[136] a loan given to enable Menelaos, a merchant, to pay a freight charge to an unidentified third party (De Romanis);[137] and as the advance payment to Menelaos, a *nauklēros*, of a freight charge (*vectura pro mutua*) (Jakab).[138] My own interpretation of the document, which I have developed at more length elsewhere, falls back upon the transactional structures described by the *nauklēroi* in Nov. 106 and the loan documentation in the Graeco-Roman papyri, which demonstrate that it was not uncommon for credit and transport contracts to be interlinked by parties with variegated interests in moneylending, the carriage of goods, and overseas trade.[139] In brief, we know that: the advance of 1,000 *d.* was couched in language normally used in other documents to describe the giving and receiving of loans; it was given in connection with a *naulotikē eksfragismenē*, or contract of affreightment; and that Primus was a slave owned by a certain P. Attius Severus, whose trading interests between Italy and Baetica have been established through attestations in the *tituli picti*.[140] We also know from shipwreck evidence that it was common for merchant-carriers to transport their own goods alongside those of other merchants, and that the lenders who financed maritime trade (certainly at Piraeus in the fourth century BCE and likely also in the Roman context, even if they were operating from a *peculium*) frequently had either active or former trading interests.[141] All this makes it possible to interpret the underlying transaction as one in which Menelaos (a *nauklēros*) received 1,000 *d.* as a loan (possibly, though not necessarily, at the lender's risk) and agreed in the contract of affreightment to offer his services partly or wholly in place of paying a financial yield. The result was an 'interlinked contract'—credit for carriage—in which a credit agreement and freight contract were rolled into one.

135. Gerhard Thür, "Die Aestimationsabrede im Seefrachtvertrag: Diskussionsbeitrag zum Referat Dimitri C. Gofas," in *Symposion 1993. Vorträge zur griechischen und hellenistischen Rechtsgeschichte (Graz-Andritz, 12–16 September 1993)*, ed. Gerhard Thür (Vienna: Böhlau, 1994), 267–71.

136. Jones, *The Bankers of Puteoli*, 103–17; Dominic Rathbone, "Merchant Networks in the Greek World: The Impact of Rome," *Mediterranean Historical Review* 22, no. 2 (2007): 315.

137. Federico De Romanis, "Timoteo, Apollodoro e i chirographa di TPSulp. 78," in *Uomini, istituzioni, mercati. Studi di storia per Elio Lo Cascio*, ed. Marco Maiuro et al. (Bari: Edipuglia, 2019), 443–48; also, De Romanis, *Pepper Trade*, 193–98.

138. Jakab, "Vectura pro mutua," 253–54.

139. See, generally, Candy, "Credit for Carriage" (with literature).

140. *CIL* XV 3642–5 and 4748–9 (Dressels 7–11 and 20): on which, Camodeca, *TPS*, 2:179. Cf. Rosario Rovira Guardiola, "El Archivo Sulpicio y los tituli picti β: Circulación de comerciantes en el Mediterráneo," in *Acta XII congressus internationalis epigraphiae graecae et latinae (Barcelona, 3–8 Septembris 2002)*, ed. Marc Mayer i Olivé, Giulia Baratta, and Alejandra Guzmán Almagro (Barcelona: Institut d'Estudis Catalans, 2007), 1264–65.

141. See, in this connection, chapter 2.

Conclusion

The evidence for the financial structure of maritime lending arrangements shows a discernible pattern: loans were customarily given *atokos*, which is to say either by capitalizing the yield or partly or wholly in return for a *quid pro quo*. In general, loans to merchants who were not also *nauklēroi* were likely to be purely financial since they lacked control of a vessel and therefore the capacity to offer any meaningful performance to the creditor besides the payment of a pecuniary yield. In this scenario, besides an acknowledgment of the debt, the terms of the arrangement were set out in a *nautikē syngraphē*, such as the one referred to in SB XIV 11850 and of which the Callimachus contract serves as a good example. However, where the borrower was a merchant-carrier (in the papyri, *nauklērokybernētēs*),[142] it was sometimes mutually advantageous for the parties to bundle the credit arrangement together with a contract of affreightment, setting the yield and freight charge off against one another in the process. Where contracts were interlinked, one would expect to find the acknowledgment of debt connected to a *naulotikē syngraphē*, of which *TPSulp.* 78 might be an example. Possibly the arrangement documented by SB III 7169 also featured an element of interlinkage (Wilhelm's hypothesis), though any conclusions drawn from this fragmentary document must necessarily be tentative.

The Condition '*si salva nave*'

The special and distinguishing feature of a maritime loan contract, which was the economic justification for the creditor's demand for an elevated yield and the reason for its falling outside the scope of the legal limit on interest rates (not only at Rome, but apparently also at Rhodes, which, unlike Athens, regulated interest rates too), was that the obligation to repay principal and yield was conditional upon the safe arrival of the ship at its destination. Demon, in *Against Zēnothemis*, says that the condition that the money was to be paid back if the ship reached port safely was "usual in all such cases;" and again, in both the orations *Against Phormiōn* ("When the ship reaches port in safety . . .") and *Against Dionysodōros* ("And if the ship arrives safe at Piraeus . . .") the contract is likely quoted verbatim.[143] The absence of any explicit evidence for the clause

142. See Casson, *Ships and Seamanship*, 316.

143. Dem. 32.5; 56.31, 36, 41. Cf. Carey and Reid, who doubt the authenticity of the two quotations given from the contract at Dem. 56.36 because they are not whole clauses: Christopher Carey and R. A. Reid, *Selected Private Speeches* (Cambridge: Cambridge University Press, 1985),

in any of the contractual documentation from the Roman period is not entirely surprising: in the only *nautikē syngraphē* for which we have any evidence of the terms (i.e., the contract entered into by Callimachus), it was implied in Scaevola's statement that the borrower received the money "*nautica*." In any case, there is no doubt that the usual form of the condition continued to refer to the safe arrival of the ship: the jurist Paul explicitly refers to loans given on terms that the debt would only become owing "*si salva nave . . . pervenerit*"; and again that recovery was only possible "*ut salva nave*."[144] Diocletian's statements in the Code make the position abundantly clear: the risk remained with the creditor "until the ship runs into the harbor" and again "before the ship arrives at its destination."[145] In the later texts, the tendency is to speak of the creditor's assumption of the risk (*periculum creditoris*), which of course presupposes the inclusion of the condition in the contract.[146]

The one exception to the otherwise uniform convention that the debtor's obligation to repay was made contingent upon the safe arrival of the ship occurs in the contract produced in the speech *Against Lakritos*, in which the borrowers were only obliged to repay "if the goods [were] brought safe to Athens . . ."[147] In Ashburner's view, the framing of the condition depended upon the subject of the security: if security was taken over the ship, then the repayment of the loan was made contingent upon the safe arrival of the vessel, and correspondingly if security was over the cargo, so too the condition was framed in that relation.[148] Probably, however, we should not make too much of the difference: both contingencies were clearly intended to make repayment conditional upon the successful completion of the enterprise. That said, a condition framed in relation to the ship narrowed the scope for fraud and benefited the creditor: preventing the safe arrival of the ship, in the safety of which others might also have an interest, was in almost every case a more difficult task than achieving the destruction or disappearance of the goods.[149] This explains some of the difficulties in Androklēs' case against Lakritos, since it was left open to the latter to argue, in spite of the borrowers' safe arrival (albeit in a different ship and

228. However, there are good reasons why Dareios, in the context of his argument, would have chosen to quote the *syngraphe* selectively. See below, 121–25.

144. D.22.2.6 (Paul. 25 *quaest.*); D.22.2.7 (Paul. 3 *ad ed.*).

145. C.4.33.2 (Diocl./Maxim. AA. Scribonio Honorato); C.4.33.5 (Diocl./Maxim. AA. et CC. Pullio Iuliano Eucharisto).

146. See, e.g., PS.2.14.3.

147. Dem. 35.11.

148. Walter Ashburner, *ΝΟΜΟΣ ΡΟΔΙΩΝ ΝΑΥΤΙΚΟΣ. The Rhodian Sea-Law* (Oxford: Clarendon Press, 1909), ccxiv.

149. Though even this was not enough to deter the most determined fraudsters. See, for example, the allegations made against Zēnothemis and his collaborator, the *nauklēros* Hēgestratos, whose attempts to sink the vessel ended in farce: Dem. 32.5–9.

not directly at Piraeus, but at the Thieves' Harbor nearby), that the goods were lost due to shipwreck and that a good case could be made that the debtors had faithfully observed the terms of the agreement.[150] The framing of the condition in relation to the goods therefore placed the burden upon the creditor to show that, notwithstanding the failure of the condition, the borrowers' obligation to repay had still arisen for breach of the agreement (e.g., failure to load a return cargo, using the proceeds of the loan to make a loan of their own).

Another feature of the contract produced by Androklēs, which is unique in the ancient evidence, is the inclusion of several terms intended to qualify the operation of the condition in the event of jettison, ransom, and salvage.[151] In the case of jettison and ransom payments, the contract states that the debtors will be liable in full if the goods arrived safely, "except for such jettison (*plēn ekbolēs*) as those sailing in the ship may have made by common agreement, and anything they may pay to enemies."[152] The brevity of the language and the need for common agreement suggests that the principles governing the distribution of the losses among those who benefited from the jettison were both customary and widely recognized. If these rules were consistent with the *lex Rhodia de iactu*, then this would imply that the borrowers were entitled to deduct their net loss after contribution from the amount to be repaid. The exact method by which this sum was arrived at is open to conjecture: in the simplest case, we can imagine that the debtor was entitled to deduct the sum paid by each participant as contribution, or indeed toward the ransom, as though the payment had been incurred as an expense. Although the clause appears to amount to a concession on the part of the creditors, it must principally have been intended to incentivize risk aversion on the part of the debtors. On the other hand, the creditors were also careful to protect against fraud, by stipulating that the debtors would only be entitled to deductions if the jettison had been made by common consent (and therefore not solely by their own initiative).[153] Finally, the contract also provided that any goods that were lost in transit and later salvaged should become the property of the creditors, so that even though the debtors were relieved of the obligation to repay on failure of the condition *salva nave*, they would not be unjustifiably enriched at the lenders' expense.[154]

150. Dem. 35.30.

151. See, generally, Paoli, *Studi di diritto*, 82–84; De Ste Croix, "Maritime Loans," 57–58; Schuster, *Das Seedarlehen*, 64–66.

152. Dem. 35.11.

153. For this point, see David Haubner, *Studien zur lex Rhodia de iactu* (Munich: C.H. Beck, 2021), 119–20.

154. Dem. 35.13. For the intention behind the clause, see Gerhard Thür, "Ownership and Secured Credit in Athens: A Response to Mark J. Sundahl," in *Symposion 2013: Vorträge zur griechischen und hellenistischen Rechtsgeschichte (Cambridge MA, 26.-29. August 2013)*, ed. Michael Gagarin and Adriaan Lanni (Vienna: VÖAW, 2014), 242–43.

Time Limits, Events Triggering the Debtor's Obligation to Repay, and Grace Periods

Besides the condition *salva nave*, maritime loan contracts also typically contained a maximum time limit for the duration of the voyage and internal time limits for departure from certain ports or sea zones along the way. Very often these time limits were customary: in the trade between the Red Sea and Malabar coasts, for example, Pliny the Elder wrote that ships were required to leave Egypt around 20 July and begin their return journey from Muziris by the next 13 January, arriving at Alexandria within a year of their original departure.[155] In the Callimachus loan contract, the money was given for "the whole period of 200 days of sailing," which is to say that if the merchant, having left Brentesium before 13 September, had still not returned to Berytus more than 200 days after his original departure from Syria, the lender would no longer assume the risk. As we have already seen, the contract produced in the oration *Against Lakritos* also provided for adjustable interest rates that changed according to the debtor's rate of progress.[156] The obvious point is that the time limits were designed to circumscribe the period during which the creditor shouldered the risk by providing for deadlines that were aligned with points in the sailing season.[157]

The combination of the condition *salva nave* with time limits for the maximum duration of the voyage produced two events that would trigger the debtor's obligation to repay.[158] The first of these events was the passing of the due date introduced by the maximum term of the loan (i.e., the *dies praestitutus*). While it is true, as De Romanis has argued, that the *dies praestitutus* was seldom, if ever, specified as a calendric date, it was nevertheless calculable with reference to the occurrence of a definite event, such as the ship's departure from the homeport.[159] In the Roman context, both the jurists Paul and Papinian anticipated the possibility that the borrower might still be at sea when the term expired.[160] That the merchant might be so long delayed, even if he left the trading port in good time, was a real possibility: vessels could be blown significantly off course, detained at stopovers by customs officials, and so forth.[161]

155. Plin. *HN*. 6.104–6: on which, De Romanis, "Time to Repay," 80–81; De Romanis, *Pepper Trade*, 168–69. See, also, *Peripl. M. Rubr.* 14.

156. Dem. 35.10, 13.

157. See, e.g., Sirks, "Sailing in the Off-Season," 142–49.

158. Jakab, "Loans and Securities," 142; also, Konstantin Tanev, "Some Highlights on the Problem of 'Maritime Loans,'" in *Règle et pratique du droit dans les réalités juridiques de l'Antiquité*, ed. Isabella Piro (Soveria Mannelli: Rubbettino, 1999), 540, fig. 1. Cf. De Romanis, who argues that maritime loan contracts "never specify the deadline for the loan repayment with an a priori calendric date": De Romanis, *Pepper Trade*, 159, also 166.

159. De Romanis, *Pepper Trade*, 159.

160. D.22.2.4 (Pap. 3 *resp.*) and D.22.2.6 (Paul. 25 *quaest.*).

161. Q. Cervidius Scaevola, for example, reported the case of a ship that was detained in Aqui-

The concession in the loan given for the journey to the Arōmatophoros makes sense in this light.[162] There, even if the *synploi* returned to the Red Sea coast after the one-year term had elapsed, Archippos agreed not to charge any interest for a period of perhaps 50, 70, 80, or 90 days, ostensibly to give them time to transport the goods across the desert to Koptos and from there downriver to Alexandria. If we interpret the term as being for the voyage, then the creditor's aim may have been to curtail his exposure to the sea-risk (notwithstanding the absence of any evidence for a condition *salva nave* in the document); though once his debtors had arrived in Egypt, it remained good business to incentivize the associates to complete the expedition in good haste by delaying the moment at which terrestrial interest began to run.

The second event that could trigger the debtor's obligation to repay was the arrival of the ship at its destination within the time limit. Strictly, the borrower's obligation became enforceable immediately on the fulfillment of the condition *salva nave*, and therefore as soon as the ship came in. In practice, however, it was customary for lenders to allow their borrowers a grace period (usually 20 days, but longer if transshipment was involved) within which to sell the cargo and satisfy the debt.[163] It is possible that the 20-day turnaround allowed by the authorities at the port of Kaunos during which a carrier would be exempted from certain taxes hints at a broader truth: that this period was widely considered by the ancients to have been a reasonable period within which to arrive at a port, conduct business, and depart again.[164]

Security

In both the contract produced in the speech *Against Lakritos* and Cervidius Scaevola's report of the Callimachus loan, the transaction was structured (to

leia for nine months: D.19.2.61.1 (Scaev. 7 *dig.*). On the possibility of a wide variation in sailing times along the same route, Peter Campbell, "Contingent Seas: Seafaring, Contracts and Law," in *Roman Law and Maritime Commerce*, ed. Peter Candy and Emilia Mataix Ferrándiz (Edinburgh: Edinburgh University Press, 2022), 27–28.

162. De Romanis, "Time to Repay," 76–77; De Romanis, *Pepper Trade*, 165–68; cf. Wilcken, "Punt-Fahrten," 94; also, Bogaert, "Banquiers," 149.

163. Twenty days in Dem. 35.11 and Nov. 106, two sources separated by almost a millennium. Cf. Schuster, *Das Seedarlehen*, 66–67.

164. George E. Bean, "Notes and Inscriptions from Caunus (Continued)," *JHS* 74 (1954): 102, C.8–10; also, Christian Marek, *Die Inschriften von Kaunos* (Munich: C.H. Beck, 2006), 185, C.8–10. Cf. fifteenth-century English shipping contracts, which typically called for a turnaround of 21 working days (i.e., just over one calendar month): Stuart Jenks, "Capturing Opportunity, Financing Trade," in *The Routledge Handbook of Maritime Trade around Europe 1300–1600: Commercial Networks and Urban Autonomy*, ed. Wim Blockmans, Mikhail Krom, and Justyna Wubs-Mrozewicz (London: Routledge, 2017), 36.

use English terminology) as an acquisition mortgage, in which security was taken over the goods acquired with the proceeds of the loan.[165] Creditors might, of course, demand further security: in one arrangement documented by the Roman jurist Paul, the lender demanded that his rights should extend not only to the goods purchased with the loan but also to all the cargoes owned by the same merchant loaded aboard other vessels, notwithstanding that they were already secured to other lenders.[166] Where the recipient of the money was a *nauklēros*, security might be taken over the ship, the crew (if they were slaves),[167] and (in some cases also) the freight charges owed to the carrier by other merchants. In the loan given by Keler and Charēs (whose debtors were '*synnauklēroi*' of a seagoing vessel), security was taken over "the vessel and all of its equipment and the freight charges from its last voyage (*eschaton naulon*)."[168] The same arrangement appears to have been negotiated in a maritime loan contract referred to briefly in the speech *Against Lakritos*, in which Antipater, co-owner with Hyblesios of the vessel in which the Phaselites' goods were shipped, lent money to Hyblesios "upon the freight to Pontus and on the vessel itself."[169] In only two instances does it appear that security was taken only over the ship to the exclusion of the cargo.[170] One text, preserved in the *Basilica*, though probably based upon the missing constitution at the beginning of the title *de nautico fenore* in the *Code*, suggests that creditors sometimes demanded landed security as well.[171] Alongside real security, lenders frequently sought to reinforce their position by extracting personal guarantees from third parties; though the only contract in which security was taken exclusively in the form of sureties is the Archippos loan, the special context of which makes broader conclusions hard to draw.[172] In one exceptional case, it is likely that the *nauklēros* Nikippos, who gave a maritime loan to the trierarch Apollodōros to finance the payment of his crew's wages for a voyage from Sestos to Athens, did not demand any security, but relied solely upon his borrower's good reputation.[173]

The documentary evidence shows that lenders were careful to safeguard

165. See, e.g., Dem. 32.12; 34.6; 35.11; D.45.1.122.1 (Scaev. 28 *dig.*).

166. D.22.2.6 (Paul. 25 *quaest.*): on which, see below, 100. Cf. Dem. 35.52.

167. Dem. 33.8 (though not a loan given on maritime terms).

168. SB XIV 11850.

169. Dem. 35.32: on which, see Casson, "New Light" (1956), 92; also, Julia Vélissaropoulos Karakostas, *Les nauclères grecs: Recherches sur les institutions maritimes en Grèce et dans l'Orient hellénisé* (Geneva: Droz; Paris: Minard, 1980), 311.

170. Dem. 32.14; 56.3.

171. Bas. 53.5.16: on which, Pontoriero, *Il prestito marittimo*, 53–55. See also Ashburner, *Rhodian Sea-Law*, ccxviii. If the text does indeed represent the missing constitution, then its placement in the *Code* suggests that it is late third century at the latest.

172. SB III 7169.

173. Dem. 50.17: on which, Schuster, *Das Seedarlehen*, 106–7 (with literature).

their rights by means of a variety of different contractual protections. In the contract produced in the speech *Against Lakritos*, the creditors demanded exclusivity in terms that the borrowers neither owed money on the 3,000 jars of Mendean offered as security, nor would use it as collateral to raise additional loans (*epidaneizein*).[174] Lenders also frequently demanded that the value of the security should exceed the value of the loan: in both the speeches *Against Lakritos* and *Against Phormiōn*, the creditors took security over merchandise worth double the sum lent.[175] This does not necessarily mean (as has sometimes been assumed) that the recipient of the loan was obliged to find some other source of funds to make up the difference: rather, it is possible that the value of the security anticipates the purchase of a second cargo at the outport, which lenders expected would typically be worth up to twice the value of the original investment.[176]

One clause that appears in Cervidius Scaevola's report of the Callimachus loan, but not in the contract in *Against Lakritos*, concerns the extension of the lender's rights to the merchandise acquired at the outport using the proceeds from the sale of the original cargo (i.e., replacement cargoes in *amphoteroploun* loans).[177] The explanation for this difference is that, unlike the Romans, the Athenians recognized a so-called surrogation principle, by which it was understood that a creditor automatically benefited from the creation of a hypothec over goods purchased with the borrowed money and their replacement without the need for express agreement.[178] Since Roman law did not recognize such a principle, lenders were required to stipulate clauses that made the subject of the security explicit.

Penalties

Penalty clauses were a standard, though not ubiquitous, feature of maritime loan contracts (the *syngraphē* produced in the speech *Against Lakritos*, for

174. Dem. 35.11, 21, 52; also, 34.6, 50.

175. Dem. 34.6 (ἐπὶ ἑτέρᾳ ὑποθήκῃ); also, 35.18.

176. Edwin Carawan, "The Athenian Law of Agreement," *GRBS* 46, no. 4 (2006): 354; cf. Signe Isager and Mogens H. Hansen, *Aspects of Athenian Society in the Fourth Century B.C.: A Historical Introduction to and Commentary on the Paragraphe-Speeches and the Speech against Dionysodorus in the Corpus Demosthenicum (XXXII-XXXVIII and LVI)* (Odense: Odense University Press, 1975), 76–77. Ashburner thought that this clause was intended to provide a margin of comfort for the lender in case priority claims should arise during the course of the expedition, for example in connection with loans taken for the preservation of the goods, contribution, and so forth: Ashburner, *Rhodian Sea-Law*, ccxiii–ccxiv. According to Ulpian, a later creditor who lent, for example, so that the cargo might be saved, or freight paid, or warehousing costs met, took priority: D.20.4.6 (Ulp. 73 *ad ed.*).

177. So, in D.45.1.122.1 (Scaev. 28 *dig.*): ". . . with security by way of *pignus* and *hypotheca* over the cargo bought at Berytus for transport to Brentesium and that which he would buy at Brentesium for transport by sea to Berytus."

178. Schuster, *Das Seedarlehen*, 103.

example, did not include a penal condition; though it did provide for an adjustable interest rate in the event the borrowers became delayed beyond a certain point).[179] In general, penalties (ἐπιτίμια, *epitimia*) were designed to incentivize the debtor to abide by the terms of the agreement and to provide for liquidated damages (and potentially the accrual of additional interest and costs) in the event of breach.[180] The Roman jurists Labeo and African observed that the inclusion of a penalty was the "usual" practice (*uti solet, uti adsolet*), often—as Papinian indicates—in connection with clauses that provided for a daily rate for the lender's representative and a rate of interest that would accrue once the risk had reverted to the borrower.[181]

Examples of penalty clauses:

Dem. 34.33 (against Phormiōn):[182]

". . . to put on board the ship the goods purchased, or else to pay a penalty of 5,000 dr." (i.e., two-and-a-half times the value of the original loan of 2,000 dr.).

Dem. 56.38 (against Dionysodōros):[183]

"if . . . they [the debtors] do not present the security plain to see and free of any encumbrance, or if they do anything contrary to the contract, let them pay twice the sum."

SB III 7169:

"If instead they do not repay within the time-limit they will pay at the same time the debt with a penalty of half (*hemiolion*) and interest of two drachmas per mina each month beyond the expiration of the time-limit according to the royal decree."

[And possibly] ". . . If they do not abide by the terms of the agreement . . ."

179. For the Greek context, see, generally, Paoli, *Studi di diritto*, 136–37; Schuster, *Das Seedarlehen*, 123–30.

180. For Biscardi's thesis that creditors during the Roman period relied upon penal stipulations to avoid the unenforceability of pacts for interest, see below, 186–89.

181. D.22.2.9 (Lab. 5 *pith. a Paulo epit.*); D.44.7.23 (Afr. 7 *quaest.*); also, D.22.2.4 (Pap. 3 *resp.*).

182. For an extended discussion (with literature), Schuster, *Das Seedarlehen*, 126–29. See, also, below, 125–27.

183. Cf. Dem. 56.20. The expression "free from any encumbrance" was relevant for the purposes of *embateusis*, or entry into possession: on which, see David Phillips, *The Law of Ancient Athens* (Ann Arbor: University of Michigan Press, 2013), 264–65.

D.45.1.122.1 (Scaev. 28 *dig.*):

> "... And it was agreed between them, that after Callimachus had arrived at Brentesium he himself would depart for Syria before what would then be the next *ides* of September with other goods having been purchased and loaded onto a vessel, or, if by the aforementioned date he had not replenished the merchandise nor sailed out from that *civitas*, that he would return the whole sum as if he had completed the voyage without interruption and pay all the costs of those escorting the money so that they might take it to Rome."

Penalty clauses were framed as conditions: whether the penalty fell due depended upon the realization of the condition. Depending upon the relationship between the condition *salva nave* and the penal condition, it was also possible (as envisaged in both the speech *Against Phormiōn* and the Callimachus loan) that the debtor might be relieved of the obligation to pay back the original debt while incurring the obligation to pay the penalty. It is therefore not surprising that a good number of the Athenian and Roman sources bearing upon maritime loan contracts from a legal perspective are concerned with the very precise but practically significant questions concerning the interpretation of contractual conditions (for which, see chapter 4).

Praxis-*Clause*

Three of the four documents addressed at the beginning of this chapter certainly contained so-called *praxis*-clauses, granting the creditor(s) extensive enforcement rights against the debtor(s).[184] Generally, it appears to have been normal for creditors to demand access to the goods on landfall; if the borrowers defaulted, to have the right to pledge or sell the property to satisfy the debt; and to proceed against the debtor's personal assets to make up the shortfall. In both the contract reported in the speech *Against Lakritos* and the acknowledgment of debt recorded in SB III 7169, the *praxis*-clause contains a special "καθάπερ ἐκ δίκης" formula purporting to empower the creditors to enforce their rights (including the right to seize the debtor's personal property) as if a court of law had already passed judgment in their favor. The interpretation of this term

184. Dem. 35.11–12, SB III 7169, and SB XVIII 13167. The contract reported by Cervidius Scaevola in D.45.1.122.1 might have contained such a clause, since it is clear that the jurist only reported those provisions that were relevant to the legal issue at stake.

(which appears many times in the Ptolemaic and Graeco-Roman papyri but also in sources outside Egypt) is controversial. The orthodox interpretation, which has since been restated by Meyer-Laurin in response to H. J. Wolff, is that the clause was intended to empower creditors to proceed against their debtors extrajudicially as stated.[185] Wolff had earlier suggested that the clause had no practical significance and only meant that the creditors would enforce their rights in a manner that was consistent with due process.[186] Probably, however, Thür is right (after an examination of the sources outside Egypt) that the phrase had a great variety of meanings, ranging from its literal application to practical insignificance, depending upon the context.[187]

Kyriōteron-*Clause*

Only one contract, reported in the speech *Against Lakritos*, contains a so-called *kyriōteron*-clause, providing that nothing should have greater legal authority (i.e., should be treated as *kyriōteron*) than the terms of the *syngraphē*. However, a reference to an identical term in the speech *Against Dionysodōros* makes it likely that such clauses featured regularly in fourth-century-BCE maritime loan contracts.[188] Later in the speech *Against Lakritos*, the speaker interprets this provision to exclude the litigants even from bringing forward any *nomos* or *psēphisma* (law or decree) in court proceedings that would contravene the contract's provisions.[189] Whether this statement was intended merely to establish the contract's priority as evidence of the parties' mutual obligations,[190] or

185. Harald Meyer-Laurin, "Zur Entstehung und Bedeutung der καθάπερ ἐκ δίκης-Klausel in den griechischen Papyri Ägyptens," in *Symposion 1971: Vorträge zur griechischen und hellenistischen Rechtsgeschichte*, ed. Hans J. Wolff (Cologne: Böhlau, 1975), 189–204; and as set out in Andreas B. Schwarz, *Die öffentliche und private Urkunde im römischen Ägypten: Studien zum hellenistischen Privatrecht* (Leipzig: Sächsischen Akademie der Wissenschaften, 1920).

186. Hans J. Wolff, "Some Observations on Praxis," in *Proceedings of the Twelfth International Congress of Papyrology (Ann Arbor, Michigan, 13–17 August 1968)*, ed. Deborah H. Samuel (Toronto: Hackert, 1970), 534 n. 36; Wolff, "The Praxis-Provision in Papyrus Contracts," *TAPhA* 72 (1941): 427–28.

187. Gerhard Thür, "The Phrase Καθάπερ Ἐκ Δίκης in Greek and Hellenistic Documents," in *Our Beloved Polites: Studies Presented to Peter J. Rhodes*, ed. Delfim F. Leão et al. (Oxford: Archaeopress, 2022), esp. 192–93.

188. Dem. 56.26.

189. Dem. 35.39.

190. See, generally, Julia Vélissaropoulos-Karakostas, *Λόγοι Ευθύνης. Ιστορική γένεση και σύγχρονη αμφισβήτηση των πηγών της ενοχικής δεσμεύσεως* (Athens: Ant. Sakkoulas, 1993), 176–79; Athina A. Dimopoulou, "Ἄκυρον Ἔστω: Legal Invalidity in Greek Inscriptions," in *Symposion 2013: Vorträge zur griechischen und hellenistischen Rechtsgeschichte (Cambridge MA, 26.-29. August 2013)*, ed. Michael Gagarin and Adriaan Lanni (Vienna: VÖAW, 2014), 265–73.

to override jurisdictional law more generally,[191] is disputed. Whatever the truth of the matter, the clause is indicative of the international character of long-distance trade and the interconnectedness of *emporia* in the fourth-century Mediterranean. There is no evidence for the inclusion of such a clause in contracts from the Roman period: though the evidence is too thinly dispersed to draw any conclusions from this.

191. Edward E. Cohen, "Commercial Law," in *The Cambridge Companion to Ancient Greek Law*, ed. Michael Gagarin and David Cohen (Cambridge: Cambridge University Press, 2005), 298–99; Cohen, "Private Agreements Purporting to Override Polis Law: A Response to Athina Dimopoulou," in *Symposion 2013: Vorträge zur griechischen und hellenistischen Rechtsgeschichte (Cambridge MA, 26.-29. August 2013)*, ed. Michael Gagarin and Adriaan Lanni (Vienna: VÖAW, 2014), esp. 278–82.

CHAPTER TWO

Maritime Loan Contracts and Long-Distance Trade

The structure of the ancient system of long-distance trade is essentially visible in the standard form contracts that served as stable connective links between commercial actors. In addition to maritime loan contracts, contracts of affreightment connected merchants with carriers, and as the evidence from the Roman period suggests, contracts between merchants and warehousemen were also based upon standard forms. The focus of this chapter is upon the role of maritime loan contracts in sustaining emporic trade during the ancient period. The chapter is in three parts, examining the origins of the standard form, its function in the context of the *emporion* at Athens, and how it was adapted to suit the needs of merchants and financiers during the Roman period.

The Origins of Maritime Loan Contracts

The first definite evidence for a maritime loan contract at Athens comes from the last quarter of the fifth century BCE. If Harvey's reading of the words "*to nautikon*" in a fragment of Eupolis' *Marikas* is correct, then the terminology was already familiar by 421.[1] The earliest sure evidence comes from a speech by the orator Lysias, composed in about 400, in which the Athenian Diodotos, who was killed in battle at Ephesos in 409, is said to have had over seven talents out as maritime credit (*nautika . . . ekdedomena*).[2] Probably, as Erxleben has suggested, a roughly contemporaneous passage by Isokratēs stating that the wealthy provide aid to the poor by helping them to enter *emporía* and the "trades" can be read in this light to imply their participation in maritime finance.[3]

1. P. Oxy. 2741, fr. 1 B col. ii 16–18: on which, F. D. Harvey, "The Maritime Loan in Eupolis' 'Marikas' (P. Oxy. 2741)," *ZPE* 23 (1976): 233.
2. Lys. 32.6–7. The large sum suggests that the total must have comprised more than one loan.
3. Isok. 7.32–35: on which, E. Erxleben, "Die Rolle der Bevölkerungklassen im Aussenhandel

Several other fragments dating to the fifth and sixth centuries BCE have been cited as evidence for the earlier existence of maritime loan contracts. According to Hasebroek, the words "*to nautikon*" in the *Constitution of the Athenians* (latter half of the fifth century, by an unknown author) refer to maritime financing; though the expression is better understood in the context to refer to the role of metics in the fleet.[4] For the sixth century, Bravo rather doubtfully interprets some lines by Theognis as referring to maritime lending;[5] and Calligas has suggested that a collection of lead tablets recovered near to the ancient walled port at Korkyra on the island of Corfu, at the site of what may have been a sanctuary to Poseidon, were documents recording the debts incurred by the borrowers of "bottomry loans."[6] The tablets, however, which are dated from the form of the letters to about 500 BCE, only contain simple acknowledgments of debt that record only the identity of the parties and the sum owed. Apart from the island context, there is therefore nothing to link the records to the practice of creditors lending at their own risk or even to the financing of overseas trade more generally.[7] None of these interpretations is sufficiently well made out to persuade of an earlier date than the final decades of the fifth century for the appearance of *nautikai syngraphai* in the historical record.

Notwithstanding that the existence of maritime loan contracts is only attested from the end of the fifth century BCE, it is clear that *nautikai syngraphai* were already central to the financing of the Athenian grain trade and were familiar not only at Athens, but at locations with a Greek presence around the seaboards of the Mediterranean and the Black Seas (at least in connection with voyages from those places to Piraeus). The origins of the contract have been attributed variously to the growth in the Athenian grain trade in about the second quarter of the fifth century (De Ste Croix);[8] or slightly earlier to the sixth or seventh centuries BCE (Purpura).[9] As to the inspiration for the

Athens im 4. Jahrhundert v.u.Z.," in *Hellenische Poleis: Krise, Wandlung, Wirkung*, ed. Elisabeth C. Welskopf, vol. 1 (Berlin: Akademie-Verlag, 1974), 469.

4. Arist. [*Ath. Pol.*] 1.12: on which, Johannes Hasebroek, *Trade and Politics in Ancient Greece*, trans. L. M. Fraser and D. C. Macgregor (London: G. Bell & Sons, 1933), 24 and n. 3.

5. Thgn. 1197–1202: on which, Benedetto Bravo, "Remarques sur les assises sociales, les formes d'organisation et la terminologie du commerce maritime à l'époque archaïque," *Dialogues d'histoire ancienne* 3 (1977): 4–5.

6. British Museum Collection, no. 1868,0110.6: on which, P. Calligas, "An Inscribed Lead Plaque from Korkyra," *Annual of the British School at Athens* 66 (1971): 84–85.

7. Also urging caution, M. M. Austin and Pierre Vidal-Naquet, *Economic and Social History of Ancient Greece: An Introduction* (Berkeley: University of California Press, 1977), 155 n. 21; Charles M. Reed, *Maritime Traders in the Ancient Greek World* (Cambridge: Cambridge University Press, 2003), 41.

8. De Ste Croix, "Maritime Loans," 44.

9. Purpura, "Ricerche," 202.

structure of the transaction, this has been traced to provisions in the so-called Law Code of Manu, a seminal Hindu text, brought to Europe by Indo-Aryan migrants (Matthiass);[10] and to Mesopotamian precedents, namely, loans made in connection with the so-called Telmun trade centered on modern Bahrain during the Dynasty of Larsa (c. 1900–1750 BCE) (Oppenheim);[11] and a form of transaction regulated by the Code of Hammurabi, possibly of Sumerian origin and which was used to finance the caravan trade (Dauvillier).[12]

It is quite possible that the technique of making repayment of a debt conditional upon the successful outcome of some enterprise was used by traders in other cultures before the first millennium BCE. However, whether any of these models provided direct inspiration for the Attic maritime loan contract is unprovable; and in any case, does not account for the special phenomenon of the written standard form contract, which (as Finley observed) "in the speculative world of maritime loans . . . became more or less universal."[13]

The broad context for the development and standardization of maritime loan contracts was most likely in the expansion of the Phoenician and Greek colonies from about the eighth century BCE and the growth in the long-distance trade in commodities (*emporía*) during the same period. The starting point here is the shipwreck data from the eastern Mediterranean, which shows that by the time maritime loan contracts enter the record at the end of the fifth century BCE, the volume of seaborne traffic crossing the Mediterranean basin had already been steadily increasing for three full centuries.[14] This increase,

---

10. Bernhard Matthiass, *Das foenus nauticum und die geschichtliche entwicklung der bodmerei* (Würzburg: Druck der Thein'schen druckerei (Stürtz), 1881), 2–4. The theory is in keeping with the late-nineteenth-century vogue for migration theories more generally. For criticism, Paul Huvelin, *Études d'histoire du droit commercial romain (histoire externe-droit maritime)* (Paris: Recueil Sirey, 1929), 205–7; Jean Dauvillier, "Recherches sur un contrat caravanier babylonien et sur les origines du prêt à la grosse aventure dans l'Antiquité grecque," in *Mélanges dédiés à Gabriel Marty* (Toulouse: Université des sciences sociales de Toulouse, 1978), 360–62; Purpura, "Ricerche," 201.

11. A. Leo Oppenheim, "The Seafaring Merchants of Ur," *Journal of the American Oriental Society* 74, no. 1 (1954): 6–7 and 10. Oppenheim identifies eight cuneiform tablets containing a conditional clause equivalent to the Roman '*santa eunte nave*.' Cf. De Ste Croix's caution that it is not clear from the language whether the clause was intended to have conditional or merely temporal force: De Ste Croix, "Maritime Loans," 59.

12. Dauvillier, "Recherches," 379. The regulations are at Arts. 100, 101, and 103 of the Code: for which, see Mervyn E. J. Richardson, *Hammurabi's Laws: Text, Translation and Glossary* (London: Bloomsbury, 2004), 72–73. The contract involved the assumption of the risk by the creditor for certain chance events, but also guaranteed him a minimum degree of profit if the expedition was successfully completed (i.e., either by taking a share of the profits or by activation of the penalty). This is closer to the participatory model that might have obtained in SB III 7169.

13. Moses I. Finley, *Studies in Land and Credit in Ancient Athens, 500–200 B.C.: The Horos Inscriptions* (New Brunswick, NJ: Rutgers University Press, 1952), 96.

14. See, generally, Andrew I. Wilson, "Developments in Mediterranean Shipping and Maritime Trade from the Hellenistic Period to AD 1000," in *Maritime Archaeology and Ancient Trade in the Mediterranean*, ed. Damian Robinson and Andrew I. Wilson (Oxford: Oxford Centre for Mari-

which starts to become truly noticeable from the late ninth-century BCE, corresponds directly with intensification of long-distance trading activity by merchants from the Levantine cities of Arwad, Byblos, Sidon, and Tyre (in particular), which emerged from the Bronze Age crisis and began to pursue a policy of trade and colonization throughout the Mediterranean.[15] The expansion of the so-called Phoenician *koiné*, which extended from the Levant to Cyprus, parts of North Africa (including Carthage), Sardinia, the Balearics, and southern Iberia, was accompanied during roughly the same period (c. 750–550 BCE) by a similar process of Greek colonization that extended northward from the Aegean to the northwest coast of the Black Sea and the Crimea, and westward to Sicily, southern Italy, and the south coast of France.

The nature of seaborne commerce was also changing during this period, from *prēxis* to *emporía* (ἐμπορία).[16] Whereas *prēxis*, the traditional mode that was still prevalent in the eighth and seventh centuries, involved small fleets carrying precious cargoes that were headed by aristocrats engaged in gift exchange and mutual hospitality; *emporía* was characterized by the shipment of commodities such as wine, olive oil, and grain (the so-called Mediterranean triad) by merchants (*emporoi*) and merchant-carriers (*nauklēroi*). From as early as the middle of the eighth century BCE both Phoenician and Greek merchants were engaged in this kind of trade: the two Phoenician shipwrecks (*Tanit* and *Elissa*) discovered off the coast of Ashkelon in the late 1990s (dated to the mid-eighth century BCE), for example, were each carrying consignments of c. 400 amphorae of wine;[17] and by the last quarter of the fifth century, the Greek Peristera wreck, which sank off the islet of Peristera near Alonessos with a cargo of 3,000–4,000 wine amphorae from Mendē and Skopelos, shows the scale that had been achieved by the time *nautikai syngraphai* first appear in the record.[18]

Several other factors may account for the specific practice of producing pri-

time Archaeology, 2011), 33–39; and now Taco T. Terpstra, *Trade in the Ancient Mediterranean: Private Order and Public Institutions* (Princeton: Princeton University Press, 2019), 3–8.

15. Carolina López-Ruiz, *Phoenicians and the Making of the Mediterranean* (Cambridge, MA: Harvard University Press, 2021), 29–30. Cf. Quinn's skepticism, that the peoples later known as Phoenicians shared among themselves a sense of collective identity: Josephine C. Quinn, *In Search of the Phoenicians* (Princeton: Princeton University Press, 2018).

16. Gabriele Cifani, *The Origins of the Roman Economy: From the Iron Age to the Early Republic in a Mediterranean Perspective* (Cambridge: Cambridge University Press, 2020), 184; Cifani, "Aspects of the Origins of Roman Maritime Trade," in *Roman Law and Maritime Commerce*, ed. Peter Candy and Emilia Mataix Ferrándiz (Edinburgh: Edinburgh University Press, 2022), 16–17.

17. Robert D. Ballard et al., "Iron Age Shipwrecks in Deep Water off Ashkelon, Israel," *AJA* 106 (2002): 151–68; also, Jeffrey P. Emanuel, "Seafaring and Shipwreck Archaeology," in *The Oxford Handbook of the Phoenician and Punic Mediterranean*, ed. Brian R. Doak and Carolina López-Ruiz (Oxford: Oxford University Press, 2019), 425–27.

18. E. Hadjidaki, "Underwater Excavations of a Late Fifth Century Merchant Ship at Alonnesos, Greece: The 1991–1993 Seasons," *Bulletin de Correspondance Hellénique* 2 (1996): 561–93.

vate written agreements, which in the context of oral cultures was a significant development in its own right. First, the growth in emporic trade brought Phoenician and Greek merchants, migrants, and colonists into regular contact, often in the context of small, close-knit, trading communities.[19] Archaeological excavations at different locations around the Mediterranean seaboard have shown the extent to which trade flourished between ports on the Syrian and Levantine coasts on the one side and the Aegean islands and the Greek mainland on the other. At the north Syrian coastal settlement of Al Mina, for example, which sat near to the mouth of the Orontes, the discovery of Cycladic and proto-Corinthian sherds together with later developments of early Greek vases show that between the late ninth and seventh centuries BCE, (Greek) merchants were importing various commodities including Euboean fabrics and pots from (among other places) Corinth and Attica.[20] On the Greek side, recent excavations similarly show that a sizeable Phoenician enclave grew up in the mid to late sixth century at Phalēron, a sheltered bay that served as Athens' main harbor until the construction of Piraeus at the beginning of the fifth century.[21] In the early fourth century, a decree honoring Straton, king of Sidon, as a *proxenos* of the city, granted metic Sidonians (i.e., those living as resident foreigners in the city) exemptions from certain taxes and other duties.[22] From an early stage, contact between Phoenician and Greek traders was therefore well established, cultivating an environment in which contractual practices could be mutually developed.

Second, long-distance trading in commodities was an extraordinarily complex affair that relied heavily upon finance for its vitality.[23] In the Greek context, the two most significant commercial actors were merchants (*emporoi*) and merchant-carriers (*nauklēroi*).[24] As the fourth-century orations show, both regularly took loans to finance all aspects of the enterprise. How long-distance trade was financed outside Athens before the late fifth century remains an open question; but given the intimate relationship between *nautikai syngraphai* and the financing of *emporía* at Athens, it seems reasonable to conjecture that mari-

19. López-Ruiz, *Phoenicians*, 32.

20. See, generally, Alexander Vacek, "Ugarit, Al Mina, and Coastal North Syria," in *A Companion to the Archaeology of Early Greece and the Mediterranean*, ed. Antonis Kotsonas and Irene S. Lemos (Newark, NY: John Wiley & Sons, 2020), 1176–79.

21. Mark Woolmer, *A Short History of the Phoenicians*, 2nd ed. (London: Bloomsbury, 2021), 186; also, Robert Garland, *The Piraeus: From the Fifth to the First Century B.C.* (Bristol: Bristol Classical Press, 1987), 62–67.

22. *IG* II^2 141 (= AIUK 11, no. 1).

23. Edward E. Cohen, *Athenian Economy and Society: A Banking Perspective* (Princeton: Princeton University Press, 2011), 146–47.

24. For the commercial activities of *emporoi* and *nauklēroi*, see below, 53–54.

time loan contracts and trading in commodities (which spanned the Phoenician and Greek contexts) were closely connected from the start; the former possibly even providing the mechanism that made it viable for merchants, who might not be able to afford a large cargo, or, even if they could, to shoulder the substantial risk of total loss due to force majeure, to engage in *emporía* in the first place.

Third, there is indirect evidence contained in the Talmud that the Phoenicians wrote legal texts touching upon topics such as ship sales and contracts of affreightment.[25] And fourth, as for the use of writing, it is difficult to see how the forms recognizable by the fourth century BCE can have predated the adoption by Greek communities of the Phoenician alphabet, likely no earlier than the late ninth or early eighth century BCE.[26]

Though the origins of the standard form maritime loan contract ultimately remain obscure, the whole context of the Phoenician and Greek colonization of key locations along the Mediterranean and Pontic seaboard, together with the growth in the overseas trade of commodities in bulk from about the late ninth century BCE, make it plausible that they were first developed in this context, if not essential to the vitality of the trade in commodities from the very beginning.

Late-Fifth- and Fourth-Century-BCE Athens

World of the Emporion

Athens' main emporium, or commercial harbor, was situated at Piraeus, which served not only as the chief conduit for imports and exports to the city from the early fifth century but also as an entrepôt for goods being distributed throughout the Mediterranean.[27] From about the second quarter of the fifth century BCE, the city began to import large quantities of grain from Sicily and locations around the Black Sea to supplement its own domestic production, such that by the mid-fourth century, Demosthenes implies that Athens was importing c. 800,000 *medimnoi* (26,368 tons) annually: enough to feed (on Moreno's esti-

25. See, generally, Jean Dauvillier, "Quelques règles retrouvées du droit maritime phénicien," *RHD* 29 (1951): 296–98; Dauvillier, "Le droit maritime phénicien," *RIDA* 6 (1959): 33–63.

26. See, generally, Roger D. Woodard, *Greek Writing from Knossos to Homer: A Linguistic Interpretation of the Origin of the Greek Alphabet and the Continuity of Ancient Greek Literacy* (Oxford: Oxford University Press, 1997), 133–39.

27. Isager and Hansen, *Aspects*, 62–64.

mates) more than 105,000 people.[28] If Casson's calculation that a typical merchant vessel from the period could carry c. 3,000 *medimnoi* is accurate, this would imply the arrival of more than 250 incoming shiploads of grain each season.[29] The total number of incoming vessels, however, was probably at least double this figure, considering that Athens was also a net importer of timber and some 3,000–5,000 slaves each year.[30]

Emporia were populated by resident mercantile communities consisting of (among others) *emporoi*, *nauklēroi*, and (to a lesser extent) professional moneylenders (*daneizontes*). The community at Piraeus during this period probably numbered between about 5,500 and 7,500 active businessmen, made up of Athenian citizens, metics, and foreigners. While the broad mercantile community was bound together (if somewhat loosely) by their mutual occupations and dependency, closer, tight-knit groups of businessmen also coalesced around shared ethnic and geographic origins together with their associated religious and cultural values.

Emporoi were fundamentally interregional traders who traveled with their merchandise.[31] At its simplest, their main business was to purchase goods in bulk for transport (usually, though not exclusively) overseas to a foreign *emporion*, where the wares could be sold and the money reinvested in a return cargo, which was then shipped back for sale at the homeport. More elaborate itineraries were of course possible, if an *emporos* made multiple stopovers during the season. Although *emporoi* bought goods in large quantities and preferred to dispose of them in one lot, they were not wholesale dealers, and often needed to sell cargoes by fractions to willing buyers in the marketplace.[32] Importantly, *emporoi* did not have control of a ship themselves (e.g., as owner, rentier) and so were

28. Demosthenes' figure of 800,000 *medimnoi* is reached by combining the two statements given at Dem 20.31–32. Moreno corroborates Demosthenes' implied figure by his own estimates and calculations with respect to land area, land use, crop yields, population, and consumption: Alfonso Moreno, *Feeding the Democracy: The Athenian Grain Supply in the Fifth and Fourth Centuries BC* (Oxford: Oxford University Press, 2007), 32–33. Other estimates range from Garnsey's conservative figure of 400,000 *medimnoi* (enough to feed c. 90,000 people): Peter Garnsey, "Grain for Athens," *History of Political Thought* 6, nos. 1–2 (1985): 74; to 1,200,000 *medimnoi* per year: Arnold W. Gomme, *The Population of Athens in the Fifth and Fourth Centuries B.C.* (Oxford: Blackwell, 1933), 28–33.

29. Casson, *Ships and Seamanship*, 183–84. Isager and Hansen assumed more than 600 incoming shiploads of grain alone, for grain imports significantly in excess of 800,000 *medimnoi*: Isager and Hansen, *Aspects*, 63.

30. Garland, *The Piraeus*, 85.

31. See, generally, Mark Woolmer, "Emporoi Kai Nauklēroi: Redefining Commercial Roles in Classical Greece," *JAH* 3, no. 2 (2015): 150–72; also, Isager and Hansen, *Aspects*, 65. Cf. Wim Broekaert, *Navicularii et Negotiantes: A Prosopographical Study of Roman Merchants and Shippers* (Rahden, Nordrhein-Westfalen, Germany: Verlag Marie Leidorf, 2013), 216–22 and 257–58.

32. See, e.g., Dem. 34.8–9; Isager and Hansen, *Aspects*, 65.

dependent upon engaging *nauklēroi* for the carriage of their goods. A *nauklēros*, meanwhile, was a merchant-carrier who used his own vessel for the purpose of engaging in overseas trade. Almost always he was the owner of a single ship, though occasionally we find a shipowner's agent in charge of a vessel rather than the owner himself.[33] Although their primary business was the transport of their own wares, *nauklēroi* also offered their services as carriers to *emporoi*.[34]

As for financiers, there is only limited evidence for the casual involvement of citizens who were not otherwise engaged in maritime trade: in Hypereidēs' speech *Against Demosthenes*, Demosthenes was accused of using state funds to engage in maritime lending for his own personal gain; and in Demosthenes' prosecution of his own guardians in *Against Aphobos I*, his father's estate is said to have included 7,000 drachmae lent out as maritime investments "with Xouthos" (*para Xouthōi*) who may have been either a middleman with some experience of maritime trade or a banker.[35] Possibly the contribution of propertied Athenian citizens (like Demosthenes' father) to the finance of maritime trade has been downplayed: Isokratēs' statement, made in general terms, that the wealthy helped the less well off by assisting them to enter *emporía* suggests that it was relatively normal even by the late fifth century BCE for the rich to provide seed capital (maybe even on maritime terms) to aid budding entrepreneurs in their fledgling careers.[36] Certainly, bankers did sometimes engage in maritime lending: most famously Pasiōn, who began his career as a slave of Antisthenēs and Archestratos, co-owners of a banking firm in the Piraeus, before being manumitted and becoming owner of the bank himself; and later his freedman Phormiōn, who took over the business on his former master's death.[37]

The main source of maritime credit at Piraeus appears to have been professional moneylenders.[38] In Lysias' speech *Against Diogeitōn* (401 BCE),

---

33. The *nauklēros* Lampis, for example, was a slave (of Diōn): Dem. 34.6. Cf., also, the example of Phormiōn, one of the wealthiest men in Athens, who owned several ships: Dem. 45.64. See, generally, Isager and Hansen, 73–74.

34. In the catalogue of *emporoi* and *nauklēroi* assembled by Reed, 10 *nauklēroi* are listed as having engaged in trading activities, and five as borrowers of loans on maritime terms: Reed, *Maritime Traders*, 13.

35. Probably the total sum was made up of multiple loans: Dem. 27.11. Middleman: Bogaert, "Banquiers," 141–46; Erxleben, "Die Rolle der Bevölkerungklassen," 493; Isager and Hansen, *Aspects*, 84, 88; also, Millett, *Lending*, 192. Banker: Cohen, *Athenian Economy*, 136–60; Schuster, *Das Seedarlehen*, 39–43.

36. Isok. 7.32–35.

37. Phormiōn, Dem. 45.64 and 49.31; Pasiōn, Dem. 27.8–11. On the latter, see John K. Davies, *Athenian Propertied Families, 600–300 B.C.* (Oxford: Oxford University Press, 1971), 428–29, no. 11672.

38. See, generally, Millett, *Lending*, 188–96. For the debate concerning the difference between moneylenders and bankers, see Bogaert, "Banquiers;" Millett, *Lending*; Cohen, *Athenian Economy*. The main difference appears to have been that while bankers accepted money on deposit and were

Diogeitōn and his brother Diodotos are both characterized as moneylenders, the latter of whose estate was worth at least 15 talents at his death, of which 7 talents and 40 minae was lent out at a maritime yield.[39] Nikoboulos in Demosthenes' speech *Against Pantaenetos* was also certainly a lender, probably a provider of maritime credit, and possibly traveled with his borrowers to protect his investment "to keep his money from slipping through his fingers unawares."[40] Many of the creditors who made a business of maritime lending were also actively engaged or had some prior history of involvement in maritime commerce. The unnamed speaker who begins the speech *Against Apatourios* gives the following brief account: "I . . . have by now been engaged for a long time in overseas trade, and up to a certain time risked the sea in my own person; it is not quite seven years since I gave up voyaging, and, having made a moderate sum of money, I try to put it to work in maritime loans."[41] In the oration *Against Dionysodōros*, the creditor Dareios similarly begins by referring to those "who are engaged in long-distance trade and who lend our money to other people."[42] In the suit *Against Phormiōn*, several remarks indicate that Chrysippos and his brother were *emporoi*, the former opening the oration by appealing to the good will of the jury, who he argues should be well disposed toward him and his partner because they have been dispensing maritime loans at the *emporion* for many years without becoming involved in a single court case.[43] Androklēs, the speaker in *Against Lakritos*, also declares himself to be an *emporos*.[44]

Merchants and carriers also turned their hand to casual lending to supplement their main sources of income. In the oration *Against Lakritos*, for example, Androklēs alleges that the borrowers, both *emporoi*, breached their contract with him by using some of the funds to make a loan to a fellow Phaselite (though whether the loan was maritime is not made explicit).[45] The same allegation is repeated by the speaker Pamphilos in the speech *Against Dionysodōros*, in which it is claimed that the debtors, Dionysodōros and Par-

therefore sometimes able to offer nonproductive loans, moneylenders did not take deposits and were only concerned with making profits from interest payments.

39. Lys. 32.6.

40. Dem. 37.52–54: on which, Paul Millett, "Maritime Loans and the Structure of Credit in Fourth-Century Athens," in *Trade in the Ancient Economy*, ed. Peter Garnsey, Keith Hopkins, and C. R. Whittaker (London: Chatto & Windus, 1983), 50–51; Millett, *Lending*, 193–96.

41. Dem. 33.4.

42. Dem. 56.1.

43. Dem. 34.1.

44. Dem. 35.49. The same Androklēs appears in two inscriptions, which show him to have been the brother of Xenocles of Sphettos, one of the foremost citizens of Athens in the latter half of the fourth century, and a substantial figure in his own right: Stephen D. Lambert, "Ten Notes on Attic Inscriptions," *ZPE* 135 (2001): 57–58; also, MacDowell, *Demosthenes*, 130.

45. Dem. 35.52–53.

meniskos, had used the money to make loans at maritime yields of their own.[46] Meanwhile, in the speech *Against Phormiōn*, Phormiōn is accused of breaching the contract by taking two further loans on the same security, one from Lampis, slave of Diōn and the *nauklēros* of the vessel chartered to carry the goods, the other from a Phoenician called Theodōros, who was also on board (in an unspecified capacity).[47] Finally, in the speech *Against Kallippos*, Lycōn, a merchant from Heraklea, is reported to have lent at maritime interest; and it is possible that Zēnothemis, who is alleged to have given a loan to the *nauklēros* Hēgestratos, was also an *emporos* (though he might equally have confined his activities to lending). It is hardly surprising that a good number of maritime lenders were either active or former *emporoi*: once a merchant had accumulated enough capital to scale back his trading activities, it made good sense to take advantage of the relative safety of port and to exploit their knowledge and contacts by putting the money to work as loans (just as the speaker in *Against Apatourios* implies).[48]

The Market for Maritime Credit

We have no quantitative evidence that could deliver an insight into the proportion of trading enterprises at Piraeus that relied either wholly or in part on the availability of maritime lending.[49] Isager and Hansen are right to point out that the nature of the surviving evidence (i.e., chiefly forensic speeches composed against the background of disputes between the parties to maritime loan contracts) should make us cautious about underestimating the number of *emporoi* and *nauklēroi* who plied their trade without the need to borrow.[50] Even so, there are several indications that both merchants and merchant-carriers took loans to finance their commercial activities on a fairly routine basis. The evidence most commonly cited in this direction consists in the closing remarks of the speaker at the end of the speech *Against Phormiōn*, who reminds the jury that "the resources of those involved in trade come not from those who borrow but from those who lend; and neither ship nor *nauklēros* nor passenger can put to sea, if you take away the part contributed by those who lend."[51] This could

---

46. Dem. 56.17.
47. Dem. 34.6.
48. Johannes Hasebroek, *Staat und Handel im antiken Griechenland* (Tübingen: Mohr Siebeck, 1928), 10; Isager and Hansen, *Aspects*, 66.
49. For this discussion, see Mark Woolmer, "The Athenian Mercantile Community: A Reappraisal of the Social, Political, and Legal Status of Inter-Regional Merchants during the Fourth Century" (PhD diss., Cardiff University, 2008), 163–65.
50. Isager and Hansen, *Aspects*, 73.
51. Dem. 34.51. Cohen cites this passage as evidence that "Virtually all of these cargoes [coming into Athens] were dependent on loans:" Cohen, *Athenian Economy*, 140–41.

be rhetorical exaggeration; except that in the four speeches in the Demosthenic corpus aimed at defaulters on maritime loan contracts the speakers refer to more than 20 other maritime credit agreements during the course of their orations,[52] several of which were concluded at locations other than Piraeus.[53] In addition, the familiar way in which maritime finance is referred to, not only in the forensic speeches but also in other literary sources, speaks to the pervasiveness of *nautikai syngraphai* in the conduct of interregional overseas trade.[54]

What factors motivated merchants to take loans? One theory, originating with Hasebroek, is that traders were driven to seek maritime credit through poverty.[55] Others have emphasized the insurance element of maritime loan contracts, arguing in broad terms that the purpose of the transaction was to "spread the risk" across those who could most afford to bear it.[56] More recently, Cohen and now Bresson and Bresson have argued that merchants also took loans to gear (or leverage) their investments.[57]

This latter suggestion warrants further attention. Gearing refers to the practice of borrowing money to invest, where the anticipated returns on the investment outstrip the cost of servicing the loan. The result is to increase or decrease the return on equity (i.e., the money invested from the borrower's own capital), depending upon whether the cost of the debt is lower (positive gearing) or higher (negative gearing) than any profits generated by the enterprise. In this context, the chief advantages for the merchant were the opportunity to supplement their own capital with borrowed money, increasing their purchasing power in the market as bulk buyers of commodities and multiplying the potential returns. In other words, if the expedition came off, the merchant

52. Woolmer, "Athenian Mercantile Community," 164.

53. E.g., the maritime loan contracts concluded by Zēnothemis and his accomplice Hēgestratos at Syracuse: Dem. 32.4–5.

54. See, e.g., the passages in forensic orations identified by Millett (Isok. 17.42; Dem. 27.11; 33.4; 52.20; Lys. 32.6; and Hyp. 5.4): Millett, "Maritime Loans," 41. See, also, Theophr. *Char.* 23; Diog. Laert. 7.13; Schol. Eupolis' *Marikas* (P. Oxy. 2741, fr. 1 B col. ii 16–18); Ath. 7.292b; Xen. *Por.* 3.9: on which, Woolmer, "Athenian Mercantile Community," 165.

55. The main proponents of this view were Hasebroek, *Staat und Handel*; Millett, "Maritime Loans," 46; and now Reed, *Maritime Traders*, 34–42.

56. Finley, *Studies*, 87; Finley, *The Ancient Economy* (Berkeley: University of California Press, 1973), 141; De Ste Croix, "Maritime Loans," 42–43; Gerhard Thür, "Law and Rhetoric in Commercial Shipwreck Cases: Isolating the Facts," in *Ιουλίαν Βελισσαροπούλου Ἐπαινέσαι. Studies in Ancient Greek and Roman Law*, ed. Athina A. Dimopoulou, Andréas Helmis, and Dimitris Karambelas (Athens: ΕΛΛΗΝΙΚΗ ΕΠΙΓΡΑΦΙΚΗ ΕΤΑΙΡΕΙΑ, 2020), 289; Nikol Žiha, "The Insurance Function of Roman Maritime Loan," in *Maritime Risk Management. Essays on the History of Marine Insurance, General Average and Sea Loan*, ed. Phillip Hellwege and Guido Rossi (Berlin: Duncker & Humblot, 2021), 35–60.

57. See Cohen, *Athenian Economy*, 135 and n. 105; also, Wesley E. Thompson, "The Athenian Entrepreneur," *L'Antiquité Classique* 51 (1982): 65–66; and Alain Bresson and François Bresson, "Max Weber, la comptabilité rationnelle et l'économie du monde gréco-romain," *Les Cahiers du Centre de Recherches Historiques* 34 (2004): § 21–41.

increased the return on their capital contribution (i.e., they achieved a positive return on the investment).

Although the claim that ancient Greek merchants borrowed money to gear their investments is theoretically sound, its evidential basis is less secure.[58] The interpretation proceeds from a passage in the speech *Against Lakritos*, which is taken to show that the borrowers Artemōn and Apollodōros leveraged their investment in a cargo of Mendean wine by part-financing the acquisition of half the merchandise from their own capital (3,000 dr.) and by taking a loan for the remainder (a further 3,000 dr.).[59] This interpretation, however, potentially misunderstands the term in the contract by which the creditor took security over merchandise worth double the value of his investment: the clause may well have been intended to cover the value of the (more expensive) surrogate return cargo, not extra merchandise purchased by the debtors at the homeport. If this is right, then the passage does not support the claim that the two brothers geared their investment, because the clause does not by itself provide evidence that they purchased additional cargo at the homeport beyond that acquired with the original loan.

It seems to me that a more nuanced perspective on merchants' motivations for borrowing is possible. Maritime loan contracts combined lending with an element of insurance.[60] The dominant pattern is of *emporoi* seeking investments over several seasons with a view to making profits, accumulating capital, and then putting their savings to work by making loans of their own. Given the considerable personal risk associated with overseas travel, it is hardly surprising that successful merchants would be keen to retire to the relative safety of port to exploit their knowledge and contacts as moneylenders. This suggests that most *emporoi* seeking credit required it because they had not yet accumulated enough wealth to retire from active trade. Gearing would likely only have been possible for those who were sufficiently enriched by several seasons' trading. Most traders probably operated solely as *emporoi* only for so long as they did not possess the capital to make a business of lending. The mercantile

58. Bresson and Bresson's claim is that "by using a leverage of 50 per cent, a merchant with 6,000 drachmas in equity could launch two expeditions and expect a total net income of twice 4,800 drachmas, or 9,600 drachmas, instead of the 5,700 [he would receive] by financing a single trip or 2,850 by financing a small expedition of 3,000 drachmas. . . . He could also choose to diversify his risk, by investing 3,000 drachmas in a maritime expedition (with leverage) and 3,000 in agriculture (without leverage), the latter investment earning him a rate of 12 per cent p.a. (the standard rate for *eggeios tokos*, landed interest), that is to say 360 drachmas, to be added to the 4,800 drachmas generated by his maritime activities. In this case, this merchant could hope to earn almost 5,160 drachmas, with a significant decrease in his financial risk" (my own translation): Bresson and Bresson, "Max Weber," § 29.

59. Dem. 35.18.

60. For the suggestion of a dual solution, Isager and Hansen, *Aspects*, 74–75.

community was not a static entity made up of categorically distinct merchants, financiers, carriers, and so on, but rather dynamically composed of traders starting out with hopes of wealth and success and more experienced hands, who once they had accumulated enough capital turned increasingly to the risky but lucrative business of moneylending.[61]

As for the insurance function, the default position in a regular loan was that the borrower shouldered *omne periculum*. For most potential merchants, whose starting capital must usually have been relatively modest, the chance of total loss would have been intolerable, owing to the manifold and totalizing risks associated with overseas trade. However, by securing the lender's agreement that he should assume the risk for *periculum maris* (i.e., by the inclusion of the condition *salva nave* in the contract), the risks were spread between the parties: the creditor taking the main sea-risks (shipwreck, foundering, piracy), the borrower the remaining perils.[62] Whereas exposure to *omne periculum* would have made the enterprise unviable for many, spreading the chance of loss between the moneylender and the merchant expanded the opportunities for both to profit: the creditor by demanding a higher yield; the borrower by the opportunity to finance a venture without shouldering the risk of force majeure. Without maritime loan contracts, the number of merchants willing to take on overseas ventures must surely have been much reduced: it was only by the creditor's assumption of the risk that the market for maritime financing was both generated and sustained.

The Roman World

Structure and Scale

The crucial point to grasp about overseas trade in the Mediterranean and Black Seas during the Roman period is that the ordinary conduct of *emporía*, the long-distance trade in commodities that had begun to take shape in the

61. For traders' aspirations in the Roman period, see André Tchernia, "Dreams of Wealth, Loans, and Seaborne Trade," in *The Romans and Trade*, trans. James Grieve and Elizabeth Minchin (Oxford: Oxford University Press, 2016), 131–39.

62. The merchant could further negotiate for the allocation of some of these remaining risks (for example, cargo damage) to the *nauklēros* in the contract of affreightment: see, generally, for the Roman period: Roberto Fiori, "L'allocazione del rischio nei contratti relativi al trasporto," in *Diritto romano e economia: Due modi di pensare e organizzare il mondo (nei primi tre secoli dell'Impero)*, ed. Elio Lo Cascio and Dario Mantovani (Pavia: Pavia University Press, 2018), 507–67; Pascal Arnaud, "Aux marges du formalisme juridique romain: Le contrat de naulisme," *Annuaire de droit maritime et océanique* 38 (2019): 365–88.

eighth, seventh, and sixth centuries BCE, continued unabated and largely undisturbed.[63] The arrival of the Romans into the Mediterranean sphere, while significant for many reasons, did little to alter the seasonal rhythm of maritime communities and their orientation around trade.[64] Importantly, the same structural separation of production and distribution that had produced such a high degree of fragmentation at the Athenian *emporion* also characterized the structure of the economy of the Mediterranean world under Rome. According to D'Arms, the aversion of the Roman landowning elites to direct visible involvement in maritime commerce was informed by a combination of social *mores* and legal sanctions, which characterized trade as an activity deserving of social opprobrium: both the *plebiscitum Claudianum* (218 BCE) and the later *lex Iulia de repetundis* (59 BCE) placed restrictions on the capacity of senators to own and operate ships.[65] Senatorial landowners therefore typically engaged in long-distance trade indirectly, operating through dependents and freedmen so as to avoid being tainted by association. The basic continuity in the structural separation between productive and distributive activities in the interconnected economies of the Mediterranean basin, however, points toward a deeper explanation than the Romans' cultural idiosyncrasies. As Tchernia has pointed out, one weakness of D'Arms' thesis is that if heads of household and patrons used their dependents and freedmen as a veil to conceal their involvement, it was not a very effective strategy, because in almost every case their identity was transparent to the third party.[66] It is therefore more likely that the choice of landowning elites to avoid direct involvement in maritime trade was ultimately motivated by economic considerations that kept productive and distributive activities largely separate.[67]

This basic structural continuity is reflected in the composition of mercan-

63. As the steady climb in the numbers of shipwrecks attests.

64. Probably the most significant impact would have been felt in the levying of taxes, especially *portoria*: see, generally, Nicholas Purcell, "The Ancient Mediterranean: The View from the Customs House," in *Rethinking the Mediterranean: Papers from a Conference Organized by the Columbia University Center for the Ancient Mediterranean, September 21–22, 2001*, ed. William V. Harris (Oxford: Oxford University Press, 2005), 200–232; Purcell, "Taxing the Sea," in *The Sea in History—The Ancient World*, ed. Pascal Arnaud and Philip de Souza (Woodbridge, UK: Boydell & Brewer, 2017), 319–34.

65. See, generally, John H. D'Arms, *Commerce and Social Standing in Ancient Rome* (Cambridge, MA: Harvard University Press, 1981). On the *plebiscitum Claudianum*, see André Tchernia, "Le plebiscitum Claudianum," in *Vocabulaire et expression de l'économie dans le monde antique*, ed. Jean Andreau and Véronique Chankowski (Bordeaux: Ausonius, 2007), 253–78; also, James R. Townshend, "Lex Claudia," in *The Oxford Classical Dictionary*, 4th ed., ed. S. Hornblower, A. Spawforth, and E. Eidinow (Oxford: Oxford University Press, 2012).

66. André Tchernia, "Landowners and Traders," in *The Romans and Trade*, trans. James Grieve and Elizabeth Minchin (Oxford: Oxford University Press, 2016), 37.

67. Tchernia, "Landowners and Traders," 26.

tile communities. *Emporoi*, *nauklēroi*, and moneylenders all continued to ply their trade. These remained, as one would expect, highly international, moving with changes in the direction of trade flows (as they always had done); while some trade diasporas also continued to maintain stable communities of resident merchants at major nodes in the network (such as the much-heralded Tyrian merchants who occupied a *statio* at Puteoli).[68] Individuals engaged in *emporía* were also frequently members of associations of mutual trust and solidarity organized around shared professional, ethnic, and religious characteristics (later formalized as *collegia*). As social networks, these associations also functioned to exert pressure on their members to behave honorably, lest they acquire a reputation for dishonesty. These organizations provided an ideal setting in which to make new contacts, cultivate business relationships—and to seek credit.[69]

Despite these continuities, there are two significant differences that need to be accounted for. The first concerns the structural involvement of members of the Roman landowning elite in maritime trade, and therefore the porousness of the screen interposed between production and distribution. At a glance, the merchants and carriers who can be identified as maritime debtors are fairly diverse. The only definite evidence of shipowners taking receipt of a loan on maritime terms is contained in a document from the Fayyum (second century CE), which records the disbursement of over seven talents to four *synnauklēroi* (co-owners) of an *akatos*-type merchant galley (evidently peregrines) in connection with a *nautikē syngraphē*.[70] Other borrowers were certainly merchants and possibly also in control of the vessel being used to transport their goods. The circumstances surrounding the departure of Callimachus, probably also a foreigner, from Brentesium suggest that he had control over the timing of the ship's leaving port, making it likely that he was not only a merchant (which is in any case certain), but a shipowner-trader.[71] The same inference may be drawn in connection with the debtor mentioned in a Diocletianic constitution of the late third century, whose responsibility for changing course implies that he had control of the vessel in which he was traveling.[72] Menelaos, the recipient of

68. See, generally, Terpstra, *Trade*, 33–82.

69. Annalisa Marzano, "The Personal Infrastructure of Maritime Trade," in *Roman Law and Maritime Commerce*, ed. Peter Candy and Emilia Mataix Ferrándiz (Edinburgh: Edinburgh University Press, 2022), 67–68; also, generally, Jane Sancinito, *The Reputation of the Roman Merchant* (Ann Arbor: University of Michigan Press, 2024).

70. SB XIV 11850.

71. D.45.1.122.1 (Scaev. 28 *dig.*). As Jakab has pointed out, the use of *promittere* instead of *spondere*, which was reserved for Roman citizens, suggests the involvement of a peregrine: Jakab, "Loans and Securities," 144.

72. C.4.33.4 (Diocl./Maxim. AA.).

1,000 *denarii* in *TPSulp.* 78, another peregrine, was probably a merchant-carrier and possibly also took the money as a loan (though the terms on which it was taken cannot be determined). Finally, the anonymous borrower who appears in the second-century Muziris papyrus (who may not have been the owner of the entire cargo enumerated on the verso), might have been the *nauklēros* of the *Hermapollon*.[73]

As for maritime creditors, the evidence supports Andreau's view that these tended to be elite *faenaratores* (moneylenders) and merchant-financiers.[74] The fictional Trimalchio, for example, is depicted as a freedman who turned his hand to making loans to other freedmen involved in overseas trade following the success of one of his maritime ventures.[75] In the *Satyricon*, Trimalchio's seed capital comes from two sources: his former master (by whom he was manumitted on death) and his wife. Petronius' story hints at the reality, that the ultimate source of finance for maritime traders was usually members of the elite acting through agents or intermediaries. Plutarch's report of the maritime loans made by the elder Cato (second century BCE) through his freedman Quinctio is well known and will be considered in more detail in the next chapter.[76] The owner of 'Stichus,' the moneylending slave (likely a *faenarator*) who financed Callimachus probably owned property at Rome, where the contract provided for the money to be taken in the event that the borrower was required to make early repayment. Some three centuries later, the 7 tal. 5,160 dr. transferred to the four *synnauklēroi* of the *Antinoos Philosarapis Sōzōn* was issued through the bank of Marcus Claudius Sabinus at Alexandria on behalf of C. Longinus Keler and Ti. Claudius Charēs, two members of the "entrepreneurial elite" in Roman Egypt who Rathbone's prosopographical research shows were concurrently involved in "landowning, tax-collecting, state supply contracts, and maritime and other loans."[77] Staying in second-century Egypt, the original sum lent in connection with the goods listed on the verso of the Muziris papyrus must have been very substantial (perhaps between one and three million sesterces), since the return cargo, which was probably on its way to Alexandria from Koptos at the time the document was drawn up, was valued at almost HS seven million after the deduction of the 25 percent tax (*tetartē*). The financier's contractual option to purchase the goods from the merchant at the conclusion of the enterprise in the event of default (i.e., for the valuation given in the document) implies that

73. De Romanis, *Pepper Trade*, 313.
74. Andreau, *Banking*, 151.
75. This can reasonably be taken to imply lending at maritime rates: Petron. *Sat.* 76.
76. See below, 92–97.
77. Rathbone, "Financing," 218–19.

he must have had at least several million sesterces available for this purpose (i.e., besides the initial outlay), qualifying him as one of the wealthiest men in the empire.[78] On a much smaller scale, the payment to Menelaos in *TPSulp.* 78 was made by Primus, slave of Publius Attius Severus, the appearance of whose name in the *tituli picti* indicates that he was a trader in olive oil between Baetica and Rome.[79]

The sparsity and geographical distribution of the evidence makes conclusions difficult to draw. However, one feature that emerges is that while the individuals who took on maritime debts tended to be foreigners, their creditors appear often to have been slaves or freedmen of the Roman landowning elite. This raises an interesting discrepancy, because the collective weight of the epigraphic, archaeological, and other evidence suggests that slaves and freedmen (in particular) were just as active as merchants and carriers as professional moneylenders. We can perhaps draw two inferences: first, it would appear that peregrines were generally most involved in overseas trade as merchants and *nauklēroi* and did not compete with professional moneylenders who had the backing of a wealthy master or patron; and second, it also seems that slaves and freedmen, when they operated as *emporoi* and *nauklēroi*, did not make such ready use of maritime lending, either because they were operating out of a *peculium* if they were a slave or, in the case of freedmen, the capital acquired by them on manumission or in some cases by way of inheritance. No doubt these inferences are too strong, not least because the evidence is so thin that even one or two more data points might change the picture considerably. Nonetheless, it appears on this evidence that the Roman elites were well positioned to tap *emporía* for profit by setting up their slaves and freedmen as professional moneylenders financing peregrine members of the trading diaspora.

The second difference between interregional commerce in the Roman period and in those which preceded it is one of scale. Entering into this discussion, we need to be careful not to imply that the ordinary conduct of *emporía* experienced a scalar revolution: in general, smaller ships of less than 75 tons capacity (approximately 1,500 amphorae) made up the great majority of vessels in the merchant fleet at any given time.[80] Rather, the key difference consists in the growth of specific trade flows in key areas of the economy that involved the distribution of the produce generated by intensive agricultural production. The most tangible of these, owing to the trail of Dressel I amphorae scattered across the seabed of the coasts of northwest Italy and the south of France, was

78. Rathbone, "Financing," 221.
79. See above, 35.
80. Wilson, "Developments," 39.

the wine trade with Gaul, which peaked in the last decades of the second and the first half of the first century BCE.[81] As several famous shipwrecks (like the *Madrague de Giens* and the *Albenga*) show, the specialization and repeat nature of this trade encouraged the construction of vessels capable of carrying many thousands of amphorae, well in excess of the capacity of a typical merchant galley.[82] Though less visible in the archaeological record (because of the perishability of the cargo), the import of Egyptian grain from Alexandria to Puteoli and then Rome was no less susceptible to economies of scale. In addition to the surge in certain trade flows, the growth of the India trade, which dealt in higher-value goods such as pepper and spices, is attested to not only by the Muziris papyrus, but in the archaeological record by the impressive development of the infrastructure serving the overland route between the ports on the Red Sea coast and the Nile.[83]

As Rathbone has observed, the continued use of maritime loan contracts in the context of the India trade shows their adaptability to new contexts:

> The net result is that, while the legal forms of the contract were fairly traditional, the economic structure was quite different. Instead of a merchant planning a venture and seeking capital where he could find it, we have a financier investing in the trade with India who recruited merchants to run individual trips. . . . These landowners invested directly, organized the shape of the venture, had their own agents involved, and bore the principal capital risk. Both our financier and these landowners could have run the ventures entirely directly. They used third-party contractors partly to spread some, but not much, of the risk (the running costs), but above all to secure management which was expert, and had a personal incentive (legal liability for loss, profit motive) in running the venture efficiently, which a subordinate employee would not have had.[84]

When elucidated in these terms, the structure of the arrangement perfectly illustrates the more-or-less routine separation of production and distribution

81. See, generally, André Tchernia, "Wine Exporting and the Exception of Gaul," in *The Romans and Trade*, trans. James Grieve and Elizabeth Minchin (Oxford: Oxford University Press, 2016), 277–96.

82. Madrague de Giens (south coast of France, c. 75–60 BCE): 375–400 tons, laden with between 6,000 and 7,000 Dressel I amphorae filled with red wine, apparently stowed underneath crates of black gloss wares, as well as coarse and cooking pottery. Albenga (near to Ligurian settlement of Albenga, c. 100–80 BCE): 500–600 tons, made up of c. 11,500–13,000 Dressel I amphorae together with sacks of hazelnuts and grain. See, for both, Wilson, "Developments," 39–40.

83. See, e.g., Wilson, "Red Sea Trade," 13–32.

84. Rathbone, "The 'Muziris' Papyrus," 43.

in the Roman world. The reasons for preferring this arrangement are transparent in light of Rathbone's remarks: financiers provided merchants with capital with which to purchase a cargo (or multiple cargoes), possibly even with the intention of reacquiring the incoming goods on the merchant's return. When interpreted from this perspective, it would appear that merchants engaged in this way were acting in something like the capacity of a modern freight forwarder: that is, persons who offer their services as experts in the logistics network, dealing with the transportation and delivery of goods through supply chains.[85] Their essential activities include organizing warehousing, transport (including transshipment), and customs documentation.[86] The key to the success of the freight-forwarding business is knowledge, not only of the distribution process and how to move goods through it effectively but also of which warehousemen and carriers to engage, how to configure multiple contractual relationships so as to integrate them from the perspective of risk allocation, and so forth.

The decision by landowner-financiers to dispose of produce and reinvest part of the proceeds as maritime loans was perfectly rational from an economic perspective. If the producer elected to keep the distribution of his produce in-house, his default position was to assume the entire risk for the enterprise and correspondingly to retain the whole profit. The main drawbacks of this approach were that the landowner had to provide (by capital investment or hire) the infrastructure himself (ships, crews, camels, storage, guards, and so forth); and to put the work in the hands of his own agents, who lacked incentives. By pursuing a strategy of reinvestment, the landowner chose instead to divest himself of some of the risk and to split the profit with the merchant (or *nauklēros*) accordingly. Again, there were drawbacks: not only was the lender exposed to a whole suite of risks associated with lending (for which, see chapter 3); but in the context of a very large loan given on security of the goods acquired with the proceeds, its size meant that the risk for the loss of the cargo (by whatever means) was *de facto* inextricably linked to the ability of the other parties to the enterprise to meet their potential liabilities. Both these considerations explain the close supervision by the creditor of the merchant: in addition to mitigating against fraud, it was in the lender's interests to monitor and control the progress of the merchandise to ensure the safety of his investment.

85. Casson refers to the shepherding of the goods overland as "the sort of task a shipping agent would undertake:" Lionel Casson, "P. Vindob G 40822 and the Shipping of Goods from India," *BASP* 23 (1986): 76.

86. Michael Browne and Julian Allen, "Logistics Out-Sourcing," in *Handbook of Logistics and Supply Chain Management*, ed. Ann M. Brewer, Kenneth J. Button, and David A. Hensher, vol. 2 (Amsterdam: Elsevier, 2001), 257.

These negatives, however, were outweighed by the significant advantages of outsourcing logistics to seasoned merchants. As Rathbone notes, merchants had both expert knowledge (as 'freight forwarders') and a personal incentive to maximize the profits of the venture, assuring the creditor of a lucrative yield. In addition, a merchant equipped with capital was in a much better position to diversify cargoes (essential also for practical reasons like stowage) and to calibrate them to meet changing sources of demand.[87] When one considers the possible sale of the return cargo back to the lender at the conclusion of the enterprise, the effective outcome of the Muziris contract was that the producer was paying for the merchant's contacts, trading knowledge, and logistical expertise to transform capital into cargoes and successfully move them through the distribution network.

Significance of Maritime Lending in the Roman World

All the indications are that maritime loan contracts were no less dispensable to the conduct of overseas trade in the Roman Mediterranean than they had been previously, albeit on a different dynamic.[88] Once again, the evidence defies quantification: but the range in the value of cargoes attested to have been purchased on credit shows that finance had a part to play across the full spectrum of transactions. Moreover, although no loan documents explicitly connected to maritime loan contracts have survived in the archive of the Sulpicii, there is a strong possibility that a number of the tablets record the details of bridging loans taken out to repay maritime lenders.[89] The most compelling evidence, however, is provided by the legal texts (albeit only indirectly). First, it was Biscardi's great insight to see that from the late Republic onwards the Roman jurists treated the interpretation of penal stipulations included in *nautikai syngraphai* as the material basis for thinking about the application of the *actio ex stipulatu*, even referring to the remedy by the alternative *actio traiecticiae pecuniae*. This can only have been possible if the use of maritime loan contracts was

87. On the practicalities and legal implications of bulk transport, see Gianfranco Purpura, "Roman Documentation Concerning Shipping in Bulk," in *Roman Law and Maritime Commerce*, ed. Peter Candy and Emilia Mataix Ferrándiz (Edinburgh: Edinburgh University Press, 2022), 109–36.

88. For a similar statement to this effect, Rougé, *Recherches*, 345.

89. Jakab, "Loans and Securities," 156–57. Jakab also suggests that the anxiety of the merchants whose grain was lost with Saufeius' ship in the well-known late-Republican *responsum* given by Alfenus/Servius (D.19.2.31 (Alf. 5 *dig. a Paulo epit.*)) could be explained if, despite the loss of their merchandise after arrival, they were still obliged to repay their maritime creditors: Jakab, "Loans and Securities," 142–43; though cf. Peter Candy, "'Judging beyond the Sandal': The Use of Rhetoric in D.19.2.31 (Alf. 5 Dig. a Paulo Epit.)," *ZRG RA* 138 (2021): 310–37.

so widespread and standardized that it was intelligible for the jurists to treat them to this degree of abstraction.

To this we may add that the whole structure of the remedies relevant to the conduct of maritime trade that were developed over the last century and a half of the Republic presuppose that maritime loan contracts were readily available to merchants for divesting themselves of *periculum maris*. A good example is the relationship between the condition *salva nave* and the carrier's liability under a *receptum nautarum*, which made him responsible for cargo damage during transit, irrespective of fault.[90] If the merchant had acquired the goods using the proceeds of a maritime loan and simultaneously engaged a carrier subject to a *receptum*, the financier assumed the risk for loss of the goods in the event that the vessel was prevented from arriving safely, the carrier (after the introduction of the *exceptio Labeoniana*) for loss or damage only if the ship had not been lost to wreck or piracy.[91] In other words, the allocation of the risk was neatly delimited by the structure of the remedies themselves, which anticipated that the carrier's liability ended where the maritime lender's began. All this suggests that maritime loan contracts continued to occupy a special and significant space within the broader structure of maritime commerce during the Roman period.

Conclusion

Though the first definite evidence for the existence of *nautikai syngraphai* comes from the last quarter of the fifth century BCE, they likely originated in the conduct of *emporía* (i.e., the long-distance trade in commodities) as early as the eighth century BCE. At Athens, maritime loan contracts were the basis upon which merchants sought financing for the acquisition of cargoes and were essential to supporting (among other things) the import of grain into Attica. Since the transaction combined credit with insurance, it provided a flexible mechanism by which merchants could raise capital and divest themselves of the sea-risk at the same time. The price for this was a maritime yield, fixed as a proportion of the sum lent and usually more expensive than landed rates. The credit function of the transaction retained its significance in the context of the *emporion*, since merchants tended to pursue active trading only for so long as they had not built up the capital required to retire to port and become lenders themselves.

90. See, generally, the texts collected in D.4.9.
91. For the *exceptio Labeoniana*, D.4.9.3.1 (Ulp. 14 *ad ed.*).

At Rome, emporic trade continued to be financed by loans given on maritime terms. However, maritime loan contracts were also now adapted to new routes and to trade on a different scale to that witnessed in classical Athens. In the systematic trades between the Red Sea coast and India and likely also the distribution of the produce of villa estates both in Italy and later the provinces, wealthy financiers (or their proxies) appear to have been more actively invested than their Athenian counterparts had been in the *emporion* at Piraeus. This participation was in part facilitated by the decision of some members of the Roman elite to set up their dependents as *faenaratores*, whose lending activities sometimes extended to maritime finance. They also seem to have developed methods for making larger investments, which were designed to exert a greater degree of control over the debtor by closer monitoring and boilerplate clauses that contained provisions more favorable to the creditor (e.g., in terms of security, options to buy). In these transactions, the borrowers fulfilled a function much closer to a modern freight forwarder than to the adventitious merchants who frequented Piraeus during the fourth century BCE.

CHAPTER THREE

Commercial Practice and Dispute Resolution

This chapter examines the relationship between maritime commercial practice and dispute resolution at classical Athens and Rome. It traces a single thread in the experience and practice of traders through from the moment of striking the bargain to completion of the enterprise or (if needed) resolution of a dispute by arbitration or in the law courts. By accommodating this process within a single frame, the continuity of practice with litigation and the dynamic interplay between commercial activity and legal institutions comes more clearly into view.

Risk

The default position in respect of risk in money loans at Athens and Rome was straightforward, in that the borrower was liable in all circumstances to repay what was due.[1] When a loan was made subject to a maritime loan contract, the position was varied by the inclusion of the condition *salva nave*, by which the creditor assumed the risk of the ship's failure to arrive at its destination. Though on its face, the condition was blind as to the reason for the ship's failure to arrive safely, its function was to shift the sea-risk to the creditor, the magnitude of which was priced into the yield.

The main sea-risks are shipwreck, foundering, and enemy action (chiefly piracy).[2] For obvious reasons, there are no statistics that we can draw upon to provide a clear picture of the proportion of voyages that ended in disaster. According to Gibbens, the annual rate of losses during the Hellenistic period

1. See Geoffrey MacCormack, "Periculum," *ZRG RA* 96 (1979): 160–62.

2. On piracy generally, see Philip de Souza, *Piracy in the Graeco-Roman World* (Cambridge: Cambridge University Press, 1999). For the practice of luring ships onto rocks by the erection of false lighthouses, D.47.9.10 (Ulp. 1 *Opin.*): on which, Emilia Mataix Ferrándiz, *Shipwrecks, Legal Landscapes, and Mediterranean Paradigms: Gone under Sea* (Leiden: Brill, 2022), 146–48.

probably ran between about 3 percent and 5 percent;[3] while Bresson and Bresson calculate an absolute minimum rate of attrition of 2 percent of all voyages, based upon the 1,200 wrecks (in Parker's set) from the same period together with the assumption that c. 60,000 voyages were made during that time.[4] To this we may add (with due caution) a comparative perspective: of the total number of sailings (2,171) made by vessels belonging to the British East India Company traveling England–Asia–England (1749–50 and 1813–14), just under 5 percent were lost;[5] of the ships traveling between the Netherlands and Asia in connection with the Dutch East India trade (1595–1795), around 3.5 percent perished;[6] and of the vessels sailing on the Atlantic route between Spain and Mexico (1550–1650), 2.45 percent were lost.[7] Though it would be unwise to place too much reliance on these figures, the headline rate is reassuringly similar to those that have been suggested for the ancient period. This also accords with Cohen's suggestion, that the relatively modest rates on maritime loan contracts (once one takes into account all the many costs and risks that could eat into the profit) indicate that the parties to the agreements perceived only a relatively low likelihood that the enterprise would meet with total failure.[8]

There were, in addition to these, marine risks (not assumed by the lender) that might result in the loss of, or damage to, the cargo, without preventing the safe arrival of the vessel. Goods stowed on deck, for example, might be swept overboard (flotsam) and those in the hold sustain water damage.[9] Similarly, as both the orations *Against Zēnothemis* and *Against Phormiōn* show, adverse changes in prices—in the latter case, owing to the outbreak of war—represented a significant risk, together with volatility in exchange rates.[10] These remained with the borrower.

---

3. David Gibbins, "Shipwrecks and Hellenistic Trade," in *Hellenistic Economies*, ed. John Davies and Zosia H. Archibald (London: Routledge, 2001), 277–78.

4. Bresson and Bresson, "Max Weber," § 36.

5. Just over three-fifths of these were foundered, lost at sea, or verifiably wrecked, and a further quarter perished to enemy action: Huw V. Bowen, "The Shipping Losses of the British East India Company, 1750–1813," *International Journal of Maritime History* 32, no. 2 (2020): 323–36.

6. See Jacobus R. Bruijn, Femme S. Gaastra, and I. Schöffer, *Dutch-Asiatic Shipping in the 17th and 18th Centuries*, vol. 1 (The Hague: Martinus Nijhoff, 1987).

7. See Huguette Chaunu and Pierre Chaunu, *Séville et l'Atlantique (1504–1650)*, vol. 6 (Paris: A. Colin, 1956); also, Pierre Chaunu, *Les Phillippines et le Pacifique des Ibériques (XVIe, XVIIe, XVIIIe siècles)* (Paris: S.E.V.P.E.N., 1960). Cf. the 12.6 percent of galleons lost between Manila and Acapulco as part of the Manila Galleon trade (1565–1815), the higher rate of attrition due to inefficient cargo loading and delayed ship departure brought about by widespread corruption: Fernando Arteaga, Desiree Desierto, and Mark Koyama, "Shipwrecked by Rents," *Journal of Development Economics* 168 (2024).

8. Cohen, *Athenian Economy*, 142–43; also, Campbell, "Contingent Seas," 29.

9. For a discussion of the effect of water damage on the calculation of contribution under the *lex Rhodia de iactu*, see D.14.2.4.2 (Call. 2 *quaest.*).

10. Dem. 32.25; 34.8–9.

In addition to shifting the sea-risk to the creditor, the condition *salva nave* created increased opportunities for dishonesty and fraud. Scuttling the ship to avoid paying a debt appears to have been a well-known tactic. In *Against Zēnothemis*, Zēnothemis is accused of collaborating with the *nauklēros* Hēgestratos to perpetrate a fraud by holing the vessel during the night before making their escape.[11] Livy similarly describes how three *societates* bid for state contracts to supply grain and equipment to the Roman army in Spain during the Second Punic War, but only on condition that (among other things) the risk to the cargoes of storm and enemy action should be borne by the *res publica*.[12] Later it transpired that two partners had conspired to make fraudulent claims, by falsely reporting wrecks and by misrepresenting the value of worthless cargoes that were loaded onto ships and then scuttled.[13] Literary sources also pick up the theme of disreputable and dishonest merchants and ship's captains, quick to claim credit for a successful enterprise but equally to resort to fraud, even at the expense of others' lives, when it suited their interests.[14]

Creditors in maritime loan transactions were also exposed to the ordinary commercial risks associated with moneylending. In general, these included the risk of the debtor's nonperformance (performance risk) and the risk of their turning out not to be solvent (credit risk). These were especially acute for maritime creditors, not only because lending is necessarily always asynchronous (the creditor always performing first), but also because of the difficulties created by the international nature of the trade and the mobility of both merchants and their assets. The resulting fragility of creditor confidence is most clearly expressed by the speaker Dareios in the oration *Against Dionysodōros*, who emphasizes the dependency of lenders on the robustness of both the law courts and the laws, in upholding contracts and protecting creditors from fraud.[15]

The response of maritime creditors to this unique combination of risks was to develop increasingly sophisticated risk-mitigation techniques. These

11. Dem. 32.5–6. Thür quite plausibly argues that the episode has been fabricated for argumentative reasons and that more likely (as we later discover at §27) the ship ran into further trouble having left Kephallēnia, leading to Hēgestratos' death: Thür, "Law and Rhetoric," 292; also, Jakab, "Loans and Securities," 147.

12. Livy, 23.49.1–3. Probably Rougé is right that these partnerships ought to be interpreted as *societates publicanorum* and should not therefore be counted as evidence for the formation of partnerships explicitly for the purposes of maritime transport: Jean Rougé, "Prêt et société maritimes dans le monde romain," in *The Seaborne Commerce of Ancient Rome: Studies in Archaeology and History*, ed. John H. D'Arms and E. Christian Kopff (Rome: American Academy in Rome, 1980), 292. On the insurance aspect of the arrangement, see Dominique Gaurier, *Le droit maritime romain* (Rennes: Presses Universitaires de Rennes, 2004), 129–30.

13. Livy, 25.3.14–19.

14. E.g., Philostr. *V.A.* 4.32.2.

15. Dem. 56.1–2.

included making and keeping written records of the contract, together with the use of witnesses, the implementation of monitoring arrangements, the taking and exercise of rights in security, and (in the last resort) to the enforcement of the contract, by a process of negotiation, arbitration, and litigation through the courts. We turn to these now.

Late-Fifth- and Fourth-Century-BCE Athens

Commercial Practice

The Written Contract

Maritime loan contracts typically contained standard clauses that were then modified by the parties to suit their particular needs. Many of the more bespoke terms defined the circumstances in which the creditor was willing to bear the marine risk. These typically concerned specification of the route and the inclusion of (customary) time limits, almost always reinforced by a conventional penalty for breach of the agreement or failure to perform in certain respects. In general, lenders appear to have been cautious about assuming the risk of sailing in the offseason, at least for certain routes.[16] They also sometimes prohibited the borrower from unloading their goods in certain ports;[17] or from shipping cargoes of grain to any destination other than Athens (to comply with the grain laws).[18] If the borrower was an *emporos*, the selection of the *nauklēros* and the vessel was also material. In the contract produced in the speech *Against Lakritos*, Artemōn and Apollodōros were bound to ship their goods in Hyblesios' merchant vessel, just as Phormiōn was likely also obliged to sail with the *nauklēros* Lampis.[19] Probably, like Chrysippos and Lampis (before their relationship broke down), lenders nurtured relationships with trusted *nauklēroi* whom they required their debtors to sail with.

16. Notwithstanding that sailing did not altogether cease during the winter months: see, generally, James Beresford, *The Ancient Sailing Season* (Leiden: Brill, 2013). Cf. Dem. 56.29–30, in which the speaker Dareios complained that some other more unscrupulous lenders had agreed to terminate their previous agreements with the debtors in order to relend to them on new terms for multiple winter sailings Rhodes–Egypt–Rhodes. Similarly, at Dem. 35.10, the term that provided for an increased yield if the debtors set off from Pontus after c. 19 September shows that winter sailing was negotiable, only at higher interest rates.

17. Dem. 35.13.

18. Dareios and Pamphilos insist upon Athens and not Rhodes as the destination port: Dem. 56.6.

19. The debtors Artemōn and Apollodōrus, for example, were only to use ports where the property of Athenian citizens was not subject to seizure: Dem. 35.10; also, 34.7.

Documentation

In the opening to *Against Dionysodōros*, Dareios reminds the jury that all that the creditor was left holding following the ship's departure from the homeport was a scrap of papyrus or writing tablet bearing the terms of his agreement with the debtor.[20] This made it imperative for the creditor to ensure that the transactional documents were not only legally effective but also capable of being verified as genuine should a dispute arise. These aims were typically achieved by constructing loan dossiers that were both designed to achieve legal effects and guaranteed as authentic by the use of witnesses, trusted depositories (e.g., bankers and other financial intermediaries), and seals.

The importance of the written *syngraphē* for the enforceability of claims arising under the contract (for which, see below) made it essential for creditors to take precautionary measures to ensure that they could prove both the existence and contents of the contract in case of dispute.[21] The document was normally drawn up on a writing tablet (a γραμματεῖον or γραμματεῖδιον) or sheet of papyrus, signed or sealed by witnesses, and sealed by the parties.[22] It was then deposited with a third party (usually a banker or money changer) under the supervision of witnesses, on the understanding that the depository was only entitled to surrender the document with both the creditor's and debtor's consent.[23] Copies of the contract were also made and distributed to the parties for their own records.[24] If a dispute gave rise to arbitration or court proceedings, it was common for witnesses (together with the depository) to be called to attest to the authenticity of the *syngraphē*. In the speech *Against Lakritos*, the production of the document is followed by the reading of depositions by the three witnesses to the contract, the depository (Archenomidēs of Anagyros), and the witnesses to the deposit.[25] Once the transaction had been successfully con-

20. Dem. 56.1–2.

21. For a discussion of the legal status of contractual documents at classical Athens and during the Hellenistic period, see Elizabeth A. Meyer, *Legitimacy and Law in the Roman World: Tabulae in Roman Belief and Practice* (Cambridge: Cambridge University Press, 2004), 12–20.

22. For an agreement recorded on a *grammateion*, see Lys. 32.7: on which, Douglas M. MacDowell, *The Law in Classical Athens* (Ithaca, NY: Cornell University Press, 1978), 233–34; Stephen C. Todd, *The Shape of Athenian Law* (Oxford: Clarendon Press, 1993), 334–37. For the use of either writing tablets or papyrus, Dem. 56.1. For witnesses as signatories, see, e.g., Dem. 35.13.

23. For the deposit of the contract with a third party, Dem. 33.36; 48.9–10, 12–18; Hyp. 3.5–11, 18, 21–22; and with bankers in connection with maritime loan contracts, Dem. 34.6; 35.14. Dem. 32.16 is sometimes understood to mean that Hēgestratos "deposited a contract with" another of the merchants on board; but cf. Isager and Hansen, who rightly point out that the expression indicates that he "entered into a contract with" the merchant: Isager and Hansen, *Aspects*, 140; also, Paoli, *Studi di diritto*, 133–36.

24. See, e.g., Hyp. 3.5–11, 18, 21–22.

25. Dem. 35.14. Some of the witnesses to the contract also served as witnesses to the deposit, though the two sets do not overlap entirely.

cluded, it was customary for the parties to symbolize the termination of their engagement by destroying the *syngraphē* (again in the presence of witnesses).[26]

Witnesses

Witnesses (*martures*) played an important part in Athenian jury trials, both by attesting to the truth of the litigants' claims and lending their support to one or other of the protagonists through their appearance on his behalf.[27] It was therefore normal for the parties to provide for the attendance of their own witnesses at relevant stages of the transaction. In the oration *Against Phormiōn*, Chrysippos attacks Phormiōn's argument by drawing attention to his inability to produce witnesses, both in connection with the moment at which the ship left port and to corroborate Phormiōn's claim to have settled the debt in Bosporos.[28] The implication of the passage is that it was normal for witnesses to be called to observe both the moment at which the risk transferred to the lender and when payments were being made. Chrysippos' wry comment that "men borrow with few witnesses, but, when they pay, they take care to have many witnesses present, that they may win a reputation for honesty in business dealings" indicates the tactical way in which both lenders and borrowers might seek to strengthen their own position at the expense of their counterpart.[29] In addition to witnessing the sealing and deposition of documents, witnesses were also brought by plaintiffs to observe the issuing of the summons (*proklēsis*), which was only valid if it was served in the presence of one or more of them.[30]

Monitoring Debtors

When the borrower was a single individual, lenders almost always chose to send a representative (χερμαχόλουθος, *kermakolouthos*), sometimes a slave, to monitor the debtor and safeguard their interests while the enterprise was ongoing. In the speech *Against Zēnothemis*, Demon alleges that the man sent by him and his partner as their representative on board, a certain Aristophōn, had con-

26. For a general statement to this effect, Dem. 56.15; also, 34.31; 33.12. See Schuster, *Das Seedarlehen*, 136 (with literature); also, Ashburner, *Rhodian Sea-Law*, ccxvi.

27. Though not under oath, witnesses were liable to be sued by *dikē pseudomarturion* if their testimony was subsequently shown to be false or improper: Todd, *Shape*, 96–97.

28. Dem. 34.28, 30. For the moment at which the risk transferred to the creditor, cf. D.22.2.3 (Mod. 4 *reg.*), in which Modestinus refers to the time at which it was agreed that the ship should set sail, not the actual date of sailing. See below, 170–71.

29. Dem. 34.30.

30. Dem. 53.15. At Dem. 34.13, Chrysippos describes serving the summons on Phormiōn in front of witnesses at the perfume shops. See, also, Dem. 56.17–18.

spired against them to help orchestrate the fraud perpetrated by Zēnothemis, Hēgestratos, and ultimately Protos.[31] In the oration *Against Phormiōn*, the lender Chryssipos refers to both a slave and a partner stationed at the outport in Bosporos, to whom Phormiōn was charged with delivering missives that were apparently never forthcoming.[32] Perhaps more unusually, there is some indication that Nikoboulos, a professional moneylender of loans at both maritime and landed rates at Athens, sometimes personally monitored his debtors on their voyages. As Millett points out, it may be material that Nikoboulos made the voyage in question during the month of Elaphēboliōn, before the beginning of the sailing season, in which case the practice may have been confined to speculative lending during the offseason.[33]

Both *emporoi* and lenders frequently operated in pairs.[34] In contrast to the Roman world, there is no evidence for larger associations formed with the specific purpose of operating maritime businesses.[35] When the borrowers were partners, it was standard to state their joint and several liability expressly in the contract.[36] Armed with this clause in the agreement, an alternative practice to sending representatives developed, in which one of the debtors was required to stay at the homeport under the watchful eye of the creditor(s).[37] In the event that the traveling merchant failed to return, the partner who had stayed behind could still be pursued for repayment, failing which they could be sued.

Security

In respect of money loans, the Athenians recognized a principle whereby the creditor not only retained the right to reclaim the money lent but also acquired security rights in any surrogate property purchased with the loan proceeds.[38]

31. Dem. 32.11, 24.
32. Dem. 34.8, 28.
33. Dem. 37.6, 10, 52–54: on which, Millett, *Lending*, 193–96.
34. Protos and Fertatos (Dem. 32.17); Massiliote citizens (Dem. 32.8); Athenian citizens (Dem. 32.14); Chrysippos and his brother (Dem. 34.39); Androklēs and Nausikratēs (friends) (Dem. 35.10); Artemōn and Apollodōros (brothers) (Dem. 35.10); Hyblesios and Apollonidēs (Dem. 35.33); Megaklidēs and Thrysyllos (brothers) (Dem. 52.20); Dareios and Pamphilos (Dem. 56.1); Dionysodōros and Parmeniskos (Dem. 56.7). See, generally, Isager and Hansen, *Aspects*, 74.
35. See below, 92–97.
36. See, e.g., Dem. 35.12.
37. Artemōn required to stay at Piraeus (Dem. 35.3–4); Dionysodōros required to stay at Piraeus (Dem. 56.7).
38. See, generally, Schuster, *Das Seedarlehen*, 91–104; also, Arnold Kränzlein, *Eigentum und Besitz im griechischen Recht des fünften und vierten Jahrhunderts v. Chr.* (Berlin: Duncker & Humblot, 1963), 89; Max Kaser, "Stellvertretung und 'notwendige Entgeltlichkeit,'" *ZRG RA* 91 (1974): 168. The precise nature of the rights of the parties to secured transactions has been the subject of debate, summarized by Mark J. Sundahl, "Secured Credit in Athens: Reopening the Debate,"

The principle evidently applied to maritime lending (at least during the fourth century BCE) and even extended to the return cargo, the value of which under normal conditions would exceed the original loan. As soon as the debtor purchased the return cargo the lender acquired a hypothec over the surrogate property without the need for an express term in the contract. Although the borrower was granted far-reaching authorization (*kyrios*) to deal with the property while the enterprise was ongoing, this ceased once the contractual grace period for payment of the debt had expired. If the borrower was a *nauklēros*, the lender might additionally take security over the ship, the crew (if they were slaves), and any money owed to the carrier as freight.

Creditors went to great lengths to safeguard their interests in security. In the absence of any significant statutes governing secured transactions, the parties' rights were left to be established by contract and custom.[39] In the contract produced in the speech *Against Lakritos*, the debtors were required to admit the security to the creditors' control as soon as they arrived at Athens until they had paid what they owed; that once 20 days had elapsed, the creditors were entitled to sell the cargo or to give it as security to raise loans of their own; and that if the proceeds were insufficient to satisfy the debt, to pursue the debtors personally "as if judgment had been given against them."[40] The existence of networks of contacts and agents (such as the slave and partner of Chrysippos stationed at Bosporos) throughout the trading network ensured that information concerning a vessel's impending arrival could travel ahead. Equipped with this information, creditors were able to anticipate a vessel's arrival in order to exercise their rights as soon as the ship put in. In the speech *Against Zēnothemis*, Demon describes how, on news of the vessel's arrival from Kephallēnia (an island in the

in *Symposion 2013: Vorträge zur griechischen und hellenistischen Rechtsgeschichte (Cambridge MA, 26.-29. August 2013)*, ed. Michael Gagarin and Adriaan Lanni (Vienna: VÖAW, 2014), 227–31. Harris concludes that "the Greek form of real security was in its essential features identical to *hypotheca* in Roman law:" Edward M. Harris, "Hypotheca in Roman Law and ὑποθήκη in Greek Law," in *Transferts culturels et droits dans le monde grec et hellénistique (Actes du colloque international, Reims, 14–17 mai 2008)*, ed. Bernard Legras (Paris: Éditions de la Sorbonne, 2012), 440. Thür is right to doubt the usefulness of retrojecting an absolute conception of ownership back into the Athenian legal context: rather, the Athenian conception was more elastic, allowing for the parties to contest their rights through a ritualized process of intrusion and ejection followed by the raising of a *dikē exoulēs* for a penalty of double the property's value by the intruder: Gerhard Thür, "Kannte das altgriechische Recht die Eigentumsdiadikasie?," in *Symposion 1977: Vorträge zur griechischen und hellenistischen Rechtsgeschichte (Chantilly, 1.-4. June 1977)*, ed. Józef E. Modrzejewski and Detlef Liebs (Cologne: Böhlau, 1982), 55–69; Thür, "Sachverfolgung und Diebstahl in den griechischen Poleis (Dem. 32, Lys. 23, IC IV 72 I, IPArk 32 u. 17)," in *Symposion 1999: Vorträge zur griechischen und hellenistischen Rechtsgeschichte (Pazo de Mariñán, La Coruña, 6.-9. September 1999)*, ed. Gerhard Thür and Francisco Javier Fernández Nieto (Cologne: Böhlau, 2003), 58–60; Thür, "Ownership and Secured Credit," 239.

39. Finley, *Studies*, 16; Sundahl, "Secured Credit," 225.

40. Dem. 35.11–12. For *praxis*-clauses, see above, 44–45.

Ionian Sea where she had stopped for repairs), those who had lent money on the ship and its cargo of grain rushed to the port to intercept and take possession of the property.[41]

When the lender's rights in security were in the cargo, the practice was for the goods to be unloaded into a warehouse straight off the ship, which ensured that both parties retained shared access and the ability to exercise their respective rights.[42] Though we have no direct evidence for this at Athens, both the Muziris papyrus and (possibly) some tablets in the archive of the Sulpicii attest to the integral part played by warehouses both as secure environments and neutral spaces for storing goods in which both parties retained a legal interest.[43] Thus, for several of the tablets documenting security over goods stored in warehouses at Puteoli, one possible explanation (offered by Jakab) is that the warehouse units were hired to store goods kept as security in connection with "a network of transmarine and land loans."[44] In the speech *Against Zēnothemis*, storing the goods in a warehouse was likely the merchant Protos' first action upon arrival at Piraeus.

Once the goods were in the warehouse, the borrower had the duration of the grace period (usually, 20 days) to sell the cargo to willing buyers. If the borrower had failed to sell the goods or to raise sufficient funds by the end of the grace period, the lender was entitled to take the law into his own hands and to formally eject (*ēxagein*) the debtor using ritualized violence from (any remaining) property.[45] If the debtor resisted ejection, the creditor was entitled to raise a *dikē exoulēs* against him (to settle legitimate possession of the goods). To avoid ejection, debtors sometimes took bridging loans at landed rates from third parties so that they could pay off the maritime lender before the grace period expired. In the speech *Against Apatourios*, for example, Apatourios, who was about to default on a maritime loan of 40 *minae* taken on security of his ship and crew of slaves, avoided falling into default by taking two further loans (10 *minae* from a foreigner called Parmenōn and a further 30 *minae* from Hērakleidēs' bank), the proceeds of which were used to pay off the original lender.[46]

41. Dem. 32.14.

42. Kränzlein, *Eigentum und Besitz*, 89–90; also, Thür, "Sachverfolgung und Diebstahl," 60 n. 16 and 64–65; Thür, "Ownership and Secured Credit," 241; Jakab, "Loans and Securities," 147.

43. For this aspect of the function of warehouses in ancient trade, see Renzo P. Corritore, Brigitte Marin, and Catherine Virlouvet, "Fonctionnement administratif et économique," in *Entrepôts et trafics annonaires en Méditerranée: Antiquité-Temps modernes*, ed. Marin Brigitte and Catherine Virlouvet (Rome: École française de Rome, 2016), 159–61.

44. The two portfolios at issue are those of the creditors C. Novius Eunus (*TPSulp.* 45 and 51/52) and L. Marius Iucundus (*TPSulp.* 46, 53, and 79).

45. Dem. 32.14, 17, 20. See below, 82.

46. Dem. 33.6–12: on which, see Phillips, *Law*, 392–93. See, also, the loan that Phormiōn claimed to have taken to pay the penalty owing to Chrysippos and his partner as Bosporos: Dem.

Once the creditor had seized the property, his actions in respect of it depended upon whether his rights in security were substitutive or collateral.[47] Under a substitutive arrangement, the creditor was entitled to seize the secured property in satisfaction of the debt, whatever the relation of the value of the security to that of the amount owed. It follows that, because the creditor's entry into possession discharged the borrower's liability, the lender could choose to either keep or dispose of the property as he liked (taking any loss or profit that ensued). By contrast, collateral arrangements preserved a link between the security and the debtor's personal liability: once in possession, the creditor had the right to dispose of the property, either by sale or by giving it as security to raise loans, and to retain the proceeds so far as they went toward satisfying the debt. If, however, the amount raised fell short of the amount owed, the creditor retained the right to recover the deficit from the debtor's personal property; but he was equally obliged to hand over any excess funds to the debtor, if the disposal of the security raised more than the debt was worth. Both types of arrangement are attested to in the context of maritime loans: whereas the security for the original loan taken by Apatourios appears to have been substitutive in relation to the ship (which would explain his eagerness to avoid the ship's seizure by the original lender),[48] the contracts between Protos and the brothers Artemōn and Apollodōros and their creditors provided for collateral arrangements.[49]

Dispute Resolution

In the event of default, by far the creditor's preferred option was to recover as much money as possible through the exercise of his rights in security. However, if (in a collateral arrangement) the disposal of the secured property was insufficient to satisfy the debt, or he was kept out of the security altogether, the lender had no option but to fall back on personal claims founded on the contract. All three of the cases in the Demosthenic corpus concerned with breaches of maritime loan contracts only arose because the lender was kept out of his security: Androklēs and Nausikratēs by Apollodōros' alleged decision to put in at Thieves' Harbour and to attempt to sell the cargo by sample at Piraeus;[50] Chrysippos and his partner by Phormiōn's choice to leave the Bosporos "with-

34.23. For the bridging loans detected by Jakab in the Sulpician tablets: Jakab, "Loans and Securities," 154, 156, and 157–58.

47. See, generally, Phillips, *Law*, 373; also, Isager and Hansen, *Aspects*, 82.

48. Dem. 33.6.

49. Dem. 32.25–26, 30; 35.12.

50. Dem. 35.28–29.

out loading marketable goods in the ship and (thus) with no security;"[51] and Dareios and Pamphilos' failure to detain their debtors' ship. These forensic speeches provide us with a colorful insight into how contractual disputes at Athens typically unfolded: beginning with several rounds of tactical negotiation, attempts at mediation through private arbitration, and only finally ending up before a court.

Negotiation

Disputants usually attempted to negotiate a resolution before proceeding to private arbitration or litigation. Sometimes creditors were willing to compromise to their mutual benefit: in the speech *Against Dionysodōros*, Dareios expresses his frustration at the willingness of his debtors' other creditors to let them off at a reduced yield for the early termination of the voyage at Rhodes, claiming that their generosity was motivated by the prospect of further round-trips Rhodes–Egypt–Rhodes during the offseason.[52] However, if like Dareios and Pamphilos the creditor tried to hold the debtor to terms, the dispute could transform into a tactical battle, in which the parties explored the possibility of a negotiated settlement while at the same time maneuvering themselves into position to arbitrate and eventually litigate. The nuances of these encounters are best illustrated by the accounts of these wrangles in the speeches. In the oration *Against Phormiōn*, Chrysippos claims that his debtor had initially agreed to satisfy the debt, only to renege on that commitment.[53] He therefore summoned Phormiōn to court but was persuaded just before the court date to submit the dispute to arbitration instead. An arbitrator was appointed but declined to reach a decision. By this time (Chrysippos alleges), Phormiōn had colluded with Lampis to testify that the latter had received payment on Chrysippos' behalf in Bosporos. The case has now come to trial. The negotiations described in the oration *Against Dionysodōros* are even more involved.[54] When Dareios discovered that Parmeniskos had put in at Rhodes instead of Athens, he confronted his partner Dionysodōros and demanded satisfaction of the debt. Dionysodōros made a counteroffer, that he would repay the principal together with a reduced yield, to reflect the early termination of the voyage. Dareios refused. Dionysodōros, however, continued to press the offer, bringing with him "a host of witnesses" to

51. Dem. 34.22. See, further, Carawan, "Athenian Law," 354.

52. Dem. 56.29–30. The original loan had been given in the month of Metageitnion (roughly August), already near to the end of the traditional sailing season: Dem. 56.5.

53. Dem. 34.12–21.

54. Dem. 56.11–18.

exert pressure on his adversary. Having listened to the advice offered by some bystanders, Dareios accepted but retained the right to sue for the remainder. Dionysodōros countered by making his offer conditional upon the destruction of the contract, which would bar a future suit. Again, Dareios refused; but this time took the initiative by issuing a formal challenge (*proklēsis*) that Dionysodōros pay the principal together with the reduced yield and submit to a panel of one or more arbitrators, selected from among the merchants at Piraeus, for the rest.[55] This time Dionysodōros declined, and the case was brought to trial.

Several features emerge from these examples. First, it was not uncommon for creditors to summon their debtor to court in full contemplation that a negotiation and possible settlement would follow. The raising of the suit, which required the creditor to set out his charges in the plaint, therefore served the initial function of setting the clock running and establishing an opening bargaining position. Second, negotiations were sometimes conducted in public, with each side making tactical use of witnesses to exert pressure on the other.[56] Third, in both the speeches discussed above, the creditors were keen to emphasize their reluctance in bringing the dispute to court;[57] but in the conduct of the negotiations, they were equally wary of conceding too much ground, in case that might jeopardize their chances in front of a jury.

Private Arbitration

In many disputes private arbitration played a key role.[58] Unlike public arbitration, which was imposed by law in the preliminary stages of certain classes of lawsuit, private arbitration was initiated and sustained by the consent of the parties. The terms on which the arbitration was to be conducted (including, for example, the number of panelists, apparently up to five, their identity, how they should be selected, and the terms on which they were to issue an opinion) were recorded in a written agreement that, like *nautikai syngraphai*, was also witnessed, sealed, and deposited with a third party.[59] The essence of the agreement was that the parties would accept the decision of the arbitrator (*diaitētēs*) as

55. *Proklēsis* was an opportunity for the challenger to provoke his adversary into making binding statements before witnesses that could later be relied upon at trial: see Gerhard Thür, *Beweisführung vor den Schwurgerichtshöfen Athens: die Proklesis zur Basanos* (Vienna: VÖAW, 1977).

56. Cf. D.45.1.122 pr. (Scaev. 28 *dig.*).

57. See, e.g., Dem. 34.1 and 56.14.

58. See, generally, Isager and Hansen, *Aspects*, 107–8; Todd, *Shape*, 123–25; Virginia J. Hunter, *Policing Athens: Social Control in the Attic Lawsuits, 420–320 B.C.* (Princeton: Princeton University Press, 1994), 55–62; also, generally, A. Steinwenter, *Die Streitbeendigung durch Urteil, Schiedsspruch und Vergleich nach griechischem Recht* (Munich: C.H. Beck, 1925).

59. Dem. 33.15–18.

final and therefore give up their right to take the case to court. From the beginning of the fourth century BCE, specific legislation provided that the decisions of arbitrators and the *dikastai* had equal validity, preventing either party from reopening the case.[60] At any point until just before the herald was about to read out the result of the jury vote, the parties could agree to submit the dispute to an arbitrator.[61]

Unlike the jurors in a jury trial, arbitrators could conduct the hearing in private and on a flexible basis, inquiring into the facts and asking questions; the parties could assemble a panel on their own terms and with knowledge of trade and commercial custom; and the process could be conducted expeditiously. On the other hand, arbitration suffered from a lack of sanctions for bearing false witness and susceptibility to accusations of corruption (although the contract could require the arbitrator to swear an oath). Though we have no way of knowing how effective arbitration proved at resolving disputes, the dysfunctional attempts at mediation described in the forensic speeches necessarily overrepresent the likelihood that proceedings would break down (otherwise the case would not have come to court).[62]

Litigation

The enforceability of maritime loan contracts at Athens was potentially affected by several pieces of legislation of general significance:

1. A law that stated that all private agreements (*homologiai idiai*) were to be binding (*kyria*) upon the parties to them.[63] Although the law's origins are obscure, there is little doubt that it was in place by the end of the fifth century BCE and that it applied (at a minimum) both to business dealings (including maritime loan contracts) and arbitration agreements.[64]
2. An archaic law attributed to Solon, that confirmed the right of creditors to charge interest without restriction.[65]

60. Dem. 21.94; Isok. 18.11.

61. Dem. 33.13.

62. See, e.g., the allegations that the arbitrator was corrupt (Dem. 33.16) or biased (Dem. 34.21).

63. For a survey of the evidence, see Phillips, *Law*, 376–78.

64. Phillips suggests that the statute was "probably of Archaic date and quite possibly the work of Solon:" Phillips, 372. Cf., e.g., Carawan, who dates its original enactment to shortly after the instalment of the new democracy in c. 403 BCE: Carawan, "Athenian Law," 339–74. The law was restated in the legislation establishing the *dikai emporikai* in about the middle of the fourth century BCE.

65. Lys. 10.18. Whether or not Solon was the author of the law, the use of the term '*stasimon*' for 'lent' indicates its archaic origins: Billeter, *Geschichte*, 5; Jan Korver, *De terminologie van het*

In addition, a series of laws regulating the grain trade also touched upon the enforceability of maritime loan contracts:[66]

3. Solon's law forbidding the export of any agricultural produce other than olive oil;[67]
4. A law forbidding the purchase of more than 50 *phormoi* of grain at a time;[68]
5. A law that imposed "the most extreme penalties" (i.e., capital punishment) upon Athenian residents who conveyed grain to any place other than Piraeus;[69]
6. A law requiring two-thirds of every grain cargo arriving at Piraeus to be conveyed to the city of Athens;[70]
7. A law forbidding Athenian residents from lending money (e.g., on maritime terms) on any voyage except for those importing grain to Piraeus.[71]

Although the precise impact of the inclusion of a *kyriōteron*-clause in the contract is difficult to ascertain, it is possible that they were intended to disapply any *nomos* or *psēphisma* that would affect the legality or enforceability of the agreement.[72]

If a party to a maritime loan contract wanted to sue, they had first to raise a lawsuit (*dikē*) against their adversary. In the forensic speeches that have to do with maritime loan contracts, three of the cases were brought as a *dikē blabēs* (i.e., a suit for damage)—a wrong-based remedy that treated breach of contract as the commission of a tort requiring compensation[73]—and one (*Against Zēnothemis*) a *dikē exoulēs* (for ejectment).[74]

The procedure for bringing a private lawsuit was divided into two stages: the

crediet-wezen in het Grieksch (Amsterdam: Arno Press, 1934), 114; Millett, *Lending*, 49–50; Delfim F. Leão and P. J. Rhodes, *The Laws of Solon: A New Edition with Introduction, Translation and Commentary* (London: I.B.Tauris, 2015), 113.

66. See, generally, Isager and Hansen, *Aspects*, 28–29; Phillips, *Law*, 375.

67. Plut. *Vit. Sol.* 24.1: on which, Leão and Rhodes, *Laws of Solon*, 108–9.

68. Lys. 22.6.

69. Dem. 34.37; 35.50; Lycurg. 1.27.

70. Arist. [*Ath. Pol.*] 51.4.

71. Dem. 35.51; 56.6, 11.

72. Dem. 35.13, 39; 56.26. For *kyriōteron*-clauses, see above, 45–46.

73. For the *dikē blabēs*, see Todd, *Shape*, 279–82; Phillips, *Law*, 286–88 (with literature). Cf. Pringsheim's conclusion that the suit in the case *Against Dionysodōros* was a *dikē daneiou*: Fritz Pringsheim, *The Greek Law of Sale* (Weimar: H. Böhlaus Nachfolger, 1950), 53.

74. According to Harpokration, the *dikē exoulēs* was the name of a lawsuit brought by those claiming to have been ejected from their own property against the person who had ejected them: Harp. s. v. εξουλης, on which see Phillips, *Law*, 266–67.

first before public officials who controlled access to the courts; and the second a trial conducted in a court of justice (*dikastērion*) before a jury.[75]

To initiate a lawsuit, the plaintiff was required to summon his opponent orally in the presence of one or more summons witnesses (*klētēres*), informing him of the substance of the claim and requiring him to appear before the magistrate on a certain day. On the day in question, the parties appeared before the magistrate, to whom the plaintiff presented a written plaint (*enklēma*) containing the names of the parties to the dispute, the desired remedy, a specification of the punishment or damages demanded, and a detailed account of the alleged offense.[76] If the defendant failed to appear, it was open to the magistrate to issue a default judgment.

If certain conditions were met, the plaintiff was entitled to raise the suit as an expedited *dikē emporikē* (mercantile suit).[77] The broad aim of the procedure appears to have been to resolve commercial disputes quickly and fairly, particularly in connection with the Athenian grain trade. The most significant feature was that it was open not only to Athenian citizens but also to metics and foreigners.[78] Actions could only be raised as *dikai emporikai* between the months of Boēdromiōn and Mounichiōn (i.e., September and April, during the sailing offseason, when merchants and *nauklēroi* wintered in port).[79] All of the actions

75. For a concise yet detailed account of the stages of Athenian legal procedure, see Phillips, *Law*, 33–43; also, Gerhard Thür, "Griechische Zivilverfahren," in *Handbuch zur Geschichte der Konfliktlösung in Europa*, ed. Nadine Grotkamp and Anna Seelentag, vol. 1: *Konfliktlösung in der Antike* (Heidelberg: Springer, 2019), 207–18.

76. Athenian complaints were not altogether different in style from the Roman *formula*. See, e.g., the specimen preserved at Dem. 45.46: "Apollodōros, son of Pasion, of Archanai v. Stephanos, son of Meneklēs, of Archanai. Action for perjury. Damages: one talent. Stephanos gave false testimony, attesting to that contained in the memorandum." See, also, the partial complaint preserved at Dem. 37.22, 25–26, 28–29. On the parallel, Gerhard Thür, "Review of Michael Gagarin, Writing Greek Law (Cambridge, 2008)," *ZRG RA* 126 (2009): 489.

77. See, generally, Edward E. Cohen, *Ancient Athenian Maritime Courts* (Princeton: Princeton University Press, 1973); and the detailed account by Vélissaropoulos-Karakostas, *Les nauclères grecs*, 235–67.

78. See., e.g., Dem. 21.176, in which Demosthenes refers to the judgment of two talents won by Euandros of Thespiae against Menippos of Karia in a *dikē emporikē*. All four of the parties described in *Against Dionysodōrus* were probably metics. At Dem. 56.47, Dareios anticipates that Athenian citizens could be involved as litigants in lawsuits at Rhodes: see Edward M. Harris, "Law and Economy in Classical Athens: [Demosthenes], 'Against Dionysodorus,'" in *Athenian Law in Its Democratic Context*, ed. Adriaan Lanni, 2003, § 1.5.

79. Dem. 33.23. According to Paoli, the names of the months in the text should be reversed, to show that *dikai emporikai* could only be raised during the sailing season (i.e., between April and September): Ugo E. Paoli, "Zur Gerichtszeit der δίκαι ἐμπορικαί im attischen Recht," *ZRG RA* 29 (1929): 473–77; followed by Louis Gernet, *Démosthène. Plaidoyers civils*, vol. I: *Discours XXVII–XXXVIII* (Paris: Les Belles Lettres, 1954), 141 n. 2; and Alick R. W. Harrison, *The Law of Athens*, vol. 2: *Procedure* (Oxford: Clarendon Press, 1971), 86. Against the transposition: Cohen, *Maritime Courts*, 42–59; MacDowell, *The Law*, 232; Mogens H. Hansen, "Two Notes on the Athenian Dikai Emporikai," in *Symposion 1979: Actes du IVᵉ Colloque International de Droit Grec et Hellénistique*

in the Demosthenic corpus brought in connection with maritime lending were styled as *dikai emporikai*.[80] For a mercantile suit to be successfully raised, three legislative conditions had to be met. (1) one of the litigants had to be an *emporos* or *nauklēros*; (2) the dispute had to involve trade either from or to Athens; and (3) there had to be a *symbolaion* or any wrong committed in these circumstances.[81] The meaning of the word *symbolaion* in this context is contested. For a long time, the prevailing view has been that the plaintiff was required to present a contractual document (e.g., a *nautikē syngraphē*) when filing a *dikē emporikē*.[82] Alternatively, it has been argued that the word refers instead to the need for a "liability relationship" ("Haftungsbeziehung") between the parties, requiring the plaintiff to show the existence of an "actionable liability" arising from either a breach of contract or the commission of a civil wrong.[83] The two views are not mutually exclusive: almost certainly a plaintiff who brought a mercantile suit for damage in respect of a maritime loan contract was required to produce the *syngraphē* as proof that the alleged debt was still (at least potentially) outstanding.[84] However, while necessary, production of the *syngraphē* was not by itself sufficient to establish the defendant's liability, which could still be denied on substantive grounds (for example, that the conditions on which the debt and any penalties became due had failed to materialize). The structure of the arguments for and against the existence of a *symbolaion* in these cases is picked up in the next chapter.

(Égine, 3–7 Septembre 1979), edited by P. Dimakis, 170–75 (Cologne: Böhlau, 1983); and Carey and Reid, *Speeches*, 234–35. If my arguments concerning the timing of Justinian's legislation in 540/1 CE are correct, this would suggest that the litigation that provoked the repeal of Nov. 106 was also being conducted during the offseason. See below, 181–82.

80. A *dikē blabēs* brought as a mercantile suit might therefore be styled a *dikē emporikē blabēs*.

81. For the law, Dem. 32.1; 33.1–3, 23; 34.3–7, 42. See, generally, Phillips, *Law*, 375–76; together with Edward Harris, "The Meaning of the Legal Term Symbolaion, the Law about Dikai Emporikai and the Role of the Paragraphe Procedure," *Dike* 18 (2015): 18. For an account of the earlier debates concerning the precise scope of *dikai emporikai*, see Vélissaropoulos-Karakostas, *Les nauclères grecs*, 236–41.

82. See, e.g., Cohen, *Maritime Courts*, 100–157; Isager and Hansen, *Aspects*, 84–87; MacDowell, *Demosthenes*, 13; MacDowell, *Demosthenes the Orator* (Oxford: Oxford University Press, 2009), 275; and now Thür, "Griechische Zivilverfahren," 212.

83. See, generally, Hans J. Wolff, *Die attische Paragraphe: Ein Beitrag zum Problem der Auflockerung archaischer Prozessformen* (Weimar: Böhlau, 1966); Harris, "The Meaning," 17. Thür is right to point out that the distinction between contract and tort was not familiar to ancient Athenian law, which provided a remedy for breach of contract (the *dikē blabēs*) that was predicted on the (tortious) infliction of damage: Thür, "'Der Sturm' in der Rede gegen Zenothemis (Dem. 32)," in *Dike: Essays on Greek Law in Honor of Alberto Maffi*, ed. Lorenzo Gagliardi and Laura Pepe (Milan: Giuffrè Francis Lefebvre, 2019), 328–29.

84. Creditors kept *syngraphai* as proof of outstanding debts. Correspondingly, debtors sought the destruction of the *syngraphē* to symbolize the termination of the relationship (for which, see above, 73–74). See, for example, Dionysodōros' requirement that the acceptance of his offer of settlement was conditional on the destruction of the *syngraphē* as a guarantee against future suit: Dem. 56.14–15.

According to Cohen, the *dikai emporikai* developed in three stages:[85] (1) in the first half of the fourth century, mercantile suits were likely not classified as 'monthly' and handled by the *nautodikai*, a board of magistrates who oversaw trials involving men who traveled by sea;[86] (2) by the middle years of the century (between 355 [the earliest date for Xen. *Por.* 3.3] and 342 [Dem. 7.12]),[87] they had been classified as *dikai emmēnoi* ('monthly suits') and placed under the jurisdiction of the *eisagōgeis*; and (3) during the grain crisis of 330–326 they were transferred to the jurisdiction of the *thesmothetai*. Classification as 'monthly suits' probably meant that they had to be concluded no later than one month after the acceptance of the plaint by the magistrate;[88] though it is possible (as Cohen has suggested) that the designation only meant that the relevant magistrate would accept plaints on a specified date each month; and that since *dikai emmēnoi* were excepted from the requirement to go to public arbitration, cases could therefore be moved more quickly to trial and (ideally) heard before the next time plaints were accepted 30 days later.[89]

At the submission of the plaint (or possibly at the *anakrisis*), the defendant had the opportunity to submit a written response, either in the form of a denial of the substantive charge (*antigraphē*) or counter-indictment (*paragraphē*, so-called because the objection was noted 'next to' the text of the *enklēma*) directed against the original plaintiff for illegal prosecution.[90] In disputes over maritime loan contracts, there were at least two grounds for raising a *paragraphē*: (1) that the agreement was unenforceable because it was connected to a voyage that had not imported grain to Athens;[91] and (2) that if the action had been brought as a *dikē emporikē*, one or more of the legislative conditions for raising the suit had not been met.[92] Once both parties had submitted their written statements, they each swore an oath confirming their

85. See, generally, Cohen, *Maritime Courts*, 158–98, esp. 161; though cf. MacDowell, *Law*, 231–33. For the view that the development of the *dikai emporikai* had more to do with the collapse of the Athenian empire following the Social War than commercial considerations, see Claude Mossé, "The 'World of the Emporium' in the Private Speeches of Demosthenes," in *Trade in the Ancient Economy*, ed. Peter Garnsey, Keith Hopkins, and C. R. Whittaker (London: Chatto & Windus, 1983), 53–63.

86. Cohen, *Maritime Courts*, 183.

87. For the earliest and latest possible dates for the introduction of *dikai emporikai* as monthly suits, see Adriaan Lanni, *Law and Justice in the Courts of Classical Athens* (Cambridge: Cambridge University Press, 2006), 151; also, Phillips, *Law*, 376.

88. Harris, "The Meaning," 32; also, Vélissaropoulos-Karakostas, *Les nauclères grecs*, 241–45; Hansen, "Two Notes," 167–70; cf. Cohen, *Maritime Courts*, 23–36.

89. Cohen, 39–40.

90. For general accounts of the *paragraphē* procedure, see Isager and Hansen, *Aspects*, 123–31; Todd, *Shape*, 135–39.

91. For the law, see above, 82.

92. For the statutory requirements, see above, 84.

veracity. If the magistrate accepted the plaint, the claim was entered into the protocol by a secretary and a date for the *anakrisis* (literally, 'inquiry') was drawn by lot.[93] At this second preliminary stage, the main purpose of which was to clarify and polarize the positions of the parties ahead of the main hearing, the litigants questioned each other in front of the magistrate, who could compel them to answer formal questions. The litigants were also required to produce copies all the documents that they wished to rely upon in argument (e.g., laws, written testimonies, contracts) and to deposit them in clay pots (*echinoi*) that were then labeled and sealed.[94]

How the process unfolded if the defendant successfully lodged a *paragraphē* is controversial. There are three dominant theories concerning the structure of the process:[95] (1) that there were (potentially) two hearings, the first devoted only to the procedural question and the second (if the action was found to be admissible) to the substantive issue;[96] (2) that there was only one hearing, but two votes, the first on the procedural question and the second (again, if the action was found to be admissible) on the substantive issue;[97] and (3) that there was only one hearing and a single vote, in which the jurors were tasked with deciding between the inadmissibility of the suit or granting the plaintiff's *timēma*.[98] The one undisputed point is that in a *paragraphē* hearing the order of the speakers was reversed, so that the original defendant gained the advantage of defining the terms of the dispute and presenting his arguments ahead of the plaintiff.[99] The *paragraphē* hearing was therefore an opportunity for the defendant to seize the initiative, both in the (initial) hearing by speaking first and in seeking to have the case thrown out on procedural grounds.[100]

Trial was held in a jury court (*dikastērion*) composed of at least 201 lay-citizens chosen by lot, each of whom swore an oath to uphold the laws and in the absence of any relevant law, to judge the case according to their "most

93. Antiph. 6.42; Ar. *Clouds* 770.

94. Cf. James Sickinger, "Literacy, Documents, and Archives in the Ancient Athenian Democracy," *American Archivist* 62, no. 2 (1999): 167; Gerhard Thür, "The Principle of Fairness in Athenian Legal Procedure: Thoughts on the Echinos and Enklema," *Dike* 11 (2008): 51–73.

95. For an overview, see Edwin M. Carawan, "Paragraphê and the Merits," *GRBS* 51, no. 2 (2011): 255–58.

96. Wolff, *Die attische Paragraphe*, 81; also, now, Harris, "The Meaning."

97. Ugo E. Paoli, *Studi sul processo attico* (Padova: A. Milani, 1933), 77–116.

98. Mario Talamanca, *Dike ouk eisagogimos: Contributi allo studio del processo attico*, ed. Alberto Maffi (Vienna: VÖAW, 2017), 117–18; and independently, Carawan, "Paragraphê and the Merits," 290–91; followed by Thür, "'Der Sturm,'" 327–30.

99. According to Thür, defendants were willing to risk the one-sixth penalty for losing on a *paragraphē* to gain the advantage of speaking first: Thür, "Law and Rhetoric," 293.

100. For an account of the trial process, see Phillips, *Law*, 36–43.

just understanding" (*dikaiotatē gnōmē*).[101] At the beginning of the hearing the presiding officer read out the complaint, the compensation demanded, and the defendant's answers to the charges that had been made. The oral presentations of the litigants followed in earnest, each usually making two speeches in an alternating pattern starting with the plaintiff (if the defendant had lodged a *paragraphē*, the order was reversed). The length of the orations was limited by a water-clock (*klepsūdra*) to about 30 minutes for each speaker, which could be stopped when witness statements and documents were read out. Neither speakers nor witnesses were allowed to be interrupted; and there was no deliberation by the jury, who earned their pay by voting "yes" or "no" in a secret ballot conducted immediately after the end of the proceedings. Defendants who lost their case and had a judgment debt imposed upon them could be imprisoned until they paid.[102] On the other hand, to deter frivolous cases, a prosecutor who failed to obtain one-fifth of the jury vote was required to pay a fine of one-sixth of the sum sued for (*epōbelia*) and could be similarly detained pending payment.[103] Finally, the malicious prosecutor of an *emporos* or *nauklēros* was liable to *endeixis* (denunciation, leading to the offender's arrest by a magistrate) and (or) *apagōgē* (summary arrest by a private individual, who then brought them before a magistrate).[104]

Classical Rome

Naturally both the commercial practice and the legal framework within which commercial actors were operating depends upon both the period and place one has in view. While the discussion of this question at Athens was confined to a specific period and to one *polis*, to achieve comprehensive coverage for the Roman period would be to address not only the enforcement of contracts through different forms of procedure at Rome but also to consider the coexistence of local legal traditions in the provinces and their interaction with Roman

101. This was the oath taken by the Heliasts. Cf. Cohen's argument that in *dikai emporikai* special juries were assembled from members of the emporic community: Cohen, *Maritime Courts*, 93–95.

102. Dem. 32.29; 33.1; 35.46; 56.4. See, also, Dem. 21.176, in which we hear that Euandros of Thespiae arrested his adversary, Menippos of Karia, after he had initially left Athens but returned for the celebration of the Mysteries: on which, Carey and Reid, *Speeches*, 209.

103. Dem. 56.3–6. See, further, Douglas M. MacDowell, "The Athenian Penalty of Epobelia," in *Symposion 2007: Vorträge zur griechischen und hellenistischen Rechtsgeschichte (Durham, 2.-6. September 2007)*, ed. Edward M. Harris and Gerhard Thür (Vienna: VÖAW, 2009), 87–94; also, Edward M. Harris, *The Rule of Law in Action in Democratic Athens* (Oxford: Oxford University Press, 2013), 72–76.

104. Dem. 58.10–12. For *endeixis* and *apagōgē*, Phillips, *Law*, 30–31.

provincial administration. There is in addition the problem of foreigners' access to Roman law during different periods, which raises difficult questions (especially for the Republic) concerning the scope and application of *commercium*, the jurisdiction of the peregrine praetor, the relationship between the peregrine praetor and the development of the formulary procedure, the accessibility (or otherwise) of the ancient *legis actiones* to peregrines, and so forth.

Since the juristic texts, which are our main source for considering the basic questions concerning the enforcement of maritime loan contracts in Roman law, were composed during the classical period (i.e., between the last century of the Republic and the early third century CE) and from the perspective of the formulary procedure, this will be the view presented here. Adopting this point of view has three chief advantages: (1) it enables a focus on the already problematic question of the enforcement of maritime loan contracts using the formulary procedure at Rome; (2) it aligns the discussion of the juristic texts with our best sources for commercial practice in Italy during the period, namely those preserved in the Campanian archives (first century CE); and (3) it enables at least some assessment of the relationship between commercial practice and juristic activity in this limited field. The disadvantages are to introduce an artificial focus on the center at the expense of the periphery and to avoid the complexities associated with the coexistence of different forms of procedure and the involvement of peregrines in litigation, at least before 212 CE and especially during the Republic.

Commercial Practice

The Contract and Documentation

The documentary evidence from the Roman period shows that in most respects the standard forms that had already been established for centuries remained unaffected by the arrival of the Romans on the Mediterranean scene. Like the moneylenders operating at Piraeus, creditors during the Roman period continued to delimit the circumstances under which they were willing to bear the risk in much the same way as before. Changes, however, can be detected in the way in which the parties concluded and documented their transactions, with a view to making them conform to the requirements of Roman law.

Like at Athens, creditors during the Roman period (together with bankers and other financial intermediaries) constructed loan dossiers that were intended to serve as proof for those aspects of the transaction that were legally significant.[105] The best insight we have into the makeup of loan dossiers in a

105. There is a debate as to whether chirographs were binding in themselves or merely evi-

Roman context is provided by the Campanian tablets (first century CE), which were preserved at various locations around the Bay of Naples following the eruption of Vesuvius in 79 CE. Notwithstanding the limitations associated with the tablets as a source, there is no reason to doubt that the forms, material, and law used in their composition were identical to those employed at Rome and elsewhere on the Italian Peninsula.[106] As the loan documentation preserved in the Campanian tablets shows, dossiers typically consisted of several components:

1. *Chirographa*: Chirographs were one-sided written documents containing a declaration by the person issuing it (e.g., "I, Menelaos . . .") that certain legally relevant facts had taken place.[107] They were usually witnessed and sealed (normally by 3–6 individuals, in addition to the author). The document was intended to provide proof that the author had made the declarations in question (e.g., *TPSulp.* 78, in which Menelaos acknowledged the receipt of the 1,000 *d.* transferred to him "according to the sealed *naulotikē syngraphē*");
2. *Cautiones*: Documents recording the terms of agreements concluded by stipulation. These contained a formulary, usually at the end of the document, stating that the stipulator had asked whether the promisor would faithfully carry out the agreement and that the promisor had responded (in congruent terms) that he would. No *cautiones* have been preserved among the Campanian tablets, probably because (like at Athens) it was normal to symbolize the termination of the relationship between the parties by removing the document from the dossier. Juristic texts suggest that the Roman practice was for the creditor to hand over the *cautio* to the debtor, who could use it to defend proceedings brought by the creditor by adducing it as evidence of his (tacit) agreement not to sue.[108] Ulpian, for example, in a discussion of the theft of financial documents, noted that debtors frequently sought to recover *tabulae* on completion of the transaction so that they could rebut the allegation that they had failed to repay.[109]

dentiary. For chirographs as binding, see Éva Jakab, "Chirographum in Theorie und Praxis," in *Römische Jurisprudenz—Dogmatik, Überlieferung, Rezeption. Festschrift für Detlef Liebs zum 75. Geburtstag*, ed. Karlheinz Muscheler (Berlin: Duncker & Humblot, 2011), 275–92; Adriaan J. B. Sirks, "Chirographs: Negotiable Instruments?" *ZRG RA* 133 (2016): 265–85; Sirks, "Chirographs in Roman Law: Constitutive or Evidential," *TvR* 91 (2023): 93–114. Contra Johannes Platschek, *Das Edikt de Pecunia Constituta. Die römische Erfüllungszusage und ihre Einbettung in den hellenistischen Kreditverkehr* (Munich: C.H. Beck, 2013), 1–5; Hendrick L. E. Verhagen, "Chirographs in Classical Roman Law. Constitutive or Probative?," *RIDA* 65 (2018).

106. Meyer, *Legitimacy*, 126–27.

107. This is a paraphrase of the definition given by Verhagen, "Chirographs," 251.

108. D.2.14.2.1 (Paul. 3 *ad ed.*). The debtor's possession of the *cautio* would go toward substantiating an *exceptio pacti*. See, also, Meyer, *Legitimacy*, 119–20.

109. D.47.2.27 pr. (Ulp. 41 *ad Sab.*).

3. *Testationes*: Documents written as third-person narrations ("L. Sulpicius Cinnamus said that . . .") attesting to the occurrence of formal or procedural acts (e.g., *vadimonia*, *tabulae sistendi*, formulae granting *iudices*). These were often sealed by at least seven individuals, though sometimes by as many as 11. The most significant *testationes* appear in loan dossiers as *nomina arcaria*, that is, cash entries recording the paying out of the money from the lender's *arca*, or money-chest, to the borrower.[110] As Gröschler has shown, the similarity in the terminology used in Roman account-*tabulae* makes it possible to identify *nomina arcaria* as individual extracts copied from account books (i.e., *rationes*).[111]

Each document comprising the dossier might be independently witnessed, bound into a closed diptych or triptych, and sealed.[112] Witnesses (*testes*) and individuals adding their personal seal (*signatores*, typically with a personalized ring) performed separate functions until at least the second century CE.[113] In the Campanian tablets, for example, witnesses are most closely associated with documents attesting to the occurrence of formal acts (i.e., *testationes*), tasked with observing that the formalities were correctly performed.[114] *Signatores*, meanwhile, were often friends (*amici*) who added their *fides* to that of the individual making an informal declaration, commonly in the form of a chirograph. Several legal texts touch upon the nuances of Roman documentary practice in the context of maritime credit transactions. According to Labeo (Augustan period), if there was no one upon whom the creditor could serve a notice of default (*interpellatio*), a formal declaration in front of witnesses (i.e., a *testatio*) would suffice;[115] and a constitution of Diocletian and Maximian (late third century CE) provides that, if the creditor was not available for the debtor to repay, they could execute a *testatio* to that effect and, if payment was not accepted, deposit the money in a public place.[116]

To protect themselves creditors designed loan dossiers and adopted lending techniques suited to the enforcement of their loans in Roman law. In general,

---

110. See Meyer, *Legitimacy*, 137–38 with G.3.131.

111. Gröschler, *Die Tabellae-Urkunden*, 199–246 and 372 (summary).

112. For the evolution of the practice of binding and sealing *tabulae*, Meyer, *Legitimacy*, 127–32.

113. Meyer, 161.

114. The order in which individuals' names appeared in witness lists was often determined by their social status: Terpstra, *Trade*, 125–67.

115. D.22.2.2 (Pomp. 3 *ex Plaut.*).

116. C.4.32.19 pr., 3 (Diocl./Maxim. AA. et CC. Aureliae Irenaeae). This was the method of repayment attempted by the borrower in D.45.1.122 pr. (Scaev. 28 *dig.*), though to no effect.

a debtor who borrowed on maritime terms was potentially liable on two main grounds: (1) for the main debt (i.e., capital and maritime yield), subject to the condition *salva nave*; and (2) for a penalty in the event of nonperformance by a deadline, normally accompanied by a daily rate for the services of the lender's representative. The written contract also usually provided for a time-denominated rate of interest to be paid once the loan converted to a landed footing. As for the main debt, the handing over of the principal by the creditor generated an obligation *ex re* binding the debtor to return an equivalent sum, which could be sued upon using the *actio certae creditae pecuniae*. For the other clauses, however, classical Roman law only recognized the terms of the written contract as binding if they had been concluded orally by stipulation.

(i) Maritime yield. In the maritime loan contract reported in the speech *Against Lakritos*, the clause providing for the maritime yield was expressly included. From the perspective of Roman law, this clause was only enforceable if it had been concluded by stipulation. To circumvent this issue, creditors appear to have drawn up their loan documentation so as to suggest that the money had been lent *atokos* (i.e., 'without a yield').[117] (1) In the simplest case, the sum stated in the chirograph was intended to represent the whole amount of the debt (including both principal and maritime yield). The recoverability of the debt would then depend upon the relationship between the sum stated in the chirograph and the technique used for making the loan. If the lender had overstated the amount given, then the debtor could plead *exceptio doli* (after 66 BCE) or, later, *exceptio non numeratae pecuniae* (second or early-third century CE), against the creditor's *actio c. c. p.* to limit recovery to the principal (there being no obligation *ex re* beyond the sum handed over).[118] The availability of these defenses, however, could be limited by the use a technique known to the sources as the payment of future interest (*usurae futurae*), in which case an *actio c. c. p.* would be effective for the recovery of the full amount of the debt (notwithstanding that the borrower had paid the yield upfront using the original loan proceeds, probably on the basis of a pact or stipulation).[119] (2) Another possibility for loans given *atokos* is that the borrower had committed himself to some other performance in lieu of interest (i.e., an interlinked contract). Probably the chirograph would contain a reference to the interlinked contract, for example, a contract of affreightment (*naulotikē syngraphē*). The resulting transaction was likely enforceable under the classical scheme by means of an *agere*

117. See above, 10.

118. For the dating of the *exceptio doli*: Alan Watson, *Law Making in the Later Roman Republic* (Oxford: Oxford University Press, 1974), 72–75.

119. Verboven, "Sulpicii from Puteoli," 7–28. See above, 29–30.

praescriptis verbis, in which the parties set out the details of their engagement in the *praescriptio* and asked for the case to be adjudicated on that account.[120]

(ii) Additional clauses. As for the other standard clauses in the written contract, it was probably not uncommon for lenders to transform *syngraphai* into *cautiones* by the inclusion of a statement to the effect that the agreement had been concluded as a stipulation. The formulary reported by Q. Cervidius Scaevola in the *cautio* (i.e., the *nautikē syngraphē*) concluded by Callimachus is typical in this respect.[121] The inclusion of such a statement was not by itself sufficient to bind the promisor: the oral exchange of question and answer had actually to have taken place. It was, however, strong evidence to that effect, placing the burden on the promisor to adduce positive evidence to the contrary.[122]

Monitoring Debtors

Like their counterparts at Piraeus, Roman creditors continued to send representatives to monitor their debtors. The Callimachus loan provides the model in this regard: the moneylender, himself a slave, sent another slave under his command (Eros) to travel with the borrower and to take early repayment if he failed to load the goods and depart Brentesium by the appointed date. In the Muziris papyrus, though the part of the contract dealing with the journey between the Red Sea and Malabar coasts has not survived, the creditor's representatives were present at each stage of the overland route between Berenikē/Myos Hormos and Alexandria via Koptos.[123] Other juristic excerpts in the *Digest* hint at the typicality of this arrangement, since it was reportedly normal for penalties for late repayment to be introduced into the stipulation for the cost of the services of the attendant slave, which began to run alongside interest once the time limit had expired.[124]

Although we have no direct evidence in the context of maritime lending, it was apparently commonplace for merchants to operate in pairs (e.g., freedmen of the same patron, members of the same family).[125] On occasion, however,

120. For the development of this action from the time of Labeo, see Roberto Fiori, "Rise and Fall of the Specificity of Contracts," in *Nova Ratione: Change of Paradigms in Roman Law*, ed. Adriaan J. B. Sirks (Wiesbaden: Harrassowitz Verlag, 2014), 33–49.

121. D.45.1.122.1 (Scaev. 28 *dig.*): "*eaque sic recte dari fieri fide roganti Sticho servo Lucii Titii promisit Callimachus.*"

122. See, e.g., J. Inst. 3.19.12.

123. See Ron Harris, "The Organization of India-to-Rome Trade: Loans and Agents in the Muziris Papyrus," in *Roman Law and Economics*, ed. Giuseppe Dari-Mattiacci and Dennis P. Kehoe, vol. 1 (Oxford: Oxford University Press, 2020), 163–96.

124. D.22.2.4.1 (Pap. 3 *resp.*); D.44.7.23 (Afr. 7 *quaest.*).

125. See Wim Broekaert, "Joining Forces: Commercial Partnerships or Societates in the Early Roman Empire," *Historia* 61, no. 2 (2012): 221–53.

lenders could require *emporoi* and *nauklēroi* to form themselves into a club for the purpose of collective lending. The sole example of this phenomenon is attested to by a passage that comes near to the end of Plutarch's *Parallel Lives* of Aristides and Cato the Elder (d. 149 BCE):

> He [Cato] used to loan money also in the most disreputable of all ways, namely, on maritime terms, and his method was as follows: He required his borrowers to form a large club (κοινωνίᾳ), and when there were fifty members and as many ships, he took one share in the club himself, and was represented by Quin(c)tio, a freedman of his, who was in business with and sailed with the borrowers. In this way the entire capital was not imperiled, but only a small part of it, and his profits were large.[126]

The text represents the earliest evidence we have of a Roman citizen giving a maritime loan (*daneion nautikon*).[127] According to Plutarch, the elder Cato, when he was nearing the end of his life, made a practice of giving maritime loans, but only on condition that his borrowers form themselves into a fifty-strong "club" or "partnership" (κοινωνίᾳ, *koinōnia*) in which his freedman Quinctio would take a single share. Both the structure of the transaction and how it produced greater profits for Cato have proved controversial. Beginning with the juridical relationship between Quinctio and the debtors, the dominant interpretation given to the passage is that Cato encouraged his borrowers to enter into a consensual *societas*.[128] This also appears to be the implication behind von Lübtow's suggestion that the arrangement amounted to a "Kombination von Seedarlehen und Fernhandelsgesellschaft," in which losses were distributed among the participants and from which Cato's representative was entitled to a share of the profits.[129] Rathbone, too, argues that "On an unforced reading . . . the basic situation is pretty clear. Cato encouraged the formation of

126. Plut. *Vit. Cat. Mai.* 21.6 (translation by Bernadotte Perrin, adapted).

127. Cf. Francesco De Martino, *Storia economica di Roma antica*, vol. 1 (Florence: La Nuova Italia Editrice, 1979), 133; also, Broekaert, "Joining Forces," 225 n. 15.

128. See, e.g., Koenraad Verboven, *The Economy of Friends. Economic Aspects of Amicitia and Patronage in the Late Republic* (Brussels: Latomus, 2002), 282 and 285; Adriaan J. B. Sirks, "The Food Distributions in Rome and Constantinople: Imperial Power and Continuity," in *Herrschaftsstrukturen und Herrschaftspraxis: Konzepte, Prinzipien und Strategien der Administration im römischen Kaiserreich*, ed. Anne Kolb (Berlin: Akademie Verlag, 2006), 37; Luuk de Ligt, "Law-Making and Economic Change during the Republic and Early Empire," in *Roman Law and Economics*, ed. Giuseppe Dari-Mattiacci and Dennis P. Kehoe, vol. 1 (Oxford: Oxford University Press, 2020), 91; Broekaert, "Joining Forces," 225.

129. Ulrich von Lübtow, "Catos Seedarlehen," in *Festschrift für Erwin Seidl zum 70. Geburtstag*, ed. Heinz Hübner, Ernst Klingmüller, and Andreas Wacke (Cologne: Hanstein, 1975), 104.

a business association (*societas*) of fifty shipowners . . . and spread his risk by lending to them as a group."[130]

The argument that Cato's borrowers entered into a consensual partnership in which the profits and losses were shared among all the participants, be they active or sleeping partners, is less secure than is sometimes assumed.[131] As Talamanca pointed out in a response to von Lübtow, the interpretations that reach this conclusion often run the danger of conflating the question of the juridical relationship between the debtors with that concerning the effect of the association on the profitability of Cato's loans.[132] Although Rathbone, for example, is right to observe that in lending to a number of borrowers Cato was spreading the risk, this could just as well be achieved by giving loans to the same number of borrowers on an individual basis, without requiring them to enter into any kind of association. There are two positive arguments in favor of the *societas* as Cato's chosen vehicle. The first, which is textual, is that Plutarch's use of the word *koinōnia* indicates the existence of a Roman *societas*, or partnership, in the legal sense. However, as several scholars have already pointed out, the context of Plutarch's work (moralizing and didactic, not juridical) and his distance from the event (some 250 years) must surely discourage us from placing too much reliance on his choice of language in this instance.[133]

The second argument, which requires some disentangling, proceeds by analogy with the roughly contemporaneous loan contract drawn up at Ptolemaic Alexandria during the second century BCE (SB III 7169). Referring back to that discussion, it will be remembered that the original editor's conjecture was that the five *synploi* referred to in the papyrus had—possibly—entered into a partnership with each other and also into a profit-sharing arrangement with their creditor.[134] Some eight years later Heichelheim, the first to make the analogy between the arrangement described in the papyrus fragments and Cato's lending strategy, followed Wilcken's conjecture and (implicitly) relied upon the passage in Plutarch to equate the *synploi* in the Ptolemaic contract with *koinōnoi*.[135] In an influential exegesis of the Plutarch excerpt published some 40 years later again, von Lübtow argued that Cato, like Archippos, did

130. Rathbone, "Financing," 214.

131. With similar skepticism, André Tchernia, *The Romans and Trade*, trans. James Grieve and Elizabeth Minchin (Oxford: Oxford University Press, 2016), 36.

132. See, in this connection, Mario Talamanca, "Rec. di 'Festschrift für Erwin Seidl zum 70. Geburtstag,'" *BIDR* 82 (1979): 290.

133. Talamanca, "'Festschrift für Erwin Seidl,'" 290; Purpura, "Ricerche," 239–40; Konstantin Tanev, "The Real Securities in the Agreement on the 'traiecticia pecunia,'" *Orbis Iuris Romani* 4 (1998): 83–84.

134. Wilcken, "Punt-Fahrten," 93 n. 1 and 100.

135. Fritz Heichelheim, "Zu Pap. Berol. 5883 + 5853," *Aegyptus* 13, nos. 1–2 (1933): 190.

not demand interest, but rather a share of the profit. In effect, Plutarch's use of the word *koinōnia* has been relied upon as an aid to the interpretation of the more general term *synploi*; and Wilcken's profit-sharing conjecture used in the other direction to explain the method by which Cato derived his profit through Quinctio. The argument, now propped up like a wigwam (to borrow Keith Hopkins' well-known metaphor), is finally tied together at the top by the parallels drawn between Quinctio and the enigmatic Cnaeus.

No doubt there are similarities between the two enterprises: notwithstanding their contemporaneity, they both involved (maritime) loan contracts entered into by wealthy venture capitalists via intermediaries to multiple borrowers who were in some kind of association with one another. However, on closer inspection, some important differences become apparent. It is by no means clear that Quinctio, who the Plutarch text indicates was more squarely in the mold of the creditor's representative, carried out similar functions to Cnaeus, who more likely performed the role of an independent intermediary (perhaps like Xouthos, who handled the maritime investments of Demosthenes' father), facilitating the documentation of the loan and transfer of funds. It is also not apparent whether the borrowers in the Ptolemaic loan contract were operating more than one ship: probably, in my view, they were more in the character of the *synnauklēroi* who took the loan documented in SB XIV 11850, the co-owners of the vessel *Antinoos Philosarapis Sōzōn*. Most significantly, however, the ambiguity of the word *atokos*, which Wilcken interpreted literally but which subsequent scholarship has shown to have had several different possible technical meanings, ought to make us cautious in ascribing a particular structure to the Ptolemaic transaction.

All this takes us back to the drawing board. The challenge is to provide an explanation for both the juridical structure of the association between Quinctio and the debtors as well as to explain how that association tended toward the greater profitability of Cato's loans. At this point, we come back to the problem that Cato was trying to address: that is, to find an effective strategy for reducing the risks associated with maritime lending. Part of Cato's approach was entirely orthodox: a representative, Quinctio, was charged with overseeing the debtors' trading operations. Although I think it unlikely that the borrowers were required to travel in convoy (*pace* Rougé), it is possible that Cato confined his lending to a single trade route or even to the trade in a particular kind of merchandise (e.g., the Mediterranean triad or slaves).[136] Whatever the case, Cato saw an additional

136. Cf. Rougé's translation of *koinōnia* as "convoy," which has been rightly rejected: Rougé, "Prêt et société maritimes," 292–93; Rougé, *Recherches*, 427. There is good archaeological evidence that the traffic along long-distance trade routes, for example carrying wine from the Tyrrhenian

opportunity to invest a large amount of capital and spread the risk by lending to multiple traders, thereby diversifying his investment and reducing his exposure. However, even if Cato's borrowers were operating along the same route, it can hardly have been practical to send multiple representatives to monitor each of them individually. His solution was therefore to create incentives for the borrowers to monitor each other, by encouraging them to form an association, the membership of which was left at their own (and Quinctio's) discretion.

The way in which the principle of self-selection works to reduce risk can be seen by comparison with modern protection and insurance clubs. P&I clubs, which emerged in Britain in the eighteenth century, are voluntary associations of shipowners formed for the purpose of providing mutual liability insurance.[137] The association works by providing mutual cover for risks (such as loss of or damage to cargo) not included in traditional hull insurance policies. At the end of each financial year, members are called upon to contribute to cover the claims that have arisen in the previous cycle, thus distributing losses proportionately across the membership rather than suffering it to fall solely on a handful of unfortunate operators. Governance is by the shipowners themselves, who also decide which operators to accept as members.

The key to success of P&I clubs is the ability to identify substandard operators and to deny them entry into the association. Albeit in a different historical context, Cato relied upon the same principle of self-selection to mitigate against performance and credit risks, by making his debtors' receipt of the loans conditional upon their forming into a club.[138] Crucially, Cato still shouldered the sea-risk—after all, it was this that entitled him to a maritime yield—and it was therefore only indirectly that in attempting to mitigate their own exposure to each other that the codebtors simultaneously reduced Cato's exposure to risk across the board. Significantly, like modern P&I clubs, it would not have been necessary for the debtors to participate in a full partnership in which both profit and loss were shared. As a borrower's club, all that was required was that the members were in some way exposed to the losses of their associates; and since Cato assumed the marine risk, this can only have been the performance and credit risks associated with (maritime) lending. Quinctio's "share" in the asso-

coast of Italy to the south of Gaul, was already beginning to intensify rapidly by the first half of the second century BCE: Tchernia, "Wine Exporting," 279.

137. There is, so far as I can tell, a paucity of academic literature on P&I clubs. For an insight into their practical and legal operation, the following report, which was pointed out to me by Johanna Hjalmarsson at the University of Southampton, has proved illuminating: Terence Coghlin, "Maritime Transport Committee Report on the Removal of Insurance from Substandard Shipping: A Report to the Maritime Transport Committee of the OECD" (Paris: Organisation for Economic Co-operation and Development, 2004), esp. 17–21.

138. Tchernia reaches the same conclusion: Tchernia, *Trade*, 35–36.

ciation need not therefore have been the channel through which Cato's profit flowed: rather, it may simply have entitled him to a seat at the table, deciding upon the entry of debtors into the club and the settlement of claims.[139] Finally, it is unlikely that borrowers' clubs were formed *ex nihilo*: modern P&I clubs still retain strong geographical connections and rely heavily upon personal ties. In the ancient world, a club like Cato's probably built upon the existing associations of ship-operators that are known to have existed at trading hubs from at least the Phoenician period (if not much earlier), and at places like Delos, where members of the mercantile community bonded around shared ethnic, religious, and cultural identities.[140]

From a legal point of view, two alternative structures are possible: either the club was formed as a consensual *societas* (practically through a *pactum conventum societatis*) or by a series of stipulations.[141] Only one scholar, Purpura, has argued for the latter solution, which (it is proposed) took the form in parallel with Hellenistic practice of a mutual network of guarantees (*fideiussiones*).[142] On this account, Cato's borrowers stood surety for one another, guaranteeing the performance of their associates and therefore standing to be sued should one of their codebtors breach their covenant with the lender. Purpura's solution is attractive, principally because the juridical structure of the *koinōnia* would match the economic intent: namely, to drive out substandard or insolvent ship-operators by encouraging them to self-select. Provided that an operator was considered reliable by his peers and possessed of a suitable ship and crew, he could access credit while at the same time maintaining a considerable degree of autonomy and freedom to pursue his own profits. Cato, meanwhile, mitigated his exposure to risk by relying upon his borrowers to exclude untrustworthy and substandard operators.

Security

Personal security. Though it is likely that Cato took security over his borrowers' cargoes, if Purpura's suggestion that he required his debtors to form a net-

139. Again, Tchernia, 35–36.

140. See, generally, Marzano, "Personal Infrastructure," 57–76; also, Candace Rice, "Mercantile Specialization and Trading Communities: Economic Strategies in Roman Maritime Trade," in *Urban Craftsmen and Traders in the Roman World*, ed. Andrew I. Wilson and Miko Flohr (Oxford: Oxford University Press, 2016), 97–114.

141. Talamanca, "'Festschrift für Erwin Seidl,'" 290.

142. Purpura, "Ricerche," 244. Cf. Tanev, who suggests that a similar effect could be achieved by taking real security in merchandise spread across multiple vessels: Tanev, "Real Securities," 83 n. 7. On mutual guarantees, see Eva Cantarella, *La fideiussione reciproca: Allellegue e mutua fideiussio* (Milan: Giuffrè, 1965).

work of mutual guarantees is correct, then Plutarch's account shows that he was willing to rely extensively upon personal forms of security. Such reliance is not unique: in the roughly contemporaneous document drawn up in connection with the loan given by Archippos to the five *synploi* at Ptolemaic Alexandria, Archippos extracted guarantees from five other individuals (three army officers and two merchants); and the chirograph attributed to Menelaos at Puteoli (first century CE) is followed up by a second declaration, that a certain M. Barbatius Keler had agreed to stand surety for the debt.

In the Roman context, extracting a guarantee was normally achieved by requiring the surety to undertake by stipulation to perform toward the creditor in the same manner as the principal debtor.[143] Once the debt fell due, the creditor could then elect which of the debtor or sureties to sue; although it appears to have been considered bad form to sue a surety without having first called upon the principal debtor to pay. If it was a surety who satisfied the debt, they gained the creditor's claim against the debtor for recovery of the money paid out. By demanding guarantees, creditors therefore increased both their chances and the speed of recovery by providing themselves with a choice of defendants, who could be selected depending upon factors such as their availability, solvency, the nature of their assets, and so forth. The burden of recovering from the principal debtor could then pass to the surety.

In the Roman world, standing surety was considered an aspect of friendship (*amicitia*), such that an individual could feel entitled to call on his friends to lend their *fides* to his business dealings.[144] Members' associations of mutual trust and solidarity organized around shared professional, ethnic, and religious characteristics (later formalized as *collegia*) provided a perfect venue to cultivate these relationships.[145] It may even be that the subscribers to Cato's borrowers' club were already members of an existing consortium, so that he was effectively lending to a group of traders who were already known to each other not only by profession but also by their shared ethnicity and cultural values. This would explain how Cato was able to find 50 merchants and *nauklēroi* willing to enter into legal relations with one another: in the context of long-distance trade, it is almost inconceivable that so many individuals would be willing to guarantee (let alone enter into a partnership with!) so many others without

143. See, generally, David Johnston, *Roman Law in Context*, 2nd ed. (Cambridge: Cambridge University Press, 2022), 106–8.

144. A failure to live up to this expectation could engender considerable bitterness. See, for example, the epitaph of L. Licinius Nepos, a businessman who had "hoped to become rich through trading but was deceived by hope and by many friends . . :" *CIL* VI 9659 (= ILS 7591). For further discussion, see Broekaert, *Navicularii et Negotiantes*, 79–80, no. 115.

145. Marzano, "Personal Infrastructure," 67–68.

some degree of confidence in their sharing a common outlook (i.e., just like the early P&I clubs).

Real security. Roman law recognized three types of real security by the classical period:[146]

1. *Fiducia*, in which the debtor transferred ownership of the secured property to the creditor, who undertook to reconvey it once the debt was repaid;
2. Pledge (*pignus*), in which the debtor retained ownership of the pledged property but gave over possession. If the debtor defaulted, the creditor was entitled to satisfy the debt by disposing of the property in his possession. If he had lost possession, two remedies (both probably dating to the first century BCE) provided legal means to recover the property, either from the debtor (*interdictum Salvianum*) or from third parties; and,
3. Hypothec (*hypotheca*), in which the debtor retained both ownership and possession of the pledged property. Once the debt fell due, the creditor had the same remedies for acquiring possession of the property as if the security had been received as a pledge.

Since the proceeds of loans given on maritime terms were typically used to buy cargoes for the debtor to trade with, it was standard for the purchased goods to be hypothecated (rather than conveyed or pledged) to the creditor. In addition, because the Romans recognized no equivalent to the surrogation principle in Athenian law, a creditor who lent money as a *mutuum* transferred ownership of the funds to the borrower and did not automatically have a remedy for expulsion (the *dikē exoulēs* of Athenian law) to recover the purchased goods. Apart from some specific exceptions, the nature and extent of the security taken by the creditor had to be expressly agreed upon: Roman financiers had to state, for example, that their rights in security would extend to merchandise bought by the debtor.[147]

Like Athenian law, Roman law also recognized that it was competent for the creditor to create rights in security over goods that the debtor would acquire in the future. As Verhagen has shown, these so-called general pledges can be regarded as a floating charge: that is, a hypothec over stock-in-trade that could

146. See Johnston, *Roman Law*, 108–15.

147. See, e.g., the phrasing in D.45.1.122.1 (Scaev. 28 *dig.*) (though cf. Dem. 35.53, which uses the same formulation).

conceivably also apply to goods acquired during a long-distance trading enterprise.[148] This was essential in return loans for acquiring security rights over the goods purchased at the outport. The recognition of the legal validity of general pledges was also important for creditors who took security over the "last freight": once the debt fell due, the creditor was entitled to serve notice on the carrier's customers, who were then barred from paying the *nauklēros* and could be sued by the financier using an *actio utilis*.[149]

Another prospect raised by the flexibility of the hypothec was the opportunity for the debtor to offer the same property as security for more than one debt. The complications that could arise were explored by the jurist Paul:

> D.22.2.6 (Paul. 25 *quaest.*):
>
> A lender made a loan at a maritime yield (*pecuniam usuris maritimis mutuam dando*) and took security over the goods in the ship. If they were not sufficient to pay the whole, he took security over the goods, pledged to their own lenders in other ships. The question was whether, if the first ship was lost within the time limit and the whole could have been paid from that ship, the loss fell on the creditor or the shortfall could be made up from the other ships. I replied that a diminution of secured property falls on the debtor, not the creditor. But when (or since?) *pecunia traiecticia* is given on terms that the creditor can sue for it only if the ship arrives safely within the time limit, on failure of the condition the debt itself is discharged. Hence, there is no action even to realize the goods not lost. The ship is lost within the time limit; the condition fails; and the action for the possession of the goods in the remaining ships is without cause (*sine causa*). When, then, could the creditor sue for the possession of those further goods? When the condition is realized, but the goods originally taken as security are lost by some other accident, or sold off cheap, or the ship is lost after the time limit has passed.

Identifying the structure of the underlying transaction is not straightforward. Both Purpura and Rathbone conclude that the goods distributed across the several vessels must have belonged to multiple debtors, bound together by

148. See Hendrick L. E. Verhagen, *Security and Credit in Roman Law: The Historical Evolution of Pignus and Hypotheca* (Oxford: Oxford University Press, 2022), 268–316, esp. 310; also, William W. Buckland, *A Text-Book of Roman Law from Augustus to Justinian*, ed. Peter G. Stein, 3rd ed. (Cambridge: Cambridge University Press, 1963), 478; Johnston, *Roman Law*, 110–11.

149. Verhagen, *Security*, 286–89.

mutual guarantee or as partners respectively.[150] The basis of Rathbone's interpretation in particular is unconvincing: to say that the condition added by the lender (that he took the goods loaded on other ships as security) would have been redundant if they had belonged to a single merchant, for the creditor would have in any case been able to recover from them as part of the merchant's general property, misses the considerable practical difference between a realizable right in security and reliance upon a personal right in respect of the debt. A more compelling interpretation has been offered by Benincasa, who argues that each of the cargoes on the different ships belonged to a single merchant, who had financed their acquisition by taking loans from several creditors, at least one of whom took security over the all the debtor's merchandise, subject to the condition that they should recover out of the cargo acquired with their own capital first.[151] The situation contemplated here bears similarities to a series of passages in the Demosthenic corpus, in which creditors complained about their debtors charging the goods acquired with the loan proceeds as security for debts owed to other lenders.[152] Though the ambiguous use of the word *proprius* makes it difficult to determine who owned the vessels, it may be that they belonged to the debtor, who borrowed money to finance the acquisition of multiple cargoes.[153]

In any case, the question posed by Paul was whether the creditor was entitled to call up his security in the cargoes loaded onto the other vessels if the first ship was lost before the time limit. His answer was that because the debtor's obligation to repay was suspended to the safe arrival of the ship within the time limit (i.e., the condition *salva nave*), it followed that the lender's rights in security, which were accessory to that obligation, would also be prevented from materializing on failure of the condition before the *dies praestitutus*. The creditor would only be entitled to recover from the goods on the other vessels if the ship had arrived safely or, if lost, it had perished after the time limit had expired. Once the condition that the debt should be satisfied out of the main cargo first had been taken into account, the only circumstances in which the creditor could recover from the extra merchandise were therefore if the main

150. Purpura, "Ricerche," 273–78; Rathbone, "Financing," 214–15.

151. Zuzanna Benincasa, "Prawo zastawu jako zabezpieczenie roszczenia o zwrot pożyczki morskiej w D. 22,2,6," *Zeszyty Prawnicze* 11 (2011): 112–13. Cf., also, Tanev, "Real Securities," 77–81; Jakab, "Loans and Securities," 141–42.

152. See above, 41.

153. For this suggestion, Henryk Kupiszewski, "Sul prestito marittimo nel diritto romano classico: Profili sostanziali e processuali," *Index* 3 (1972): 371; see, also, Tanev, "Real Securities," 79. The example would not be without parallels: see, e.g., Petron. *Sat.* 75–76; and the attestations of multiple ship-ownership provided by inscriptions on ship anchors collected by Broekaert, *Navicularii et Negotiantes*, (e.g.) 455, no. 1206.

cargo was not sufficient for this purpose, because it had been lost or damaged after the *dies praestitutus* or sold off cheaply.

Dispute Resolution

Notwithstanding that no speeches composed for delivery in cases concerning maritime loan contracts have survived from the Roman period, the combined evidence furnished by epigraphic material and the juristic texts indicates that the gradual escalation of disputes from negotiation, to arbitration, to litigation, was just as typical at Rome as it had been at Athens.

Negotiation and Private Arbitration

Like in Athens, the parties to complex disputes engaged in tactical rounds of negotiation before proceeding either to arbitration or court. In his speech *pro Caecina* Cicero indicates that the trial had already been adjourned twice and had been preceded by a period of tactical maneuver in which the parties attempted to fortify their legal position (e.g., by soliciting favorable opinions from jurists).[154] Similarly, in *pro Tullio* he alleges that his client's adversary in the suit, Publius Fabius, had sought to influence the praetor, first directly and then through the tribune of the plebs, to amend the terms of the *formula* to his advantage.[155] As several of the tablets preserved in the Sulpician archive suggest, parties normally agreed to meet near to the court in advance of the trial in order to leave open the opportunity for a negotiated settlement.[156]

Arbitration also remained significant as a method of dispute resolution.[157] In the Sulpician tablets one document records the terms of a *compromissum* and a further five are listed by Camodeca as *diei dationes ad audiendum*, recording the date, time, and location of the hearing (usually one of the main *chalcidica* in the settlement).[158] One remarkable feature of *TPSulp.* 34 is that legal proceedings had already progressed *apud iudicem* before the parties agreed to submit to

---

154. See, generally, Bruce W. Frier, *The Rise of the Roman Jurists. Studies in Cicero's* pro Caecina (Princeton: Princeton University Press, 1985).

155. Cic. *Tull.* 38–39.

156. *TPSulp.* 1–19. See, generally, Johnston, *Roman Law*, 135–36; also, Alfons Bürge, "Zum Edikt de edendo," *ZRG RA* 112 (1995): 1–50; Ernest Metzger, "Republican Civil Procedure: Sanctioning Reluctant Defendants," in *The Oxford Handbook of Roman Law and Society*, ed. Paul J. du Plessis, Clifford Ando, and Kaius Tuori (Oxford: Oxford University Press, 2016), 245–56.

157. See Johnston, *Roman Law*, 143–44; also, Leanne Bablitz, "Roman Courts and Private Arbitration," in *The Oxford Handbook of Roman Law and Society*, ed. Paul J. du Plessis, Clifford Ando, and Kaius Tuori (Oxford: Oxford University Press, 2016), 234–44.

158. *TPSulp.* 34–39: on which, see Camodeca, *TPS*, 2:103–11.

arbitration instead.[159] Like their counterparts at classical Athens, Roman arbiters were not bound by the instructions laid down in the *formula*, but possessed the flexibility to arrive at a compromise.[160] In the arbitration agreement, it was standard for each of the disputants to stipulate a penalty for failure to carry out the decision. Once, therefore, an arbitrator had reached a *sententia*, it was the breach of the penal stipulation *ex compromisso* that provided the grounds for raising an action (again, *stricti iuris*) before a judge, not the maritime loan contract itself. A trial before a judge on the terms of the original *nautikē syngraphē* would therefore only occur if the arbitrator declared that he could not decide the case (*non liquet*), the proceedings collapsed, or the parties elected not to go to arbitration in the first place.

Litigation

The procedural aspects of the enforcement of maritime loan contracts depend upon the time and place one has in view. For the reasons given at the beginning of this section, the time under consideration will be limited to the classical period of Roman law. For the most part this limits our attention to the formulary procedure; though it is likely that in the provinces cases may have at some point become subject to the governor's *cognitio*. The aim here is to track the course of an action raised to enforce a maritime loan agreement through to the time of judgment. This section will therefore only discuss issues material to the achievement of that objective.

Like the procedure at Athens, the formulary process was split into two stages: the first before a magistrate (*in iure*); the second in front a of a judge or a panel of judges (*apud iudicem*).

Proceedings *in iure*. To initiate a lawsuit the plaintiff was required to issue an oral summons to his opponent calling him to law (*in ius vocatio*). Here *ius* not only meant the proceedings but referred especially to the place where a magistrate chose to exercise his *iurisdictio*.[161] For the city praetors this meant their tribunals *in foro*; in the provinces the location at which the governor conducted his legal administration while on *conventus*. In municipalities across the empire, lawsuits could also be raised before local magistrates, though colonial and municipal charters routinely limited their jurisdiction to particular types of claim below a certain value. And it was also possible in

159. Camodeca, *TPS*, 2:104–6.
160. Cic. *QRosc.* 4.10–11: on which, Bablitz, "Roman Courts" (with literature).
161. D.1.1.11 (Paul. 14 *ad Sab.*).

many places under Roman rule to continue to seek redress under preexisting local traditions and laws.[162]

The days on which legal business could be conducted were determined by the calendar. Sometimes the parties agreed to meet ahead of time on a day designated for the conduct of legal business at a place near to the praetor's tribunal. This agreement was known as *vadimonium* (bail) and was typically concluded on the basis that the defendant would be liable to pay a penalty for failure to appear. Meetings at or near to the *forum* provided opportunities for negotiations and, if these failed, for the plaintiff to issue the summons and lead the defendant to the magistrate's tribunal.[163] One way to settle the dispute at this late stage was for one of the parties to challenge the other to swear an oath (*iusiurandum deferre*) disclaiming liability in the name of the gods and the genius of the emperor.[164] If the recipient of the challenge swore (*paratus esse iurare*), this barred any future proceedings on the same claim. At this extrajudicial phase, while the swearing of oaths was strictly voluntary (*voluntarium*) it was still open to the recipient of the challenge to refuse to swear without consequence; though as two tablets preserved in the Sulpician archive show, the parties could agree for one of them to swear an oath in advance, such that refusal would amount to breach of contract.[165] Another option was for the recipient of the challenge to issue a counter (*referre iusiurandum*), challenging the tenderer of the original oath to swear himself. For this reason, it was presumably common for the oath-tenderer to swear that he was not proceeding vexatiously (*calumniae causa*) in advance. In the context of negotiations leading up to *in ius vocatio*, challenging one's adversary to swear an oath was a way to up the ante: though it terminated the possibility of suing on the same claim (a borrower who swore had an *exceptio*, and in any case the praetor would deny the plaintiff an action, *denegare actionem*), an oath-breaker could be sued using an edictal *actio ex iureiurando*; in the early classical period probably also *de dolo*; and in addition could be made the subject of criminal proceedings (for perjury, *periurium*; and if the oath referred to the emperor, *crimen laesae maiestatis*).

162. See Kimberley Czajkowski and Benedikt Eckhardt, "Introduction," in *Law in the Roman Provinces*, ed. Kimberley Czajkowski, Benedikt Eckhardt, and Meret Strothmann (Oxford: Oxford University Press, 2020), 1–15.

163. Kaser, *RZ*, 231; cf. Metzger, who maintains the possibility that *vadimonia* could be entered into for this purpose, but who denies that there is any positive evidence to this effect: Ernest Metzger, *Litigation in Roman Law* (Oxford: Oxford University Press, 2005), 37.

164. In a dispute over a loan, the borrower swore that he did not owe (*sed dare non oportere*); the creditor that he was owed (*sibi dari oportere*): Johannes Platschek, "Formularprozess: Verhandlung in iure," in *HRP*, 1:408. For the contents of oaths, Thomas Finkenauer, "Eid (iusiurandum)," in *HRP*, 1:560.

165. *TPSulp.* 28 and 29.

Once called, the *vocatus* was required either to appear or supply a *vindex* as surety. It is possible that still by the classical period the plaintiff could use force to compel a recalcitrant defendant to appear; but the Praetor's Edict also provided for additional sanctions.[166] The edict itself was displayed on whitewashed wooden boards at eye level in the forum, setting out the various actions, defenses, and other devices that the magistrate was willing to entertain in the conduct of his official duties. Each device had its own template pleading that could be used toward the construction of a negotiated *formula*. Among other things, typical *formulae* began by nominating the judge or judges to hear the case, before stating the claim and any defenses pleaded by the defendant and finishing with an instruction to the judge(s) to condemn or absolve the defendant on that basis. In these respects, the *formula* had the effect of a "mini-statute" ("kleine-Satzung") establishing an *iudicium* and setting the limits of the judge's decision-making power.[167]

Having issued the summons, the plaintiff was required to inform the defendant of the action he wanted to bring (*editio actionis*) and of the evidence that he would rely upon in support of his claim (e.g., documents and witnesses; *editio instrumentorum*).[168] The problem of identifying the actions that were available to and used by lenders to enforce maritime loan contracts is complex. My conclusion on this point is that the only remedies available to lenders during the classical period were those conventionally used to enforce loan contracts: that is, the *actio certae creditae pecuniae* and the *actio ex stipulatu*. (Readers interested in my reasoning should see the essay in appendix I.) In practice, maritime loan contracts were part of a more extensive loan dossier that included a *chirographum* in which the borrower acknowledged his indebtedness (probably cross-referring to the contract) and a *nomen arcarium* providing evidence of the disbursement of the funds. Creditors moreover typically required their debtors to acknowledge the whole amount of the debt (capital and yield) in a *chirographum* that could then be sued upon as a *certum* using the *actio c. c. p.* For sums that were *incerta* (e.g., interest accrued after the passing of the risk and a daily rate for the services of the lender's representative), the *actio ex stipulatu* lay insofar as the relevant clauses had been concluded by stipulation.[169]

---

166. According to Gaius, an *actio in factum*. The plaintiff could also seek *missio in possessionem* leading to *bonorum venditio*. See Cicero *pro Quinctio*.

167. Platschek, "Verhandlung in iure," in *HRP*, 1:382. For comparison with the Athenian plaint (*enklēma*), see above, 83.

168. Ernest Metzger, "Formularprozess: Verfahrenseinleitung," in *HRP*, 1:370. It is not known if the plaintiff could be sanctioned for failing to disclose relevant evidence at *editio*, nor if there was a parallel duty on the defendant to produce evidence that would support an *exceptio*. Cf. the Athenian rules concerning the production of documents in litigation, above, 86.

169. For the *formula*, Lenel, *EP*^{3}, 151–54; Dario Mantovani, *Le formule del processo privato romano: Per la didattica delle istituzioni di diritto romano* (Como: New Press, 1992), 45.

A creditor seeking to bring an action would therefore have had his eyes drawn to two consecutive titles in the edict: XVII *de rebus creditis* (concerning things owed); and XVIII *Quod cum magistro navis, institore eove, qui in aliena potestate erit, negotium gestum erit* (Concerning transactions entered into with shipmasters, business managers, and those who are in someone else's power).[170] In short, the first title dealt with issues relating to claims for a *certum* (i.e., a certain sum of money or thing); the second with modifications to remedies that the praetor was willing to grant in certain circumstances, some of which were common to maritime trade.

Under the title *de rebus creditis* were included several rubrics, the first of which was that *si certum petetur* (if a certain [sum or thing] is sought). The rubric consisted of three parts: (1) an edict concerning the tendering of oaths; (2) the *formula* of the *actio c. c. p.*; and (3) provisions regarding the reciprocal exchange of *sponsiones* promising a penalty equal to one-third of the sum claimed in case of defeat (*sponsio et restipulatio tertaie partis*).[171] Taking each in turn:

(i) Once *in iure* it was still possible for the parties to tender oaths to one another; only now this took place under the supervision of the praetor, who stated in the edict that if the plaintiff issued a challenge, he would compel the defendant to either pay, swear, or refer the oath back to the plaintiff.[172] If the defendant swore (*iusiurandum necessarium*), or the plaintiff swore on referral, the dispute was resolved on the praetor's refusal to grant an action (*denegatio actionis*). If the plaintiff declined to swear on referral the action was similarly lost; though like oath-tenderers in the extrajudicial phase, it was probably usual for the creditor to swear in advance that they were acting in good faith (*iusiurandum calumniae*). Refusal to cooperate could lead to an order allowing seizure of the refuser's goods (*missio in possessionem*) leading to sale (*bonorum venditio*). This machinery of compulsory oath-taking likely only applied in actions seeking a *certum*, most especially the *actio c. c. p.*, the *formula* for which was displayed next in the edict.[173]

170. Lenel, *EP*^{3}, 257, esp. 257–86.

171. "*Si paret* N^m N^m A^o A^o *sestertium decem milia dare oportere*:" Lenel, *EP*^{3}, 232.

172. Ulpian's report of the edict in D.12.2.34.6 (Ulp. 26 *ad ed.*), which says only that the praetor would compel the recipient to either pay or swear, is demonstrably interpolated and probably incomplete: Lenel, *EP*^{3}, 235–37; Platschek, "Verhandlung in iure," in *HRP*, 1:410–12.

173. For the emendation ". . . *a quo* <*certum*> *petetur* . . . :" Otto Gradenwitz, "Schiedseid und Beweiseid im römischen Civilprozesse, Beitrag zur Erörterung der Eidesfrage von Dr. Gustav Demelius," *ZRG RA* 8 (1887): 275; and with modern literature, Platschek, "Verhandlung in iure," in *HRP*, 1:410–11 n. 177.

(ii) If the dispute was not to be decided by oath *in iure*, it was for the plaintiff to raise the *actio c. c. p.* on the claim that the defendant ought to give to the plaintiff a certain sum of money.[174] The abstract framing of the *intentio* gave it potentially a very wide scope, the omission of any reference in the *formula* to a *causa* enabling the action to be brought on a variety of different grounds. This was an advantage to the creditor, who was not required to state the ground upon which he was claiming the money, but only to produce evidence of the existence of the debt (e.g., a *chirographum*). At a minimum it is clear from Gaius that the action lay whenever the plaintiff claimed a right to the return (*repetere* or *condicere*, hence *condictio*) of a certain sum of money; and therefore (*inter alia*) to the moneylender *condicere pecuniam numeratam*, for example, on the strength of having made a loan for consumption (*mutuum*). Insofar as the action was aimed at *petere* (i.e., a positive claim), it was apparently available to enforce the debtor's obligation to pay specific sums entered against him in the form of a debt note (*nomen*) in the creditor's accounts (*codex accepti et expensi*); and probably also specific sums agreed upon in clauses that had been concluded by stipulation.[175]

(iii) The procedure under the formulary *actio c. c. p.* could be made penal by the parties' reciprocal exchange of *sponsio et restipulatio tertaie partis*. Whether the process was compulsory or at the election of the plaintiff is unclear: though the opportunity for a hold-out debtor to concede the action by acceding to the praetor's order to pay the debt instead of swearing an oath would juxtapose sensibly with the alternatives of swearing without justification or (hypothetically) proceeding to trial at the risk of condemnation for both debt and penalty. Examples of the *formulae* of the *actio c. c. p.* and an accompanying *actio ex sponsione tertiae partis* for one-third of the sum sued for have been preserved in the Sulpician archive.[176]

Immediately after the rubric *si certum petetur* was another *de eo quod certo loco dari oportet* (concerning that which ought to be given at a certain place).[177]

---

174. Lenel, *EP*³, 237; Mantovani, *Le formule*, 43.

175. On this last point, Julius C. van Oven, "Les Actions Issues de la Stipulation," *TvR* 27, no. 4 (1959): 391–411.

176. *TPSulp.* 31. For the identification of the *sponsio*, see Raimondo Santoro, "Le due formule della Tabula Pompeiana 34," *AUPA* 38 (1985): 333–50. The sums were HS 18,000 (*actio c. c. p.*) and 6,000 (*sponsio tertiae partis*).

177. Lenel, *EP*³, 240–47; and generally, Francesca Pulitanò, *De eo quod certo loco* (Milan: Giuffrè, 2009).

As Gaius noted, the danger of a claim for a *certum* was that, owing to the strict application of the *formula*, the plaintiff might overclaim in some respect and so not only lose his case, but any right of action on the same claim.[178] There was overclaim when the plaintiff sought (*inter alia*) more than was owed, or payment before it was due, or when what was due in one place was claimed in another. In the rubric *de eo . . .*, however, the praetor relaxed the requirement that the action had to be brought at the place of performance (*locus solutionis*), by allowing the plaintiff to sue elsewhere while instructing the judge to take account of both parties' interest in performance at the place stipulated for.[179] As Ulpian remarked, this could include the creditor's interest in the payment of a penalty due under a maritime loan contract at a particular location, where he might owe money on security of a pledge or penal stipulation, which sum became due owing to the debtor's failure to perform at that place.[180] Underclaim (*minus petitio*), on the other hand, was not fatal: if the plaintiff claimed too little, he could sue again on the difference, but not during the same magistracy, in which case he could be met by *exceptio litis dividuae et rei residuae*.[181]

An additional concern for the plaintiff was if the defendant at the time of concluding the transaction stood in some agency-like relationship with a third party. If the defendant was simply a mandatary then this posed few issues: the plaintiff could sue the mandatary, though the mandatary could require the mandator to defend the action on his behalf (*procuratio in rem suam*). More relevant to maritime trade were the praetorian edicts contained in the title *Quod cum magistro navis . . .* facilitating suits against those who were either in someone else's power (e.g., slaves and sons-in-power) or who had been appointed to the role of shipmaster (*magister navis*) or business manager (*institor*). Thus, if the plaintiff contracted with someone trading from a *peculium*, the praetor offered an action up to the limit of the fund's value (*de peculio*) and also to trace any assets taken back into the master's or *paterfamilias*' main estate (*de in rem verso*). So too the praetor promised that if a contract was made with a shipmaster in connection with the matters for which he had been appointed, he (the

178. On *plus petitio*, G.4.53–60; Giuseppe Sacconi, *La 'pluris petitio' nel processo formulare* (Milan: Giuffrè, 1977).

179. The first evidence for the inclusion of the rubric in the Praetor's Edict is from Labeo, who appears to have interpreted the *condemnatio* to instruct the judge not only to take account of the defendant's interests (as previously), but also the plaintiff's: D.13.4.2.8 (Ulp. 27 *ad ed.*). The whole question as to how the *condemnatio* in an action for *certum* could be made subject to the judge's *arbitrium* is controversial. For a plausible reconstruction (modeled on the *formula* of the *condictio certae rei*), see Pulitanò, *De eo*, 344–45.

180. D.13.4.2.8 (Ulp. 27 *ad ed.*). Cf. the creditor's interest in performance at Brentesium in D.45.1.122.1 (Scaev. 28 *dig.*).

181. G.4.122; Lenel, *EP*^{3}, 502.

praetor) would grant an *iudicium* to an unlimited extent (*in solidum*) against the person with the right to exploit the vessel (the *exercitor*). Probably these worked by transforming the *formula* of the main remedy (e.g., the *actio c. c. p.* or *ex stipulatu*) into a so-called Rutilian *formula*, such that although the claim (*intentio*) still identified the original contractor as the obligor, the *condemnatio* named the person against whom the praetor promised the *iudicium*.[182] Presumably reliance on these edicts will not have been uncommon in disputes arising from maritime loan contracts.

One final consideration for the plaintiff was whether the defendant was the correct person against whom the claim should be brought (i.e., passive legitimation). Normally this was a matter for the *iudex*; but in some cases it was open to the plaintiff to put questions to the defendant under the supervision of the praetor (*interrogatio in iure*).[183] The answer (*responsio*) was then treated as *prima facie* true for the purposes of adjudication. The chief area of relevance in which the praetor would supervise an *interrogatio* was in matters in which the plaintiff sought to establish whether and to what extent the defendant was heir to the debtor. The answer, either negative or confirming that they were the sole or partial heir, was then treated as true for the purposes of the suit.[184] If the defendant's answer was unclear or turned out not to be true, then they would be treated as the sole heir (and therefore liable *in solidum*) *apud iudicem*.

Now turning to the defendant, one option that was always available was simply to accept liability (*confessio in iure*), whether voluntarily or in response to the tendering of an oath. In a claim for *certum*, a defendant who made *confessio* was treated as *iudicatus*, that is, as though he had been condemned at trial.[185] The amount due was now a judgment debt subject to the *actio iudicati*. In a claim for an *incertum*, it is likely that the confessor was treated as *indefensus* unless he gave full security against whatever amount he owed. This was perhaps mitigated by the rule that the defendant would not be deemed to have accepted liability unless he had conceded both on the merits and with respect to the sum due.[186] Reluctant defendants who failed to participate in the proceedings due to

182. For discussion of the procedural aspects (with literature), see Peter Candy, "Limits of Juristic Argument in the Exercitorian Edict," in *Principle and Pragmatism in Roman Law*, ed. Benjamin Spagnolo and Joe Sampson (London: Hart, 2020), 147–48.

183. Kaser, *RZ*, 252–53. There may be some similarity with the Athenian *anakrisis*. Such would have been useful in the suit *Against Lakritos*, one of whose arguments was that he could not be liable as the debtor's heir since he had yet to enter onto the inheritance: see below, 127–30.

184. *Testationes* attesting to *interrogationes in iure* have been preserved in the Sulpician archive: *TPSulp.* 23–26; on which, Camodeca, *TPS*, 2:79–87.

185. Lenel, *EP*^{3}, 410; Platschek, "Verhandlung in iure," in *HRP*, 1:377–78.

186. Platschek, 1:378–79; and, generally, Laura D'Amati, *L'inattività del convenuto nel processo formulare: Indefensio, absentia e latitatio* (Naples: Jovene, 2016).

their own inaction were also *indefensus*, liable to execution against the person (*ductio*) and *missio in possessionem* leading to *bonorum venditio*.

If the dispute was not to be decided by oath and the defendant chose to contest the case, he could elect to plead a defense (*exceptio*) selected from among those contained in the edict. The necessity for the defendant to seek the inclusion of an explicit defense in the *formula* arose from the *stricti iuris* nature of the *actiones c. c. p.* and *ex stipulatu*, neither of which permitted the judge to consider extenuating circumstances (e.g., considerations of good faith) in reaching his decision. The chief defenses available to a defendant disputing a debt owed on a maritime loan contract are as follows:

1. *Doli mali*: After c. 66 BCE, "... if in this matter nothing was done or is being done through [the plaintiff's] *dolus malus* ...," for example, if the creditor sued on an acknowledgment of debt *sine causa*; or on a penal condition in the contract, and the defendant alleged that the fulfilment of the condition had been induced by the creditor's fraud (cf. D.22.2.8).[187]
2. *Metus*: No earlier than c. 80 BCE, "... if in the matter nothing has been done through fear ...," that is, duress.[188]
3. *Pacti conventi*: If the debtor alleged that the sum sued for was not in fact due, owing to the existence of some additional agreement between the parties, for example, a (tacit) pact not to sue, or the concession by the lender's representative for the terms of a penal condition to be amended, provided that the representative was acting within the scope of his authority (see, e.g., D.45.1.122.1).
4. *Non numeratae pecuniae*: If a defendant promised by stipulation to repay a loan but had not in fact received the principal, they could defend the action *doli mali*. This however required them to take on the difficult task of proving the negative, that is, that the money had not been paid. No later than 215 CE the *exceptio n. n. p.* was introduced, which removed the presumption against the debtor created by his acknowledgment in the *chirographum* and shifted the burden of proof to the creditor to show that the money had in fact been paid out. Though the availability of the *exceptio* much reduced the value of the *chirographum* to the creditor as evidence of the debt, this was mitigated by the requirement that it could only be pleaded within a year of the creation of the debt (i.e., it was dilatory in nature). It may not have been a feature

187. Lenel, *EP*[3], 512.
188. Lenel, *EP*[3], 512.

of the formulary system and is not included by Lenel in his reconstruction of the *Edictum perpetuum*.[189]

5. Those covered by the rubric *si quid contra legem senatusve consultum factum esse dicetur*:[190] for example,
   a. *legis Plaetoriae*: Proceeding from the *lex Plaetoria*, a law of the late third or early second century BCE that gave an *actio* and *exceptio legis Plaetoriae* to persons under the age of 25 who alleged that they had been induced into a transaction by fraud. Later the praetor promised *restitutio in integrum* where it appeared that the minor had been led into making a bad deal owing to their inexperience. By the classical period, it was common for minors to appoint a *curator* to reassure nervous creditors that they had acted reasonably and under advice.
   b. *Senatusconsulti Macedoniani*: Proceeding from a resolution of the Senate under Vespasian, which instructed magistrates to refuse an action to lenders who had made a money loan to a son-in-power, even once they had become *sui iuris*. The *senatusconsultum* was interpreted narrowly: the plaintiff might respond, for example, that the *filiusfamilias* had represented himself as a *paterfamilias*, pleading *replicatio doli*.
6. Procedural defenses: for example,
   a. *Iurisiurandi*: If the dispute on the claim had already been resolved by oath.[191]
   b. *Rei iudicatae vel in iudicium deductae*: If the *iudicium* was *imperio continens*, the defendant could plead that the plaintiff's right of action had been consumed by a previous *litis contestatio*.[192]
   c. *Litis dividuae et rei residuae*: If a plaintiff initially claimed less than he was owed (*minus petitio*), and later sued for the difference, he could be met *litis dividuae* if he tried to raise the suit during the same magistracy.[193]

It will be seen from the above that negotiating the terms of a *formula* during proceedings *in iure* was a complex affair that required the active participation of both the magistrate and the parties to the dispute, sometimes under threat of

189. See Iole Fargnoli, "Condictio aus Darlehen (mutuum)," in *HRP*, 2:1910; also, Wiesław Litewski, "'Non numerata pecunia' im klassischen römischen Recht," *SDHI* 60 (1994): 405–56; Verhagen, "Chirographs," 297–99.
190. Lenel, *EP*^{3}, 513.
191. Lenel, *EP*^{3}, 512.
192. Lenel, *EP*^{3}, 506–11.
193. Lenel, *EP*^{3}, 502.

compulsion. If the disputants could not complete their business *in iure* by the end of the day, it was open to them to make *vadimonium* to reappear on some later day, often on pain of a penalty if the defendant failed to do so. If, however, the parties could not reach their own agreement on the matter, the praetor at the close of business each day ordered the litigants in pending cases to perform a *vadimonium*, promising reappearance on the day after next.[194] The edict also allowed the plaintiff to demand a penalty of the defendant for failure to appear, subject to the limitation that it should not exceed HS 100,000 nor be vexatiously high. If the defendant failed to appear as promised, the plaintiff could sue on the *vadimonium*, either for the penalty or, if none was included, for *quanti ea res erit*. To the defendant the edict provided several defenses, for example, that the penalty was too high, or that his failure to appear had been occasioned by some force beyond his control ("*valetudine, tempestate, vi fluminis*").[195]

Once the parties had arrived at a *formula*, their final task was to decide upon the identity of the judge who would try the case. If not by consent the judge was selected from a list of potential nominees (*album iudicum*) by a process of mutual rejection (*reiectio*). Where one or both of the parties were foreigners, it is probable that these proceedings will have been before the peregrine praetor and possible that instead of *unus iudex* the case was sent to trial before a panel of judges (*recuperatores*, but there is much uncertainty). Once the terms of the *formula* had been finalized, its acceptance by the defendant led to joinder of issue (*litis contestatio*), possibly accompanied by the ancient appeal to witnesses ("*testes estote*"). If the praetor was satisfied that the *iudicium* should be granted, he then issued the *formula* for the parties to record and both authorized and ordered the person nominated as judge to hear the dispute (*iudicare iubere*).

Joinder of issue had many important effects, several of which were material to the trial of cases arising from maritime loan contracts. The most significant was that it destroyed the old obligation and replaced it with a new one. In destruction the precise effect depended on the ancient distinction between an *iudicium legitimum* (i.e., a trial conducted within a mile of Rome in a suit between citizens and adjudicated by a citizen *iudex*) and one *quae imperio continentur* (i.e., not *legitimum*, but conceived as depending for its existence upon the magistrate's *imperium*). In *iudicia legitima* joinder of issue extinguished the obligation sued upon *ipso iure*; otherwise the defendant had to rely on the praetorian *exceptio rei iudicatae vel in iudicium deductae* to defend future actions

194. For the contents of the edict, Lenel, *EP*³, 516; and for a reconstruction of the process, Metzger, *Litigation*, 81.

195. See, further, Lenel, *EP*³, 501.

on the principle *bis de eadem re agi non potest.*[196] A second effect of joinder was that it fixed the subject matter of the claim. If the plaintiff's only claim was for a *certum*, the amount sought will usually have corresponded with the amount stated in the chirograph, representing both capital and yield. However, if (as was usual) the plaintiff had also stipulated for an additional rate of interest and a daily rate for the services of his representative once the risk had passed, then the *incertum* would have to be sued upon *ex stipulatu*, producing a *strictum iudicium* for *quanti ea res est.*[197]

Proceedings *apud iudicem*. Trials granted in disputes concerning a maritime loan contract would either have been heard by a single judge (*unus iudex*) or, if one or more of the litigants was a foreigner, possibly by a panel of *recuperatores*. Though judges were laymen who swore a judicial oath to execute their office according to truth and the laws, knowledge of the law was assumed (*iura novit curia*).[198] It was therefore commonplace for a judge to act in consultation with members of their *consilium* and to solicit advice (in the form of *responsa*) from jurists on points of law. Though the controversies surrounding the institution of the so-called *ius respondendi* necessarily encourage caution, it is possible that from the time of Augustus judges were effectively bound in some circumstances to follow the opinion contained in *responsa* issued by certain jurists.[199]

The existence of the *iudicium* was determined firstly by the scope of the *formula*: any deviation, for instance, in the identity of the judge, made the proceedings a nullity. Though it was possible for the parties to change the terms upon which the *iudicium* was to be conducted (*translatio iudicii*, e.g., on the death of one of the parties), this required the cooperation of the magistrate and a fresh joinder of issue.[200] If, however, the magistrate decided that the *iudicium* should be renewed, it was within his power to compel cooperation by a recalcitrant defendant by threatening to hold them *indefensus*. The existence of *iudicia* was also time limited.[201] If the *iudicium* was *de imperio continentia*, it expired at the end of the granting magistrate's term of office unless a sooner date had

196. G.4.106–7; Lenel, *EP*³, 506–11.

197. On the question as to what should be brought into the assessment at *litis aestimatio* in a *strictum iudicium* for *quanti ea res est*: Kaser, *RZ*, 297; Kaser, *Restituere als Prozeßgegenstand* (Berlin: C.H. Beck, 1932), 99–105.

198. Kaser, *RZ*, 358.

199. Emanuele Stolfi, "Prinzipat," in *HRP*, 1:69–71. For a review of the historiography, see Kaius Tuori, "The ius respondendi and the Freedom of Roman Jurisprudence," *RIDA* 51 (2004): 295–337 (with literature at 295–96).

200. Kaser, *RZ*, 353–55; Georg Klingenberg, "Formularprozess: Verhandlung apud iudicem," in *HRP*, 1:426–28.

201. Kaser, *RZ*, 352; Klingenberg, "Verhandlung apud iudicem," in *HRP*, 1:424–25.

been fixed. Conversely, *iudicia legitima* expired after 18 months, as enacted by the *lex Iulia iudiciorum privatorum*. Especially in the more common *iudicia* resting on the magistrate's *imperium*, it was therefore common for litigants to raise suits near to the beginning of a magistrate's term of office to reduce the risk of *mors litis*.

As a rule, judges were relatively unconstrained in their conduct of the trial. They were bound to stick to the terms of the *formula* and execute their instruction in accordance with the oath. Hearings were conducted during daylight hours and could be continued over several days. Judges had it within their authority to adjourn proceedings (*diem diffindere*), probably (at least in some circumstances) at his own discretion but perhaps normally with reference to certain grounds that were enumerated in statutes from time to time.[202] If the judge breached his official duty *per imprudentiam* he could expose himself to civil liability on the allegation that he had "made the case his own" (*litem suam facere*).[203]

Although the hearing itself was largely unregulated, it typically consisted of speeches delivered by rhetors (for the plaintiff, an *oratio*, in reply, an *altercatio*) seeking to persuade the judge of their client's case. Like at Athens, the time for speeches was regulated by a water-clock (*clepsydra*), which in the case of judicial *clepsydrae* consisted in simple outflow vessels that could be stopped for short periods to allow for the reading out of documents.[204] Unlike the orations of Pseudo-Demosthenes, however, no speeches (for example, by Cicero) composed for delivery in suits concerning maritime loan contracts survive. Be that as it may, similar cases must have arisen; and there is additionally the intriguing possibility that Demosthenes' speeches on the topic might have been known to the Roman orators.[205]

The burden of proof was on the plaintiff in respect of his *actio*; and on the defendant to prove his *exceptio*. Only evidence that had been edited *in iure* was admissible at trial.[206] The best evidence was classified by the rhetors as *probationes inartificiales* (i.e., sources external to the speaker, such as documents and

202. See, e.g., XII tables, tab. II.2. Chap. 95 of the *lex Ursonensis* lists seven possible excuses for a litigant's failure to appear, which may have constituted sufficient grounds for adjournment. The *lex Iulia iudiciorum privatorum* probably also contained similar excuses: Ernest Metzger, *A New Outline of the Roman Civil Trial* (Oxford: Clarendon Press, 1997), 94–100.

203. Philipp Klausberger, "Klagen aus Quasidelikten," in *HRP*, 1:2654–57; cf. Lenel, *EP*[3], 168–69.

204. Andrew M. Riggsby, "For Whom the Clock Drips," *Arethusa* 42, no. 3 (2009): 283.

205. See, e.g., Cic. *Brut.* 9.35: "For one could easily say that Demosthenes is clearly perfect and in no way lacking in anything"; also, Cecil W. Wooten, "Cicero and Quintilian on the Style of Demosthenes," *Rhetorica: A Journal of the History of Rhetoric* 15, no. 2 (1997): 177–92.

206. On evidence, see, generally, Kaser, *RZ*, 367–69; Klingenberg, "Verhandlung apud iudicem," in *HRP*, 1:436–46.

witnesses), in contrast to the testimony of the speaker himself. Although the documents were in most cases strictly probative, they were nonetheless strong evidence that the conduct giving rise to the obligation (e.g., the handing over of a sum of money, the oral conclusion of a stipulation), had in fact taken place. *Tabulae* in particular were the subject of legislation, such that from 61 CE they were required to be perforated and bound in a certain way (in addition to the witnesses, seals, interior and exterior writing, and so forth) to be of any value at all.[207] Witnesses, who were not compellable (at least in civil trials), generally gave evidence after the end of the advocate's speech and could give their testimony either orally or in writing by means of a *testatio* (though the former was preferred, since the witness' presence allowed for questioning). Expert witnesses could also be called to testify on technical matters. In a trial concerning a monetary debt evidenced by a suite of documents and perhaps also witnesses, the defendant's routes to absolution were therefore limited to attacking the form of the document; showing that the contents of the document or any witness testimony was factually and materially inaccurate; or proving an *exceptio*. During proceedings, it was open to the parties to challenge each other to swear to the veracity of certain facts (*iusiurandum in iudicio*),[208] or to concede points voluntarily (*confessio*).[209] If the concession was sufficient for either of the parties to prove their case this led to condemnation or absolution accordingly.[210]

Judges were tasked with deciding questions of both fact and law. The judge's opinion (*sententia*) was delivered by oral pronouncement (*pronuntiatio*) and conveyed his decision to condemn or absolve. The content of the judgment was called *iudicatum* and the settled dispute *res iudicata*. There was no right of appeal.[211] Absolution meant either that the plaintiff had failed to discharge his burden of proof; or that there had been overclaim (*plus petitio*); or that the defendant's *exceptio* had been upheld (*summovere*).[212] Condemnation was always for a sum of money: if for a *certum*, the amount fixed in the *formula*; if *incertum*, an amount estimated by the judge (*litis aestimatio*), but limited by the inclusion of a *taxatio* or, if the *actio* had been modified *de peculio* and *de in rem verso* to the extent of the *peculium* and any assets that could be traced back into the master's or *paterfamilias*' estate.[213] In *formulae* containing an arbitral clause

207. Klingenberg, 443; Meyer, *Legitimacy*, 165–68.

208. Klingenberg, "Verhandlung apud iudicem," in *HRP*, 1:446–47.

209. Kaser, *RZ*, 366; Klingenberg, "Verhandlung apud iudicem," in *HRP*, 1:445–46.

210. One of Cicero's main arguments in *pro Tullio* is that his adversary's *confessio* is sufficient to justify condemnation under the (contested) terms of the *formula*: Paola Ziliotto, "Dolo e iniuria nella pro Tullio di Cicerone," *BIDR* (2017–18): 133–48.

211. Kaser, *RZ*, 370–71; Klingenberg, "Verhandlung apud iudicem," in *HRP*, 1:458–60.

212. Klingenberg, "Verhandlung apud iudicem," in *HRP*, 1:457–58.

213. Kaser, *RZ*, 316 and 372–74; Klingenberg, "Verhandlung apud iudicem," in *HRP*, 1:452–56.

(for example, if the *actio* had been modified under the edict *de eo quod certo loco dari oportet*), then it was open to the interested party to swear to the value of the claim (*iusiurandum in litem*); though the judge was not bound to fix the value at the amount sworn to by oath.[214] In the case of interest-bearing money debts, interest continued to run through the period to judgment; but once the decision was pronounced, the obligation was novated into a judgment debt, which if it had not been satisfied within 30 days could be sued upon using the *actio iudicati* and made the subject of execution procedures.[215]

Conclusion

Commercial practice and dispute resolution exist in a continuum. From a Braudelian perspective, commercial practice in respect of long-distance trade in the ancient Mediterranean is best understood as an aspect of the *longue durée*, that is, "man in relation to his environment." In that long-durational context, the legal cultures that were engaged in the economic system from time to time appear as conjunctural phenomena, each coming into contact with the world of overseas trade and adapting in their own culturally specific ways. In terms of the relationship between the economic and legal systems, it was generally the case that commercial actors were quick to adapt to the legal framework in which they were operating, by including clauses in their contracts dealing with jurisdiction, providing for enforceable security rights, compiling loan dossiers designed to afford them maximum protection, and so forth. It was also the case that the legal institutions of different cultures were adapted to the needs of maritime traders, at Athens (for example) by the introduction of *nautodikai* and later the *dikai emporikai*; and at Rome by the introduction of the peregrine praetor and subsequent edictal developments. The result at both classical Athens and Rome was the gradual convergence of the economic and legal systems by a process of mutual adaptation.

214. Kaser, *RZ*, 372; Klingenberg, "Verhandlung apud iudicem," in *HRP*, 1:448–49.

215. For the *actio*, Kaser, *RZ*, 384–86; Constantin Willems, "Formularprozess: Vollstreckung," in *HRP*, 1:479.

CHAPTER FOUR

The Interpretation of Maritime Loan Contracts

The paucity of documents having to do with maritime loan contracts surviving from commercial practice is at least partially offset by the comparative richness of the legal texts. The two most voluminous bodies of texts consist in several speeches of the Attic orators, composed in about the middle of the fourth century BCE, and a cluster of Roman legal texts, comprising mainly juristic writings from the late Republican and classical periods (i.e., first century BCE to early third century CE) and imperial constitutions issued by the emperors Diocletian (late fourth century CE) and Justinian (sixth century CE). Within this body of material, however, there is significant variety: while for Athens, the speeches provide us with an insight into litigation in the courts, for Rome, instead of speeches from civil trials, we have juridical texts composed at least one step removed from actual civil proceedings.

Notwithstanding this variety, there is a common thread that runs through both the Attic speeches and the majority of the Roman texts, *viz.*, that each represents the response of a different legal culture to the problem of resolving disputes between commercial actors over the interpretation of contracts. More specifically, both the Athenian and Roman materials are animated by the problem of the interpretation of contractual conditions, most especially the condition *salva nave* and penalty clauses, both of which were typically included as standard terms in maritime loan contracts. Like the previous two chapters, the analysis will be divided into two parts, the first focusing on the speeches of the Attic orators, the second on the juridical texts from the Roman period.

Late-Fifth- and Fourth-Century-BCE Athens

In coming to the speeches of the Attic orators there are few better places to start than Wolff's remarks in his famous lecture on "Demosthenes as Advocate," given in Berlin in 1967.[1] In that lecture, Wolff developed his method of *Gesamtinterpretation* ("wide angle analysis"), which involved peeling back the rhetorical layers in the speeches to gain new insights into the legal institutions lurking behind them. With that technique in mind, a more recent contribution by Thür shows how in the so-called shipwreck cases (i.e., Dem. 56, 32, 34, and 35), *logographoi* (speechwriters) employed a rhetorical strategy of isolating and concealing facts to their advantage, which was especially effective when the speaker had the benefit of delivering their presentation first.[2] In substance, this strategy consisted in identifying the key facts that were material to deciding the case and manipulating them in ways that tended to undermine their opponent's argument while strengthening the speaker's own.

The argument of this section is that, in a subset of these shipwreck cases (*viz.*, those which were suits for damage flowing from an alleged breach of a maritime loan contract: Dem. 56, *Against Dionysodōros*; Dem. 34, *Against Phormiōn*; and Dem. 35, *Against Lakritos*), the facts isolated by the speaker were those material to the legal arguments turning on the interpretation of conditions in the contract.[3] Before coming to these cases it is necessary to make two points regarding their context. The first concerns their procedural background. Though all the speeches that concern us were raised as suits for damage using the mercantile procedure (i.e., as a so-called *dikē emporikē blabēs*), only the case *Against Dionysodōros* had proceeded to a trial on the merits (*euthydikia*); the others having been the object of a counter-indictment (*paragraphē*). In these two hearings the order of the speakers was reversed (the original plaintiff in the suit speaking second); and the issue before the court was also changed, from an exclusive focus on the merits to a focus also on the admissibility of the suit, particularly in respect to the provability of the existence of a *symbolaion* between the parties.[4]

The second concerns the nature of legal argumentation in the courts. The rigid formalism of the Athenian civil trial produced an environment that was essentially agonistic, in the sense that each of the speakers was pitted against the other in an oratorical combat or contest.[5] There was no assumption that the

1. Hans J. Wolff, "Demosthenes as Advocate: The Functions and Methods of Legal Consultants in Classical Athens," in *The Attic Orators*, ed. Edwin Carawan, trans. Jess Miner (Oxford: Oxford University Press, 2007), 91–115.

2. Thür, "Law and Rhetoric."

3. In treating these cases I have excluded discussion of the speech *Against Zēnothemis*, which concerns a dispute over the possession of a cargo taken as security against a maritime loan, but which does not raise any questions of contractual interpretation directly.

4. For the meaning of the term *symbolaion*, see above, 84.

5. See, e.g., Louis Gernet, "Sur la notion du jugement en droit grec," *Archives d'histoire du droit oriental* 1 (1937): 119–22; Paoli, *Studi sul processo*, 66–72.

members of the jury knew the law: rather, it was for the litigants to adduce the statutes that they wished to rely upon as a type of artless proof (*atechnos pistis*) of the *nomoi* that they contended ought to be applied in the case. In this adversarial system the art of forensic oratory, in the words of Protagoras, was that of "making the weaker argument the stronger."[6] But while rhetorical skill could enhance an argument it could not by itself define the issue, the legality of which was ensured by the jurors' oath to observe the laws in reaching judgment. The complicating factor in this is the role of the concept of *epieikeia* or 'fairness' as a basis for arguing against the strict application of a law on the grounds that to do so in a particular case would produce injustice. Certainly the notion that laws provided general rules to which exceptions ought sometimes to be made on grounds of fairness was discussed by the philosophers;[7] but the extent to which arguments of this type featured in the courts (and in what context) is controversial.[8] Though a comprehensive discussion of this problem is beyond our scope, the analysis of the speeches discussed here shows how *logographoi* mobilized these arguments in the context of specific questions of contractual interpretation.

In these three cases then the legal issue before the court was whether either or both of the condition *salva nave* and penalty clause should be treated as realized. When the facts allowed it, the arguments advanced by the speakers on this question were sometimes framed either as an appeal to a literal interpretation of the contract in accordance with the laws or (by contrast) as an appeal for an exception to be made on grounds of fairness (*epieikeia*). The most significant law for this purpose was the piece of legislation that stated that all private agreements (*homologiai idiai*) were to be binding (*kyria*) upon the parties to them. The effect of the law was to put the emphasis on the parties' choice of language, making the specific formulation of the clauses the focus of interpretation. However, where a strict or literal reading of a particular clause would appear to lead to an unjust result, it was open to the parties to argue for an exception to the

6. Arist. *Rh.* 2.24.10; cf. Pl. *Tht.* 166d.

7. Pl. *Plt.* 294a; cf. Arist. *Eth. Nic.* 1137b; also, Arist. *Rh.* 1.13.13–18: on which, Annie Hewitt, "Universal Justice and Epieikeia in Aristotle," *Polis* 25 (2008): 115–30.

8. See, e.g., Edward M. Harris, "How Strictly Did the Athenian Courts Apply the Law? The Role of 'Epieikeia,'" *BICS* 56 (2013): 26 (with literature at notes 2–4); Harris, "The Athenian View of an Athenian Trial," in *Use and Abuse of Law in the Athenian Courts*, ed. Chris Carey, Ifigeneia Giannadaki, and Brenda Griffith-Williams (Leiden: Brill, 2018), 56–57. For a classic statement, read Paul Vinogradoff, *Outlines of Historical Jurisprudence*, vol. II: *The Jurisprudence of the Greek City* (Oxford: Oxford University Press, 1922), 63–71. Cf. especially Harald J. Meyer-Laurin, *Gesetz und Billigkeit im attischen Prozess* (Weimar: H. Böhlaus Nachfolger, 1965), the first four chapters of which are translated into English in Meyer-Laurin, "Law and Equity in the Attic Trial," in *The Attic Orators*, ed. Edwin Carawan, trans. David Mirhady (Oxford: Oxford University Press, 2007), 116–39.

general rule established by the written law (i.e., that the contract should be binding) on grounds of *epieikeia*, which could (for example) take the form of pleas of necessity or good intent. In all these cases, the legal issues defined which factual details were material to resolving the dispute, while the speakers employed rhetorical strategies to undermine their opponent's case and strengthen their own. What is clear is that in all three cases the position taken by each of the parties was at least arguable as a matter of law (which may explain why the litigants were willing to risk the *epōbelia*), even if the details presented by the speakers as factual support were of doubtful veracity or even manufactured.

Dem. 56 (Against Dionysodōros)[9]

The speech *Against Dionysodōros* was composed during one of the last years of the grain crisis (330–320 BCE) in about the middle of 322.[10] Although several stylistic and technical features of the composition make Demosthenes' authorship unlikely,[11] there are several indications that it was written by the same unidentified individual as the author of the speech *Against Phormiōn*.[12] The speech was composed for delivery at a trial on the merits (*euthydikia*), at which both the defendant's liability and the amount of damages to be awarded were at issue.[13]

The facts (according to the plaintiff) are as follows. Dareios and Pamphilos, business associates, agreed to lend 3,000 dr. to Dionysodōros and Parmeniskos, two partners, on security of the ship for a voyage Athens–Egypt–Athens (6). Apparently, all four individuals were metics, so that the grain laws would apply.[14] This explains why, when the borrowers requested that the port of destination should be either Rhodes or Athens (i.e., at their election) (5), the creditors insisted upon the latter as the final destination and expressly stipulated in the *syngraphē* that the ship should sail to no other port besides Athens (6). The contract also contained a penalty clause that stated "if . . . they [the debtors] do not present the security plain to see and free of any encumbrance, or if they do anything contrary to the contract, let them pay twice the sum" (20, 38).[15]

9. For a translation with brief commentary, see Victor Bers, *Demosthenes, Speeches 50–59* (Austin: University of Texas Press, 2003), 92–106. For the Greek text with commentary, see F. A. Paley and J. E. Sandys, *Select Private Orations of Demosthenes*, 2nd ed., vol. 1 (Cambridge: Cambridge University Press, 1886), 228–58; also, Carey and Reid, *Speeches*, 56–67.

10. Isager and Hansen, *Aspects*, 208–9; Carey and Reid, *Speeches*, 201–4.

11. Bers, *Demosthenes*, 92.

12. Friedrich Blass, *Die Attische Beredsamkeit*, vol. III.1 (Leipzig: Teubner, 1893), 525.

13. In a *dikē blabēs*, the plaintiff was entitled to double damages if he could show that the breach was intentional, but only simple compensation if the breach was deemed unintentional: Dem. 21.43.

14. For the laws, see above, 82.

15. Dem. 56.38. For Carey and Reid's doubts about the authenticity of the supposed quotes from the contract in (36), Carey and Reid, *Speeches*, 228; and see above, 36.

Finally, the parties agreed that Dionysodōros would stay at Athens and that the debtors were jointly and severally liable (6–7).[16]

Dareios, the speaker in the case,[17] gives a colorful version of events. When the day for sailing arrived, Parmeniskos departed for Egypt, leaving Dionysodōros behind (7). Dareios then alleges (as was apparently unbeknownst to him at the time the loan was made) that Dionysodōros and Parmeniskos were in league with Kleomenēs (the ruler of Egypt installed by Alexander the Great), whose network of agents spread across Mediterranean ports sent updates on grain prices back to Egypt, from where he manipulated the market and mercilessly exploited the price differentials for his own profit (7–8).[18] Armed with new information that the price of grain at Athens had collapsed, but that the Rhodian market remained buoyant, Parmeniskos therefore made for the latter, where he sold the cargo at a high price (9–10). Once news came back to Athens of these events, Dareios claims to have confronted Dionysodōros, who refused to pay back the full amount of the debt, but only the principal at a reduced yield, to reflect the early termination of the voyage at Rhodes (11). Dareios rejected the counteroffer, on the grounds that to accept would be tantamount to an admission that he had colluded with his debtors to break the grain laws (12–13). The negotiations then descended into a wrangle (14–16), which ended when Dionysodōros refused a challenge (*proklēsis*) to bring the ship to Athens (40) and submit to arbitration (17–18), leaving Dareios with no option but to raise a mercantile suit (18).

The next part of the speech is dedicated to legal arguments and rebuttals. Dareios anticipates that Dionysodōros will make three arguments in his defense (21–22), to which he proceeds to offer a series of counterarguments. Although several of the arguments are run together and much of the focus is on points of factual detail, two of the disputed issues (the first and third) turn on the interpretation of conditions in the contract. For simplicity, I will examine all three; but paying particular attention to these two.

(1) The first argument concerns the interpretation of the penal condition in the contract, which stated that the penalty would become due if: (a) they [the debtors] did not present the security (i.e., the ship) to the creditors free from third party rights; or (b) they violated the agree-

16. This appears to have been an alternative strategy to sending a representative to monitor the debtor.

17. The name appears in the Hypothesis but not in the speech itself. Carey and Reid suggest that the information may have come from a document that was reproduced in full in a branch of the manuscript tradition now lost. This cannot have been the *syngraphē*, which Dareios says he was not named in (6). It may therefore have been the *proklēsis* (17): Carey and Reid, *Speeches*, 195 n. 38.

18. See, e.g., Arr. *Anab.* 3.5.2–5; Curt. 4.8.5.

ment in any other respect (38). In outline, Dareios' argument is that both conditions for the imposition of the penalty have been realized; and that the penalty ought therefore to be imposed according to the law stating that private agreements are to be treated as binding (2). Near the end of the speech, Dareios asks the jury to impose the penalty provided for by the contract (i.e., the 6,000 dr. payable as damages on fulfillment of the penal condition) and not to let the debtors off by requiring them only to pay the original debt (*opheilomena*) (44). Since the penal condition is framed in the alternative, his submissions break into two parts.

(a) Dareios' argument with respect to the first limb is that the condition has been realized because the debtors have failed to produce the security. This argument seems dubious; and it is perhaps telling that the speaker appears to deliberately quote the condition out of context at the relevant point in the speech (38). Although we do not have the full text of the agreement, it is likely that the penal condition was connected with another clause in the contract, similar to one in the *syngraphē* reported in *Against Lakritos* requiring that "if the goods are brought safe to Athens . . . until such time as they [the debtors] shall have paid the money due in accordance with the contract they shall admit the creditors' control over the goods offered as security, which must not be liable to any (other) seizure."[19] In that speech the condition *salva nave* and the clause establishing the creditors' right to take possession are linked by the connective *kai*: the intention is clearly that the creditors' right to take possession of the goods offered as security should only arise on the debt becoming due (i.e., when the ship had put in at its final destination). The penalty in the present *syngraphē* was likely also intended to reinforce this right: to provide an avenue for recovery for creditors who had been kept out of their security once the ship had returned. Crucially, this made the realization of the penalty clause dependent upon the fulfillment of the condition *salva nave*: if the latter condition failed, there was no debt; and if there was no debt, the creditor had no right to take possession of the security and therefore no right to seek a penalty for having been kept out.

(b) The second limb of the condition provided that "if they [the debtors] violated the agreement in any other respect" the debtors

19. Dem. 35.11.

should pay a fine of 6,000 dr. Dareios' claim is that it is an express term of the agreement that the ship "should sail to no other port than to Athens" (11); and that since Parmeniskos sailed to Rhodes, the debtors are in breach of the agreement, realizing the condition for payment of the penalty. According to Dareios, the defendant's counterargument is that Parmeniskos' decision to put in at Rhodes was made out of necessity (21): on his way back from Egypt, the ship was "wrecked" (*ragēnai*), so that he was "forced" (*anagkasthēnai*) to stop for repairs and unload his cargo at the port.[20] Dionysodōros continues that this is corroborated by the fact that some of the cargo was later forwarded to Athens on charter vessels. Dareios, however, counters that even if the damage done to the ship occurred against Parmeniskos' will (*akousion symptōma*), he has since been able to repair (*epanorthoumenoi*) the vessel and continue to trade (23), showing that he acted willingly and therefore not under compulsion (*hekontes kai ouk ex anankēs*) (42). In fact, Parmeniskos only sent on merchandise that would fetch a higher price at Athens than at Rhodes; and that this did not include the grain, which had already been sold off, showing that profit was the chief motivation for putting in at the port (24–25).

The back-and-forth between the litigants over the second limb of the condition is a classic example of legal argumentation in which the literal interpretation of the contract as encouraged by statute is counterposed to arguments motivated by *epieikeia*.[21] The issue is finely balanced: the defendant argues that Parmeniskos put in at Rhodes out of necessity; the plaintiff that, notwithstanding the involuntary character of the initial decision, Parmeniskos' subsequent decision to stay on in the port put the defendants in breach. Though the arguments concentrate on factual detail, the implication is that if the jury should find that Parmeniskos did in fact hold over at Rhodes beyond the need for repairs, then they should reject the defendant's argument of necessity and find for the plaintiff.

(2) The second argument may be disposed of quickly. According to Dareios, Dionysodōros will argue that it was incumbent upon the credi-

20. "ῥαγῆναι" can also mean "be holed," "spring a leak": Carey and Reid, *Speeches*, 221. The implication is that the ship was incapacitated, even if it did not sink.

21. Harris, "How Strictly," 36.

tors to accept the defendants' counteroffer of a reduced yield (22). Dareios, however, points out that the lenders who agreed to compromise were in a position to negotiate new loans for further voyages between Rhodes and Egypt, so that they ultimately benefited from the change of plans (26).[22] In any case, he continues, the claim was no defense since the borrowers' relationship with other creditors was irrelevant to the interpretation of the present agreement. The submission therefore amounts to the (baseless) claim that the defendants should be released from the terms of the agreement for no other reason than that they had made reasonable efforts at compromise.

(3) Dareios' third argument refers to Dionysodōros' claim that he is not obliged to repay the original debt, because the failure of the ship to arrive at Piraeus means that the condition *salva nave* has failed to materialize (22). Again, the dispute is over the interpretation of a contractual condition; but this time the roles are reversed. Now it is Dionysodōros who seeks to rely on a literal interpretation of the condition supported by the law concerning private agreements: the contract says, ". . . if the ship arrives safe at Piraeus"; the ship has not arrived; therefore, there is no debt to repay. Dareios responds that Dionysodōros' earlier offer to pay back the principal with a reduced yield suggests that even the defendant does not believe in the force of his own argument (31–37); and further, that the failure of the condition to materialize is due to the debtors' own fault (41–42). This latter argument—that a condition prevented from materializing by the promisor's own fault should be treated as satisfied—puts the case for an exception to the general rule of giving effect to the agreement as expressly stated, impliedly on grounds of *epieikeia*.

Although much of the plaintiff's argumentation in the speech is given over to points of factual detail, the facts that are in dispute (e.g., the extent of the damage to the ship and the nature of Parmeniskos' decision to put in at Rhodes, and whether the ship had made later voyages) are precisely those that are material to questions concerning the interpretation of the conditions in the contract. The two conditions at issue were those upon which the creditor was dependent for the contract's enforcement: namely, the penalty clause and the condition

22. The implication is that the other lenders, unlike Dareios and his partner, were *xenoi* and therefore not subject to the grain laws. The creditors' problems were likely exacerbated by the decision not to send a representative, who might have been authorised to make some (limited) decisions on their behalf; though cf. D.45.1.122.1 (Scaev. 28 *dig.*).

salva nave. For each, the plaintiff and defendant alternated roles, arguing for a strict interpretation on the basis of the written law against appeals to *epieikeia* and vice versa. We do not know how the case was decided.

*Dem. 34 (*Against Phormiōn*)*[23]

Like that oration *Against Dionysodōros*, the speech *Against Phormiōn* (327/26 BCE) also concerns a dispute over the interpretation of a maritime loan contract.[24] Chrysippos and his brother had raised a *dikē emporikē blabēs* against Phormiōn, a metic and merchant in cheap perfumed goods and dyes (*rōpos*, ῥῶπος) to whom they had lent money, for breach of contract.[25] Phormiōn objected that the suit was inadmissible and filed a *paragraphē*. Phormiōn therefore speaks first and Chrysippos replies. As the latter relates in the opening sections of the speech,[26] Phormiōn's principal objection is that there was no *symbolaion* binding him to any performance, because he had been released from payment of the original debt by the failure of the condition *salva nave* and had already discharged what was owed on the penalty at Bosporos (a kingdom in the Crimea). The plaintiff's aim was therefore to establish the suit's admissibility by showing the existence of a *symbolaion*.

In the first half of the oration, Chrysippos relates the events that have led up to the court case. He claims that he and his brother lent 2,000 dr. to Phormiōn for an expedition Athens–Bosporos–Athens, taking security over merchandise worth 4,000 dr. in anticipation of the increase in value of the return cargo (6). Chysippos then alleges that Phormiōn proceeded to take two further loans of

23. For a translation with brief commentary, see MacDowell, *Demosthenes*, 110–29. See also the commentary to the Greek text by Paley and Sandys, *Private Orations*, 5–48.

24. For the date, Isager and Hansen, *Aspects*, 169.

25. For Phormiōn's identity as a metic, Dem. 34.13 (resident at Athens) and 50 (not an Athenian citizen); and for the connotations of *rōpos*: Str. 4.5.3; Arist. [*Mir.*] 844a19; Hsch. s. v. ῥῶπος. Chrysippos and Lampis track down Phormiōn at the perfume stalls in the *agora* on his return (13). Isager and Hansen speculate that he was an exporter of perfumed olive oil: Isager and Hansen, *Aspects*, 157.

26. It is generally agreed that Chrysippos delivered the first 17 sections of the speech and the portion from section 33 to the end. In the intervening sections 18–32, the presence in the text of the demonstrative pronouns οὗτος and ὅδε, which seem undoubtedly to refer to Chrysippos, has given rise to various theories concerning the possibility of a change of speaker. The chief of these are that: (1) the intervening sections were delivered by a second speaker (despite the absence of a request to the jury for leave to this effect): Arnold Schaefer, *Demosthenes und seine Zeit*, vol. III:2 (Leipzig: Teubner, 1885), 304–5; (2) it was not clear by whom the speech would be delivered when it was composed: Blass, *Die Attische Beredsamkeit*, III.1:580–81; and (3) Chrysippos was the speaker throughout, but that he used demonstrative pronouns to refer dramatically to himself: John O. Lofberg, "The Speakers in the Case of Chrysippus v. Phormio," *Classical Philology* 27, no. 4 (1932): 333. To avoid confusion, I shall generally refer to the speaker as Chrysippos, though subject to the above qualification.

1,000 dr. and 4,500 dr. (total, 5,500 dr.) from different lenders on similar terms; but that he defrauded all three of his creditors by only purchasing cargo worth 5,500 dr., so that the value of the security was not even sufficient to cover the debts (which had risen to 7,500 dr.) (7). Having produced the *syngraphē*, witness statements, and customs records from Piraeus to substantiate the claim, the speaker describes how Phormiōn traveled with the goods to Bosporos, only to find that the market for his wares had collapsed following the outbreak of war (8). When the *nauklēros* of the vessel told Phormiōn to re-embark his goods on the ship as the agreement required, he refused, claiming that he was unable to find a buyer for his "trash." He therefore instructed his slave or business partner to go instead (9). In a tragic turn of events, the ship was wrecked shortly after leaving port to a considerable loss of life.[27] However, Lampis the *nauklēros* survived and made it back to Athens on another boat, where he reported to Chrysippos what had happened (10). When Phormiōn eventually returned, Chrysippos confronted him; and after some wrangling, they agreed to submit the dispute to private arbitration (18). When the arbitrator declined to declare a result (μηδὲν αποφηνάμενος), allegedly out of partiality to Phormiōn, the only option left to Chrysippos was to raise a lawsuit (21).

All this builds to the issue in contention, which was whether Phormiōn was bound by a *symbolaion* for the purposes of establishing the admissibility of the suit under the mercantile procedure. According to Chrysippos, Phormiōn argued that his obligation to pay the original debt had never arisen, because the condition in the contract, that he should pay "when the ship reaches port in safety," had failed to materialize (33). Chrysippos states that he is willing to concede to Phormiōn the failure of the condition *salva nave*: the fact of the shipwreck was beyond dispute. However, he counters that notwithstanding that Phormiōn is not obliged to repay the main debt, the condition that he should "put on board the ship the goods purchased, or else pay a fine of 5,000 dr." has been realized.[28] Phormiōn's failure to load a new cargo at Bosporos has there-

27. The figures for the number of dead and their identity differ in the manuscript tradition. A (Monacensis 485, tenth century CE) reads "200 free souls" (*diakosia sōmata eleuthēra*). S (cod. Parisinus 2934, late ninth or early tenth century CE) has "300 souls" (*triakonta sōmata*). For reasons largely predicated on assumptions about the capacity of ancient sailing vessels, modern textual editions emend "300" to "30" and retain "free" (*eleuthēra*). If, however, as some have argued, the reading of the generally more authoritative S ought to be preferred, then Dem. 34.10 might refer to the sinking of a vessel to the loss of "more than 300 slaves:" David M. Lewis, "A Cargo of Slaves? Demosthenes 34.10," *Mariner's Mirror* 108, no. 2 (2022): 135–48; also, Charles T. Penrose, *Select Private Orations of Demosthenes* (Cambridge: The University Press, 1843), 180.

28. The sum of 3,900 dr. that Phormiōn claims to have paid at Bosporos is 50 percent greater than that of the original debt (2,600 dr.). Bogaert infers that the principal, interest, and penalty amounted to 3,900 dr., that is, the 2,600 dr. due at Athens plus a fine of 50 percent, the *hēmiolion*: Raymond Bogaert, "Le cours du statère de Cyzique aux Ve et IVe siècles avant J.-C.," *L'Antiquité*

fore made any discussion of the failure of the condition *salva nave* "null and void"; the existence of any *symbolaion* turns on the question of the satisfaction of the penal condition. At least one of Phormiōn's arguments (as reported by Chrysippos) against the existence of a *symbolaion* is that he has already discharged his liabilities (including the full amount of the penalty) as contemplated by the agreement by paying Lampis at Bosporos (32, 34).

The case is therefore a delicate one. According to Chrysippos, the reason for Phormiōn's failure to load the goods at Bosporos was that he could not find any buyers for his goods following the outbreak of war, with the intention of following closely behind once the market had recovered. However, if Phormiōn had loaded a cargo onto the original ship, it would have perished, in which case there would be no *symbolaion*, either for repayment of the original debt or for the penalty. In fact, those left on shore considered Phormiōn to have been "lucky" not to have loaded a fresh cargo (10). Now the creditor seeks to rely on the penalty clause, notwithstanding that condition *salva nave* has failed to materialize. In the speech *Against Dionysodōros*, the fulfillment of the penalty clause was linked to the realization of the condition *salva nave* by connecting it to the creditors' entitlement to take possession of the goods on arrival. By contrast, the clause agreed to by Phormiōn did not link its fulfillment to the realization of the condition *salva nave*: it states only that if Phormiōn failed to load a new cargo at the outport, he would be liable to pay 5,000 dr. The case therefore turns on Phormiōn's contention that he has already discharged his liabilities at Bosporos.

*Dem. 35 (*Against Lakritos*)*[29]

The speech *Against Lakritos* cannot have been composed before 355 BCE (when the legislation establishing *dikai emporikai* was enacted). On the other hand, it was certainly composed before 338 (the year of Isokratēs' death)[30] and probably before 348, when Philip II of Macedon successfully besieged Olynthos and completed his conquest of the Chalcidian League, making trade between Athens and Chalkidikē perilous.[31] A date in the late 350s is most plausible.

Classique 32 (1963): 100–102. Isager and Hansen maintain that the figure of 3,900 dr. is erroneous, the speakers having miscalculated the exchange rate with Cyzicene staters: Isager and Hansen, *Aspects*, 163. Thompson argues that the figures in 25–26 imply the existence of a second penalty: Wesley E. Thompson, "An Athenian Commercial Case: Demosthenes 34," *TvR* 48, no. 2 (1980): 142.

29. For a translation with brief commentary, see MacDowell, *Demosthenes*, 130–49. See also the commentary to the Greek text by Paley and Sandys, *Private Orations*, 49–88.

30. Dem. 35.40.

31. MacDowell, *Demosthenes*, 130; cf. Isager and Hansen, *Aspects*, 169–70.

Though there is no positive evidence that Demosthenes was not the author of the speech, many scholars have doubted his authorship for stylistic reasons.

Androklēs, an Athenian citizen, and Nausikratēs of Karystos, his friend and partner, had lent money on maritime terms to Artemōn and Apollodōros, two young brothers from Phaselis on the coast of Lykia, for a trading expedition from Athens to Pantikapaion on the eastern shore of Crimea, via Mendē and Skionē, and from there back to Athens. When the borrowers returned to the Aegean, they did so on a different vessel, which instead of Piraeus put in at the Thieves' Harbor along the coast. After 25 days, having failed to take possession of any goods as security or to recover any of the money he had lent, Androklēs issued a summons to Apollodōros and separately to Lakritos, brother to the two debtors and heir to Artemōn, who had since died. In contrast to the original borrowers, who were probably *xenoi*,[32] Lakritos was resident at Athens (and therefore a metic) and likely an orator, having been a student of Isokratēs.[33] Androklēs raised a *dikē emporikē blabēs* against the two men, to which Lakritos responded by entering a counter-indictment (*paragraphē*). Lakritos' two main claims, as implied by Androklēs' arguments, are that: (1) because he had not entered into Artemōn's estate as the rightful heir, he could not be held personally liable for any claims against his deceased brother; and (2) even if he could be held liable, there was in any case no *symbolaion* between them, because the loss of all the debtors' merchandise on the return journey in a shipwreck had led to the failure of the condition *salva nave*.

To preserve a focus on the interpretation of contractual conditions in these speeches I will focus on only the second of these claims.[34] As a result of the *paragraphē*, Androklēs will have spoken second, with the task of showing the existence of a *symbolaion* in the case. According to Androklēs, Lakritos' claim is that the debtors were unable to repay the loan, because the goods that they had purchased as a return cargo at Bosporos had been lost in a shipwreck along the coast between Pantikapaion and Theodosia (30–31); and that since the money had been borrowed subject to the condition that it should only be repaid "if the goods are brought safe to Athens" (11), their loss in the Black Sea meant that the condition had failed to materialize.

However, Androklēs gives an entirely different version of events. Before even reaching Pantikapaion, he alleges that the borrowers had already breached

32. The speaker, for example, does not accuse them of violating the grain laws, which applied only to citizens and metics: Isager and Hansen, *Aspects*, 170. For the laws, see above, 82.

33. Dem. 35.15, 40–43; also, Plut. *Vit. Dem.* 28, quoting Hermippos of Smyrna (third century BCE).

34. For the claim concerning Lakritos' status as Artemōn's heir, see Isager and Hansen, *Aspects*, 172–75.

the contract on two counts: first, by taking an additional loan against the same security of 3,000 jars of Mendean wine, when they had already promised that Androklēs and Nausikratēs would have exclusive rights in this respect (21–23); and second, by purchasing only 450 jars of wine at Mendē, and so failing to furnish the required security (18–20). Once at Pantikapaion, Androklēs alleges a third breach, when the borrowers elected (on his account) not to acquire a return cargo, but instead to travel on with Hyblesios to Theodosia with a small cargo of wool, salt fish, and hides, and (at least) 100 Cyzicene staters in cash (24–25, 34). After surviving the wreck of Hyblesios' vessel on the way to Theodosia (31–33), Androklēs claims that the two brothers found a *nauklēros* (a fellow Phaselite) who would take them to Athens; but instead of investing their remaining funds in merchandise, they chose to lend it to the *nauklēros*, at the same time allowing priority in security to another creditor (a merchant from Chios), who would only give the loan on condition that his security extended over all the goods at his borrowers' disposal (36–37, 52).[35] Finally, when the new vessel eventually made it back to Attica, the *nauklēros* chose to put in at the Thieves' Harbor instead of Piraeus (28, 53), probably to avoid being compelled to unload his cargo of grain and to sell two-thirds of it on the spot, as required by Athenian legislation (51–52).[36] After more than 25 days in the Thieves' Harbor, during which time the borrowers have been seen wandering around the sample market at Piraeus, the ship set sail for Chios, without the lenders having taken possession of any secured goods or repayment of the loan.

In the final analysis, the dispute concerning Lakritos' second claim is framed by two competing arguments: Lakritos contends that there is no *symbolaion* because the loss of the goods in a shipwreck meant that the condition suspending the brothers' duty to repay had failed to materialize; Androklēs that the condition ought to be treated as realized because it had been prevented from materializing by the debtors' own blameworthy conduct.[37] At a factual level, the critical question was therefore whether Artemōn and Apollodōros had purchased a return cargo at Pantikapaion that was lost on the way to Theodosia. If they had, they would be relieved of the obligation to repay because the condition *salva nave* had failed to materialize; but if, as Androklēs submits, they had not, then they ought not to be relieved because its nonfulfillment was not due to the occurrence of the shipwreck, but rather to their failure to acquire a return cargo and to install it on board. In the absence of a penal condition such as the

35. Cf. the lending arrangement described by Paul in D.22.2.6 (Paul. 25 *quaest.*): on which, see above, 100–102.

36. For the law, see above, 82.

37. For the Roman approach to this problem, see below, 147–49.

one relied upon by the creditors in the speech *Against Phormiōn*, Androklēs' only option was to argue against the operation of the condition by which he and his partner had assumed the risk. This explains Androklēs' introduction of numerous depositions of those involved in the wreck and the subsequent voyage, to prove that the merchandise lost on Hyblesios' ship did not belong to the borrowers but to other merchants (33–34). From this perspective, the borrowers' loan to the second *nauklēros* would be a marvelous piece of opportunism: having arrived empty-handed in Attica following the wreck, Artemōn and Apollodōros could avoid paying back the original loan while profiting from lending out the capital to another trader.

The discussion of these cases allows for some brief reflections before heading to Rome. In each the central question before the jury was whether one or more of the conditions in the contract should be treated as satisfied. In a *euthydikia* the question was straightforwardly material to the determination of the defendant's liability; in cases that featured a *paragraphē*, to the admissibility of the suit in respect of the existence of a *symbolaion*. In general, the tension that existed in the interpretation of the contract was between the literal approach encouraged by the law concerning private agreements and arguments that an exception should be made on grounds of *epieikeia*. For the condition *salva nave*, it was typically the debtor who argued that on a literal interpretation the condition had failed to materialize (i.e., Dionysodōros, Phormiōn, and Lakritos); and the creditor who argued that the condition had been prevented from materializing by the debtor's own fraud or fault (especially Dareios and Androklēs). However, in the interpretation of penal conditions the positions were reversed: now the creditor argued that on a literal interpretation the condition was satisfied; the debtor that they should be excepted from liability on grounds of fairness (e.g., Dionysodōros, that they had been driven to breach the contract by necessity).

Classical Rome

The problem of the interpretation of contractual conditions was taken up again some three centuries later by the Roman jurists. Almost certainly these cases had continued to be litigated in the intervening period, not just at Athens but around the Mediterranean seaboard. They provide a rare opportunity to study the response of two different antique legal systems and cultures to precisely the same problem (i.e., the interpretation of conditions in a standard form contract). The Roman and Attic material is distinguished most fundamentally by the nature of the texts: whereas for Athens we are required to view the problem through speeches composed for delivery in jury courts, for Rome, what we lack for speeches of counsel is made up for by the preservation of a small collection of juristic texts and imperial constitutions in the sixth-century *Digest* and *Code*. Of the juristic texts, the majority of those authored before the Severan period are principally concerned with the interpretation of penal conditions. These formed the basis of a juristic debate concerning their interpretation, beginning (in our evidence) in the late Republic and continuing through the classical period of Roman law. Two points of context provide a route into the problem.

First, almost all the texts concerned with the interpretation of penalty clauses in maritime loan contracts approach the problem through the lens of stipulation, an old oral contract of the Roman *ius civile*. In a stipulation, the promisor bound himself by making an oral promise in response to a question put to him by the stipulator or promisee. In the context of the classical formulary procedure, the remedies for the enforcement of stipulations were *stricti iuris* (i.e., their *intentio* did not contain a clause *ex fide bona*). In practice, this meant that, in deciding the case, the judge was limited to interpreting the parties' express language, without taking account of arguments motivated by considerations of good faith. Extenuating circumstances could therefore only be taken into account if the promisor inserted one of the recognized defenses (*exceptiones*) into the *formula* from the list in the Praetor's Edict (see those enumerated in chapter 3). Without pressing the parallel too far, the interpretive context generated by the conclusion of agreements as stipulations was therefore not dissimilar to the one created by the Athenian law concerning *homologiai idiai*: that is, the parties were bound by the words used to conclude their agreement, unless they could show that an exception ought to be applied (at Rome these took the form of edictal *exceptiones*, at Athens, appeals to *epieikeia*).

Second, in the fragments that have come down to us, the jurists seldom, if ever, set out to interpret penal stipulations in maritime loan contracts in individual cases, but used them rather as material examples for the conduct of discussions about the interpretation of stipulations more generally. In several texts we therefore find penalty clauses in maritime loan contracts discussed alongside analogous terms in both arbitration agreements and *vadimonia* (i.e., promises to appear in the context of legal proceedings), because the relevant clauses in these types of agreement were highly standardized and therefore provided a stable basis for juristic analysis. However, while the texts therefore have at first the appearance of being somewhat technical and abstract in nature, the problems that occupied the jurists were ultimately rooted in the same interpretive issues as those at the heart of the disputes that gave occasion to the speeches of the Attic orators and would have been material to the resolution of cases in Roman law courts.

Two Rules

The following two excerpts by Ulpian have been separated in Justinian's Digest, but originally belonged together as part of his commentary on *vadimonium sisti* in the Praetor's Edict:[38]

> D.50.17.161 (Ulp. 77 *ad ed.*):
>
> In the Civil law, the received view is that, whenever a person with an interest in this happening is responsible for a condition not being fulfilled, it is treated as if the condition is fulfilled. This rule is extended to grants of freedom, bequests, and the naming of heirs. On these models, stipulations also are binding when the promisor is responsible for the stipulator's not complying with a condition.
>
> D.22.2.8 (Ulp. 77 *ad ed.*):
>
> . . . Servius says that no action can be brought for the penalty on [a loan of] *pecunia traiecticia*, if it is the creditor's responsibility that repayment within the prescribed time limit was not received.

In the first excerpt Ulpian states the received view that a condition prevented from materializing by a person interested in its nonfulfillment should be treated as realized.[39] In the context of conditions in good faith contracts (e.g., sale), it was uncontroversial by the time of Ulpian, if not much earlier, that the rule should freely apply. This much was straightforward, because responsibility for preventing a condition's satisfaction could be interpreted as contrary to good faith. In stipulation, however, the actions for which did not contain a good faith clause, there was no *prima facie* basis upon which such an argument could be advanced. This potential for inequity was addressed by the classical jurists who, according to Ulpian, first carried over the rule equating prevention with satisfaction to stipula-

38. Lenel, *Pal*, 2:869. On both texts, see now Bruce W. Frier, *A Casebook on the Roman Law of Contracts* (Oxford: Oxford University Press, 2021), 75.

39. The leading texts having to do with this rule are D.35.1.24 (Iul. 55 *dig.*) and D.50.17.161 (Ulp. 77 *ad ed.*). Both have been excerpted from passages on *vadimonium sisti:* Lenel, *Pal*, 1:460; Lenel, *Pal*, 2:869.

tion by analogy with rules developed in the context of the interpretation of conditions in wills. We know that the rule originated in the case where an heir made it impossible for a *statuliber* to fulfill the condition of his freedom; and that it was extended to similar situations in conditional legacy and conditional institution of an heir.[40] The analogous case in stipulation occurred when a promisor made fulfillment of the condition under which the promisee was to be paid impossible by his fraud or fault.[41] By Julian's time, we are told that "some" (*quidam*, including Julian) applied the rule to stipulation; and Daube suggests that by the time of Ulpian its application was beyond dispute.[42]

In the second excerpt, Ulpian reports the Republican jurist Servius' view that a penal condition in a maritime loan contract ought not to be treated as realized if the stipulator was responsible for his debtor's nonperformance. In his discussion of the text Daube asks why Servius denies the creditor an action (*peti non posse*) rather than allowing the debtor *exceptio doli*; and so, too, why instead of referring to *dolus* he prefers a wider formulation involving the creditor's responsibility. The explanation, he suggests, must have to do with the peculiar features of the penalties concluded in maritime lending arrangements.[43] However, the more likely explanation is that Servius adopted the conservative view that while it was inappropriate to introduce equitable considerations into a trial on a strict law *formula*, it was open to the praetor to deny an action *in iure* on grounds beyond those covered by the *exceptio*. Further, this put the debtor whose performance has been prevented by his creditor in the same position as one affected by (for example) supervening impossibility; and this not only on account of the creditor's *dolus*, but for any reason whatever owing to his culpable conduct or inaction. In both cases the response is to deny the stipulator a remedy. By the first century CE, Servius' rule had been generalized to cover penal stipulations in any context, not just those in maritime loan contracts.[44]

Both rules, each the converse of the other (i.e., prevention equals satisfaction; inducement equals nonsatisfaction), had a field of application in respect

40. David Daube, "Condition Prevented from Materializing," *TvR* 28 (1960): 276 (with literature).

41. See Julian's formulation in D.35.1.24 (Iul. 55 *dig.*): ". . . *cum per promissorem factum esset, quo minus stipulator condicioni pareret.*"

42. Daube, "Condition Prevented," 276.

43. Daube, "Condition Prevented," 280.

44. See D.4.8.40 (Pomp. 11 *ex var. lect.*), which contains a general restatement of Servius' opinion in D.22.2.8. On both texts, Daube, "Condition Prevented," 280; Salvatore Riccobono Jr., "Profilo storico della dottrina della mora nel diritto romano," *AUPA* 29 (1962): 154–62; Alan Watson, *The Law of Obligations in the Later Roman Republic* (Oxford: Oxford University Press, 1965), 2; Amalia Sicari, *Pena convenzionale e responsabilità* (Bari: Cacucci, 2001), 337–45; Massimo Miglietta, *'Servius respondit': Studi intorno a metodo e interpretazione nella scuola giuridica serviana. Prolegomena I* (Trento: Universita degli Studi di Trento, 2010), 449–50; Pontoriero, *Il prestito marittimo*, 107–8.

of the interpretation of conditions in maritime loan contracts. The first rule, which equated prevention with satisfaction, was material to the interpretation of the condition *salva nave:* if a merchant prevented the ship from arriving safely, and then tried to argue that they owed nothing to the creditor on account of the failure of the condition, it was accepted that the merchant's prevention of the fulfillment of the condition should be treated as satisfaction. Meanwhile the second rule, which stated that a condition the fulfillment of which had been induced by the person who stood to benefit ought not to be treated as realized, was material to the interpretation of penalty clauses: for example, if a creditor was responsible for his debtor's failure to perform such that a penalty fell due. The next two subsections treat the juristic interpretation of each of these standard clauses in reverse order, starting with penal stipulations before moving on to the condition *salva nave*.

Penal Stipulations

Notwithstanding the variety of the specific terms that could be contained in penalty clauses, in general the penalties included in maritime loan contracts were made conditional upon the failure of the debtor to perform in some certain respect by a deadline (*dies*). The penalties themselves normally consisted of a fixed sum, the same clause frequently providing for a daily rate for the services of the creditor's representative (and costs) once the deadline had passed.

The juristic treatment of the interpretation of penal stipulations in this context focuses on two broad issues: *viz.*, the timing of their satisfaction and (relatedly) the timing of the onset and consequences of *mora* (default).[45] On the question of the timing of satisfaction, the interpretation differed depending upon whether the condition contained a time limit or not. If the condition did not contain a time limit, it was arguable when the condition should be treated as satisfied, which point was the subject of juristic debate. Since none of the texts having to do with this problem refer to penal stipulations in maritime loan contracts directly (which in any case normally contained a time limit), I do not propose to discuss them here. As for penal stipulations containing a time limit, the general rule was that the condition was realized as soon as the deadline passed without performance. There were, however, exceptions. If, for example, it became impossible for the debtor to perform before the appointed day owing to some occurrence that was not attributable to his fault (i.e., the

45. See generally Rolf Knütel, *Stipulatio poenae: Studien zur römischen Vertragsstrafe* (Cologne: Böhlau, 1976), 224–37.

case of supervening impossibility), the stipulation was ineffective such that the stipulator had no action for its enforcement.[46] Similarly, if the realization of the condition had been induced by a person interested in its fulfillment, the rule first suggested by Servius in the specific context of maritime loan contracts and generalized to all penal stipulations by Pomponius was that it ought not to be treated as satisfied (D.22.2.8).

These exceptions provided relief for the debtor whose failure to perform by a deadline was due to reasons beyond their control. A text drawn from African's *quaestiones* introduces for the first time a more generalized framework for establishing when penal stipulations should become actionable:

> D.44.7.23 (Afr. 7 *quaest.*):
>
> In connection with a loan of *traiecticia pecunia*, a penalty (as was usual) was introduced into the stipulation for the services of the person who would claim the money, if it was not repaid on the appointed date; the person who claimed the said money recovered part thereof and then ceased to claim, but subsequently, after passage of an interval, he served an *interpellatio*. On being consulted, he [Julian] replied that the penalty can be claimed also in respect of the period during which a claim was not made; what is more, this is so even if no *interpellatio* had been made at all; the stipulation has not come into operation except when it was through the fault of the debtor that payment was not made; otherwise, it must be ruled that if the person who had commenced his demand ceased to continue when prevented by ill-health, the penalty was not incurred. However, it clearly can be questioned whether, if the person against whom the demand was made was himself in default, the penalty nonetheless is incurred, even though he tenders the money afterward; and it is said that the more correct view is that it is so. For also if an arbitrator in arbitration proceedings ordered money to be paid on a specified date and there was not failure to pay through the fault of the one who was ordered to pay, he gave as his opinion that the penalty was not incurred; so much so that Servius too considered it most correct that if the date on which payment was to be made was not included in the arbitrator's award, a moderate period appears to have been allowed. This same ruling must be applied also when something has been sold on condition that unless the price shall have been paid on a certain date, the thing shall become unbought.

46. See, e.g., Frier, *A Casebook on the Roman Law of Contracts*, 84.

The seventh book of African's *quaestiones* contains a series of texts on different topics, some concerned with questions of timing in the context of contractual conditions.[47] Here the parties to a maritime loan contract stipulated for a penalty that would fall due if the debtor had failed to repay by a certain date; when the date arrived without payment, the creditor (or his representative) recovered a part of what was owed and then let the matter lie for an interval before instituting a fresh demand (*interpellatio*). The question is, can the creditor seek payment of the penalty (including a daily rate for the services of the representative) for the time between his ceasing to claim and the service of the demand? According to African, the response of his mentor Julian was that he could: the stipulation would only be treated as effective once the debtor was responsible for his own failure to perform. If the condition contained a time limit that had subsequently elapsed the consequences of the debtor's *mora* began at the same time, *viz.*, when his failure to perform could be attributed to his fault. The creditor was therefore not required to interpel the debtor to put him into delay;[48] for if it were otherwise a debtor could be relieved of the consequences of his delay through his creditor's misfortune, for example, because he had fallen ill and was therefore unable to institute a demand (an *argumentum ad absurdum*).[49]

The response then turns to consider two examples of the application of the rule: first, in which the debtor was responsible for his own default, though he tendered repayment after fulfillment of the condition (conclusion: penalty due);[50] and second, in which the debtor was not responsible for his failure to abide by an arbiter's award, notwithstanding that the date specified in the condition had passed (conclusion: penalty not due). Accordingly, Servius is reported to have held that, even though a *poena compromissi* that did not include a due date should fall due immediately (*statim*) on conclusion of the proceedings, it was most correct (*rectissime*) that the condition should not be

47. Lenel, *Pal*, 1:20.

48. On the question of the necessity or otherwise of a demand: Heinrich Siber, "Interpellatio und Mora," *ZRG RA* 29 (1908): 47–113; cf. Agostino Elefante, "'Interpellatio' e 'mora,'" *Labeo* 6 (1960): 30–49; Elefante, "La 'mora ex re' e l''interpellatio,'" in *Mnemeion S. Solazzi* (Naples: Jovene, 1964), 397–431; see, also, Jan D. Harke, *Mora debitoris und mora creditoris im klassischen römischen Recht* (Berlin: Duncker & Humblot, 2005); Harke, "Die interpellatio als Synonym für den Tatbestand des Schuldnerverzugs—Spuren der Rechtspraxis in den Digesten," in *Usus Antiquus Juris Romani: Antikes Recht in lebenspraktischer Anwendung*, ed. Wolfgang Ernst and Éva Jakab (Berlin: Springer, 2005), 77–85.

49. On the use of *reductio ad absurdum* by African/Julian, Mario Bretone, "Note minime su Celsus filius," *Labeo* 9 (1963): 337–38; cf. Pietro Cerami, "Considerazioni sulla cultura e sulla logica di Caecilio Africano (A proposito di D.35.2.88 pr.)," *IVRA* 22 (1971): 136–37.

50. The fact pattern is analogous to that presented by Cervidius Scaevola in D.45.1.122 pr. (Scaev. 28 *dig.*), with the same result.

treated as satisfied until a reasonable time (*modicum spatium*) had passed for the loser to abide by the award. The passage ends with an observation, likely added by African, that the same rule should apply in a sale made conditional upon payment of the price by a certain time, such that satisfaction of the condition would be postponed until responsibility for the failure to pay could be attributed to the buyer.

This somewhat complicated text contains the elements of a generalized framework covering issues of timing in penal stipulations. The rule that a penal stipulation will not come into operation except when it was through the fault of the debtor that payment was not made is attributed elsewhere to the Augustan jurist Sabinus.[51] It would appear to have two chief advantages:

(1) Harmonization of the treatment of penal stipulations across different contexts. At Rome there were three standard form contracts that typically contained penalty clauses: arbitration agreements, maritime loan contracts, and *vadimonia*. By the late Republic, the treatment of stipulations in these different contexts was affected by a degree of unevenness. First, there were juristic opinions that suggested the denial of an action to the creditor in certain circumstances (e.g., supervening impossibility, Servius' opinion in D.22.2.8). Second, there were *exceptiones* of general application contained in the Praetor's Edict (e.g., *doli*, *pacti*), which potentially overlapped with the juristic opinions suggesting the denial of an action in the same circumstances (e.g., when a creditor had deliberately induced the fulfilment of a penal condition by not accepting payment: a situation covered by both Servius' opinion in D.22.2.8 and *exceptio doli*). Third, if the penalty had been stipulated in connection with a promise to appear (*vadimonium*) that had been entered into on the praetor's order, the edict provided an additional, special *exceptio* to the defendant that his failure to appear had been occasioned by some force beyond his control ("*valetudine, tempestate, vi fluminis*").[52] There was, however, no equivalent *exceptio*, excusing the promisor if their performance had been prevented by *vis maior*, for penal stipulations entered into in other contexts (e.g., in arbitration agreements or maritime loan contracts). The uneven terrain created by

51. D.45.1.115.2 (Pap. 2 *quaest.*).

52. The reason for the special availability of the *exceptio* in this context must be that the defendant had little choice but to heed the praetor's instruction to promise to reappear on postponement of the proceedings *in iure*. See, further, D.2.11.2.3–8 (Ulp. 74 *ad ed.*); Lenel, *EP*[3], 501; Reinhard Zimmermann, *The Law of Obligations: Roman Foundations of the Civilian Tradition* (Cape Town: Juta, 1990), 106.

these juristic opinions together with the combination of *exceptiones* of both general and special application, created space for further *interpretatio* to regularize the approach across the field. The effect of Sabinus' rule, to postpone actionability to the promisor's fault, was therefore to produce a single regulatory framework that defined when a penal stipulation should be treated as realized, regardless of the context in which the agreement was made.

(2) Alignment of the moment at which the stipulation becomes actionable with the onset of *mora*. A debtor was deemed to be in default (*mora*) as soon as he was at fault for his failure to perform.[53] This was a question of fact; though in practice a creditor could put the debtor on notice by serving him with a legitimate demand (*interpellatio*). In the above text, the question is raised whether such a demand is required to put the debtor into default: to which Julian replies in the negative. It has sometimes been held that, when a condition contained a deadline, the passing of the deadline substituted for the personal service of the demand (*dies interpellat pro homine*). But in circumstances when the actionability of the stipulation was postponed, notwithstanding that the deadline had passed, it can hardly have been the case that the notional demand triggering *mora* occurred on the *dies*, though the debtor was not yet at fault for his failure to perform. By making the timings of the actionability of the stipulation and the onset of *mora* concurrent, that is, by making both depend upon the promisor showing fault, Sabinus unites actionability and *mora* into a general regulatory framework.

D.45.1.122.1 (Scaev. 28 *dig.*): A Case Study

At the end of the Papinianic mass in D.45.1, the compilers have inserted an extended passage (taken from the appendix mass) from the 28th book of Q. Cervidius Scaevola's *digesta*. In the fragment after the *principium*, a response has been included by the epitomator of the *digesta* that was given by Scaevola in response to a question arising from the interpretation of a maritime loan contract entered into by a merchant called Callimachus.[54] The text is corrupt

53. See, generally, Mario Varvaro, "Stipulationsklage mit unbestimmten (actio ex stipulatu) und bestimmten Klageinhalt (condictio)," in *HRP*, 2:1933. A brief summary of the Roman rules may be found in David Johnston, "Breach of Contract," in *A History of Private Law in Scotland*, ed. Kenneth Reid and Reinhard Zimmermann (Oxford: Oxford University Press, 2000), 176.

54. For a discussion of the *cautio* reported in the text, see above, 4–7.

at points. In the late nineteenth and early twentieth centuries, it was mainly assumed that this was due to interference by the sixth-century compilers of Justinian's *Digest*. As von Lübtow argued in a thorough and detailed exegesis of the fragment in the mid-1970s, however, those alterations that can be detected more likely originated in the process of compilation of Scaevola's *digesta*, which consisted of an anthology of the jurist's *responsa* that was put together posthumously from the papers comprising his estate in about the middle of the third century CE.[55] The replies themselves, which are often given in response to questions asked in the context of Greek materials (contracts, wills, and so forth) but from the perspective of Roman law, are characterized by brevity and frequently related without justification.

Von Lübtow's proposed amendments to Mommsen's edition of the text are mostly persuasive.[56] In appendix II (no. 2) I have presented von Lübtow's version of the text with changes indicated, alongside the text of the Mommsen edition. The translation below follows upon the alterations suggested by von Lübtow. The translation will be followed by a discussion of the basis for those changes and the implications for our interpretation of the legal problem that Scaevola was asked to address.

> D.45.1.122.1 (Scaev. 28 *dig.*):
>
> Callimachus took from Stichus, slave of Seius, a money loan on maritime terms (*nautica*) in the province of Syria for a sea voyage from Berytus to Brentesium. It was lent for the full two hundred days of sailing under pledge and hypothec over the goods purchased at Berytus to be transported to Brentesium and over those that would be bought at Brentesium for carriage by ship to Berytus. And it was agreed between them, that after Callimachus had arrived at Brentesium he himself would depart for Syria before what would then be the next *ides* of September with other goods having been purchased and loaded onto a vessel, or, if by the aforementioned date he had not replenished the merchandise nor sailed out from that *civitas*, that he would return the whole sum as if he had completed the voyage without interruption and pay all the costs of those escorting the money so that they might take it to Rome. And this is what Callimachus promised in faith to Stichus, slave of Lucius Titius, would be properly given and done in response to his question.

55. von Lübtow, "Das Seedarlehen," 330–31; cf. Marina Frunzio, "Il caso della Sfortunata navigazione di Callimaco: D.45.1.122.1 (SCAEV. 28 DIG.)," *SDHI* 83 (2017): 271–97 (with literature).

56. See, generally, von Lübtow, "Das Seedarlehen."

> And when, pursuant to the agreement, the goods were loaded onto the ship before the aforementioned ides, he sailed out ostensibly for Syria <after the ides> with Eros, fellow slave of Stichus <, who had been sent with him and to whom nothing more concerning the money previously mentioned was permitted or authorized after the agreed date, than that he should take receipt of it and convey it to Rome>, the question arose:–since Callimachus had sent the goods to be carried to Berytus onto the ship according to the agreement <, but had sailed out> at the time he ought to have paid back the money at Brentesium to be taken to Rome, whether, the ship having sunk, Eros' consent was to his benefit or whether Callimachus could nevertheless be held to an *actio ex stipulatu* concerning the money by the master of Stichus? He [Scaevola] replied that according to what was put forward he was bound. Likewise, I asked if the above-mentioned Eros had given his consent to Callimachus to set sail after the appointed date, whether he could deprive his master of an action already acquired? He replied that he could not, but that there was room for an *exceptio* if the slave had been granted the discretion to have the money returned at whatever time in whatever place.

Few substantive issues are raised by the part of the text in which Scaevola relates the terms of the loan agreement. The switching of the (stock) name of the master of Stichus from Seius to Lucius Titius is well known and insignificant. In the sentence *aliis mercibus . . . proficiscatur* von Lübtow would have *missis* for *mercis*, Biscardi *impositis*: either is acceptable as a replacement for the errant noun.[57] Von Lübtow would also have the grammatically correct *ipsam* for *ipse*, though Biscardi would preserve this as a common Graecism. The more significant problems arise in the passage following the report that the contract was concluded as a stipulation. First, it is apparent that the words *et cum ante idus* cannot refer to *enavigavit*, since if Callimachus had left Brentesium before September 13 there would be no potential breach and no question could arise. The blunt solution proposed by Alciatus was to introduce a *non* into the phrase (i.e., *et cum <non> ante*).[58] More plausibly, Huschke, who von Lübtow follows on this point, suggested that the words *post idus* have been eliminated after *impositis*, the letters POSTID in the original manuscript looking much like a

57. For both this and the next point, Arnaldo Biscardi, "Pecunia traiecticia e stipulatio poenae," *Labeo* 24 (1978): 295.

58. Alciatus, *Parerga* X.19. Hugo Donellus proposed [*cum*] <*non*> *ante idus*. On this point, see C. F. von Glück, *Ausführliche Erläuterung der Pandecten nach Hellfeld: Ein Commentar* (Erlangen: Johann Jacob Palm, 1820), XXI:178; also, Huvelin, *Droit commercial romain*, 201–2.

repetition of POSITIS (after *impositis*).[59] If so, this would bring out the contrast between Callimachus' success in loading the goods before September 13 and his failure to depart before that date. Next, the expression *quasi in provinciam Syriam enavigavit* has produced a variety of interpretations. Where De Martino would delete it altogether, most scholars (von Lübtow and Biscardi included) would retain it.[60] Robert took the phrase to mean that Callimachus had changed his route to Syria in midsail.[61] As Krampe points out, there is nothing in the facts to suggest this, and the surest interpretation remains that *quasi* only indicates that although Callimachus left Brentesium intending for Syria, that intention was never fulfilled.[62] Von Lübtow would then move the relative clause *qui cum . . . Romam perferret* to the *narratio*, though to no great effect since in either case the clause would refer to the extent of Eros' authority without prejudice to the substance of the *quaestio*.

The sentence *cum secundum . . . deberet* calls for emendation. Mommsen's text indicates that Callimachus had kept to the terms of the agreement by remaining at Brentesium after the debt had become due, which plainly contradicts the earlier statement that he had set out for Syria (after the ides). Not satisfied by the suggestions made by earlier scholars that the sentence ought to be excised as a suspected interpolation, von Lübtow argued (following Cujas, Duarenus, and Robert), that the problem more likely proceeded from a scribal error, that mistook *in navem misisset* for *in nave mansisset*.[63] Reading the former, the sentence would now indicate that Callimachus had complied with the terms of the contract by loading the goods before the ides. Von Lübtow further suggested (following Cujas, Huschke, and Amann) that the word *set* (*sed*) was eliminated as a repetition after the termination of *misisset*, after which *enavigasset* may be supplied to bring out the contrast with Callimachus' delayed departure.[64] He concluded that the clause under discussion therefore originally contained two conditions: first, that Callimachus stow the merchandise he had purchased at Brentesium on board the ship before September 13; and second, that he was required to leave for Syria by the same date.[65] If he failed to perform in these terms, he would be obliged to pay the whole amount of the debt (*universa pecunia*, including costs) immediately to Eros, who had been instructed

59. Ph. Eduard Huschke, "Das Schifflehen des Callimachus," *Zeitschrift für Civilrecht und Prozeß* Neue Folge 10 (1853): 11; also, von Lübtow, "Das Seedarlehen," 340.
60. Francesco De Martino, "Sul foenus nauticum," *RDN* 1, no. 3 (1935): 242.
61. Jean Robert, *Receptae iuris Civilis lectionis, libri II* (Helmstadt: Lucius, 1586), Lib. I.I.
62. Krampe, "Der Seedarlehensstreit," 220.
63. For the older literature, see von Glück, *Ausführliche Erläuterung*, XXI:178–79.
64. von Lübtow, "Das Seedarlehen," 344.
65. von Lübtow, "Das Seedarlehen," 345.

to transport the money to Rome. Correspondingly, the facts were that although Callimachus had loaded the goods before the ides, he had failed to depart on time, albeit with Eros' consent. The ship then sank along the route, preventing the condition *salva nave* from materializing, so that Callimachus' obligation under the main contract to pay back the debt never arose. Scaevola was therefore asked whether the creditor still had an action for the recovery of a sum of money equivalent to the amount of the whole debt (including the costs incurred in connection with the services of his slave Eros) under the terms of the (penal) condition, notwithstanding that the original debt had not become due because the condition *salva nave* had failed to materialize.

Like Biscardi, I am substantially in agreement with the main substance of von Lübtow's interpretation.[66] Further, the plausibility of von Lübtow's conjectures is supported by additional contextual considerations. The contract likely had real origins.[67] The issue also bears striking parallels with the question of the existence of a *symbolaion* in *Against Phormiōn*.[68] In that case, Chrysippos claimed that the contract contained a clause binding Phormiōn to pay a fine of 5,000 dr. if he did not load goods into the ship at Bosporos for return to Athens. The vessel having perished on its way back to Piraeus, Phormiōn claimed relief under the condition *salva nave*; the creditors argue that the obligation to pay the penalty has arisen notwithstanding the failure of the condition; Phormiōn responds that he had in any case discharged his liabilities to Chrysippos by paying Lampis at the outport. Like Phormiōn, Callimachus, too, may well have sought shelter under the failure of the condition *salva nave*; the creditor argues that the penalty is in any case owing; Callimachus responds that the goods were loaded in time and that he only departed after September 13 with Eros' consent; the creditor points out that Eros was not authorized to give that consent: Scaevola is asked his opinion. We do not know what the jury decided in Phormiōn's case. We do, however, know Scaevola's decision—penalty due.

The report of Scaevola's opinion is typically laconic and gives no indications

66. Biscardi, "Pecunia traiecticia," 294.

67. For the arguments in support of this view, see above, 6–7.

68. According to Paoli, the transactions described in *Against Phormiōn* and D.45.1.122.1 are structurally different and do not bear comparison: Paoli, *Studi di diritto*, 30–33. Paoli cites Dem. 34.30 to show that Phormiōn was contractually entitled to discharge his liabilities at reduced interest at the outport. He then contrasts this with the Callimachus contract, which made the debtor liable to repay a sum equivalent to the whole debt with costs if he failed to load a cargo and leave by September 13: a penalty rather than an option. At Dem. 34.30, however, there is no indication that Phormiōn is entitled to pay a reduced yield: rather, Chrysippos expresses surprise that Phormiōn would not take care to have witnesses present when (so he claims) he paid back "both the debt and the yield for both journeys." The tenor of the agreement therefore appears to have been that Phormiōn was entitled to pay back *universa pecunia* at any point by paying the carrier, Lampis (Dem. 34.32). Having failed to sell his wares, Phormiōn's choice at Bosporus was either to pay the whole debt early or load a fresh cargo: if he did neither, the penalty would fall due.

as to his reasoning. The key to unlocking the legal problem at the heart of the text is to begin by scrutinizing its palingenetic and compilatorial context. We have already said that the text's inscription indicates that it was drawn from the private collection of the jurist's *responsa*, which consisted in a large part of replies constructed upon the interpretation of Greek documentary materials through the prism of Roman law. The process by which the text came to be included by the sixth-century compilers in the *Digest* title on stipulation (D.45.1) yields further information. In the *editio maior*, Mommsen indicates in the margins of the folios the mass (according to Bluhme's *Massentheorie*) from which each text is supposed to have been drawn.[69] In the 45th book of the *Digest* (*de verborum obligationibus*), the first text of the Papinianic mass is D.45.1.115, the second paragraph of which is dedicated to Papinian's discussion of the debate concerning the timing of the satisfaction of conditions not containing a time limit. Later in the same mass, the passage excerpted from Scaevola's *digesta* has been inserted, but from a different mass altogether (the appendix). In other words, the compilers deliberately inserted D.45.1.122 at the end of a run of texts drawn from a different mass, which were introduced by a leading text on the timing of the satisfaction of penal stipulations. Now, the connection between the two texts—insofar as the compiler's may have inferred one—is slight, and therefore ought not to be pressed too far.[70] However, it remains a possibility that the compilers saw some connection between Scaevola's *responsa* preserved in D.45.1.122 and the surrounding fragments, which were introduced by the passage from Papinian's *quaestiones*.

The compiler's conscious placement of the text at the end of the Papinianic mass suggests that it had a particular analytical context, that is, the interpretation of penal stipulations and the timing of their fulfillment. The structure of the analysis should therefore proceed on this basis. We recall that, like Phormiōn, Callimachus was relieved of his obligation to pay the main debt on failure of the condition *salva nave*, so that the creditor was compelled to seek recovery on other grounds. The creditor's contention is that Callimachus is liable under the contract for failing to depart Brentesium by the appointed date; and further, that he therefore owes a sum equivalent to the total amount of the debt (i.e., both the capital and the fixed yield), together with the cost of taking the money to Rome. The utility of a penal stipulation that enumerates a liability for the promisor equivalent to the one it secures is that, notwithstanding that the creditor might bring suit on different contractual grounds (*mutuum*, *stipulatio*), the documentation produced by the creditor at the *editio* stage of pro-

69. I am indebted to Prof. Jakob Stagl for his observations on this point.

70. See, also, D.45.1.122.2 (Scaev. 28 *dig.*), which concerns the timing of the forfeiture of a penal stipulation: on which, Knütel, *Stipulatio poenae*, 172–74.

ceedings would be the same in either event (i.e., whether the suit was brought for the main debt or the sum due on fulfillment of the condition).

The starting point for the analysis is the clause in the contract, which Scaevola summarizes as follows:

> . . . after Callimachus had arrived at Brentesium he himself would depart for Syria before what would then be the next *ides* of September with other goods having been purchased and loaded onto a vessel, or, if by the aforementioned date he had not replenished the merchandise nor sailed out from that *civitas*, that he would return the whole sum as if he had completed the voyage without interruption and pay all the costs of those escorting the money so that they might take it to Rome.

The question is whether the condition should be treated as realized, such that Callimachus will be liable to pay the whole amount of the debt with costs. The starting position is that the condition will be treated as realized if Callimachus has failed to perform by the appointed date (*dies praestitutus*), that is, September 13. Since it is established that the date had passed before Callimachus sailed out from Brentesium, he is *prima facie* in breach. He does however have two possible counterarguments at his disposal: (1) that notwithstanding the breach, the condition ought not to be treated as realized; or (2) (in the alternative) successfully pleading an *exceptio*.

In connection with (1), Callimachus has two possible arguments: (a) that the two limbs of the condition should be interpreted as cumulative, not alternative (a construction point); and (b) that an action ought to be denied to the creditor because its satisfaction was induced by the person who stood to benefit. Since we are told that Scaevola held for the creditor, it follows that he must have rejected these arguments. How did Scaevola reach these conclusions?

(a) *The interpretation of the two limbs of the condition as cumulative or alternative.* The first part of the relevant clause stipulates that Callimachus is bound to perform two separate acts by September 13: *viz.*, (1) to purchase a fresh cargo and load the goods onto a vessel; and (2) to sail out from the port at Brentesium for Syria. The facts are that Callimachus accomplished (1) but failed (2). The interpretive question that arises is whether (as a point of construction) the penalty should fall due on the promisor's failure to perform only one or both of the required acts. As Krampe has pointed out, another text by Scaevola drawn from the 12th book of his *quaestiones* provides some insight into the jurist's views on this point:[71]

71. Krampe, "Der Seedarlehensstreit," 218–19.

D.45.1.129 (Scaev. 12 *quaest.*):

> If someone stipulates as follows, "do you give 10 pounds if the ship arrives and Titius becomes consul," the sum is not due unless both happen. Conversely, "do you promise to pay if the ship does not arrive and Titius does not become consul" requires that neither should happen. The formulation "if neither the ship arrives nor Titius becomes consul" is similar. But if it goes, "will you pay, if the ship comes or Titius becomes consul," one is enough. Conversely, "will you pay if the ship does not come or Titius does not become consul" is satisfied if one does not happen.

According to Scaevola, in a condition with two actions joined by a conjunctive, the condition ought only to be treated as satisfied when both events have occurred (or not occurred, as the case may be). In the Callimachus loan, the framing of the condition is analogous to the formulation "if neither the ship arrives nor Titius becomes consul," which Scaevola says is analogous to the first formulation. The consistent application of this reasoning would produce the conclusion that Callimachus was not bound under the condition, since he had only failed to perform in respect of one of the two required actions. Scaevola's decision, however, is to the contrary: the jurist interprets the two limbs of the condition as alternative. Krampe's suggestion is that Scaevola reaches this interpretation by referring directly to the parties' intentions as they appear from the whole context of the agreement. This makes sense: from the creditor's perspective, it was not enough that Callimachus should depart before the ides but without the goods, nor that he should load the goods but fail to leave on time. The parties' intention was that Callimachus should leave with a return cargo before or on September 13, after which date, the creditor was not willing to tolerate the increased risk of sailing in the offseason. Notwithstanding the parties' chosen formulation, the interpretation that gave proper effect to their intentions was therefore that the limbs of the condition should be understood as alternative.

(b) *Fulfillment of the condition induced by the interested party.* The second argument potentially open to Callimachus is that the creditor ought to be denied an action because the condition's satisfaction was induced by the person who stood to benefit from its fulfillment. The substance of the claim is that Callimachus only departed Brentesium after the deadline because he had obtained the permission of Eros, the lender's representative. The *exceptio doli* must be excluded because it only lay if the stipulator had acted *dolo malo*, which is not in evidence. However, it might have been open to Callimachus to argue on the strength of the juristic opinions of Servius and later

Pomponius (D.22.2.8 and D.4.8.40) that the creditor ought to be denied an action, because it was his responsibility that Callimachus had departed late from Brentesium such that the realization of the condition had been induced by the person standing to benefit.

Scaevola (impliedly) rejects this argument on the basis that Eros was not authorized to do anything with the money, other than to transport it to Rome after the time limit had passed. The reasoning suggests that the jurist had in mind the following question, *viz.*, whether a condition should be treated as satisfied if its fulfillment had been brought about by the creditor's representative, where the representative was acting beyond the scope of his authority. Scaevola decides not—the creditor's plea of lack of authority (with no evidence of knowledge on his part) is sufficient to remove this case from the scope of Servius' opinion. Scaevola then goes on to suggest that had Eros possessed the appropriate authorization, an *exceptio* (probably *pacti*) would have been available to Callimachus to defend the action. This would suggest that the principle behind Servius' opinion did not extend to the case in which the creditor was *ignorans* but would have if his representative had acted *ex voluntate*. We are left in the dark as to the position if it were possible to trace Eros' exercise of his apparent authority back to some act or omission of the principal (or perhaps his *scientia* or *patentia*).

Viewed from a distance, the problem explored by Scaevola is that which in the modern world animates the doctrine of apparent or ostensible authority. In the modern law, a principal is normally only bound by the acts of their agent performed within the scope of their authority. But from the early nineteenth century, a doctrine was developed whereby a principal could be bound by acts outside of the scope of an agent's authority, if (for example) the principal had by his conduct or representations created the impression in the third party's mind that the agent possessed the authority to act.[72] In the ancient world, the problem of agents acting beyond the scope of their authority manifested itself most acutely in maritime trade. But in both cases where it is approached—that is, in the context of the exercitorian edict and maritime loan contracts—the discussion is conducted through the lens of the interpretation of the particular edict or contract from which the issue arose. In this text, the question is therefore whether the condition should be treated as realized, when its fulfilment was induced by the representations of an agent acting beyond the scope of their authority. In the absence of any information to show the principal's knowledge

72. A similar problem is raised in the context of the exercitorian edict, where the question is whether the subappointee of a *magister navis* could bind the principal in contract, if the *magister* was not authorized to make the subappointment but acted with the principal's knowledge and acquiescence (*scientia et patientia*): D.14.1.1.5 (Ulp. 28 *ad ed.*). See Candy, "Limits," 149–51.

of, or acquiescence to, Eros' representations, Scaevola decided in the negative. But had Scaevola introduced this information into the problem, we might have had the makings of the modern doctrine.

*Condition (*salva nave*) Prevented from Materializing*

The Roman materials provide only one example of a case in which the decision turned on the interpretation of the condition *salva nave*. The details are provided in a constitution issued by the Emperors Diocletian and Maximian in response to a petition brought by a certain Aurelia Juliana, probably in the late 280s:

> C.4.33.4 (Diocl./Maxim. AA. Aureliae Iulianae):
>
> Since you say that you gave a maritime loan on condition that, after the voyage, which the debtor affirmed was directed at Africa, the money loaned at interest would be repaid to you on the ship's arrival into the port of the Salonitani, so that you assumed the risk of the voyage insofar as its destination was Africa; and that through the fault of the borrower, who did not even pay attention to the destination of the voyage, the *fiscus* confiscated the ship which was holding illicit goods he had purchased: the *ius publicum* does not permit the loss of the lost merchandise, which is affirmed not to have happened as the result of a storm at sea, but of the debtor's reckless avarice and impetuous boldness, to be ascribed to you.

The constitution is usually cited for its unique attestation of a female engaged in maritime finance.[73] It is also a rare example of a single (*heteroploun*) loan: possibly the money raised from the sale of the goods in Africa was intended for transport back to Salona (modern-day Split, Dalmatia) without being reinvested in a second cargo.[74] Despite the dubious economics of such an arrangement, the chronological distribution of shipwreck sites with evidence of coins among the assemblage do show that the physical transport of coinage was a more common occurrence by the late third century CE than previously.[75]

73. See, e.g., Verena Halbwachs, "Ipsae sibi negotia tractant: Zur Frau als Geschäftpartnerin im Spiegel römischrechtlicher Quellen," in *Règle et pratique du droit dans les réalités juridiques de l'antiquité*, ed. Isabella Piro (Catanzaro: Rubbettino, 1999), 349–63.

74. Cf. D.13.4.2.8 (Ulp. 27 *ad ed.*), which envisages a loan of *pecunia traiecticia* given for a one-way trip that was repayable at the voyage's destination.

75. Harris, "A Strange Fact," 150–55.

The text may be taken in three parts. The first part—the *narratio*—is relatively straightforward: Aurelia Juliana gave a loan on maritime terms to a debtor for an expedition from Dalmatia to Africa and assumed the risk for the outbound leg of the journey. If the transaction was in any way conventional, there would have been a loan dossier including a loan contract concluded as a stipulation. We know, for example, that the money was lent "at interest" (*fenebris*), which suggests that the loan was purely financial in structure and that it was given at the lender's risk by the inclusion in the agreement of a condition *salva nave*.

The middle part of the text describes the conduct of the debtor. Though the phrasing is a little awkward, the sense is relatively clear: having taken the money, the borrower used it to acquire "illegal" goods, after which he intentionally sailed somewhere other than the agreed destination. Perhaps, as Rathbone has suggested, the goods were not illicit when they were acquired, but only made so by the borrower's evasion of customs duties.[76] In any case, the fisc intervened to make a seizure (*fiscum occupasse*). At this point, ambiguity in the text allows for two possible interpretations: either the fisc only seized the merchandise (as per Rathbone's translation), or they also confiscated the ship (as per the translations by Blume and now Frier). The latter interpretation is confirmed by a text originating from the roughly contemporaneous *Sententiae* of [pseudo-]Paul:

> PS.5.1a.12:[77]
>
> If either the owner of a ship or passengers on it bring anything on board illegally, the ship is forfeit to the imperial treasury as well. But if something of the sort is done, in the absence of the owner, by the master or steersman or the pilot or any of the sailors, the latter are liable to capital punishment, and the goods are confiscated, but the ship is returned to its owner.

If, as would appear from the adventitious nature of the enterprise, Aurelia Juliana's debtor was a *nauklēros*, the discovery of contraband by the fisc would have entitled them to confiscate both the offending cargo and the ship.[78]

76. Rathbone, "Financing," 217.

77. = D.39.4.11.2 (Paul. 5 *sent.*). Translation by Alan Watson. The rule that a shipowner's vessel might be forfeit despite their having no knowledge of, or involvement in, the illegal use of the property, continues to apply in various jurisdictions. The rationale is, at least in part, to impose an obligation on the shipowner to prevent the illegal use of the property.

78. Cf. D.19.2.61.1 (Scaev. 7 *dig.*), in which a ship that was detained at a port in the African

The case bears similarities with the speech *Against Dionysodōros*. In that case, the borrowers had put into the port at Rhodes, allegedly for repairs, only to claim (among other things) that by not returning to Athens the condition *salva nave* had failed to materialize, relieving them of their obligation to pay. Aurelia Juliana's debtor appears to have run the same argument. While the contract between Dionysodōros and his creditors had included a penalty clause, however, Aurelia Juliana does not seem to have protected her interests in the same manner (just like the debtors in the speech *Against Lakritos*), placing the onus upon her to argue against the operation of the condition. In the suit *Against Dionysodōros*, the creditors framed the issue in the following terms:

> For who other than this fellow [Dionysodōros] is to blame, men of the jury, if the ship did not arrive safe at Piraeus? Are we to blame, who lent our money expressly for a voyage to Egypt and to Athens, or is it the fault of this fellow and his partner, who after borrowing money on these terms, that the vessel should return to Athens, then took her to Rhodes? And that they did this of their own will and not of necessity is clear on many grounds . . . [79]

The only response available to Aurelia was therefore that the reason that the condition had been prevented from materializing was not an event beyond the debtor's control (like, for example, shipwreck), but rather one that came about because of his blameworthy conduct (*vitium debitoris*).[80] In other words, the question was whether a condition that had been prevented from materializing by the person who stood to benefit from its nonfulfillment should be treated as realized. As D.50.17.161 shows, the "received view" by the time of Ulpian was that a rule equating prevention with satisfaction existed in the field of stipulation. Assuming that Aurelia Juliana had concluded her *nautikē syngraphē* by stipulation (recorded in a *cautio*), the case reported in C.4.33.4 would appear to have been one in which this civil law rule could straightforwardly have been applied. While the emperors reach a decision consistent with the rule (in Aurelia Juliana's favor), however, they cite the *ius publicum*, not the civil law, as the source of their finding. The question as to whether the emperors had in mind the civil law rule in making their decision must therefore be left open.

---

province of Cyrene was eventually allowed to sail on to Aquileia, but only after its cargo of olive oil and grain had been confiscated by the authorities.

79. Dem. 56.42. Translation by Norman W. DeWitt.

80. If the debtor had been fraudulent the *actio de dolo* might lie. "*Vitium debitoris*" must therefore refer to the debtor's fault.

Conclusion

Conditions in maritime loan contracts were at the heart of their commercial operation. In the fourth-century Athenian courts, disputes arising from the interpretation of these conditions were played out against the backdrop of two pieces of legislation: the first establishing the *dikai emporikai* and the second providing for the enforceability of private agreements. Against this background, litigants argued over the admissibility of suits and the interpretation of the contract, in the latter case balancing the strict operation of the condition against considerations of fairness (*epieikeia*). The problem was then thrown upon the jury to weigh up the parties' competing arguments. At Rome, the same contracts must have continued to generate litigation, only in a different legal context. If the agreement was concluded as a stipulation, similar interpretive problems arose, especially when the exclusion of considerations of good faith in the adjudication of the dispute would appear to produce injustice. To some extent, at least from the first half of the first century BCE, the potential for inequity was reduced by both juristic and praetorian interventions, in the latter case through the introduction of edictal *exceptiones*. However, the unevenness in coverage provided the space for further juristic work, particularly the development of rules—often by analogy with rules already established in testamentary succession—concerning the timing of the fulfillment of conditions and the circumstances in which they should be treated as realized. Together with the available *exceptiones*, the evolution of these rules provided a basis for bringing equitable considerations into civil proceedings where an otherwise literal approach to the interpretation of contractual conditions would appear to produce injustice.

CHAPTER FIVE

Financial Terminology and the Regulation of Interest Rates

It is commonly assumed that both the Athenians and the Romans drew a fundamental distinction between different types of loan for consumption (*daneismos*, *mutuum*): that is, between ordinary or landed loans on the one hand, and maritime loans on the other.[1] This is reflected in the modern terminology, which refers to loans given subject to a *nautikē syngraphē* as maritime or nautical loans, *prêts maritimes (à la grosse aventure)*; *prestito marittimo*, *Seedarlehen*, or the like. In English, the terms *bottomry* and *respondentia*, which became popular as a form of financing in the sixteenth and seventeenth centuries, are sometimes also used.[2] The same assumption continues to inform studies into "sea loans" in both the Greek and Roman contexts.[3] In textbooks of Roman law, maritime loans often feature after *mutuum* as (for example) "der Sondertyp des Seedarlehens" ("the special type of sea loan").[4]

This chapter argues that the supposed primacy of the distinction between different types of loan for consumption was not familiar to the ancient mind but is rather the product of modern (especially Pandectist) thinking. The argument in brief is that the ancients (both Greek and later Roman) had only the single conception of a loan for consumption, that could generate either a maritime or landed yield. A yield was maritime when it was produced by a loan given on maritime terms, that is, subject to a maritime loan contract. A contract was maritime when it included a condition *salva nave*, which had the unique effect of producing a yield that was not susceptible to denomination by time, because

1. My remarks in this chapter are confined to loans for consumption. The ancients did, of course, distinguish between loans for consumption and loans for use (i.e., *chrēsis*, *commodatum*). For the Greek distinction, see Arist. *Eth. Nic.* 1131a2–5: on which, Phillips, *Law*, 371–72. For the Roman law, see G.3.90 together with 4.47.

2. Strictly these latter two terms refer to loans taken out by shipmasters to fund urgent repairs to a vessel on security of the ship (bottomry) or the cargo (respondentia). Like loans given at a maritime yield, however, they share the basic similarity that they too were given subject to a condition *salva nave*, so that their use in this context is perfectly sensible: De Ste Croix, "Maritime Loans," 41.

3. See, e.g., Schuster, *Das Seedarlehen*; Pontoriero, *Il prestito marittimo*.

4. Kaser, *RP*, 1:532–33; and cf. now Fargnoli, "Condictio," in *HRP*, 2:1910–11.

the duration of the voyage was uncertain. If the loan was not given on maritime terms, it produced a yield that was susceptible to denomination by time, which because it stood in contrast to a maritime yield was conceived (originally by the Greeks) as landed. The *fons et origo* of this terminological framework was the *nautikē syngraphē*, which produced the contrast between a maritime yield (i.e., a yield that was not susceptible to denomination by time) and the time-denominated interest produced by loans given on conventional terms.

To make this argument out we need to work through both the Greek and Roman material. On the Greek side, this consists mainly of the speeches of the Attic orators together with a handful of fragmentary commercial documents. Significant headway has already been made on these by Cohen, whose analysis I shall consider in detail in the next section. On the Roman side, more work is required, mainly owing to the nature of the sources, which consist chiefly of juridical texts requiring careful examination. The chapter concludes with a reappraisal of Justinian's legislative interventions into the regulation of maritime lending.

Financial Concepts in Ancient Greek Thought

The ancient Greeks viewed the world of trade through the prism of a constellation of concepts that structured their understanding of commercial activity. The mental framework inhabited by the Greeks, though it may have been original to ancient Greek thought, was deeply influential on later civilizations, not least the Romans, whose own conception came to be shaped by it. The whole question of Greek commercial thought was considered about 30 years ago by Cohen, who had many important insights.[5] Though it was already known that the ancient Greeks made a distinction between landed and maritime yields, for a long time it was thought that this was secondary to the distinction between types of loan, which depended upon the nature of the security on which they were given.[6] In the traditional account, landed loans were those given on real security, maritime loans standing simply in contrast.[7] The nature of the yield

5. Edward E. Cohen, "Athenian Finance: Maritime and Landed Yields," *Classical Antiquity* 8, no. 2 (1989): 207–23; Cohen, *Athenian Economy*, 44–60.

6. Cohen traces the interpretation at back to at least A. Bernhard Büchsenschütz, *Besitz und Erwerb im griechischen Altertum* (Halle: Verlag der Buchhandlung des Waisenhauses, 1869), 490. See, also, Korver, *De terminologie*, 150. For further discussion, see Cohen, *Athenian Economy*, 45 n. 24.

7. Cf. Paoli, who saw that 'landed loans' were not characterized by their being given on real security, but by their "simple antithesis" ("semplice contrapposto") to 'maritime loans': Paoli, *Studi di diritto*, 60 n. 5 and 93 n. 1.

was therefore determined by the type of loan that produced it: landed yields proceeding from loans made on real security, maritime yields from maritime loans. Cohen, however, saw that the fundamental distinction in Greek commercial thought was not between types of loan, but types of yield. On his account, the distinction turned upon the method by which the yield was calculated (by time or as a fixed sum). A loan was therefore maritime when it produced a yield that was not susceptible to denomination by time, and conversely landed when it generated one that was. Crucially, Cohen preserved the distinction between different types of loan, but simply reversed the hierarchy by making the distinction between types of loan secondary to the distinction between yields.

Though I agree with Cohen's analysis on many points, my interpretation of the evidence differs in several important respects. To take the discussion forward, I will begin by following Cohen's argument, before indicating the moment at which I depart and explaining my reasons for doing so. The starting point here is the tendency in Greek thought toward binary opposition and polarization.[8] Comprehending the world through the prism of contrast and antithesis, particularly by setting up pairs of complementary opposites, was a dominant feature of Greek classical culture and thought. The doctrine of contrastive opposition was a feature of Greek philosophy from an early stage,[9] manifesting itself in the Greek language, in particles (such as the *men* . . . *de* . . . construction) that operated in the balancing or opposition of two elements; and in Greek literature, theater, and art, which depended to a great extent upon linked polarity (e.g., male/female, mortal/divine, man/beast, city/wild) to generate dramatic effect. The opposition of land and sea was also physically and culturally built into the very layout and location of Greek settlements: the main inland city (*to astu*), organized around its landed business center (*agora*), set apart from the often-subsidiary maritime commercial center (*emporion*), usually situated on the coast. As Cohen writes, "In a world perceived in opposites, no structural polarity was more basic than the fundamental contrast between land and sea, between the nonmaritime and maritime spheres."[10]

The fundamental antithesis of land and sea also pervades Greek financial terminology. Cohen's opening statement on this theme is that "this physical separation [between *agora* and *emporion*] was paralleled in financial matters

8. Geoffrey E. R. Lloyd, *Polarity and Analogy: Two Types of Argumentation in Early Greek Thought* (Cambridge: Cambridge University Press, 1966), 15–85; Richard Garner, *Law and Society in Classical Athens* (London: Croom Helm, 1987), 76; Cohen, *Athenian Economy*, 46–52; Cohen, "Commercial Law," 290–92.

9. Nicholas Rescher, *Cosmos and Logos: Studies in Greek Philosophy* (Frankfurt: Ontos Verlag, 2005), 33–46.

10. Cohen, *Athenian Economy*, 47.

by a corresponding, pervasive conceptualization of all loans as either landed (*eggeia*) or maritime (*nautika*)."[11] This is followed by the similar observation that "a contract can be 'landed' (*eggeion*) or 'maritime' (*nautikon*)."[12] Now, for reasons that I will explain in a moment, I think that neither of these statements is accurate, at least for fourth-century BCE Athens. On the other hand, Cohen is right to identify the significance of the contrast in other areas. Assets were grouped according to whether they were maritime or nonmaritime: in Xenophon's *Symposion*, maritime and landed possessions are juxtaposed;[13] and in the contract produced in the speech *Against Lakritos*, the creditors were entitled to proceed against the debtors' property "both landed and maritime."[14] Similarly, in Demosthenes' speech *Against Aphobos I*, Demosthenes lists the assets comprising his father's estate, categorizing them either as domestic (*tauta oikoi panta*) or maritime (*nautika*).[15] The same was true of investments: in Hypereidēs' criticism of Demosthenes' investment activity, his accusations distinguish between his involvement in real-estate and maritime finance; and again, the orator Lysias, in two separate cases, levels criticism at individuals who have invested childrens' assets in high-risk maritime ventures instead of land.[16] Finally, landed and maritime yields are set in contrast: at Lysias 32, for example, Diodotos' estate is said to consist in large part of the income derived from loans, which are categorized as either being at maritime or landed interest. The contrast also finds expression in the speeches collected in the Demosthenic corpus: in the oration *Against Dionysodōros*, Parmeniskos is accused of relending the money that he had borrowed to other traders "at a maritime yield";[17] while in the oration *Against Phormiōn*, the eponymous debtor borrows 120 Cyzicene staters "at landed interest" in an attempt to pay off the debt to his original (maritime) lender.[18]

As I mentioned a moment ago, Cohen's insight was to challenge the traditional account by turning the hierarchy between loans and yields on its head. His starting point was to return to the basic conception of interest in Greek and Roman thought. The word used by the ancient Greeks to denote the return

11. Cohen, *Athenian Economy*, 48.
12. Cohen, *Athenian Economy*, 49.
13. Xen. *Symp.* 4.31.
14. Dem. 35.12.
15. Dem. 27.11. As Hopper observes, "the stress on 'papers' should be noted, just as 'ship's papers' are stressed in connection with maritime loans": Robert J. Hopper, *Trade and Industry in Classical Greece* (London: Thames & Hudson, 1979), 122.
16. Lys. 32; also, Lys. frag. 428 (Carey).
17. Dem. 56.17.
18. Dem. 34.23.

on money lent out was *tokos*, which as Aristotle explained was a metaphorical extension from the original meaning of the word—a "bringing forth" or "birth"—the yield on a money loan being as the offspring (τὸ γιγνόμενον) of a parent.[19] The Romans, too, conceived of financial yields in the same terms: the word *faenus*, according to Varro, deriving "from *fetus*, or 'offspring,' and from a birth, as it were, from money, producing and giving increase."[20] As Cohen noted, to translate *tokos* (and indeed *faenus*) as interest is somewhat misleading, since in modern parlance interest is generally defined as a rate of payment for the use of money expressed as a percentage per unit of time.[21] The concept of *tokos*, however, is not inherently time-related, and is therefore better translated into English by the word yield rather than interest.

This insight provided Cohen with the platform to develop the thesis that the basic distinction drawn by the Athenians was not between different types of loan, but rather maritime and landed yields (i.e., *tokoi nautikoi* and *tokoi eggeioi*). By placing the yield at the heart of the distinction, Cohen reversed the relationship between loans and yields: whereas in the traditional account a yield was landed because it was produced by a loan given on real security, now a loan was landed only for so long as it generated a landed yield. The distinction between yields turned upon the way in which they were calculated:

> Athenian 'maritime yield' bore no relationship to time-denominated 'interest.' In turn, for the Athenians, with their tendency to antithetical but imprecise financial conceptualization, 'landed yield' derived meaning essentially through contrast to 'maritime yield.' Extensions of credit were conceived and grouped antithetically ('maritime loans,' *daneismata nautika*, and 'landed loans,' *daneismata eggeia*), and each group was characterized by a different method of calculating financial return: a 'maritime yield,' normally used in sea finance, determined by entrepreneurial factors; and a 'landed yield,' calculated on the basis of the passage of time. The term 'landed yield' is strictly a counterpoint to 'maritime yield': the Athenian tendency to antithetical conceptualization resulted in characterization of loans and yields as 'landed,' in contexts where the alternative financing was 'maritime,' even where the 'landed' loan lacked any special real-property context.[22]

19. Arist. *Pol.* 1.1258b5.
20. Gell. *NA*. 16.12.
21. Cohen, *Athenian Economy*, 45.
22. Cohen, *Athenian Economy*, 45.

To see that the basic distinction made by the Greeks was between the yields that loans generated, rather than between different types of loan, was an important step. However, the analysis can be further developed. Before setting out my own position, I need to raise two objections. Earlier I quoted two statements that I claimed were inaccurate, at least with respect to the fourth-century evidence. The first statement was that the Greeks held a "pervasive conceptualization of all loans as either 'landed' (*eggeia*) or 'maritime' (*nautika*)." Cohen leads with this statement; but without substantiating it with any evidence that directly attests to a contrast between different types of loan.[23] Further, where the division is between types of asset, the word sometimes used is *ekdosis*, which might just as well refer to money lent at a maritime yield as a maritime loan.[24] In fact, as Schuster has pointed out, the term 'δάνειον ναυτικὸν' (*daneion nautikon*) only enters the historical record for the first time in the second century CE:[25] in Plutarch's account of Cato the Elder's lending activities and in a banker's receipt preserved on papyrus dated to 149 CE.[26] This leads him to speculate that "presumably δάνειον ναυτικὸν was already known as the name for the sea loan during Demosthenes' time . . . It is not unlikely that this adjective was used early on to distinguish a sea loan from a simple loan (δάνειον, *daneion*)."[27] But all this assumes that the fourth-century Athenians drew a distinction between different types of loan, when the only firm evidence we have is that they only distinguished between landed and maritime yields.

The second objection concerns Cohen's juxtaposition of maritime with landed contracts. The first and only attestation of the expression *nautikē syngraphē* in the fourth-century evidence is in Demosthenes' oration *Against Lakritos*, in which the speaker opens by referring to a "συγγραφὴν . . . ναυτικήν."[28] The significance of the expression, however, is amply attested to by later sources.[29] Cohen adduces two fragments to make out the supposed con-

23. In the footnote appended to this statement, attention is immediately diverted to evidence for the distinction between landed and maritime assets: Cohen, *Athenian Economy*, 48 n. 36.

24. See Dem. 27.11; 29.36; 52.20. Schuster conjectures that *ekdosis* indicates that the investment was made through a banker: Schuster, *Das Seedarlehen*, 26 n. 17.

25. Schuster, *Das Seedarlehen*, 26.

26. Plut. *Vit. Cat. Mai.* 21.6: "δανεισμῶν ἐπὶ ναυτικοῖς." See, also, SB XIV 11850; Bas. 23.3.74.

27. Schuster, *Das Seedarlehen*, 26 (my translation): "Vermutlich war δάνειον ναυτικὸν als Name für das Seedarlehen schon zu Zeiten des Demosthenes geläufig . . . Es ist nicht unwahrscheinlich, dass man sich dieses Adjektivs schon früh zur Unterscheidung des Seedarlehens vom einfachen Darlehen (δάνειον, *dáneion*) bedient hat."

28. Dem. 35.1.

29. In SB XIV 11850 (second century CE), two bankers order the payment of the balance on a "maritime loan according to a maritime loan contract" ("εἰς ἔκτεισιν δάναιον ναυτικὸ(ν) κατὰ ναυτικὴν συνγραφὴν"). In SB XVIII 13167 (second century CE), the "contracts of loan" ("δα[νείου σ]υνγραφαῖς") mentioned at recto.ii.13 likely refer to (among other things) a maritime loan contract. The expression '*contractus traiecticius*' in C.4.32.26.2 (Iust., 528 CE) is synonymous with the Greek '*nautikē syngraphē*.'

trast with landed contracts. The first claim is that "when the speaker in Demosthenes 33 is justifying his use of a jurisdictional objection (the *paragraphē*), he insists that there is no agreement (*symbolaion*)—'neither maritime nor landed'—between himself and his adversary."[30] However, as Harris has argued, the word *symbolaion* "does not mean 'contract' but in legal contexts designates all 'actionable liabilities' arising either from a delict or from breach of contract or 'disputes about such liabilities.'"[31] If this is right, then the distinction at Dem. 33.3 is between "actionable liabilities" arising in maritime and landed contexts, not between maritime and landed contracts. The second document adduced by Cohen is (again) the bankers' receipt preserved on papyrus dated to 149 CE (SB XIV 11850). Here, in Cohen's words, we do find "contiguous reference . . . to . . . a 'maritime' contract, and a 'landed' contract;"[32] but the two do not stand in contrast. Rather, the landed contract refers only to the copy of the maritime loan contract that was deposited with the bankers on land.[33]

There is therefore no firm evidence for distinctions in classical Greek thought between either landed and maritime loans or landed and maritime loan contracts. Instead, what we find are references to *nautikai syngraphai* and loans productive of either landed or maritime yields, which are sometimes categorized as landed or maritime assets or investments as part of a person's estate. All this points to the centrality of the maritime loan contract as the *fons et origo* of the constellation of financial terminology that developed around it.[34] Cohen's argument was that the Greeks distinguished between yields by the way they were calculated (i.e., as a fixed proportion of the sum lent, and interest denominated by time). The problem with this distinction is that it is possible for a loan to be given for a fixed yield and for a certain term, in which case the lender's return can just as easily be expressed as a percentage rate over a period.[35] The susceptibility of a yield to denomination by time does not therefore depend upon the simple method of calculation (*pace* Cohen), but rather the underlying financial structure of the transaction. Specifically, if a loan's repayment is made conditional upon the occurrence of an uncertain event (e.g., the safe arrival of the ship or merchandise at its destination), the yield will not be susceptible to conversion to an annual rate at the outset, because the duration of the voyage

30. Dem. 33.3; Cohen, *Athenian Economy*, 49.

31. Generally, Harris, "The Meaning," 7–36, esp. 13–14. Cf., e.g., MacDowell, *Demosthenes*, 99.

32. Cohen, *Athenian Economy*, 52.

33. See, e.g., Rathbone, "Financing," 197–229.

34. Cf. Finley, who noted that the practice of committing private agreements to writing *in extenso* probably first developed in the context of maritime loan contracts: Finley, *Studies*, 96.

35. E.g., a fixed yield of one-fifth on a loan given for a term of 200 days (such as was the maximum term of the loan extended to Callimachus reported in D.45.1.122.1 (Scaev. 28 *dig.*)) is equivalent to an annual rate of 36.5 percent. It is only in virtue of the condition *salva nave* that the yield cannot be denominated by time.

is at that point unknown. The heart of the distinction between maritime and landed yields was not how, but rather why, the yield was expressed as a fixed sum: a maritime yield was one brought forth by a loan, the repayment of which was conditional upon the occurrence of an uncertain event (*viz.*, the safe arrival of the ship or the merchandise at its destination).

The source of the distinction between landed and maritime yields was therefore the inclusion of the condition *salva nave* in the (*nautikē*) *syngraphē*. It did not depend, for example, upon where or for what reason the loan was given. The loan taken by Phormiōn at the outport in Bosporos, for example, was at landed interest, even though it was given in the *emporion* in connection with a maritime venture.[36] Rather, if the loan was given on terms that the borrower was only obliged to repay if the ship returned safely, the yield was maritime because it was subject to an uncertain condition and therefore not susceptible to denomination by time.

The conclusion must be that the Athenians started with a single conception of a loan for consumption (*daneismos*). With the growth of *emporía*, loans began to be given on a new basis: that is, subject to a condition *salva nave* with the entire agreement recorded in writing in a *syngraphē*. And since these contracts were the lifeblood of *emporía*, and therefore part of the foundations upon which the whole financial world of the *emporion* was built, it is hardly surprising that this inextricable link should be expressed by the description of the *syngraphē* as *nautikē*. Considering that the defining feature of a maritime loan contract was the inclusion of a condition *salva nave* (which played a critical role in making *emporía* financially viable in the first place), this produced a fundamental distinction between yields by their susceptibility to denomination by time. It followed that a loan given subject to a *nautikē syngraphē* produced a maritime yield (*tokos nautikos*), creating a contrast with loans given on conventional terms, the interest on which was susceptible to denomination by time. Having already identified yields generated by loans given on maritime terms as *nautikoi*, the Greek tendency toward polarization dictated that interest on loans not given subject to a condition *salva nave*, if not maritime, must be landed. For the classical Greeks, loans for consumption were singular in their capacity to produce either landed or maritime yields, which distinction had its roots in the mutual development of maritime loan contracts and *emporía*.

36. Dem. 34.23.

Financial Concepts and the Regulation of Interest Rates at Rome

The traditional view expounded in the Romanist literature is that the Romans drew a primary distinction between different types of loan for consumption. Having already assumed the primacy of the distinction between different types of loan, the question for scholars has therefore been what, if anything, distinguishes a maritime from an ordinary loan, in the context of the Roman contractual system.

This debate, concerning the place of maritime loans within the Roman contractual system, has further been conducted through the prism of the distinction between the essential and accidental features of contracts.[37] If the creditor's assumption of the risk was an essential feature of a maritime loan, then their separate contractual identity would explain the derogations from the ordinary principles that governed *mutuum* (e.g., the possibility of demanding *usurae ex pacto*). On this account, both the expressions *pecunia traiecticia* and *faenus nauticum* were used synonymously (together with, e.g., *pecunia nautica*) as the *nomen iuris* of the transaction that occupied its own place within the Roman contractual system.[38] If, however, the creditor's assumption of the risk was only accidental, then maritime loans had no special contractual identity apart from the conventional framework of *mutuum* and *stipulatio*.

The original thesis that maritime loans were a special type of *mutuum* can be traced at least as far back as von Glück, who interpreted *pecunia traiecticia* as a special loan for which interest could be recovered *ex pacto*.[39] The essential feature of *pecunia traiecticia*, that differentiated it from an ordinary loan, was the creditor's assumption of the risk (*periculum creditoris*), which also justified the exception of maritime loans from the legal limit on the rate of inter-

37. See, e.g., Purpura, "Ricerche," 281: "The fundamental question in the understanding the institution—whether *periculum creditoris* was essential [to] differentiate the maritime loan from the ordinary *mutuum* and to legitimize the payment of interest exceeding the legal limit . . ." ("Questioni fondamentali per la comprensione dell'istituto—come l'essenzialità del *periculum creditoris*, che valeva a differenziare il prestito marittimo dal commune mutuo ed a legittimare la corresponsione di interessi superiori al limite legale . . ."). As Coing and others have shown, using the idea of the *natura contractus* and the accompanying terminology to interpret the classical texts carries its own danger of anachronism, since the conceptual apparatus appears only to have been adapted from Aristotelian philosophy into the legal realm at the earliest by the Byzantine lawyers: Helmut Coing, "Zum Einfluß der Philosophie des Aristoteles auf die Entwicklung des römischen Rechts," *ZRG RA* 69 (1952): 32–33.

38. See, e.g., Pontoriero, *Il prestito marittimo*, 191; also, Bruce W. Frier, ed., *The Codex of Justinian: A New Annotated Translation, with Parallel Latin and Greek Text*, vol. 2 (Cambridge: Cambridge University Press, 2016), 955 n. 165.

39. von Glück, *Ausführliche Erläuterung*, XXI:151–69.

est. Through the remaining years of the nineteenth century, the assumption that *pecunia traiecticia* was a special type of loan subject to exceptional rules remained largely unchallenged: the only question concerned the remedies available for its enforcement.[40] In the first decades of the twentieth century Pringsheim advanced the 'special type' thesis one step further: maritime loans were an example of a legal transplant, grafted into Roman from Greek law.[41] Again, the defining feature of the contract that set it in contrast with *mutuum* was the creditor's assumption of the risk. As a creature of Greek commercial practice, maritime loans were therefore subject to special rules that were familiar to Greek law, such as the break from the principle *ex nudo pacto non oritur actio* to allow the enforcement of pacts for interest. In this sense, Pringsheim interpreted the maritime loan as a "foreign legal institution" ("das fremde Rechtsinstitut") that the jurists had difficulty accommodating within the contractual system and that continued to be governed according to Greek customs though now from within the Roman legal framework.[42]

In the mid-1930s, De Martino attacked Pringsheim's thesis at its root, arguing that the creditor's assumption of the risk was only an accidental feature of Roman maritime loans (i.e., *accidentale negotii*).[43] Adopting a radical text-critical approach, De Martino drew attention to texts showing that *pecunia traiecticia* could be given *sine periculo creditoris* and argued that the fragments that appeared to show that interest could be demanded on a pact were interpolated. Maritime loans, he concluded, were not recognized by the Roman lawyers as an independent contract but rather as formless agreements, the enforceability of which depended upon the conventional actions associated with *mutuum* and *stipulatio*.

Almost one century later De Martino's contribution continues to define the terms of the debate. In the late 1930s it provoked an immediate response from Biscardi, who reaffirmed *periculum creditoris* as an essential feature of the contract.[44] A number of other scholars, meanwhile, have either supported or offered variations on De Martino's argument:[45] that the jurists differed among them-

40. In France, for example, the thesis was taken up by Jean-Marie Pardessus, *Collection de lois maritimes antérieures au XVIII siècle*, vol. 1 (Paris: Imprimerie Royale, 1828), 70–71 and 115–16. For further literature, see Pontoriero, *Il prestito marittimo*, 6 n. 1.

41. Pringsheim, *Der Kauf*, 146–47; and following: Huvelin, *Droit commercial romain*, 215–18; Paoli, *Studi di diritto*, 69–71; Riccobono, "Stipulatio ed instrumentum," 359–60 (= *Corso di diritto romano*, 415).

42. Pringsheim, *Der Kauf*, 146.

43. De Martino, "Sul foenus nauticum," 217–47; reaffirmed (contra Biscardi) in De Martino, "Ancora sul foenus nauticum," *RDN* 2, no. 4 (1936): 433–45.

44. Biscardi, "La struttura," 343–71; reaffirmed in Biscardi, *Actio*.

45. In support: Vittorio De Villa, *Le 'usurae ex pacto' nel diritto romano* (Rome: Foro italiano, 1937), 105; Johan A. Ankum, "Some Aspects of Maritime Loans in Old-Greek and in Roman Law,"

selves as to whether *periculum creditoris* was an essential element of the contract, depending upon their place of origin (Litewski);[46] and that it was not *periculum creditoris*, but the demand for interest, that was *naturale negotii* to a maritime loan (Kupiszewski).[47] Purpura and now Pontoriero have offered further arguments in support of Biscardi's position.[48] Though the thesis that *periculum creditoris* was essential appears to have achieved widespread acceptance in some quarters, no resolution has been reached, nor even appears possible: the texts brook of no consistency on the point and give the impression of being irreconcilable.[49]

In a study first published in 1881, von Jhering described the apparent doctrinal problems thrown up by the *sedes materiae* as a "riddle."[50] For von Jhering, who was focused upon the interpretation of two especially problematic texts that I shall consider in more detail below, the "solution to the riddle" was to recognize that the Roman lawyers made a primary distinction between yields and not between types of loan.[51] Building upon von Jhering's (and Cohen's) insights, my basic proposition is that the Romans, just like the Greeks, had only the single conception of a loan for consumption (*mutuum*) that could produce either a maritime or landed yield (i.e., *faenus nauticum* or *usurae communes*, respectively).[52] Put another way, for the Romans (like the Greeks) there were only loans for consumption (*mutua*), productive at any given time of either *usurae communes* (the equivalent to the Greek concept of *tokos eggeios*) or *faenus nauticum* (a direct translation of *tokos nautikos*).

---

in *Timai Iōannou Triantaphyllopoulou* (Athens: Ant. Sakkoulas, 2000), 299; though cf. Ankum, "Observations," 62. See, also, Sicari, *Pena convenzionale*, 231–49.

46. Litewski suggested that Ulpian, Cervidius Scaevola, and Modestinus all thought *periculum creditoris* essential on account of eastern Mediterranean backgrounds; whereas Paul, Papinian, and Diocletian (or his chancery) did not: Wiesław Litewski, "Römisches Seedarlehen," *IVRA* 24 (1973): 135; reaffirmed (contra Biscardi) in Litewski, "Bemerkungen zum Römischen Seedarlehen," in *Studi in onore di Cesare Sanfilippo*, vol. 4 (Milan: Giuffrè, 1983), 381–97. Biscardi condemned the thesis as "very weak:" Biscardi, "Pecunia traiecticia," 282.

47. Kupiszewski, "Sul prestito marittimo," 378.

48. Purpura, "Ricerche," 285; Pontoriero, *Il prestito marittimo*, 193.

49. See, e.g., von Lübtow, "Catos Seedarlehen," 106; Amelia Castresana Herrero, *El préstamo marítimo griego y la pecunia traiecticia romana* (Salamanca: Ediciones Universidad de Salamanca, 1982), 69–90; Giuffrè, "'Faenus' e intraprese," 136 n. 10 and 153–54; José Luis Zamora Manzano, "Algunas notas en relación a los antecedentes romanos del seguro marítimo como desviación de la 'pecunia traiecticia,'" *BIDR* 39 (1997): 673; Christoph Krampe, "Fenus nauticum," in *Der neue Pauly: Enzyklopädie der Antike*, ed. Hubert Cancik, Helmuth Schneider, and August F. Pauly, vol. 4 (Stuttgart: J.B. Metzler, 1998), 471; Schuster, *Das Seedarlehen*, 188.

50. Rudolf von Jhering, "Skizzen," *Jahrbücher für die Dogmatik des heutigen römischen und deutschen Privatrechts* 19 (1881): 4 (= "Skizzen," in *Gesammelte Aufsätze aus den Jahrbüchern für die Dogmatik des heutigen römischen und deutschen Privatrechts*, vol. 3 (Aalen: Scientia Verlag, 1969), 214).

51. von Jhering, 4: "die Lösung des Rätsels." The two texts are C.4.32.26.2 (Iust. 528 CE) and D.22.2.4 (Pap. 3 *resp.*).

52. The term *usurae communes* stands in contrast to the titular *fenus nauticum* in C.4.33.2 (Diocl./Maxim. AA. Scribonio Honorato, 286 CE): on which, von Jhering, 4–5.

Understanding the conceptual framework possessed by the Roman lawyers helps toward understanding the legal problems at the heart of the juristic texts. For the Severan jurists in particular, the existence of a legal limit on *usurae communes* raised the question as to when a loan would be productive of a maritime yield and therefore outside the scope of the regulation of interest demanded on loans made on nonmaritime terms.[53] The interpretation I wish to give of the Roman legal texts is that the classical law required two conditions to be satisfied for a loan to produce a maritime yield falling outside the scope of the regulation of *usurae communes*: it had to be (1) *traiecticia* (i.e., carried by sea and therefore exposed to *periculum maris*); and (2) carried at the lender's risk (*periculo creditoris*). Put shortly, to produce a maritime yield a loan had to be both *traiecticia* and *periculo creditoris*: as soon as one or other of these conditions did not pertain, the loan could only produce *usurae communes* up to the statutory limit.

Pecunia traiecticia

Most of the terms adopted by the Roman jurists in connection with loans given subject to maritime loan contracts are direct translations of their Greek equivalent: *pecunia nautica* for *nautika chrēmata*; and *faenus nauticum* and *usurae maritimae* for *tokoi nautikoi*. The one exception, for which there is no Greek equivalent, is the term *pecunia traiecticia*. Indeed, the Roman origins of the phrase are attested to in Nov. 106, in which Justinian retained the expression in its Latin form despite the rest of the constitution being written in Greek. Modestinus gives a definition:

> D.22.2.1 (Mod. 10 *pand.*):
>
> *Pecunia* is *traiecticia* when it is carried overseas. If it is spent where lent, it is not *traiecticia*. But are goods bought with the money in the same position? It depends upon whether they are being carried at the lender's risk (*periculo creditoris*): if so, it becomes *traiecticia pecunia*.

The text gives rise to some difficulties. Both De Martino and Biscardi offered radical reconstructions, though with greater attention to the course of their own arguments than to the language of the fragment itself.[54] Giuffrè, meanwhile, argues that a middle portion of the text has been excised by a post-

---

53. See above, 36.

54. De Martino, "Sul foenus nauticum," 230; De Martino, "Ancora sul foenus nauticum," 433–39; cf. Biscardi, "La struttura," 345–50; Biscardi, *Actio*, 108–9 n. 2.

classical epitomator.[55] Like Pontoriero, I see no reason to suspect substantial alteration: the logic of the fragment is internally coherent, even if it is not brilliantly expressed.[56]

The text repays careful and precise exegesis. In the *Palingenesia*, Lenel places the text after an excerpt from the same source, which stated that penal stipulations could not be used to circumvent the legal limit on the rate of interest.[57] Together with the present fragment, this suggests that Modestinus was broadly concerned with the scope of the regulation of *usurae communes* and defining the circumstances in which the legal limit would apply. The text starts with a definition, that money counts as *traiecticia* when it is carried by sea (*trans mare vehitur*). The literal translation of *pecunia traiecticia* as traveling money (or, as Rougé put it, "*l'argent qui voyage*") is therefore appropriate, in the sense that the loan proceeds were only *traiecticia* for so long as they were exposed to the sea-risk.[58] This is followed by the statement that money will not be *traiecticia* if it was consumed at the same location: the money itself cannot be said to be *trans mare vehitur*. The question that arises is when goods purchased with the money will count as *traiecticia*. The jurist's response is that this depends upon whether they are being carried at the creditor's risk: if so, the loan proceeds are *traiecticia*.

The text should be taken in two parts. In the first (*traiecticia ea . . . non erit traiecticia*), a plain reading indicates that the *pecunia* is only *traiecticia* for the time it is at sea, which is to say only after commencement of the voyage.[59] Modestinus' definition also implies that *pecunia* could be *traiecticia* irrespective of which of the parties shouldered the risk, provided that it was exposed to *periculum maris*. Correspondingly, money that was not exposed to the sea-risk, for example, because it had been spent where lent, was not *traiecticia*. This sets up the problem for the second part (*sed videndum . . . pecunia fit*). On this narrow definition, only the original loan proceeds could be *pecunia traiecticia*, though not if they were consumed before the voyage began.[60] If, as I have suggested, a loan needed to be both *traiecticia* and *periculo creditoris* to generate a

55. Giuffrè, "'Faenus' e intraprese e intraprese commerciali," *Seminarios complutenses de derecho romano* 7 (1995): 147–49; Giuffrè, "Il prestito ad 'interessi marittimi' nel tardo impero," in *Atti dell'Accademia romanistica costantiniana: 12. Convegno internazionale in onore di Manlio Sargenti*, ed. Giuliano Crifò and Stefano Giglio (Naples: Edizioni scientifiche italiane, 1998), 360–62.

56. Pontoriero, *Il prestito marittimo*, 25–32.

57. D.22.1.44 (Mod. 10 *pand.*): Lenel, *Pal*, 1:725.

58. Rougé, *Recherches*, 351.

59. Jakab, "Loans and Securities," 140.

60. The argument, popular among several scholars, that Modestinus' definition demonstrates that *traiecticia pecunia* originally consisted of money loans taken abroad to purchase goods for carriage back to the port of departure, is surely implausible given the reciprocal nature of maritime trade and the centrality of return loans to the profitability of the enterprise: Huvelin, *Droit commercial romain*, 196; also, Litewski, "Römisches Seedarlehen," 120–23; Schuster, *Das Seedarlehen*, 192.

maritime yield, the problem for Modestinus was that a loan used to purchase goods before embarkation could not be *traiecticia* and was therefore excluded from producing *usurae maritimae*. The jurist's response was to say that if the purchased goods were being carried by sea at the lender's risk (i.e., fulfilling both conditions for producing a maritime yield) they counted as *traiecticia*. It follows from this that items purchased with the proceeds of a loan that were not being carried at the lender's risk—for example, loans given to a shipmaster to purchase equipment *ad reficiendam causa*, like the purchase of sails discussed by African in the context of the exercitorian edict—did not count as *traiecticia*.[61]

Periculum creditoris

The double requirement that a loan had to be both *traiecticia* and *periculo creditoris* to produce a maritime yield emerges from a short passage in the *Sententiae* of [pseudo-]Paul:

> PS.2.14.3:
>
> *Traiecticia pecunia* can (*potest*) generate an unlimited rate of interest for so long as the vessel is under sail, on account of the risk assumed by the creditor (*periculum creditoris*).

The use of *potest* again discloses the true position: *traiecticia pecunia* can (i.e., is capable of) producing an unlimited yield; but only for so long as the vessel is at sea (the money is *traiecticia, trans mare vehitur*) and the loan is at the creditor's risk. The use of "*potest*" implies that *pecunia traiecticia* was equally capable of generating *usurae communes* for the time the loan was not at the creditor's risk. The *interpretatio* states the position even more clearly:

> Interpr. PS.2.14.3:
>
> So-called *traiecticia pecunia* is that which is loaded onto a ship to be transported overseas. Because the money is exposed to the sea-risk (*periculum maris*), the creditor can make the loan agreeing any rate of interest.

61. See, generally, D.14.1.1.8–11 (Ulp. 28 *ad ed.*) and D.14.1.7 pr.–1 (Afr. 8 *quaest.*): on which, Candy, "Limits," 143–58.

Like Modestinus, the author explains that *traiecticia pecunia* consists of money taken onto a ship for carriage by sea. The justification for the creditor's entitlement to demand an unlimited yield is that by assuming the risk he exposes his investment to the perils of the sea. For the time during which the loan proceeds were both exposed to *periculum maris* (i.e., *traiecticia*) and at the lender's risk, the money was capable of generating a maritime yield outside the scope of the regulation of *usurae communes*. The loan would only be outside the regulation of *usurae communes* when both conditions—that is, money carried by sea at the creditor's risk—were met. A text by Papinian explores the interaction of the two requirements:

> D.22.2.4 pr. (Pap. 3 *resp.*):
>
> It makes no difference whether traveling money (*pecunia traiecticia*) is not given at the lender's risk (*sine periculo creditoris*) or the risk ceases to be on the lender after the appointed date or the fulfillment of the condition. In these two cases, no more than the legal limit on the rate of interest is owing: in the first case, for the entire duration; in the second, after cessation of the risk. A *pignus* or *hypotheca* does not involve higher interest.

The *principium* has been a battleground for those engaged in the question concerning the place of maritime loans within the Roman contractual system. The reason is apparent: on the one hand, Papinian appears to indicate that *pecunia traiecticia* could be lent *sine periculo creditoris*; and on the other, that the creditor's assumption of the risk was a *sine qua non* for interest on the loan to exceed the legal limit. The problem is mainly for those who argue that *periculum creditoris* was an essential feature of a maritime loan: if *pecunia traiecticia* is the *nomen iuris* of a special type of loan, the essential feature of which was the creditor's assumption of the risk, some explanation needs to be found for Papinian's statement that *pecunia* could be *traiecticia* while not at the lender's risk. For Biscardi the answer was simple: the offending phrase must have been interpolated.[62] However, there are no grounds, philological or otherwise, to suspect that the principium is inauthentic.[63] Others, meanwhile, have sought to explain the phrase away by narrowing its meaning to specific contexts. Purpura, for example, argues that Papinian's statement acknowledges

62. Biscardi, *Actio*, 121–22; cf. De Martino, "Sul foenus nauticum," 226 and 241 n. 1.

63. In favor of the text's authenticity, Kupiszewski, "Sul prestito marittimo," 370–71; Litewski, "Römisches Seedarlehen," 129–30; Purpura, "Ricerche," 282; Sicari, *Pena convenzionale*, 240; Pontoriero, *Il prestito marittimo*, 41.

the times before departure and after arrival, during which the loan would still be maritime but not at the lender's risk.[64]

As von Jhering noticed, the interpretation of the text is made straightforward by recognizing that the primary distinction was between types of yield rather than loan.[65] The *principium* sets out two circumstances in which the yield on *pecunia traiecticia* would be subject to the legal limit on the rate of interest: first, if the money was traveling (i.e., exposed to *periculum maris*) but not at the creditor's risk (*sine periculo creditoris*); and second, if the loan had been given at the creditor's risk, once the *periculum* had reverted to the borrower after fulfillment of the condition *salva nave* or the passing of the *dies praestitutus*. The question that stimulated the *responsum* therefore appears to have concerned when *pecunia traiecticia* (i.e., by Modestinus' definition, *pecunia quae trans mare vehitur*) would generate only *usurae communes* subject to the legal limit. The implication of Papinian's reply is that money that was being carried by sea could only produce a yield that was not subject to the statutory maximum for so long as the risk was with the creditor. If, therefore, the risk was with the borrower, either from the outset or once the risk had reverted to him (on the so-called *dies periculi*, D.22.2.4.1), the money would only produce *usurae communes* capped at the legal maximum. It follows from this that if money was *traiecticia*, it could switch from the generation of *faenus nauticum* to *usurae communes* midvoyage: if, for example, the maximum term of the loan had expired so that the risk passed from the lender back to the borrower (e.g., as contemplated by deadline of 200 days included in Callimachus' contract in D.45.1.122.1).

The jurist Paul appears to have shared Papinian's conception of loans productive of either *usurae communes* or maritime yields. In D.22.2.6, the opening to the *narratio* makes Paul's conception explicit:[66] the loan capital was provided as a *mutuum* on terms that it would produce a maritime yield (*usuris maritimis*). Later in the text, Paul makes a general statement that is difficult to interpret (*sed cum traiecticia pecunia ita datur . . .*): either Paul intended "*cum*" to introduce a causal clause (i.e., "since *traiecticia pecunia* is given on terms that . . .");[67] or a temporal clause (i.e., "when *traiecticia pecunia* is given on terms that . . .").[68] The statement takes on significance in the debate concern-

64. Purpura, "Ricerche," 283.
65. See von Jhering, "Skizzen" (1881).
66. For a translation, see above, 100.
67. See, e.g., Biscardi, *Actio*, 121 n. 1 and 182 n. 57 ("evidente il valore causale, e non temporale, del cum!"); Biscardi, "Pecunia traiecticia," 281.
68. De Martino, "Sul foenus nauticum," 226–27; Litewski, "Römisches Seedarlehen," 130; Litewski, "rec. A. Castresana," *IVRA* 34 (1983): 119. Röhle argues that Paul used the construction *sed*

ing whether *periculum creditoris* was an essential feature of a maritime loan, because if Paul intended the clause to be causal, this would appear to indicate that it was implied in the description of *pecunia* as *traiecticia* that the creditor assumed the risk. As Röhle pointed out, Paul's use of the indicative ahead of the subjunctive (i.e., *datur*, not *detur*) suggests a temporal meaning.[69] In addition, the construction "*ita . . . ut*" indicates an alternative: namely, that *pecunia* could be *traiecticia* even if repayment was not made subject to a condition *salva nave*. On the other hand, Castresana Herrero has argued that Paul occasionally uses the construction *sed cum* with the indicative to introduce a causal clause, a usage that was increasingly common in later juristic literature.[70] Though none of these arguments are conclusive, some guidance can be derived from another of Paul's texts on the subject:

> D.22.2.7 (Paul. 3 *ad ed.*):
>
> In some contracts, interest is owed as if on a stipulation. Thus, if I lend ten as *pecunia traiecticia* on terms that I recover capital and interest at a certain rate if the ship is safe, I can sue for the capital and interest [, even if I have not taken a stipulation].

In this extract, Paul's phrasing—"*traiecticia, ut salva nave . . .*"—suggests that notwithstanding that the money was intended for carriage by sea, it fell to the parties to agree whether to include a condition *salva nave* in the contract. Paul's basic conception of the transaction in the previous text as a *mutuum* given at a maritime yield, together with the implied possibility that *pecunia traiecticia* could be *sine periculo creditoris*, suggests that the jurist shared Papinian's conception that the primary conceptual distinction was between types of yield rather than types of loan.

Finally, all these readings are consistent with the decisions contained in a series of imperial constitutions issued by Diocletian and Maximian in the last decades of the third century CE.[71]

---

cum with the indicative to denote a recurring action (i.e., *cum iterativum*, in the sense of *quotiens*): Robert Röhle, "Zum Beispiel D. 22,2,6," *SDHI* 45 (1979): 557. This view was rightly rejected by Castresana Herrero as too rigid—the usage in the texts is more flexible. On this point, Ph. E. Huschke, *Die Lehre des römischen Rechts vom Darlehn und den dazu gehörigen Materien: Eine civilistische Monographie* (Stuttgart: F. Enke, 1882), 222 n. 5; Ankum, "Some Aspects," 300 n. 25.

69. Röhle, "Zum Beispiel," 557.

70. Castresana Herrero, *El préstamo marítimo*, 79–80.

71. All the translations of imperial constitutions drawn from the *Codex* in this section have been adapted from Frier, *Codex of Justinian*, 2:955–57.

C.4.33.2 (Diocl./Maxim. AA. Scribonio Honorato, 286):

> It is clear that *traiecticia pecunia* given at the creditor's risk is free from the observance of common interest rates (*communium usurarum*) until the ship runs into port.

The constitution, which impliedly sets *faenus nauticum* in contrast to *usurae communes*, amounts to the observation that a maritime yield would only be forthcoming for so long as the ship was at sea at the lender's risk: as soon as the ship arrived at its destination, the condition *salva nave* was fulfilled and the rules concerning *usurae communes* would apply.

C.4.33.3 (Diocl./Maxim. AA. Aureliae Cosmianae, 286):

> Since you say that you loaned money on condition that it be paid back to you in the Sacred City [Rome], and you acknowledge that the uncertain danger that is customarily feared from sea-navigation did not pertain to you, there is no doubt that you cannot demand more than the legal rate of interest on the money loaned.

Conversely, a constitution issued to Aurelia Cosmiana in the same year (286) reiterates the point that although the money was exposed to the *incertum periculum* associated with travel by sea (i.e., *traiecticia*), the loan was only capable of producing interest (*usura*) subject to the legal limit since the lender had declined to assume the risk.

C.4.33.5 (Diocl./Maxim. AA. et CC. Pullio Iuliano Eucharisto, 294):

> The loss of *traiecticia pecunia*, given as a *mutuum* at the risk of the creditor (*periculo creditoris*), does not fall on the debtor before the ship arrives at its destination. But without an agreement of this type, he [the debtor] will not be released by the misfortune of shipwreck.

In a constitution issued in 294, the transaction is introduced as a loan (*mutuum*) of traveling money, which could either be lent *periculo creditoris* or *sine . . . conventione* (i.e., not subject to a condition *salva nave*). In the former case, the debtor would be released from his obligation to repay if *casus* occurred before fulfillment of the condition; whereas in the latter he would not, since the obligation was not suspended to the safe arrival of the ship. Again, the suggestion that *pecunia* could be *traiecticia* notwithstanding the absence of a condition *salva nave* in the contract is consistent with the view that the primary distinction was between types of yield rather than loan.

To summarize the results of this section: the debate concerning the essential or accidental quality of *periculum creditoris* to the designation of a loan as maritime is predicated upon a misconception as to how the Romans approached the relationship between loans and yields. The expression *pecunia traiecticia* meant only money given as a *mutuum* that was carried by sea (*trans mare vehitur*): to generate a maritime yield it had also to be at the creditor's risk. A *mutuum* therefore only produced a maritime yield for so long as two conditions were present: (1) that the money loaned, or the goods purchased with the loan, were exposed to the perils of the sea; and (2) that it was being carried at the lender's risk. In other words, it had to be both *traiecticia* and *periculo creditoris*. This made it intelligible for Papinian to say that *pecunia traiecticia* could at the same time be *sine periculo creditoris*, because for so long as the money was at sea, the yield could shift from a maritime onto a landed footing with the passing of the risk (i.e., on the *dies periculi*) even though the proceeds of the loan remained exposed to the hazards of the sea. Precisely the same conception was shared by Paul, the author of the *Sententiae Pauli*, and the Emperors Diocletian and Maximian in their constitutions.

Timelines

Maritime loan contracts essentially operated on two timelines, each corresponding to one of the two main sources of liability for the debtor. The first timeline concerned the main debt, which could produce a maritime yield for so long as the money lent (or cargo purchased with the money) was exposed to the perils of the sea and at the creditor's risk; and landed interest (at a stipulated rate) outside of this period. The second concerned the penalty and daily rate for the services of the lender's representative, which became due on fulfillment of the penal condition. The question for the jurists was therefore to identify the key moments in the life of the contract, that is, at which the risk passed between the parties, the yield converted from maritime to landed, and the penal condition materialized (considered in chapter 4). The answers to these questions had implications not only for the relationship between the parties, but also for the creditor in respect of the regulation of interest rates, which became material once the loan had converted to a landed footing.

The Main Debt

According to Modestinus, the risk passed from the debtor to the creditor on the date agreed for sailing:

> D.22.2.3 (Mod. 4 *reg.*):
>
> In *pecunia nautica* the risk is with the creditor from the day it is agreed that the ship should sail (*navem navigare conveniat*).

The expression *pecunia nautica* indicates that the loan had been made subject to a maritime loan contract. *Prima facie* a creditor who lent on these terms assumed the risk from the moment he made the advance. However, according to Modestinus the risk would only pass to the creditor on the date agreed for sailing. The effect is to align the lender's assumption of the risk with the period during which it was agreed that the ship should be exposed to the sea-risk. Taken together with a maximum time limit, the creditor's risk was therefore limited to the agreed (maximum) duration of the voyage. It follows from this that outside the agreed period (i.e., both before the agreed date of departure and after either the expiry of the time limit or the ship's safe arrival) the creditor was only entitled to demand interest up to the legal limit. What if the ship was prevented from leaving on the appointed date for a reason outside the parties' control (e.g., a storm)? Jakab says that in this case the risk would only shift to the lender on the actual date of departure.[72] This was the Athenian position: in Demosthenes' speech *Against Phormiōn*, the speaker Chrysippos calls attention to the practice of summoning witnesses to attest to the lender's assumption of the risk from the moment the ship set sail.[73] Modestinus appears to depart on this point: the risk shifts on the date agreed for sailing, notwithstanding that the ship's departure might be delayed.

As for the passing of the risk from the lender back to the debtor, this occurred on two events: (1) the satisfaction of the condition *salva nave*; or (2) the passing of the deadline for the maximum duration of the enterprise. Whichever of these events occurred earlier constituted the "risk deadline" ("*dies periculi*," D.22.2.4.1), when the risk reverted from the creditor to the debtor. The arrival of the risk deadline brought with it several consequences. At a minimum, time would begin to run for the accrual of landed interest on the loan. It might also happen that the penal condition was set to materialize if the debtor had failed

72. Jakab, "Loans and Securities," 141.
73. Dem. 34.28.

to perform by the occurrence of one or other of the events constituting the risk deadline (i.e., after the grace period following the safe arrival of the ship or the maximum term of the loan had expired). In that case, both the penalty and the daily rate for the lender's representative would also fall due from this date.[74]

In some cases, both time-denominated interest and a daily rate for the services of the lender's representative ran concurrently. Since the yield was no longer maritime the interest that the creditor could charge was capped at the statutory maximum, which for most of the classical period was 12 percent p.a. However, the question arose whether there was any limit on the daily rate for the lender's representative, which was open to abuse by creditors seeking to evade the legal limit on ordinary interest. Papinian gave the following response:

> D.22.2.4.1 (Pap. 3 *resp.*):
>
> If a daily rate is stipulated for the services of a slave traveling in connection with a loan of traveling money, the amount due is limited to the statutory maximum (*ad finem centesimae*) and to no more than double (*non ultra duplum*). If there is a separate stipulation for interest after the risk has passed, the rate can be made up to the statutory limit (*usurae legitimae*) from the stipulation for services.

The difficulties in this text arise from the inclusion of the words *non ultra duplum*. Without these words the response makes easy sense. If the contract included a stipulation for the services of the lender's representative, the daily rate could not exceed the statutory maximum. In addition, if the contract also included a stipulation providing for a rate of interest payable after the passing of the risk, this together with the daily rate for the representative could not exceed 12 percent p.a. The response is consistent with Modestinus' more general statement in D.22.1.44, that penal stipulations could not be used to circumvent the legal limit.

There are three main interpretations that have been given to the words *non ultra duplum*, *viz.*, that:[75] (1) in the special context of maritime lending, the legal limit was double the statutory maximum (i.e., 24 percent p.a.), which could be made up from both the stipulated rate of interest and the daily rate for services—one serious deficiency of this interpretation is that it would require the expression *usurae legitimae* to refer to a statutory maximum other than the

74. However, this need not be the case: cf., e.g., the penalty clause in D.45.1.122.1 (Scaev. 28 *dig.*).

75. For the older literature, see Billeter, *Geschichte*, 247–50.

conventional 12 percent p.a., which was the norm during Papinian's time; (2) it was meant to refer to the *non ultra duplum* rule, whereby the interest that could accrue on a money loan was limited to double the amount of the principal in all. An objection is that for interest accruing at 12 percent p.a., it would take many years for the interest paid to overtake the sum of the principal. This would even be so if the rule applied both to the sum of the maritime and landed yields together: if the maritime yield were one-third, then the total interest paid would only overtake the principal at the end of the fifth year. Nonetheless, Papinian may simply have referred to the rule for completeness; (3) the words have been interpolated by the compilers of Justinian's *Digest*. This argument, first proposed by Billeter, holds that the words were introduced to bring Papinian's reply into line with a constitution of Justinian issued in 528, which decreed a special limit on interest flowing from a *contractus traiecticius* at double the ordinary limit.[76] The suggestion is attractive because (as I argue in the next section) the limit in the constitution of 528 was likely intended to apply to loans of traveling money only once they had converted to a landed footing. Though the second interpretation cannot be ruled out, Billeter was probably right to suspect this phrase of interpolation.

Penalty

One problem discussed by the jurists in respect of the penalty falling due concerned the position of the creditor if the debtor had died before the realization of the condition. Two texts by Labeo, separated in the *Digest* but likely originally belonging to one passage, address the issue:[77]

> D.22.2.9 (Lab. 5 *pith. a Paulo epit.*):
>
> If a penalty is promised for a [loan of] *pecunia traiecticia*, as is usual, although at the date for payment no one is alive who owes the money, the penalty falls due as if there were an heir of the debtor.

76. C.4.32.26.2 (Iust. 528 CE): on which, see below, 177. Billeter, *Geschichte*, 249 n. 1. See, also, De Martino, "Sul foenus nauticum," 227; Litewski, "Römisches Seedarlehen," 156; Purpura, "Ricerche," 289 n. 288; Ankum, "Some Aspects," 306; and the literature cited by Pontoriero, *Il prestito marittimo*, 44 n. 14.

77. Texts originally belonging to the same passage: Biscardi, "La struttura," 359; Biscardi, *Actio*, 30–31 n. 1; Purpura, "Ricerche," 312; Giuffrè, "'Faenus' e intraprese," 152 and n. 49; though cf. Sicari, *Pena convenzionale*, 251 and 268 n. 69; and Harke, *Mora debitoris*, 53–54 n. 11.

D.22.2.2 (Pomp. 3 *ex Plaut.*):

> Labeo says that if there is no one on the side of the promisor who can be served with an *interpellatio* for [a loan of] *pecunia traiecticia*, that fact should be recorded by *testatio* as the equivalent of raising an action.

The first text is drawn from the fifth book of Paul's epitome of Labeo's *pithana*.[78] The fragment has as its background the law of succession, particularly the case in which there was no *heres necessarius* and therefore an interval in time between the death of the debtor and the entry of the *heres* into the inheritance.[79] During this interval, the *hereditas* was said to be *iacens*, pending the acceptance (*aditio*) of the person to whom the *hereditas* had been (or would be) offered. This raised conceptual issues, most especially concerning which of the *personae* of the deceased and the future *heres* the inheritance was taken to represent. The classical jurists were split on the issue (though not apparently by school), those favoring the view that the *hereditas* represented the future *heres* holding that the *aditio* was retrospective to the time of decease. Though the contrary view ultimately prevailed, it was widely accepted during the classical period that the *aditio* was retrospective, despite the logical inconsistencies associated with the position.

Labeo's view, one of the earlier surviving interventions on the issue, therefore concerned the question as to whether a penalty, the condition for payment of which materialized after the decease of the debtor but before the acceptance of the inheritance by the future *heres*, could fall due when there was no one to be bound by the obligation. His response was that the future *heres* was bound by a fiction that he had entered into the *hereditas* by the time the condition materialized.

The second text addresses the problem of the sufficiency of demands. In the absence of a person upon whom an *interpellatio* could be served, a *testatio*—that is, a solemn declaration by the creditor before witnesses, not requiring the promisor's presence—would suffice.[80] It has been argued that the two texts

78. On the nature of Labeo's *pithana*, see, e.g., J. A. C. Thomas, "Pithanon Labeonis a Paulo Epitomatorum Libri VIII," in *Daube Noster: Essays in Legal History for David Daube*, ed. Alan Watson (Edinburgh: Scottish Academic Press, 1974), 317–25; Mario Talamanca, "I 'Pithana' di Labeone e la logica stoica," *IVRA* 26 (1975): 1–40; Bruno Schmidlin, "Horoi, pithana und regulae—Zum Einfluß der Rhetorik und Kialektik auf die juristische Regelbildung," in *Aufstieg und Niedergang der römischen Welt*, ed. Hildegard Temporini and Wolfgang Haase, vol. II:15 (Berlin: De Gruyter, 1976), 101–30.

79. On the concept of the *hereditas iacens*, see Buckland, *Text-Book*, 306–10. In the context of this fragment, Pontoriero, *Il prestito marittimo*, 115–19 (with literature).

80. Pontoriero, *Il prestito marittimo*, 119–21 (with literature).

address separate issues, on the basis that there would have been no need for an *interpellatio* if the penal condition in the loan contract contained a time limit; and consequently, that the present fragment has been interpolated. But this presupposes a rule *dies interpellat pro homine*, when as we have seen, there were occasions in which the actionability of a penal stipulation would be postponed notwithstanding that the deadline had passed.

One further fragment, drawn from the ninth book of Paul's commentary *ad edictum*, reports another opinion of Julian focusing upon the duties of a *curator* tasked with administering an estate:

> D.3.5.12 (Paul. 9 *ad ed.*):
>
> A debtor of mine who owed me 50 died, I undertook to be curator of his estate and I spent (as curator) 10. After this 100 were realized by the sale of a portion of the property which he left on his death, and I put that sum by in a chest; but the money was lost without any negligence on my part. The question arose whether, on an heir eventually coming forward, I had the right to sue him, either for the sum of 50 which I had originally lent, or for the 10 which I spent. Julianus says that the essential point to consider is whether I had reasonable ground for putting by the 100, because, assuming that what I ought to have done was to pay off what was owing to myself and the other creditors who had claims against the estate, then I ought to bear the risk of not only the 60 [*sic*] but also the 40 that remained; however, I might still retain the 10 that I spent; in other words I need only make good 90. But if there was reasonable ground for keeping the whole sum of 100 by me, for example, there was a danger lest land of the deceased should be forfeited for a government debt, or, money having been borrowed on a sea-risk, the penal sum payable on failure of the condition should be increased, or payment should be demandable in pursuance of an arbitration,—then, says Julianus, I can recover from the heir not only the 10 which I spent to preserve the estate, but in addition to that my original debt of 50.

The hypothetical sets up a delicate problem: a debtor dies owing 50 to one of his creditors, who steps up as *curator* of his estate.[81] The *curator* spends 10; and

81. See, generally, Barbara Biscotti, "Custodia, amministrazione, liquidazione di bene ereditari: Il responso di Salvio Giuliano in D.3.5.12," in *Studi per Giovanni Nicosia*, vol. 2 (Milan: Giuffrè, 2007), 12; Aldo Cenderelli, "Questioni di fatto e questioni di diritto alla luce di D. 3, 5, 12," in *Nozione, formazione e interpretazione del diritto: Richerche dedicate al Prof. F. Gallo*, vol. 1 (Naples: Jovene 1997), 99–116.

having raised 100 by the sale of a portion of the inheritance, stores the proceeds in a lockbox. The *arca* is then lost through no fault of his own. The question is whether, on the acceptance of the *hereditas* by the heir, the *curator* can claim not only for the 10 (as *curator*), but also for the 50 (as creditor). According to Julian, the answer depends upon whether the *curator* can show an *iusta causa seponendi*: that is, a justifiable reason for putting the 100 to the side instead of paying off the debts of the deceased. If not, then although the *curator* could claim the 10 as expenses, he could not claim the 50, since he ought as *curator* to have attended to paying the creditors (including himself) using the 100, the risk (*periculum*) falling upon him rather than the heir for the loss of money in the lockbox (at least as regarded his own claim). If, however, he could show such an *iusta causa*, for example, because the estate was still exposed to certain risks (including the potential satisfaction of a penal condition in an arbitration agreement or maritime loan contract), then the *curator*-cum-creditor could recover both the 10 and the 50.

Julian's opinion presupposes Labeo's view that if a penal condition in a maritime loan contract materialized in the interval between the debtor's death and acceptance, there would be a fiction that the *aditio* had occurred retrospectively so that the obligation to pay the penalty could bind the future *heres*. The two fragments D.22.2.9 and D.3.5.12 are therefore consonant with one another. As Knütel well points out, the potential for the realization of the condition in this particular case was not enough to substantiate an *iusta causa* for the *curator* in itself: there must have been a risk that by failing to pay the penalty, the debt could be further increased (*augeretur*).[82] This refers implicitly to the stipulations for interest and a daily rate for the services of the creditor's representative that were regularly included alongside the penalty in maritime loan contracts, the operation of which introduced an increasing burden to the estate. Since the debts owed to the other creditors (including the *curator*) were fixed, the *curator's iusta causa* therefore consisted in his prioritizing the growing debt over those that threatened no increase.

The Regulation of Maritime Lending by Justinian

So far as we know, Justinian was the most active of the emperors in attempting to regulate maritime finance. His legislation in the *corpus iuris civilis* provides significant evidence of the antithesis in Graeco-Roman thought between mari-

82. Knütel, *Stipulatio poenae*, 231–32.

time and landed yields.[83] As von Jhering noticed, the distinction lies behind the whole structure of Justinian's legislation concerning the regulation of interest rates.[84] In both the *Digest* and the *Code*, the texts are collected in two adjacent titles: the first *de usuris* (and so forth) (C.4.32/ D.22.1); the second *de nautico faenore* (C.4.33/ D.22.2). The expression *faenus nauticum* appears elsewhere only once (in a constitution of Diocletian and Maximian dated to c. 286) and is synonymous with the Greek *tokos nautikos*, or maritime yield.[85] In another Diocletianic constitution, of the same date, the emperors refer by contrast to the regulation of *usurae communes*.[86] The implication is that, for both Diocletian and Justinian (at least), the proper contrast was between, on the one hand, the regulation of *usurae communes* (equivalent to the Hellenic concept of landed interest), and on the other, *faenus nauticum* (a direct translation of *tokos nautikos*). The placement of the titles in both the *Digest* and the *Code* therefore reproduces the original Greek distinction between landed and maritime yields and demonstrates the continued primacy of the same distinction in Roman legal thought, at least to the time of Justinian.

The first specific issue to confront in the context of Justinian's legislation is the use of the term *pecunia traiecticia*. In the introductory constitution to the *Digest*, the title *de nautico faenore* is referred to as *de . . . traiecticiis pecuniis*;[87] a constitution of 528 imposes a limit on interest flowing from a *contractus traiecticius*;[88] and in a novel issued in 540, Justinian uses the linguistically hybrid expression "νόμος *traiecticia*" (preserving *traiecticia* in the Latin script in the otherwise Greek original).[89] Normally this occurrence of the phrase is adduced as evidence of the use of the term as a *nomen iuris*. Again, however, the argument is predicated on the wrong assumption that the primary distinction was between loans. Rather, in all these cases, to refer to the "law concerning *traiecticia pecunia*" meant the whole law surrounding loans of traveling money, both during the times it was productive of a mari-

83. To which add Bas. 53.5.16, in which the legal position of a creditor who had given a maritime loan (δανεῖον ναυτικὸν) was secured using a hypothec over landed property (ἐγγείων πραγμάτων): Pontoriero, *Il prestito marittimo*, 53–55.

84. von Jhering, "Skizzen" (1881), 19–20.

85. C.4.33.4 (Diocl./Maxim. AA. Aureliae Iulianae). The constitution is usually dated to 286 on the basis of Krüger's conjecture that the consuls referred to at the end of the preceding constitution must also have been those in office at the time this constitution was issued: see Huvelin, *Droit commercial romain*, 211; and following, e.g., Ankum, "Some Aspects," 297–98.

86. C.4.33.2 (Diocl./Maxim. AA. Scribonio Honorato).

87. Const. Tanta. 5 (533 CE) (= C.1.17.2.5).

88. C.4.32.26.2 (Iust. 528).

89. Nov. 106 pr.

time and landed yield. D.22.2.4, for example, which is included in the *Digest* title, is *de traiecticiis pecuniis* in the sense that it concerns the rules applicable to loans of traveling money after the risk had reverted to the borrower when only *usurae communes* was due.

Identifying the precise regulatory framework that surrounded maritime lending during the time of Justinian has proved controversial. In addition to the texts collected in the titles *de nautico faenore* in the Digest and the Code, Justinian issued three further constitutions in 528, 540, and 541. The text that has caused most consternation is Justinian's constitution from 528, which was included in the title *de usuris* in the Code:

> C.4.32.26.2 (Iust., 528):
>
> We, therefore, order that persons of illustrious or higher rank shall not be permitted to stipulate for more than four percent in any contract, small or great; managers of shops and persons who carry on any lawful business must be satisfied to stipulate for eight percent; on maritime loan contracts (*in traiecticiis . . . contractibus*), or loans of property in species, stipulations cannot be exacted for more than twelve [and a half] percent (*ad centesimam*), though contracts in excess of this were permitted in former laws; all other persons, moreover, can stipulate for only six percent; and this rate cannot be exceeded in any other cases in which interest may be demanded without a stipulation. Nor shall a judge increase such rate by reason of any custom in any region.

The traditional reading of the text, which continues to find favor with scholars and that retains its place in the textbooks, is that the constitution set a limit on the rate of interest that could be demanded on a maritime loan. Two issues arise. First, the expression "*ad centesimam*" has sometimes been interpreted as referring to the classical *centesima usura*, which amounted to an annual rate of 12 percent.[90] It should be noted, however, that following the currency reforms of Constantine the Great in the early fourth century, the value of the gold solidus (aureus or nomisma) was set at 1/72 of a litra of gold and divided into 24 silver siliquae (*keratia*), with the result that the *centesima* ceased to be an absolute rate and was set at three siliquae (i.e., one-eighth of a nomisma) per month

90. See, e.g., Fargnoli, "Condictio," in *HRP*, 2:1910–11.

or 12.5 percent p.a.[91] The detail is significant, not least because it explains a remark in Nov. 106, to which we shall return shortly.

The second issue concerns the constitution's scope of application. The traditional interpretation holds that the expression "*contractus traiecticius*" refers to a maritime loan transaction.[92] On this reading, the statutory limit would apply to the whole transaction, and therefore even for the time during which the risk was assumed by the creditor. This is further supported by the observations that Justinian refers to earlier laws (*veteres leges*) that permitted higher rates and that in the *scholium* to the corresponding text in the *Basilica*, the scholiast states that the limit would apply for the duration of the voyage.[93] The conclusion is that Justinian had introduced legislation at the beginning of his reign that established for the first time a limit on the rates that lenders could demand on a maritime loan.

An alternative explanation, however, was proposed by von Jhering,[94] who argued that it was inconceivable that Justinian should have introduced a limit on maritime yields, which would have nullified the economic basis for the transaction. The "solution to the riddle," he argued, was to fall back upon the distinction between landed and maritime yields: Justinian must only have intended the constitution to apply to sea loans for the time during which they produced landed interest. In support of this argument, von Jhering adduced the apparent contrast between this constitution and those included by Justinian in the adjacent title *de nautico faenore*, which appeared to confirm that maritime yields were outside the scope of the regulation of *usurae communes*.[95] In addition, the placement of the constitution in the title *de usuris* indicated the legislator's intention that the limit ought only to apply to landed interest.

Von Jhering's interpretation remains controversial.[96] However, in light of

91. Notwithstanding the translation given above. On this point, Billeter, *Geschichte*, 332; F. Klingmüller, "Fenus," in *Paulys Real-Encyclopädie der classischen Altertumswissenschaft*, ed. August F. Pauly and Georg Wissowa, vol. 6.2 (Stuttgart: J. B. Metzler, 1909), col. 2198; Ernesto Bianchi, "In tema d'usura: Canoni conciliari e legislazione imperiale del IV secolo (contin. e fine)," *Athenaeum* 62 (1984): 142; Demetrios Gofas, "The Byzantine Law of Interest," in *The Economic History of Byzantium from the Seventh through to the Fifteenth Century*, ed. Angeliki E. Laiou (Washington, DC: Dumbarton Oaks, 2002), 1096–97; Francesco Fasolino, *Studi sulle usurae* (Salerno: Brunolibri, 2006), 166 and n. 30.

92. See, e.g., De Ste Croix, "Maritime Loans," 55–56; Pontoriero, *Il prestito marittimo*, 162; Fasolino, *Studi*, 172; Giovanni Luchetti, "Il prestito di denaro a interesse in età giustinianea," *Cultura giuridica e diritto vivente* 3 (2016): 8.

93. Sch. 1 and *cod. Par. Gr.* 1352 to Bas. 17.1.12 (= Herman J. Scheltema and D. Holwerda, eds., *Basilicorum Libri LX, Series B*, vol. 3, Scholia in libr. XV–XX [Groningen: J.B. Wolters, 1957], 1041–42): on which, Pontoriero, *Il prestito marittimo*, 162–63 n. 9; Luchetti, "Il prestito di denaro," 8.

94. von Jhering, "Skizzen" (1881), 18–23.

95. For criticisms of this argument, see Purpura, "Ricerche," 321–22.

96. In support: Huvelin, *Droit commercial romain*, 208; Purpura, "Ricerche," 327–28; Purpura,

the centrality of the distinction between landed and maritime yields in Graeco-Roman thought, the conclusion appears to me to be inescapable. The fundamental objection to the traditional account is that the Romans did not conceive of a maritime loan, but only of loans that could at one time or another produce landed or maritime yields. In the constitution of 528, "*contractus traiecticius*" carries the meaning of a contract concerned with a loan of *pecunia traiecticia*, which in turn carries its conventional meaning of a sum of money transported overseas (*trans mare vehitur*). In other words, the contract, just like the loan with which it was concerned, was capable of generating both a landed and maritime yield, depending upon which of the parties was bearing the risk. This interpretation is supported by the possible interpolation made by the compilers in D.22.2.4.1: there, it is likely that the words *non ultra duplum* were included to give effect to the constitution of 528, but only in connection with the interest due after the risk had passed to the borrower.[97] In addition, it is simply incoherent to say that the *centesima usura* could apply to limit a maritime yield: the *centesima* was a limit on time-denominated *usurae communes*, quite apart from the regulation of *faenus nauticum*. It was the very essence of a maritime yield that it was not susceptible to denomination by time and therefore outside of the scope of the regulation of landed interest. Together with the placement of the constitution in the title *de usuris*, the implication is that the constitution was only intended to limit the gathering of *usurae communes* to the *centesima usura* for the time during which the loan underpinning the *contractus* was productive of landed interest. As for the scholiast's remark, I take this to indicate that this higher limit—12 (or 12.5 percent) p.a.—applied while the ship was under sail (i.e., while the money was *traiecticia*). For the time during which the loan was not *traiecticia* (for example, after the ship's arrival in port and after the grace period had elapsed), it is possible that the lender was only entitled to the lower rate reserved for those running businesses on land (i.e., *ad bessem centesimae*, 8 percent p.a.).

This interpretation has the added benefit of helping to make sense of the later constitutions issued by Justinian in 540 and 541. We have met the first of these already, in chapter 1.[98] The constitution was issued in response to a petition by two moneylenders, who requested that the emperor bring clarity to the law surrounding maritime lending. Justinian acceded to the request and ordered his prefect, John the Cappadocian, to ascertain the customs, so

---

"Review of Pontoriero, I., *Il prestito marittimo in diritto romano* (Bologna: Bonomia, 2011)," *IVRA* 62 (2014): 416–17. Cf. Pontoriero, who declares von Jhering's thesis "without foundation" ("priva di fondamento"): Pontoriero, *Il prestito marittimo*, 196.

97. See above, 171–72.

98. See above, 24–26.

that they could be set down in law. John therefore convened a conference of *nauklēroi* and *emporoi*, whose account was transformed into legislation in the following terms:[99]

Nov. 106.1:

Accordingly, now that we have read the minutes and become informed on the matter, we decree that the practice, both now and for all time to come, should be as has been deposed before your excellency, because (for one thing) they are not in conflict with already enacted laws. In such cases, then, that is what must be observed in future by a special law, in suits of this nature involving shipowners and traders: the disembarkments, and all other customary observances attested before your eminence, must be as in the said agreements. That is what is to be in force, as a special law for cases involving shipowners and traders; after all, how could it not be right for what has been in use and force, unaltered, over such long periods—as the testimonies given before your excellency have declared—to be in force also for all other cases that will arise hereafter? That is to be the method of settling their affairs, in force under a special law and requiring no other directive, but in force on shipping and trading enterprises for all time. It will act as general legislation in force for transactions with shipowners or traders, and will play its due part among the laws we have laid down, so as to be the benchmark for judges in making their judgments.

The constitution was given at Constantinople on 7 September 540. However, just seven months later, on 26 April 541, Justinian abrogated the law:

Nov. 110:

[pr.] We are aware of having previously, on information from you, made a law about traveling money, which has been notified to your excellency; . . .

[1] . . . However, petitions were subsequently made to us, as a result of which we have instructed that the law is not to be in force; but having instructed it to be withdrawn from your court, we have discovered that it had already been made public in some provinces. For that reason, we are decreeing that such law should be altogether inoperative, and if it

99. The translations from the *Novels* are drawn from Miller and Sarris, *The Novels*.

> had already come to have been sent abroad, it is not to be in force there, either. The way in which we wish the matter to proceed is as if the said law had, in fact, not ever been laid down: cases are to be tried, and to gain due judgment, in accordance with the laws previously enacted by us for such matters.

Two points are of interest. First, in Nov. 106.1, we are now in a position to make sense of Justinian's claim that the constitution of 540 was "not in conflict with already enacted laws," since the setting of maritime yields to the fixed sum of one-eighth of the principal was consistent with the limit of one-eighth of a nomisma per month (i.e., 12.5 percent p.a.) on the landed interest generated by loans of *pecunia traiecticia* for the time during which the debtor shouldered the risk. Even if one accepts the traditional interpretation of the constitution of 528 (i.e., as applying to maritime loans *in toto*), the suggestion that the constitution of 540 raised the interest rate limit from 12 percent p.a. to 12.5 percent runs foul of the effect of the currency reforms.[100]

Second, if the interpretation of the constitution of 528 offered above is accepted, we can make easy sense of Justinian's brief and unsuccessful intervention into the regulation of maritime yields in 540/1. If, as von Jhering originally argued, that constitution was limited only to the regulation of landed interest, then these two novels represent Justinian's only inroad into the otherwise consistent position that maritime yields were not subject to regulation for so long as the loan was both *traiecticia* and at the creditor's risk. Though Billeter thought that the reason for the rapid repeal of the law was the ineffectiveness of extending customs specific to Constantinople elsewhere throughout the empire, I agree with Purpura that the customs attested to by the *nauklēroi* and *emporoi* were both ancient and widespread.[101] The true reason, I would suggest, is that the *nauklēroi* and *emporoi* consulted by Johannes had a vested interest (as borrowers) in misrepresenting the customary yield as the minimum usually demanded in connection with a long-distance trading enterprise: that is, one-eighth of the principal, the amount associated most closely in the sources with *heteroploun* loans or those given for short journeys of no more than a few days.

100. Cf. Mariagrazia Bianchini, "La disciplina degli interessi convenzionali nella legislazione giustinianea," in *Studi in onore di Arnaldo Biscardi*, ed. Franco Pastori, vol. 2 (Milan: Istituto Editoriale Cisalpino, La Goliardica, 1982), 418–22; Salvatore Cosentino, "Banking in Early Byzantine Ravenna," *Cahiers de Recherches Médiévales et Humanistes* 28 (2014): 252; and now Miller and Sarris, *The Novels*, 2:697 n. 1. This interpretation misses both the impact of Constantine's currency reforms and the fundamental distinction between yields calculated by time and as a fixed proportion of the sum lent.

101. Billeter, *Geschichte*, 338; also, Heinrich Sieveking, *Das Seedarlehen des Altertums* (Leipzig: Veit, 1893), 41 n. 1; cf. Purpura, "Ricerche," 326–27.

Further, the dates, which align closely with the end of the sailing season in 540 and the start of the next in 541, give the impression that the defectiveness of the law, compounded by the confusion that must have attended blunt legislative intervention into the complex domain of maritime finance, created such a degree of consternation that it had to be urgently set aside before the beginning of the next season.[102] Moreover, if the constitution of 540 gave rise to so many petitions that it had to be repealed before even one season had passed, it is difficult to see how the constitution of 528, which on its traditional reading would be even more far-reaching in its effect, could have failed to produce a similar degree of confusion with little or no legislative response. As Justinian remarked in the preamble to Nov. 111, which was issued shortly after Nov. 110 in the same year, "what medicine does for diseases, laws do in business matters: the effect may be the opposite of what is intended, and experience may prove what was thought efficacious to be useless." A salutary lesson.

Conclusion

For a long time the idea has persisted that the maritime loan was a special type of *mutuum* that had its own place in the Roman contractual system. In fact both the Greeks and later the Romans possessed only the single conception of a loan for consumption (*daneismos, mutuum*), that could be productive of either a landed or maritime yield. The evidence suggests that the earliest use of maritime as an adjective was in connection with written contracts (*syngraphai*) made in connection with the long-distance trade in commodities. The defining feature of these contracts was the inclusion of a condition *salva nave* that suspended the debtor's obligation to repay to the safe arrival of the ship at its destination. Since the yield produced by a loan made on such a condition was not susceptible to denomination by time from the outset, this produced a contrast between maritime yields and landed interest, the latter susceptible to denomination by time. It was only in virtue of the type of yield generated by the capital that the loan fell to be described as either maritime or landed. Indeed, Justinian's remark in Nov. 106 pr., that if a debt remained outstanding after the expiry of the grace period, "the nature of the loan changed at once and became a terrestrial one, as the lenders no longer had the worry over the perils of sea-going," shows that it was the change in the type of yield that determined the footing of the loan.

102. For a similar interpretation, see Pontoriero, *Il prestito marittimo*, 182; also, Purpura, "Review of Pontoriero," 417.

Recognizing the primacy of the distinction between yields transforms our understanding of the Roman juristic texts. The question that occupied the jurists concerned the circumstances in which the yield generated by a loan would be landed rather than maritime and therefore subject to the rules governing *usurae communes*. Further, it allows us to accept Papinian's statement in D.22.2.4 pr. at face value: *pecunia traiecticia* referred only to loan capital that was exposed to the perils of the sea, that was capable of generating a maritime yield (*faenus nauticum, usurae maritimae*) for so long as the lender assumed the risk. In this respect, the Romans encountered the Greeks and took over from them their mental framework, recasting it in the structures of their law.

Appendix I

The Enforcement of Maritime Loan Contracts in Classical Roman Law

The problem is to identify the remedies that were available to and used by creditors to enforce maritime loan contracts in classical Roman law. The crux of the issue is that, on the one hand, the customary structure of *nautikai syngraphai* was a matter of commercial development that had its origins well before Rome had entered the Mediterranean sphere; and on the other, that the scheme of actions contained in the Praetor's Edict appeared to leave open the possibility that aspects of a *syngraphē* agreed in the customary way might lack legal protection. Since the handing over of the principal bound the recipient *ex re* for the return of an equivalent sum, the problem concentrates on the other clauses in the contract, particularly the creditor's demand for interest, which if it was not concluded as a stipulation could not be sued upon on the principle *ex nudo pacto non oritur actio*. However, there are additionally a small number of texts in the *Digest* that seem to indicate that pacts for interest agreed in a maritime loan (contract) were directly enforceable by the late classical period.

The basic problem for the Pandectists was to explain the special rules concerning the enforceability of pacts for interest in maritime loan contracts while preserving the logical integrity of the contractual system. A convenient strategy pioneered by Glück was to interpret maritime loans as a special type of *mutuum*, making the exceptional rules concerning *usurae ex pacto* easier to justify since they were associated with their own contractual type. Accordingly, the creditor had the *actio ex stipulatu* if a stipulation had been concluded, failing which a *condictio ex lege* was available.[1] Von Savigny proposed instead that

1. von Glück, *Ausführliche Erläuterung*, 200; also, Matthiass, *Das foenus nauticum*, 53–54; Huschke, *Die Lehre des römischen Rechts*, 221–38.

maritime loans were interpreted by the Roman jurists as transactions *do ut des* (i.e., as an innominate contract), for which a *condictio* together with an *actio praescriptis verbis* lay;[2] and Karlowa and Beseler that the parties were given an *actio in factum*.[3] Into the early twentieth century, Pringsheim advanced the furthest extension of the maritime-loan-as-contractual-type thesis, in claiming that it was enforceable in its own right having been grafted into Roman law from Greek practice.[4] For these scholars, the distinguishing feature of a maritime loan that separated it conceptually from an ordinary *mutuum* was that the former was made subject to a condition *salva nave*. The claim was normally expressed in terms that the assumption of the risk by the creditor (*periculum creditoris*) was an essential feature of a maritime loan, that marked it out as an independent contractual type (alongside *mutuum*) capable of supporting its own special rules.

The first dissenter from the orthodox view was De Martino, who argued to the contrary that the assumption of the risk by the creditor (*periculum creditoris*) was merely accidental to the loan contract, such that the creditors who had made loans on maritime terms had recourse only to the conventional remedies associated with *mutuum* and *stipulatio*.[5] If the agreement was concluded only as a pact, then the default position at law was that its terms were therefore unenforceable beyond the availability of the *actio certae creditae pecuniae* for recovery of the principal. However, in denying that the maritime loan was an autonomous contractual type, De Martino had again to confront the difficulty of explaining how special rules could apply to some loans rather than others. Predictably for the period, his solution was to argue that all the texts that appear to show the possibility of enforcing pacts for interest in maritime loan contracts are interpolated.

De Martino's thesis elicited a fierce response from Biscardi, for whom the prospect that key parts of the *conventio* might be unenforceable was intolerable from a sociohistorical perspective.[6] He rejected both Pringsheim's and De Martino's theses in favor of a "middle way," in which the potential for legal diffi-

2. Friedrich C. von Savigny, *System des heutigen Römischen Rechts* (Berlin: Veit, 1847), 131 n. m; also, Hermann Kleinschmidt, *Das Foenus Nauticum und dessen Bedeutung im römischen Rechte* (Heidelberg: J. Hörning, 1878), 51; and Sieveking, *Das Seedarlehen*, 39.

3. Otto Karlowa, *Römische Rechtsgeschichte*, vol. 2 (Leipzig: Veit, 1901), 1310; Gerhard Beseler, *Das Edictum de eo quod certo loco: Eine rechtshistorische Untersuchung* (Leipzig: Deichert, 1907), 82 n. 1.

4. Pringsheim, *Der Kauf*, 146–47.

5. Francesco De Martino, "Sul foenus nauticum," 217–47; De Martino, "Ancora," 433–45.

6. Biscardi's sympathy for the importance of commercial practice is evident in Arnaldo Biscardi, "Introduction à l'étude des pratiques commerciales dans l'histoire des droits de l'Antiquité," *RIDA* 29 (1982): 21–44.

culties encountered by the parties to maritime loan contracts were met in practice by the widespread use of nongenuine conventional penalties (concluded as stipulations) that provided for their indirect enforcement by the creditor.[7] Rather than suing on the main debt and separately for the interest, creditors sued on the penal stipulation using an action styled by the jurists as *actio traiecticiae pecuniae*. Biscardi also rejected De Martino's suspicions of interpolation to maintain the maritime loan as an autonomous contractual type distinguished by the inclusion of the condition *s. n.*

Biscardi's thesis regarding the use of penalty clauses repays closer attention. His main argument depends upon the interpretation of a single text by Ulpian:[8]

> D.15.1.3.8 (Ulp. 29 *ad ed.*):
>
> If a slave, while living as a free man, agrees to a reference to arbitration, the question is raised whether an action on the peculium should be given for the penalty agreed to be paid on disobedience to the award, the case being regarded as one of voluntary agency (*negotia gesta*), just as the action lies [for the penalty] in the case of *pecunia traiecticia*. But to both Nerva *filius* and myself the better view appears to be that an action on the peculium ought not to be given on a reference by a slave, for neither is an action given against him (the master) if the slave is condemned in an action at law.

A slave believing himself to be a freeman submits to arbitration and promises a penalty for failure to abide by the award. The question is, the slave having failed to abide by the award, can the *dominus* be sued *de peculio* for the penalty—just as would be the case if the penalty had been promised in connection with a loan of *pecunia traiecticia*? Ulpian's response, which follows the view of the younger Nerva (first century CE), is that—unlike the comparable penalty in a maritime loan contract—no action lies against the master on the *peculium*, because the slave has no procedural capacity at law.[9]

According to Biscardi, the fragment shows that the application of the *actio ex stipulatu* in connection with penal stipulations in agreements to submit to arbitration was considered by the jurists to be analogous to its identical appli-

7. See the introduction to the "Postilla": Biscardi, *Actio*, 165–66.

8. Biscardi, *Actio*, 12–24.

9. On the procedural aspects, Arnaldo Biscardi, "La capacità processuale dello schiavo," *Labeo* 21 (1975): 149–52; and now Ernest Metzger, "Cum servo agere," in *Inter cives necnon peregrinos: Essays in Honour of Boudewijn Sirks*, ed. Jan Hallebeek et al. (Göttingen: V&R Unipress, 2014), 533–43 (with literature).

cation in the case of maritime loan contracts. Since, moreover, the parties to arbitration agreements routinely dispensed with creating an obligation to abide by the award, relying instead upon a penalty as a means of indirect enforcement; so too the parties to maritime loan contracts avoided the potential that aspects of the underlying agreement might be unenforceable by stipulating for the same.[10] The use of nongenuine penalties in both contexts was therefore normalized to such an extent that the *actio ex stipulatu* was referred to as *ex compromisso* and *traiecticiae pecuniae* in each case, allowing its application to be compared by the jurists across contexts. In the text cited, for example, Ulpian used the analogy as the basis to distinguish between the application of the *actio ex stipulatu* in the event the slave conducted himself as a freeman (*se pro libero gerere*): in *compromissum*, the action did not lie *de peculio*, whereas on the maritime loan contract it did.

Biscardi drew two main conclusions from the text. The first was that the expression *traiecticia pecunia*, not *fenus nauticum*, was the preferred *nomen iuris* for the maritime loan, this being the term used by the jurists to refer to the *actio ex stipulatu* in the context of maritime loan contracts. This argument is not conclusive: in my view (for which, see chapter 5), the expression *traiecticia pecunia* refers only to the loan capital, which could be productive at any given time of either *usurae communes* or *faenus nauticum*.[11] Ulpian's reference to a so-called *actio traiecticia pecuniae* in this context means only the *actio ex stipulatu* used in connection with a penalty agreed in a *nautikē syngraphē*, just as a reference to the *actio ex compromisso* means only the *actio ex stipulatu* used in connection with a penal stipulation designed to achieve the enforcement of a *compromissum*.

Biscardi's second conclusion is that the text (together with other references) demonstrates the customary use of nongenuine conventional penalties to achieve the indirect enforcement of maritime loan contracts in the Roman period. This argument in particular provoked a fierce response from De Martino, who thought it implausible that Roman financiers should have been reduced to the choice between an unenforceable pact for interest or a heavy-handed conventional penalty.[12] Biscardi responded that in addition to providing for indirect enforcement, creditors would have been well disposed toward the use of penalties to put their debtors *in terrorem* and so reduce the risk of

10. See also Zimmermann, *Obligations*, 98–99.
11. See above, 159–69.
12. Francesco De Martino, "Sull'actio pecuniae traiecticiae," *RDN* 15, nos. 1–2 (1949): 37–38.

litigation on the merits.[13] Since these interchanges the debate has lain more or less dormant, apart from a few minor interventions.[14]

My thesis both in what remains of this section and which I developed in chapter 5 is that the move from the assumption of risk by the creditor through inclusion of a condition *salva nave* in a *nautikē syngraphē* to the identification of a contractual type is an error, motivated by Pandectist concerns. In fact the inclusion of the clause in the contract had implications for the regulation of interest, but had no bearing whatsoever on the available remedies. Neither do the texts that appear to show the enforceability of pacts for interest pose a problem in this respect: the only text that can be relied upon in this regard shows only that, by the late classical period, yields calculated as a proportion of the sum lent were recoverable on the strength of the pact, this rule applying in other contexts besides loans made subject to maritime terms.[15] There is no evidence that the Roman jurists ever had a concept of a maritime loan as an autonomous contractual type; nor did they ever conceive of the issues raised by maritime loan contracts in those terms. Finally, the 'enforcement gap' left by the availability of only the orthodox remedies is a mirage: in practice, the gap was filled by carefully constructed loan dossiers, which obviated the need for the creditor to enforce a separate clause providing for the maritime yield. Though it is possible that creditors sometimes also relied upon nongenuine penalty clauses of the kind described by Biscardi, the evidence for this is confined to inferences drawn from a solitary juristic text, finding almost no corroboration in the documentary sources.

The argument depends first upon the interpretation of the texts that appear to show the possibility of *usurae ex pacto*. There are two, the earliest of which is by Q. Cervidius Scaevola (second century CE):

D.22.2.5 (Scaev. 6 *resp.*):

[pr.] In exchange for bearing a risk (*periculi pretium est*) and even if a penal condition is not realized (*non exsistente*) you may recover what you gave and moreover something besides the money, provided that [the arrangement] does not fall into the category of a game of

13. Biscardi, *Actio*, 171–72.

14. See, e.g., Károly Visky, *Spuren der Wirtschaftskrise der Kaiserzeit in den römischen Rechtsquellen* (Budapest: Akadémiai Kiadó, 1983), 85–108. Also, Giuffrè's view that an *actio in factum* may have been available in provincial practice: Giuffrè, "'Faenus' e intraprese commerciali," 146 n. 36.

15. See, e.g., Buckland, *Text-Book*, 545.

chance (<*aleae*>): for example, those [arrangements] out of which *condic<t>iones* usually arise, such as "if you do <not> manumit," "if you do not do that," "if I will not have got well," and so on. No doubt also if I give a large sum of money to a fisherman to buy equipment so that if he makes a catch, he returns (*redderet*) and to an athlete to train and compete so that if he wins, he returns.

[1.] In all these [cases] a pact is capable of increasing the obligation without a stipulation.[16]

The text is a hornet's nest of interpretive difficulties.[17] The compilers of the *Digest* ascribed it to the sixth book of Scaevola's *responsorum libri vi*, a fourth-century abridgement of the more voluminous *digesta*, itself a collection of the jurist's replies that had been preserved among the papers of his estate.[18] Though the high level of abstraction with which the problem is discussed has led several scholars to believe that the passage may originally have belonged to Scaevola's *quaestiones*, I think the attribution is probably right, not least because many of the replies collected in both the *digesta* and *responsa* are characterized by the application of Roman law to Greek materials.[19]

Several textual issues call for discussion. First, although some of the manuscripts have *alie*, *aliam*, and so forth, Mommsen's *aleae* is preferred.[20] Second, whereas the Florentine has *condiciones*, other manuscripts give *condictiones* (*vel sim.*), which as Noodt observed makes better sense as the subject of *nasci* than the alternative.[21] It may be, as Litewski suggested, that *condiciones* in the

16. [pr.] Periculi pretium est et si condicione quamvis poenali non exsistente recepturus sis quod dederis et insuper aliquid praeter pecuniam, si modo in <aleae> speciem non cadat: veluti ea, ex quibus <condictiones> nasci solent, ut "si <non> manumittas," "si non illud facias," "si non convaluero" et cetera. nec dubitabis, si piscatori erogaturo in apparatum plurimum pecuniae dederim, ut, si cepisset, redderet, et athletae, unde se exhiberet exerceretque, ut, si vicisset, redderet. [1] In his autem omnibus et pactum sine stipulatione ad augendam obligationem prodest.

17. See, generally, Pontoriero, *Il prestito marittimo*, 81–82 and nn. 25–27. The Dutch jurist Cornelis van Eck (1662–1732) included the text in his doctoral work *De septem damnatis legibus Pandectarum seu crucibus jurisconsultorum*: on which, G. C. J. J. Van den Bergh, *Die holländische elegante Schule: Ein Beitrag zur Geschichte von Humanismus und Rechtswissenschaft in den Niederlanden 1500–1800* (Frankfurt: Klostermann, 2002), 178–79.

18. Fritz Schulz, *History of Roman Legal Science* (Oxford: Oxford University Press, 1946), 232–33; Schulz, "Überlieferungsgeschichte der Responsa des Cervidius Scaevola," in *Symbolae Friburgenses in honorem Ottonis Lenel* (Leipzig: Tauchnitz, 1931); Richard Samter, "Das Verhältnis zwischen Scaevolas Digesten und Responsen," *ZRG RA* 27 (1906): 151–210.

19. Contra Huvelin, *Droit commercial romain*, 98 n. 1 and 107–8; also, Julia M. Gokel, *Sprachliche Indizien für inneres System bei Q. Cervidius Scaevola* (Berlin: Duncker & Humblot, 2014), 305–6; Andreas Wacke, "Das nach siegreich bestandenem Wettkampf zurückzuzahlende Athleten-Darlehen. Eine Entgegnung auf Éva Jakab," *RIDA* 64 (2017): 372.

20. *aleae*] *FV^a*, *alie P^a*, *aliam P^bV^bU*: μόνον μέντοι μὴ ἐπὶ κόττῳ *B*.

21. *condictiones*] ἐξ ὧν ἁρμόξει *condicticios B*, *condiciones F*. Gerard Noodt, *De foenore et usuris libri tres: In quibus multa juris civilis, aliorumque veterum scriptorum loca, aut illustrantur aut emendantur* (Lugdunum Batavorum: Fredericum Haaring, 1698), 134.

Florentine ms. is simply a copyist's error.[22] Third, all the surviving manuscripts give *si manumittas* among the examples of penal conditions in the middle part of the *principium*. Like Litewski, I think that the section "*veluti ea . . . et cetera*" is a later insertion, made to clarify the kinds of penal conditions under discussion, probably by the editor of the original *digesta*.[23] In any case, the emendation to *si <non> manumittas* was first suggested by Cujas on the basis of a manuscript now lost but is also supported by the nature of the clauses under discussion, which are those framed in the negative as nongenuine conventional penalties.[24]

Though it would be possible to treat the text in great detail, I limit myself to assessing its value as evidence for the enforcement of *nautikai syngraphai* in classical law. Beginning with the opening section of the *principium*, Scaevola considers the position of a creditor who has been left exposed because a penal condition "*non exsistente*."[25] As the examples provided in the middle section of the *principium* show (i.e., "*si <non> manumittas . . .*"), the conditions Scaevola had in mind were the nongenuine conventional penalty clauses familiar to *nautikai syngraphai*.[26] If the penalty clause had not been concluded as a stipulation it would be unenforceable under Roman law (as a *nudum pactum*). The question that arose was therefore whether the creditor could recover both the original sum together with whatever he had demanded by way of profit (conceived as the "price of the risk," *periculi pretium*), notwithstanding that the parties had failed to conclude a stipulation. Scaevola's response was that he could recover both the original sum (impliedly by *condictio*) and "something besides the money" (*aliquid praeter pecuniam*, i.e., the *periculi pretium*). This could be either a fixed yield (*certum*) or possibly an *incertum*, such as a share of the profits (on the participatory model, such as Wilcken suggested for SB III 7169).

In the second half of the *principium* ("*nec dubitabis . . .*") Scaevola expresses his conviction that the same conclusion holds for transactions in which the debtor's obligation to make the "return" (*reddere*) was made conditional upon the success of the enterprise. These transactions have been interpreted as analogous in structure to a loan at a maritime yield:[27] in each case, the creditor lends

22. Litewski, "Römisches Seedarlehen," 161 n. 224. This may be correct in light of D.39.6.35.3 (Paul. 6 *ad l. Iul. et Pap.*), for which the Florentine ms. also has *condicio* where Mommsen prefers *condictio*.

23. Litewski, "Römisches Seedarlehen," 163.

24. *si non manumittas*] *Cuiacius*: ἵνα μὴ ἐλεγθερώσῃς *B*, si manumittas *libri nostri*. For a discussion of Cujas' emendation, see Huvelin, *Droit commercial romain*, 99.

25. For a detailed discussion of the different possible meanings of the expression, Huvelin, *Droit commercial romain*, 104–6.

26. See above, 42–44.

27. Sometimes referred to in the literature as transactions *quasi faenus nauticum*. See, e.g., Billeter, *Geschichte*, 252–54; also, the exchange between Wacke and Jakab on the topic of loans given to athletes: Andreas Wacke, "Athleten als Darlehensnehmer nach römischen Recht," *SDHI* 44 (1978):

money that the borrower uses to finance some aspect of the activity (e.g., the purchase of equipment, merchandise), on condition that his obligation to pay should only arise if, for example, he lands a catch, or the ship arrives safely. This at least was the association made by the sixth-century compilers of Justinian's *Digest*, which explains the inclusion of the text in the title *de nautico faenore* (D.22.2) despite the absence of anything in the excerpt itself to link it explicitly to maritime trade.[28] Again, the lack of an enforceable penal stipulation leaves the creditor exposed, to which Scaevola responds that a pact will be sufficient to increase (*augere*) the obligation, impliedly beyond that which would in any case be recoverable using a *condictio*.[29] The conclusion suggests the availability of an *actio bonae fidei* (perhaps *agere praescriptis verbis*) in addition to the *condictio* for the purposes of recovering the whole debt.[30]

Three considerations in my view make it unwise to depend too much upon this text as the basis for propositions concerning the enforcement of maritime loan contracts during the classical period. First, the text contains no mention of maritime loan agreements, having been included in the *Digest* title *de nautico faenore* only by association. The nature of the association made by the compilers is unknowable to us: possibly, as Huvelin speculated, the text was originally preceded by remarks specific to *faenus nauticum* that were excised; or more likely its inclusion was made on the analogy with the transactions described in the second part of the *principium* (in the Pandectist literature, *quasi faenus nauticum* so-called). There is moreover no palingenetic context that can help us in this regard: Lenel did not know where to place the text.[31] Second, it is possible that the text has been interpolated to reflect the sixth-century practice, which appears to have been to allow an *agere praescriptis verbis* to enforce maritime loan contracts *in toto*. Naturally the suspicion of interpolation without any

439–52; Éva Jakab, "Geld und Sport: Rezeption griechischer Topoi im römischen Recht?," *RIDA* 59 (2012): 93–125; Jakab, "Sponsoren und Athleten im römischen Recht: Das 'Ausbildungsdarlehen' der Athleten?," in *Sport und Recht in der Antike*, ed. Kaja Harter-Uibopou and Thomas Kruse (Vienna: Holzhausen Verlag, 2014), 249–73; Wacke, "Das Athleten-Darlehen."

28. Cf. Huvelin's suggestion that the present fragment was originally preceded by a sentence that referred to *pecunia nautica*: Huvelin, *Droit commercial romain*, 107.

29. Believing D.22.2.5.1 interpolated, principally on the basis that the opinion would provide for the actionability of a *pactum nudum*: e.g., Giovanni Rotondi, "Natura contractus," *BIDR* 24 (1911): 64 and nt 3 (= *Scritti giuridici*, vol. 2 [Milan: Ulrico Hoepli, 1922], 216 and n. 3); Salvatore Riccobono, "Stipulatio ed instrumentum nel Diritto giustinianeo," *ZRG RA* 43 (1922): 358 (= *Corso di diritto romano: Stipulationes, contractus, pacta* [Milan: Giuffrè, 1935], 412); Huvelin, *Droit commercial romain*, 107; Arangio-Ruiz, *Lineamenti*, 85 n. 2; De Villa, *Le 'usurae ex pacto'*, 108–11; Fritz Schwarz, *Die Grundlage der Condictio im klassischen römischen Recht* (Münster: Böhlau, 1952), 263; Biscardi, *Actio*, 87. Purpura tries to limit the scope of the opinion to certain special cases: Purpura, "Ricerche," 198–200; but cf. Pontoriero, *Il prestito marittimo*, 92–93. Tanev challenges the assumption that the pact in question was 'naked' and therefore *prima facie* unactionable: Tanev, "Some Highlights," 540.

30. Tanev, "Some Highlights," 539.

31. Lenel, *Pal*, 2:316.

textual basis would be no evidence in itself; though it remains possible that the compilers included the text with the added remark "*in his autem omnibus . . .*" to indicate that *nautikai syngraphai* were to be treated according to Hellenistic practice. Third, even if genuine, the lack of a direct connection to *nautikai syngraphai* together with the nature of the text (a juristic reply, perhaps academic speculation) provide little insight into the enforcement of maritime loan contracts in practice.

The second text is by Paul:

> D.22.2.7 (Paul. 3 *ad ed.*):
>
> In some contracts, interest is owed as if on a stipulation. Thus, if I lend 10 as *pecunia traiecticia* on terms that I recover capital and interest at a certain rate if the ship is safe, I can sue for the capital and interest [, even if I have not taken a stipulation].

As Ankum noted, the extract was probably written shortly after the publication of the *constitutio Antoniniana* in 212 CE, which extended Roman citizenship to all the inhabitants of the empire.[32] It was also already the case that the Emperors Septimius Severus and Caracalla had decided by rescript in 200 that a debtor who voluntarily repaid the yield on a *mutuum* on the basis of a pact should not have the *condictio indebiti* for its return.[33] Paul went still further: if a loan of traveling money had been given subject to a condition *salva nave*, the yield would be owing "as though on a stipulation" (*quemadmodum per stipulationem*). The reference to the yield as *certum* indicates that Paul meant to refer to the maritime yield demanded on the capital, not the *usurae communes* that was forthcoming after the *dies periculi*.[34] The text therefore belongs with other third-century decisions concerning loans for consumption, which treated the yield as part of the principal (and therefore recoverable by *condictio*) when it consisted of produce or when the money had been given by a *civitas*.[35]

In summary, only Paul's text gives any reliable insight into the enforcement of maritime loan contracts during the classical period, showing only that by the early third century yields demanded as a proportion of the sum

---

32. Ankum, "Some Aspects," 304. For the date, Francesco M. de Robertis, "Sulla cronologia degli scritti giuristi classici," *Rivista italiana per le scienze giuridiche*, n.s. 15 (1940): 205–20 (= Robertis, *Scritti varii di diritto romano (articoli da riviste e miscelanee). II: Storia del diritto. Diritto pubblico. Epigrafia giuridica* [Bari: Cacucci, 1987], 143–66).

33. C.4.32.3 (Sev./Ant. AA. Iuliano Serpio, 200 CE).

34. See, in this connection, D.22.2.4.1 (Pap. 3 *resp.*).

35. Roberto Fiori, "Contracts, Commerce and Roman Society," in *The Oxford Handbook of Roman Law and Society*, ed. Paul J. du Plessis, Clifford Ando, and Kaius Tuori (Oxford: Oxford University Press, 2016), 591–92.

lent were in some circumstances recoverable *ex pacto*. There is therefore no evidence that any remedies other than those conventionally used to enforce loan agreements—the *actio certae creditae pecuniae* and *actio ex stipulatu*—were used to enforce *nautikai syngraphai* during the classical period. Nor do the texts require us to postulate the availability of remedies on the basis that maritime loans were an autonomous contractual type.

This leaves only the question of the 'enforcement gap.' Biscardi suggested that, given the potential unenforceability of pacts for interest, it was standard for creditors to rely upon nongenuine conventional penalties to enforce maritime loan contracts indirectly. For this he relied upon a single text by Ulpian, citing the younger Nerva, that shows that the jurists at least were interested in comparing the availability of the *actio ex stipulatu* in the context of penalties stipulated in arbitration agreements and *nautikai syngraphai*. The argument suffers from some weaknesses, though none of them fatal. First, it is not clear from the text that the penalty clauses referred to in the context of maritime loan contracts need be precisely analogous to those in *compromissa*: Ulpian's point would hold just as well for the penal condition in the Callimachus loan contract as for a nongenuine conventional penalty. Second, there is no positive evidence in the loan documentation for the inclusion of such a clause.

In my view it is the loan documentation that holds the key for understanding how maritime loan contracts were enforced in Roman law. In commercial practice, a typical dossier included a *chirographum*, acknowledging the amount of the debt; a *cautio*, containing the terms of the agreement (recorded as a stipulation); and a *nomen arcarium*, stating that a certain sum of money had been paid out. Since maritime yields were calculated as a fixed proportion of the sum lent, it was possible for creditors to make use of techniques to capitalize the yield, either by showing the loan as *atokos* or by demanding the payment of interest as a lump sum up front (*usurae futurae*). Using these lending techniques meant that the acknowledgment of debt in the *chirographum* involved both principal and yield.

Menelaos' acknowledgment of debt in *TPSulp.* 78 provides a likely template for the drafting of chirographs connected to maritime loan contracts. In that document, the debt acknowledged by Menelaos was described as having arisen from "a sealed contract of affreightment," copies of which were presumably available to the parties. SB XIV 11850 similarly consists of a receipt for money paid out "in accordance with a maritime loan contract." *Chirographa* connected to *nautikai syngraphai* will likely have contained an acknowledgment of the whole amount of the debt (capital and yield) together with a reference to the underlying contract. It is possible as Biscardi suggested that some lenders secured the debtor's performance by further exacting a penalty for failure to perform as required, in which case the *chirographum* would contain both an acknowledgment of debt together with a penal stipulation, in a manner perhaps similar to the conditional bonds that were popular in England during the Medieval period.[36] However, only one chirograph in the Sulpician archive shows this structure, and it bears no connection to commercial lending.[37]

The chief advantage of this approach to the lender was that, when it came to enforcing the contract, his only task *in iure* was to sue on the *chirographum* using the *actio c. c. p.* (which conveniently omitted any mention of the *causa* upon which the suit was being brought). It was then for the debtor either to attack the document's evidentiary value or to plead an *exceptio* (e.g., *doli*, if the debt was not yet due, for example on failure of the condition *s. n.*; *pacti*, for example, if there was a pact not to sue; or *non numeratae pecuniae*, if the money sued for had not in fact been paid out). In all these cases the burden of proof was on the defendant to show that the debt was not in fact due. This would also explain the clever drafting of the penalty clause in the Callimachus loan contract: by stating that the sum due on failure of the condition should be equal to the whole amount of the debt (*universa pecunia*), the creditor ensured that he could rely upon the *chirographum* both for suing on the main debt and, if required, also on the penal stipulation, each being equivalent to the other.

The 'enforcement gap' is therefore something of a mirage. In Roman commercial practice, maritime loan contracts did not typically include clauses providing for the maritime yield but were rather accompanied by loan documents in which the principal and yield were capitalized. The amount stated in the *chirographum* could then be sued upon using the *actio c. c. p.*, placing the burden of proof on the debtor either to attack the document as evidence or to plead an *exceptio*. The awkward fit between *nautikai syngraphai* and Roman legal forms was therefore never much of a problem in practice, where creditors developed strategies and techniques for constructing loan dossiers that were tailored for the use of *stricti iuris* remedies.

36. For conditional bonds, see David Ibbetson, *A Historical Introduction to the Law of Obligations* (Oxford: Oxford University Press, 2001), 28–30.

37. Cf. *TPSulp.* 63, a *mutuum cum stipulatione*, which includes an acknowledgment of debt secured by a nongenuine conventional penalty.

Appendix II

Selected Texts

1. Dem. 35.10–13

Text as represented in W. Rennie, ed., *Demosthenis orationes*, vol. 2, pt. 2: *Orationes XXVII–XL* (Oxford: Clarendon Press, 1921).

ΣΥΓΓΡΑΦΗ

[10] Ἐδάνεισαν Ανδροκλῆς Σφήττιος καὶ Ναυσικράτης Καρύστιος Ἀρτέμωνι καὶ Ἀπολλοδώρῳ Φασηλίταις δραχμὰς ἀργυρίου τρισχιλίας Ἀθήνηθεν εἰς Μένδην ἢ Σκιώνην, καὶ ἐντεῦθεν εἰς Βόσπορον, ἐὰν δὲ βούλωνται, τῆς ἐπ᾽ ἀριστερὰ μέχρι Βορυσθένους, καὶ πάλιν Ἀθήναζε, ἐπὶ διακοσίαις εἴκοσι πέντε τὰς χιλίας, ἐὰν δὲ μετ᾽ Ἀρκτοῦρον ἐκπλεύσωσιν ἐκ τοῦ Πόντου ἐφ᾽ Ἱερόν, ἐπὶ τριακοσίαις τὰς χιλίας, ἐπὶ οἴνου κεραμίοις Μενδαίοις τρισχιλίοις, ὃς πλεύσεται ἐκ Μένδης ἢ Σκιώνης ἐν τῇ εἰκοσόρῳ, ἣν Ὑβλήσιος [11] ναυκληρεῖ. ὑποτιθέασι δὲ ταῦτα, οὐκ ὀφείλοντες ἐπὶ τούτοις ἄλλῳ οὐδενὶ οὐδὲν ἀργύριον, οὐδ᾽ ἐπιδανείσονται. καὶ ἀπάξουσι τὰ χρήματα τὰ ἐκ τοῦ Πόντου ἀντιφορτισθέντα Ἀθήναζε πάλιν ἐν τῷ αὐτῷ πλοίῳ ἅπαντα. σωθέντων δὲ τῶν χρημάτων Ἀθήναζε, ἀποδώσουσιν οἱ δανεισάμενοι τοῖς δανείσασι τὸ γιγνόμενον ἀργύριον κατὰ τὴν συγγραφὴν ἡμερῶν εἴκοσιν, ἀφ᾽ ἧς ἂν ἔλθωσιν Ἀθήναζε, ἐντελὲς πλὴν ἐκβολῆς, ἧς ἂν οἱ σύμπλοι ψηφισάμενοι κοινῇ ἐκβάλωνται, καὶ ἄν τι πολεμίοις ἀποτείσωσιν· τῶν δ᾽ ἄλλων ἁπάντων ἐντελές. καὶ παρέξουσι τοῖς δανείσασι τὴν ὑποθήκην ἀνέπαφον κρατεῖν, ἕως ἂν ἀποδῶσι τὸ γιγνόμενον ἀργύριον κατὰ [12] τὴν συγγραφήν. ἐὰν δὲ μὴ ἀποδῶσιν ἐν τῷ συγκειμένῳ χρόνῳ, τὰ ὑποκείμενα τοῖς δανείσασιν ἐξέστω ὑποθεῖναι καὶ ἀποδόσθαι τῆς ὑπαρχούσης τιμῆς· καὶ ἐάν τι ἐλλείπῃ τοῦ ἀργυρίου, ὃ δεῖ γενέσθαι τοῖς

δανείσασι κατὰ τὴν συγγραφήν, παρὰ Ἀρτέμωνος καὶ Ἀπολλοδώρου ἔστω ἡ πρᾶξις τοῖς δανείσασι καὶ ἐκ τῶν τούτων ἁπάντων, καὶ ἐγγείων καὶ ναυτικῶν, πανταχοῦ ὅπου ἂν]ὦσι, καθάπερ δίκην ὠφληκότων καὶ ὑπερημέρων ὄντων, [13] καὶ ἑνὶ ἑκατέρῳ τῶν δανεισάντων καὶ ἀμφοτέροις. ἐὰν δὲ μὴ εἰσβάλωσι, μείναντες ἐπὶ κυνὶ ἡμέρας δέκα ἐν Ἑλλησπόντῳ, ἐξελόμενοι ὅπου ἂν μὴ σῦλαι ὦσιν Ἀθηναίοις, καὶ ἐντεῦθεν καταπλεύσαντες Ἀθήναζε τοὺς τόκους ἀποδόντων τοὺς πέρυσι γραφέντας εἰς τὴν συγγραφήν. ἐὰν δέ τι ἡ ναῦς πάθῃ ἀνήκεστον ἐν ᾗ ἂν πλέῃ τὰ χρήματα, σωτηρία δ' ἔσται τῶν ὑποκειμένων, τὰ περιγενόμενα κοινὰ ἔστω τοῖς δανείσασιν. κυριώτερον δὲ περὶ τούτων ἄλλο μηδὲν εἶναι τῆς συγγραφῆς.

Μάρτυρες Φορμίων Πειραιεύς, Κηφισόδοτος Βοιώτιος, Ἡλιόδωρος Πιθεύς.

2. D.45.1.122.1 (Scaev. 28 *dig.*)

Text as represented in Theodor Mommsen, ed., *Digesta Iustiniani Augusti.* Vol. 2 (Berlin: Weidmann, 1870).

Callimachus mutuam pecuniam nauticam accepit a Sticho servo Seii in provincia Syria civitate Beryto usque Brentesium: idque creditum esse in omnes navigii dies ducentos, sub pignoribus et hypothecis mercibus a Beryto comparatis et Brentesium perferendis et quas Brentesio empturus esset et per navem Beryto invecturus: convenitque inter eos, uti, cum Callimachus Brentesium pervenisset, inde intra idus Septembres, quae tunc proximae futurae essent, aliis mercibus emptis et in navem mercis ipse in Syriam per navigium proficiscatur, aut, si intra diem supra scriptam non reparasset merces nec enavigasset de ea civitate, redderet universam continuo pecuniam quasi perfecto navigio et praestaret sumptus omnes prosequentibus eam pecuniam, ut in urbem Romam eam deportarent: eaque sic recte dari fieri fide roganti Sticho servo Lucii Titii promisit Callimachus. et cum ante idus supra scriptas secundum conventionem mercibus in navem impositis cum Erote conservo Stichi quasi in provinciam Syriam perventurus enavigavit: quaesitum est nave submersa, cum secundum cautionem Callimachus merces debito perferendas in nave mansisset eo tempore, quo iam pecuniam Brentesio reddere Romae perferendam deberet, an nihil prosit Erotis consensus, qui cum eo missus erat, cuique nihil amplius de pecunia supra scripta post diem conventionis permissum vel mandatum erat, quam ut eam receptam Romam perferret, et nihilo minus actione ex stipulatu Callimachus de pecunia domino Stichi teneatur. respondit secundum ea quae proponerentur teneri. item quaero, si Callimacho post diem supra scriptam naviganti Eros supra scriptus servus consenserit, an actionem domino suo semel adquisitam adimere potuerit. respondit non potuisse, sed fore exceptioni locum, si servo arbitrium datum esset eam pecuniam quocumque tempore in quemvis locum reddi.

Text conjectured by Ulrich von Lübtow, "Das Seedarlehen des Callimachus," in *Festschrift für Max Kaser zum 70. Geburtstag*, ed. D. Medicus and H. H. Seiler (Munich: C. H. Beck, 1976), 329—adapted.

Callimachus mutuam pecuniam nauticam accepit a Sticho servo [Seii] <?> in provincia Syria civitate Beryto usque Brentesium: idque creditum [esse] <est> in omnes navigii dies ducentos, sub pignoribus et hypothecis mercibus a Beryto comparatis et Brentesium perferendis et quas Brentesio empturus esset et per navem Beryto invecturus: convenitque inter eos, uti, cum Callimachus Brentesium pervenisset, inde intra idus Septembres, quae tunc proximae futurae essent, aliis mercibus emptis et in navem [mercis] <missis> [ipse] <ipsam> in Syriam per navigium proficiscatur, aut, si intra diem supra scriptam non reparasset merces nec enavigasset de ea civitate, redderet universam continuo pecuniam quasi perfecto navigio et praestaret sumptus omnes prosequentibus eam pecuniam, ut in urbem Romam eam deportarent: eaque sic recte dari fieri [fide] roganti Sticho servo [Lucii Titii] <?> <fide> promisit Callimachus. et [cum] ante idus supra scriptas secundum conventionem mercibus in navem impositis, <post idus supra scriptas> cum Erote conservo Stichi<, qui cum eo missus erat, cuique nihil amplius de pecunia supra scripta post diem conventionis permissum vel mandatum erat, quam ut eam receptam Romam perferret,> quasi in provinciam Syriam perventurus enavigavit: quaesitum est nave submersa, cum secundum cautionem Callimachus merces debito <Beryto> perferendas in [nave mansisset] <navem misisset, set (sed) enavigasset> eo tempore, quo iam pecuniam Brentesio reddere Romae perferendam deberet, an nihil prosit Erotis consensus, [qui cum eo missus erat, cuique nihil amplius de pecunia supra scripta post diem conventionis permissum vel mandatum erat, quam ut eam receptam Romam perferret,] et nihilo minus actione ex stipulatu Callimachus de pecunia domino Stichi teneatur.

respondit secundum ea quae proponerentur teneri. item quaero, si Callimacho post diem supra scriptam naviganti Eros supra scriptus servus consenserit, an actionem domino suo semel adquisitam adimere potuerit. respondit non potuisse, sed fore exceptioni locum, si servo arbitrium datum esset eam pecuniam quocumque tempore in quemvis locum reddi.

3. SB III 7169

= P. Berol. 5883 + 5853. The text is that represented in the DDbDP: 'SB III 7169,' Papyri.info, accessed 30 August 2022, http://papyri.info/ddbdp/sb;3;7169. An image of the papyrus fragments can be seen on the website of the Berlin Papyrus Database: 'P. 5853 + P. 5883: Sea Loan Contracts,' Berliner Papyrusdatenbank, accessed 30 August 2022, https://berlpap.smb.museum/01632/

1 [. . . . . .]ε̣ντα ἀπὸ τῆς προκειμένης ἡμ[έ]ρ[ας] [. . . . .]δημος μὲν πρὸς χαλκὸ[ν] [—-]

2 [. . . . .]σ̣ι, Μηνοδώραι[1] δὲ ὡσαύτως πρὸς ἀρ[γύριον] [. . . . .]ας πεντήκοντα καὶ τῶν [.][—-]

3 [. . . .] ὑπάρχων τ\ῆς/ αὐτῆς ἡμέρας ἁγνευτικὰς [.]ι καὶ οὐθενὸς αὐτῶν ἐλατ[τουμένου] [—-]

4 [. . . . . .]υτου πάλιν παρ[α]διδόναι αὐτὴν ἀπὸ τῶν προκ[ειμένων] [. . . . .] [τοὺς] ἐσομένους τόκους. [—-]

5 [. . . . . .] ς ἐδάνεισεν Ἄρχιπ[π]ος Δη[μητρίωι] [. . . . .] ____ [—-]

6 [ἐδάνει]σεν Ἄρχιππος Εὐδή[μου] [. . . . .]τ̣ι [.]α̣ ὡς ἐ[τῶν] [—-]

7 [. . . . . .]ς οὐλὴ μετώπωι ἐ[ξ] [ἀρισ]τ[ε]ρ[ᾶ]ς [Δημητρίωι] [. . . . .] [. . . . .]ξεως ὡς ἐ[τῶν] [—-]

8 [. . .] [προ]σώπωι οὐλὴ μετώπωι μέσωι καὶ Ἱππ[άρχωι] [Ἱ]ππ̣ά̣ρ[χου] [. . .][—-]

9 [. . .] [ἀνα]φαλάντωι μακροπροσώπωι οὐλὴ μ[ετώπ]ωι καὶ Δ̣[. . . . .] [τῆς] ἐπ̣ι̣γ[ον]ῆς ὡς ἐ[τῶν] [—-]

10 [. . . . .][γ]ενειον[3] καὶ Σ̣[. . .]χωι Λ[υ]σιμάχου [Λακε]δαιμονίωι [. . . . .] [ὡς] [ἐτῶν] [. . . .] [κον]τα πέντε μέσωι [—-]

11 [οὐλὴ] [μετ]ώπωι ἐ[κ] δεξιῶν καὶ Τρ[. . .]ωι Τρε̣[..] [Μεσ]σαλιώτηι [.][—-]

12 [. . . . . .]κλαστωι μακροπροσώπωι οὐλὴ χ[ειρὶ] [ἀ]ριστερᾶι το[ῖς] [ε] [τοῖς] [εἰς] τὴν Ἀρω[ματο]φ[όρον] [συ]νπλοῖς διὰ Γναίου ἐξ[—-]

13 [. . . . . .]κα εἰς ἐ[νι]α[υ]τ[ὸ]ν [ἀπὸ] [το]ῦ πρ[ο]κει[μένου] μηνός. [ἀποδότωσαν] [δὲ] οἱ δεδα[νεισ]μέ[νοι] [τῶ]ι δεδανεικότι τ[ὸ] [δάνειον] [—-]

14 [..]τα. ἐὰν δ’ ἐκπε[σ]ό[ν]τ[ε]ς τοῦ χρόν[ου] παραγένω[νται] [ἀπὸ] [τῆς] [Ἀ]ρ[ω]μα[το]φόρ[ο]υ [εἰς] τὴν χώραν, ὁμοίως [..][—-]

15 [.], ἀφ’ ἧς ἂν ἡμέρας παραγένωνται [ε]ἰς τὴν χώραν [ἡμερῶν] [. . . . .]ήκοντα. ἐὰν δὲ μὴ ἀποδῶσιν ἐν τ[ῶι] [ὡρισμένωι] [χρόνωι] [,] [ἀποτεισάτωσαν] [παραχρῆμα] [τὸ] [δάνειον] [ἡμιό]-

16 [λιον] [καὶ] τοῦ ὑπ[ε]ρπεσόντος χρόνου τοὺς κατὰ τὸ διάγραμ[μα] [τόκους] [διδ]ράχμους τῆι μνᾶι τὸν μῆνα ἕκασ[τον] [.] [ἔγγυοι] [εἰς] [ἔκτεισιν] [—-]

17 [. . . . .] [Θ]εσσαλονικεὺς ἡγεμὼν ἔξω τάξεων ὡς ἐτῶν [. . . . .] [ἑπ]τὰ μέσος, μ[ε]λίχρως, τετανὸς, στρ[ογγυλοπρόσωπος] [,] [οὐλὴ] [—-] [καὶ] [— -]

18 [. . . . . .]του Ἐλεάτης τῶν μετὰ τοῦ βασιλέως καταπε[. . . . .] [δ?]ευτέρων ἐπιλέκτων ὡς ἐτῶν τεσσ[αράκοντα] [—-]

19 [. . . . . .] δεξιᾶι καὶ Κίντος [. . . .]νιος Μεσσαλιώτηι[4] τῶν αὐ[τῶν] [ὡς] [ἐτῶν] [τ]εσσαράκοντα εὐμεγεθηι[5] μελίχρο[υς] [—-]

20 [ἀριστε]ρὰν καὶ Δημήτριος Ἀπολλωνίου Καρ[χη]δόνιος [τῶν] [τὴν] [ἔξω] [θάλ?]ασσαν πλοιζομένων ὡς ἐτῶν τρία[κοντα] [—-]

21 [. . . . . .] σύνοφρυς ἡσυχῆ καὶ Κίντος Κιντο[.] [. . . . .] [τ] ακτόμισθος ὡς ἐτῶν τεσσαράκον[τα] [—-]

22 [.]ση καὶ ἡ πρᾶξις ἔστω Ἀρχίππωι ἐ[ξ] [αὐτῶν] [τε] [τῶν] [δεδανεισμ]ένων \καὶ/ \τῶν/ \ἐγγύων/ καὶ ἐκ τῶν ὑπαρχόντ[ω]ν αὐτοῖς π[άντων] [καθάπερ] [ἐκ] [δίκης] [.] [ἐπιθέτωσαν] [δὲ] [. . . . .] [ὁ]

23 [προγεγρ]αμμένος Δημήτριος καὶ Ἵππαρχος ἀπ̣[.]ιώματα τῶν ἐκ τῆς π[ρογ]εγραμ[μένης] [—-]

24 [. . . . . .], οὗ ἂν ἡ ἐξαίρεσις γένηται τῶν ἀρω[μάτων] [?][. . . . . .] [κατὰ] [τὰ] [ἐ]πιβάλλοντ’ αὐτοῖς ἐκ τοῦ αὐτοῦ πλόο[υ] [—-]

25 [.]ι τὰ παρασταθησόμενα ὑπὸ τοῦ Ἀρ[χίππου] [?][.]ς ὥστε ἀποκαταστῆσαι εἰς τὴν χώρ[αν] [—-]

26 [. . . . . .] ὁ̣λκῆς τῶν ἀρωμάτων παραγενομ[εν] [. . . . .]ε. ἐὰν δὲ μὴ {ἐὰν} {δὲ} {μὴ} ἐπιθῶσιν, καθ[ὼς] [πρόκειται] [—-]

27 [——————————]

Apparatus

1 Scribe wrote Μηνοδώραι, for which read Μηνοδώρα.
2 Scribe wrote ταυτης, then changed to τ\ῆς/ αὐτῆς.
3 Scribe wrote γ]ενειον, for which read [γ]ενείῳ.
4 Scribe wrote Μεσσαλιώτηι, for which read Μεσσαλιώτης.
5 Scribe wrote εὐμεγεθηι, for which read εὐμεγέθης.

4. SB XIII 13167

= P. Vindob. G 40822. The text is that represented in the DDbDP: 'SB XVIII 13167,' Papyri.info, accessed 30 August 2022, http://papyri.info/ddbdp/sb;18;13167. An image of the papyrus fragments can be seen on the website of the Austrian National Library: 'Muziris Papyrus (P. Vindob. G 40822),' Österreichische Nationalbibliothek, accessed 30 August 2022, http://data.onb.ac.at/rec/RZ00001642; they have been reproduced by Federico De Romanis, *The Indo-Roman Pepper Trade and the Muziris Papyrus* (Oxford: Oxford University Press, 2020), 12–13.
Recto

i

————————————

ii

1 . . . ο̣ . μένων σου ἑτέρων ἐπ[ι]τρό̣πων ἢ φροντιστῶν καὶ στήσας
2 [δώσω τ]ῷ̣ σῷ καμηλείτηι[1] ἄλλα (τάλαντα) ρο (δραχμὰς(?)) γ̣ πρὸς ἐπίθ̣εσιν τῆς εἰς Κόπτον
3 [εἰσόδο]υ̣ καὶ ἀνοίσω διὰ τοῦ ὄρους μετὰ παραφυλακῆς καὶ ἀσ̣φα̣λεί̣ας
4 [εἰς τὰ]ς ἐπὶ Κόπτου δημοσίας παραλημπτικὰς ἀποθήκας καὶ ποι-
5 [ήσω ὑ]π̣ὸ τὴν σὴν ἢ τῶν σῶν ἐπιτρόπων ἢ τοῦ παρόντος αὐτῶν
6 [ἐξουσία]ν καὶ σφραγεῖδα[2] μέχρι ποταμοῦ ἐμβολῆς καὶ ἐμβαλοῦμαι
7 [τῶι δέ]οντι καιρῶι εἰς ποταμὸν ἀσφαλὲς πλοῖον καὶ κατοίσω εἰς τὴν
8 [ἐν Ἀλεξ]ανδρείᾳ τῆς τετάρτης παραλημπτικὴν ἀποθήκην καὶ ὁ-

9 [μοίω]ς ποιήσω ὑπὸ τὴν σὴν ἢ τῶν σῶν ἐξουσίαν καὶ σφραγεῖδα[3]. ταῖς

10 [τοῦ πλο]ι̣ου ἀπὸ τοῦ νῦν μέχρι τεταρτολογίας δαπάναις πάσαις καὶ φο-

11 [ρέτρου] ὅρους καὶ ναύλων ποταμίταις καὶ τῶν ἄλλων κατὰ μέρος ἀνα-

12 [λωμά]τ̣ων πρὸς <τὸν > -ca.?- < ὄντων > -ca.?- [πρὸς] τὸ ἐνστάντος τοῦ ἐν ταῖς κατὰ Μουζεῖριν τοῦ δα-

13 [νείου σ]υνγραφαῖς τῆς ἀποδόσεως ὡ̣ρισμένου χρόνου ἐὰν μὴ δικαί-

14 [ως τότ]ε̣ χρεολυτῶ[4] τὸ προκείμενον ἐν ἐμοὶ δάνειον τότε εἶναι

15 [πρὸς σ]ὲ καὶ τοὺς σοὺς ἐπιτρόπους ἢ φροντιστὰς τὴν ἐγλογὴν καὶ ὁλο-

16 [σχερῆ] ἐξουσίαν ὡς ἐὰν αἱρῆσθε ποιήσασθαι τὰ τῆς πράξεως χωρὶς

17 [προσβ]ολῆς καὶ προσκρίσεως κρατεῖν τε καὶ κυριεύειν τὴν π̣ρ̣ο̣κ[ει-]

18 [μένη]ν ὑποθήκην καὶ τεταρτολογεῖν καὶ τὰ λοιπὰ ἐσόμενα μέρη

19 [τρία μ]εταφέρειν οὗ ἐὰν αἱρῆσθε καὶ πωλεῖν καὶ μεθυποτίθεσθαι

20 [καὶ] ἑ̣τ̣[έ]ρωι παραχωρεῖν ὡς ἐὰν αἱρῆσθε καὶ τὰ καθ' ἑαυτὴν διοικονο-

21 [με]ῖσθαι καθ' ὃν ἐὰν βούλησθε τρόπον καὶ ἑαυτῶι ὠνεῖσθαι τῆς ἐπὶ \τοῦ/

22 καιροῦ φανησομένης τιμῆς καὶ ἐκκρού[ει]ν καὶ ἐνλογεῖν τὰ πεσούμενα

23 [τοῦ προγεγραμμέν]ο̣υ̣ δανείου. τῆς πίστεως τῶν πεσουμένων

24 [οὔσης π]ερὶ σὲ καὶ τοὺς ἐπιτρόπους ἢ φροντιστάς, ὄντων ἡμῶν ἀσυκοφαν-

25 [τήτ]ω̣ν κατὰ πάντα τρόπον. τοῦ δὲ περ̣ὶ̣ τὴν ἐνθήκην ἐνλείματός

26 [τ]ε καὶ πλεονάσματος πρὸς ἐμὲ τὸν δεδανεισμένον κα̣ὶ̣ ὑποτεθει

iii

[μένον ὄντος -ca.?-]

———————————

Apparatus

[1] Scribe wrote καμηλείτηι, for which read καμηλίτηι.
[2] Scribe wrote σφραγεῖδ, for which read σφραγῖδα.
[3] Scribe wrote σφραγεῖδα, for which read σφραγῖδα.
[4] Scribe wrote χρεολυτῶ, for which read χρεωλυτῶ.

5. SB XIV 11850 (= SB VI 9571; P. Vindob. G 19792)

The text is that represented in the DDbDP: 'SB XIV 11850,' accessed 30 August 2022, http://papyri.info/ddbdp/sb;14;11850. An image of the papyrus can be seen on the website of the Austrian National Library: 'Nachricht Über Die Auszahlung Eines Seedarlehens (P. Vindob. G 19792),' accessed 30 August 2022, http://data.onb.ac.at/rec/RZ00005972. For an earlier photograph, see Arnaldo Biscardi, *Actio pecuniae traiecticiae: Contributo alla dottrina delle clausole penali* (Turin: Giappichelli, 1974), 212.

Recto

1 ἀπὸ τῆς Μάρκου Κλαυδίου Σαβείνου [δημοσ]ί̣[ας τραπέζη]ς
2 Ζωίλῳ Ζῳιγ[ᾶ]τ̣ο̣ς καὶ Κ̣αλ̣λ̣ιμ̣ή[δει] Δ̣ι̣ογ[έν]ο̣υ̣ς [Ἀσκα]λωνε(ίταις)
3 (ἔτους(?)) ι̣β̣ Α̣ὐ̣τ̣οκ(ράτορος) Καίσαρο(ς) Τίτο(υ) Αἰλίο(υ) Ἀδριανο(ῦ) Ἀντων[ε(ίνου)] Σεβ(αστοῦ) Εὐσεβοῦς Μεχεὶρ
4 [ι]θ̣. Γάιος Λονγεῖνος Κέλερ καὶ Τιβέριος Κλαύδιος Χάρης ἃς ἐπέστειλαν
5 ὑμεῖν[1] σὺν Σωστράτῳ κα̣ὶ̣ Σώσῳ ἀμφοτέροις Διοπ̣είθους Ἀσκαλωνε(ίταις)
6 συνναυκλήροις ὑμῶν πλοίου ἀκάτο(υ) ᾧ ἐπιγραφ\ὴ/ Ἀντίνοο(ς) Φιλοσάραπ(ις) Σώζων ἀλ-
7 λ̣ηλενγύοις εἰς ἔκτεισιν δά̣ν̣ιον[2] ναυτικὸ(ν) κατὰ ναυτικὴν συνγραφὴν ἧς ἡ ἔν-
8 γειος παρ' ἐμ̣οὶ τῷ τραπ(εζίτη̣) ἐπι̣.( )ω[. .]κ̣η .( )ῳ προγεγραμμένῳ πλοίῳ καὶ τοῖς τούτο(υ)
9 σκεύεσι . . . . ἐσχάτῳ ναύ[λ]ῳ ὥστε ἔχε(ιν) ὑμ̣ᾶς τοὺς τέσσαρας ἀργυρίο(υ) (τάλαντα) ζ (δραχμὰς) Ερξ
10 σὺν οἷς ἔχε̣τ̣[ε] δ̣ι̣ὰ χειρὸς (τάλαντα) ζ (δραχμὰς) [.]ρ̣ξ τὰς λοιπὰς μ̣ὴ ἐλαττουμένου το̣ῦ̣ ἑνὸς αὐτῶν

11 Γαίου Λονγẹịνο[υ] Κẹ́λερος περ̣ὶ ὧν ἄλλων ὀφείλε[ι αὐτῷ Καλλιμ̣ήδης(?)]
12 Διογένους . . . [. . . .] . . [. . . . .] . . . κ̣ατ' ἔνγ[ραφον ἀσφάλειαν (?) -ca.?-]
13 τοκ[-ca.?-]
14 (ταλαντ) [-ca.?-]
15 . [-ca.?-]

Verso (hand 2)

1 ἔχι[3] Γ̣ά̣ι̣ο̣ς Λ[ονγεῖ]ν̣ο̣ς πιττάκιον
2 προανα( ) . . κλ̣ στ( )ο̣ των π̣ . . . ω̣ν̣

Apparatus

[1] Scribe wrote ὑμεῖν, for which read ὑμῖν.
[2] Scribe wrote δά̣ν̣ιον, for which read δάνειον.
[3] Scribe wrote ἔχι, for which read ἔχει.

TPSulp. 78 (= *TPN* 68)

The text is that represented in Camodeca, *TPS*, 2:177–78. See, also, Wolf, *TPN*, 102–4. Images of the document can be seen at Camodeca, *TPS*, 1:605–8.

Tab. I, pag. 2—tab. II, pag. 3 (*graphio, scriptura interior*)

Ἐπὶ ὑπάτων Μάρκου Ἀκύλα Ἰουλι-
ανοῦ καὶ Ποπλίου Νωνίου Ἀσ-
πρήνα πρὸ τριῶν εἰδῶν
Ἀπριλίων ἐν Δικαρχήα.
Μενέλαος Εἰρηναίου Κερα-
μιήτης ἔγραψα ἀπέχιν μαι
παρὰ Πρίμου Ποπλίου Ἀττίου Σεβή-
ρου δούλου{λου} δηνάρια χίλια
ἐκ ναυλωτικῆς ἐκσφραγισμένης,
ἃ καὶ ἀποδώσω ἀκ{ου}λούθως
τῇ ναυλωτικῇ, ἥ<ν> πεποίημαι πρὸς
αὐτόν. Κατέστησα δὲ ἔνγυον

pag. 3

εἰς ἔκτισιν τῶν προγεγραμμένων δηναρίων χιλίων Μάρκον Βαρ–βάτιον Κέλερα. *Q(uintus) Aelius Romanus scripsi rogatu et mandatu M(arci) Barbati Celeris coram ipso, quod is litteris nesciret, eum sua fide iubere eos* * ∞, *q(ui)* s*(upra) s(cripti) sunt, Primo P(ublii) Atti Severi ser(vo) pro Menela–uo Irenaei f(ilio) Ceramietae, ita uti supra scriptum es*[*t*]. (S) (S) (S)

Tab. II, pag. 4, *pars dextra* (signatories)

(S) Q(uinti) [Aeli Romani]
(S) [———]
(S) [—-] Abasc[anti?]
[———]
[———]
[———]
[———]

Bibliography

Andreau, J. *Banking and Business in the Roman World.* Translated by J. Lloyd. Cambridge: Cambridge University Press, 1999.

Ankum, J. A. "Minima de Tabula Pompeiana 13." *Cahiers d'histoire. Navires et commerces de la Méditerranée antique. Homage à Jean Rougé* 33 (1988): 271–90.

Ankum, J. A. "Noch einmal: Die Naulootike des Menelaos in TP 13 (=TPSulp. 78)—Ein Seedarlehen oder ein Seefrachtvertrag?" In *Roman Law as Formative of Modern Legal Systems: Studies in Honour of Wieslaw Litewski*, edited by J. Sondel, P. Ścislicki, and J. Reszczynski, 15–23. Krakow: Jagiellonian University Press, 2003.

Ankum, J. A. "Observations sur le prêt maritime romain, sujet cher à Henryk Kupiszewski." In *Le droit romain et le monde contemporain: Melanges à la mémoire de Henryk Kupiszewski*, edited by W. Wołodkiewicz and M. Zabłocka, 59–68. Warsaw: University of Warsaw, 1996.

Ankum, J. A. "Some Aspects of Maritime Loans in Old-Greek and in Roman Law." In *Timai Iōannou Triantaphyllopoulou*, 293–306. Athens: Ant. Sakkoulas, 2000.

Ankum, J. A. "Tabula Pompeiana 13: Ein Seefrachtvertrag oder ein Seedarlehen?" *IVRA* 29 (1978): 156–73.

Arangio-Ruiz, V. *Lineamenti del sistema contrattuale nel diritto dei papiri.* Milan: Vita e pensiero, 1928.

Arnaud, P. "Ancient Sailing-Routes and Trade Patterns: The Impact of Human Factors." In *Maritime Archaeology and Ancient Trade in the Mediterranean*, edited by D. Robinson and A. I. Wilson, 61–80. Oxford: Oxford Centre for Maritime Archaeology, 2011.

Arnaud, P. "Aux marges du formalisme juridique romain: Le contrat de naulisme." *Annuaire de droit maritime et océanique* 38 (2019): 365–88.

Arteaga, F., D. Desierto, and M. Koyama. "Shipwrecked by Rents." *Journal of Development Economics* 168 (2024).

Ashburner, Walter. *ΝΟΜΟΣ ΡΟΔΙΩΝ ΝΑΥΤΙΚΟΣ. The Rhodian Sea-Law.* Oxford: Clarendon Press, 1909.

Aubert, J.-J. "Commerce." In *The Cambridge Companion to Roman Law*, edited by D. Johnston, 213–45. Cambridge: Cambridge University Press, 2015.

Austin, M. M., and P. Vidal-Naquet. *Economic and Social History of Ancient Greece: An Introduction.* Berkeley: University of California Press, 1977.

Bablitz, L. "Roman Courts and Private Arbitration." In *The Oxford Handbook of Roman Law and Society*, edited by P. J. du Plessis, C. Ando, and K. Tuori, 234–44. Oxford: Oxford University Press, 2016.

Babusiaux, U., C. Baldus, W. Ernst, F.-S. Meissel, J. Platschek, and T. Rüfner, eds. *Handbuch des Römischen Privatrechts*. 3 vols. Tübingen: Mohr Siebeck, 2023.

Bagnall, R. S. "Price in 'Sales on Delivery.'" *GRBS* 18 (1977): 85–96.

Ballard, R. D., L. E. Stager, D. Master, D. Yoerger, D. Mindell, L. L. Whitcomb, H. Singh, and D. Piechota. "Iron Age Shipwrecks in Deep Water off Ashkelon, Israel." *AJA* 106 (2002): 151–68.

Bean, G. E. "Notes and Inscriptions from Caunus (Continued)." *JHS* 74 (1954): 85–110.

Bell, C. "Credit Markets and Interlinked Transactions." In *Handbook of Development Economics*, edited by H. Chenery and T. N. Srinivasan, 1:763–830. Amsterdam: Elsevier, 1988.

Benincasa, Z. "Prawo zastawu jako zabezpieczenie roszczenia o zwrot pozyczki morskiej w D. 22,2,6." *Zeszyty Prawnicze* 11 (2011): 99–115.

Beresford, J. *The Ancient Sailing Season*. Leiden: Brill, 2013.

Bers, V. *Demosthenes, Speeches 50–59*. Austin: University of Texas Press, 2003.

Beseler, G. *Das Edictum de eo quod certo loco: Eine rechtshistorische Untersuchung*. Leipzig: Deichert, 1907.

Bianchi, E. "In tema d'usura: Canoni conciliari e legislazione imperiale del IV secolo (contin. e fine)." *Athenaeum* 62 (1984): 136–53.

Bianchini, M. "La disciplina degli interessi convenzionali nella legislazione giustinianea." In *Studi in onore di Arnaldo Biscardi*, edited by F. Pastori, 2:389–426. Milan: Istituto Editoriale Cisalpino, La Goliardica, 1982.

Billeter, K. G. *Geschichte des Zinsfusses im griechisch-römischen Altertum bis auf Justinian*. Leipzig: Teubner, 1898.

Biscardi, A. *Actio pecuniae traiecticiae: Contributo alla dottrina delle clausole penali*. 2nd ed. Turin: Giappichelli, 1974.

Biscardi, A. "Introduction à l'étude des pratiques commerciales dans l'histoire des droits de l'Antiquité." *RIDA* 29 (1982): 21–44.

Biscardi, A. "La capacità processuale dello schiavo." *Labeo* 21 (1975): 143–71.

Biscardi, A. "La struttura classica del 'fenus nauticum.'" In *Studi in memoria di Aldo Albertoni*, edited by P. Ciapessoni, 2:343–71. Padua: CEDAM, 1937.

Biscardi, A. "Pecunia traiecticia e stipulatio poenae." *Labeo* 24 (1978): 276–300.

Biscotti, B. "Custodia, amministrazione, liquidazione di bene ereditari: Il responso di Salvio Giuliano in D.3.5.12." In *Studi per Giovanni Nicosia*, edited by E. Nicosia, 2:15–66. Milan: Giuffrè, 2007.

Blass, F. *Die Attische Beredsamkeit*. Vol. III.1. Leipzig: Teubner, 1893.

Böckh, A. *The Public Economy of the Athenians*. Translated by A. Lamb. London: Sampson Low, 1857.

Bogaert, R. "Banquiers, courtiers et prêts maritimes à Athènes et à Alexandrie." *Chronique d'Égypte* 40 (1965): 140–56.

Bogaert, R. "Le cours du statère de Cyzique aux Ve et IVe siècles avant J.-C." *L'Antiquité Classique* 32 (1963): 85–119.

Bogaert, R. "Notes critiques, juridiques et économiques sur le discours contre Phormion (Démosthène, or., 34)." In *Studi in onore di Edoardo Volterra*, edited by L. Aru and G. Astuti, 3:123–34. Milan: Giuffrè, 1971.

Bove, L. *Documenti di operazioni finanziarie dall'archivio dei Sulpici: Tabulae Pompeianae di Murécine*. Naples: Liguori, 1984.

Bowen, H. V. "The Shipping Losses of the British East India Company, 1750–1813." *International Journal of Maritime History* 32, no. 2 (2020): 323–36.

Bravo, B. "Remarques sur les assises sociales, les formes d'organisation et la terminologie du commerce maritime à l'époque archaïque." *Dialogues d'histoire ancienne* 3 (1977): 1–59.

Bresson, A. *L'économie de la Grèce des cités (fin VIe-Ier siècle a. C.).* Vol. 2. Paris: A. Colin, 2008.

Bresson, A., and F. Bresson. "Max Weber, la comptabilité rationnelle et l'économie du monde gréco-romain." *Les Cahiers du Centre de Recherches Historiques* 34 (2004).

Bretone, M. "Note minime su Celsus filius." *Labeo* 9 (1963): 331–45.

Broekaert, W. "Joining Forces: Commercial Partnerships or Societates in the Early Roman Empire." *Historia* 61, no. 2 (2012): 221–53.

Broekaert, W. *Navicularii et Negotiantes: A Prosopographical Study of Roman Merchants and Shippers.* Rahden, Nordrhein-Westfalen, Germany: Verlag Marie Leidorf, 2013.

Browne, M., and J. Allen. "Logistics Out-Sourcing." In *Handbook of Logistics and Supply Chain Management*, edited by A. M. Brewer, K. J. Button, and D. A. Hensher, Vol. 2. Amsterdam: Elsevier, 2001.

Bruijn, J. R., F. S. Gaastra, and I. Schöffer. *Dutch-Asiatic Shipping in the 17th and 18th Centuries.* Vol. 1. The Hague: Martinus Nijhoff, 1987.

Büchsenschütz, A. B. *Besitz und Erwerb im griechischen Altertum.* Halle: Verlag der Buchhandlung des Waisenhauses, 1869.

Buckland, W. W. *A Text-Book of Roman Law from Augustus to Justinian.* Edited by P. G. Stein. 3rd ed. Cambridge: Cambridge University Press, 1963.

Bürge, A. "Zum Edikt de edendo." *ZRG RA* 112 (1995): 1–50.

Calligas, P. "An Inscribed Lead Plaque from Korkyra." *Annual of the British School at Athens* 66 (1971): 79–94.

Camodeca, G. "La prassi giuridica municipale: Il problema dell'effettività del diritto romano." In *Gli statuti municipali*, edited by L. Capogrossi Colognesi and E. Gabba, 515–49. Pavia: IUSS Press, 2006.

Camodeca, G. *L'archivio puteolano dei Sulpicii.* Naples: Università Napoli Federico II, 1992.

Camodeca, G. *Tabulae Pompeianae Sulpiciorum (TPSulp.): Edizione critica dell'archivio puteolano dei Sulpicii.* 2 vols. Rome: Quasar, 1999.

Campbell, P. "Contingent Seas: Seafaring, Contracts and Law." In *Roman Law and Maritime Commerce*, edited by P. Candy and E. Mataix Ferrándiz, 23–40. Edinburgh: Edinburgh University Press, 2022.

Candy, P. "Credit for Carriage: TPSulp. 78 and P. Oxy. XLV 3250." In *Roman Law and Maritime Commerce*, edited by P. Candy and E. Mataix Ferrándiz, 171–86. Edinburgh: Edinburgh University Press, 2022.

Candy, P. "'Judging beyond the Sandal': The Use of Rhetoric in D.19.2.31 (Alf. 5 Dig. a Paulo Epit.)." *ZRG RA* 138 (2021): 310–37.

Candy, P. "Limits of Juristic Argument in the Exercitorian Edict." In *Principle and Pragmatism in Roman Law*, edited by B. J. Spagnolo and J. Sampson, 143–58. London: Hart, 2020.

Canevaro, M. *The Documents in the Attic Orators: Laws and Decrees in the Public Speeches of the Demosthenic Corpus.* Oxford: Oxford University Press, 2013.

Cantarella, E. *La fideiussione reciproca: Allellegue e mutua fideiussio*. Milan: Giuffrè, 1965.

Carawan, E. M. "The Athenian Law of Agreement." *GRBS* 46, no. 4 (2006): 339–74.

Carawan, E. M. "Paragraphê and the Merits." *GRBS* 51, no. 2 (2011): 254–95.

Carey, C., and R. A. Reid. *Selected Private Speeches*. Cambridge: Cambridge University Press, 1985.

Casson, L. "New Light on Maritime Loans." In *Symbolae Raphaeli Taubenschlag dedicatae*, edited by I. Bieżuńska-Małowist and H. Kupiszewski, 2:89–93. Warsaw: Ossolineum, 1956.

Casson, L. "New Light on Maritime Loans: P. Vindob. G 19792." In *Studies in Roman Law in Memory of A. Arthur Schiller*, edited by R. S. Bagnall and W. V. Harris, 11–17. Leiden: Brill, 1986.

Casson, L. "New Light on Maritime Loans: P. Vindob G 40822." *ZPE* 84 (1990): 195–206.

Casson, L. "P. Vindob G 40822 and the Shipping of Goods from India." *BASP* 23 (1986): 73–79.

Casson, L. *Ships and Seamanship in the Ancient World*. Baltimore: Johns Hopkins University Press, 1995.

Castresana Herrero, Amelia. *El préstamo marítimo griego y la pecunia traiecticia romana*. Salamanca: Ediciones Universidad de Salamanca, 1982.

Cenderelli, A. "Questioni di fatto e questioni di diritto alla luce di D. 3, 5, 12." In *Nozione, formazione e interpretazione del diritto: Richerche dedicate al Prof. F. Gallo*, 1:99–116. Naples: Jovene, 1997.

Cerami, P. "Considerazioni sulla cultura e sulla logica di Caecilio Africano (a proposito di D.35.2.88 pr.)." *IVRA* 22 (1971): 127–37.

Charles-Picard, G., and J. Rougé. *Textes et documents relatifs à la vie économique et sociale dans l'empire romain, 31 avant J.-C.—225 après J.-C. Collection Regards sur l'histoire*. Paris: Société d'Edition d'Enseignement Supérieur, 1969.

Chaunu, P. *Les Phillippines et le Pacifique des Ibériques (XVIe, XVIIe, XVIIIe siècles)*. Paris: S.E.V.P.E.N., 1960.

Chaunu, H., and P. Chaunu. *Séville et l'Atlantique (1504–1650)*. Vol. 6. Paris: A. Colin, 1956.

Cherchi, A. *Ricerche sulle 'usurae' convenzionali nel diritto romano classico*. Naples: Jovene, 2012.

Cifani, G. "Aspects of the Origins of Roman Maritime Trade." In *Roman Law and Maritime Commerce*, edited by P. Candy and E. Mataix Ferrándiz, 11–22. Edinburgh: Edinburgh University Press, 2022.

Cifani, G. *The Origins of the Roman Economy: From the Iron Age to the Early Republic in a Mediterranean Perspective*. Cambridge: Cambridge University Press, 2020.

Cobb, M. A. *Rome and the Indian Ocean Trade from Augustus to the Early Third Century CE*. Leiden: Brill, 2018.

Coghlin, T. "Maritime Transport Committee Report on the Removal of Insurance from Substandard Shipping: A Report to the Maritime Transport Committee of the OECD." Organisation for Economic Co-operation and Development, 2004.

Cohen, E. E. *Ancient Athenian Maritime Courts*. Princeton: Princeton University Press, 1973.

Cohen, E. E. *Athenian Economy and Society: A Banking Perspective.* Princeton: Princeton University Press, 2011.

Cohen, E. E. "Athenian Finance: Maritime and Landed Yields." *Classical Antiquity* 8, no. 2 (1989): 207–23.

Cohen, E. E. "Commercial Law." In *The Cambridge Companion to Ancient Greek Law*, edited by M. Gagarin and D. Cohen, 290–302. Cambridge: Cambridge University Press, 2005.

Cohen, E. E. "Private Agreements Purporting to Override Polis Law: A Response to Athina Dimopoulou." In *Symposion 2013: Vorträge zur griechischen und hellenistischen Rechtsgeschichte (Cambridge MA, 26.-29. August 2013)*, edited by M. Gagarin and A. Lanni, 277–86. Vienna: VÖAW, 2014.

Cohn, M. *Die sogenannte actio de eo quod certo loco: Eine Untersuchung aus dem römischen Recht.* Berlin: Weidmann, 1877.

Coing, H. "Zum Einfluß der Philosophie des Aristoteles auf die Entwicklung des römischen Rechts." *ZRG RA* 69 (1952): 24–59.

Corritore, R. P., B. Marin, and C. Virlouvet. "Fonctionnement administratif et économique." In *Entrepôts et trafics annonaires en Méditerranée: Antiquité-Temps modernes*, edited by M. Brigitte and C. Virlouvet, 137–73. Rome: École française de Rome, 2016.

Cosentino, S. "Banking in Early Byzantine Ravenna." *Cahiers de Recherches Médiévales et Humanistes* 28 (2014): 243–54.

Crook, J. A. *Legal Advocacy in the Roman World.* Ithaca: Cornell University Press, 1995.

Czajkowski, K., and Eckhardt, B. "Introduction." In *Law in the Roman Provinces*, edited by K. Czajkowski, B. Eckhardt, and M. Strothmann, 1–15. Oxford: Oxford University Press, 2020.

Dale, G. "'Marketless Trading in Hammurabi's Time': A Re-Appraisal." *Journal of the Economic and Social History of the Orient* 56, no. 2 (2013): 159–88.

D'Amati, L. *L'inattività del convenuto nel processo formulare: Indefensio, absentia e latitatio.* Naples: Jovene, 2016.

D'Arms, J. H. *Commerce and Social Standing in Ancient Rome.* Cambridge, MA: Harvard University Press, 1981.

Daube, D. "Condition Prevented from Materializing." *TvR* 28 (1960): 271–96.

Dauvillier, J. "Le droit maritime phénicien." *RIDA* 6 (1959): 33–63.

Dauvillier, J. "Quelques règles retrouvées du droit maritime phénicien." *RHD* 29 (1951): 296–98.

Dauvillier, J. "Recherches sur un contrat caravanier babylonien et sur les origines du prêt à la grosse aventure dans l'Antiquité grecque." In *Mélanges dédiés à Gabriel Marty*, 341–81. Toulouse: Université des sciences sociales de Toulouse, 1978.

Davies, J. K. *Athenian Propertied Families, 600–300 B.C.* Oxford: Oxford University Press, 1971.

De Martino, F. "Ancora sul foenus nauticum." *RDN* 2, no. 4 (1936): 433–45.

De Martino, F. *Storia economica di Roma antica.* Vol. 1. Florence: La Nuova Italia Editrice, 1979.

De Martino, F. "Sul foenus nauticum." *RDN* 1, no. 3 (1935): 217–47.

De Martino, F. "Sull'actio pecuniae traiecticiae." *RDN* 15, nos. 1–2 (1949): 19–40.

De Romanis, F. *The Indo-Roman Pepper Trade and the Muziris Papyrus*. Oxford: Oxford University Press, 2020.

De Romanis, F. "Playing Sudoku on the Verso of the 'Muziris Papyrus.'" *Journal of Ancient Indian History* 27 (2012): 75–101.

De Romanis, F. "Time to Repay a Maritime Loan: A Note on SB III 7169 and SB XVIII 13167 Recto." *Sileno: Rivista semestrale di studi classici e cristiani fondata da quintino cataudella* 40 (2014): 73–89.

De Romanis, F. "Timoteo, Apollodoro e i chirographa di TPSulp. 78." In *Uomini, istituzioni, mercati: Studi di storia per Elio Lo Cascio*, edited by M. Maiuro, G. D. Merola, M. De Nardis, and G. Soricelli, 443–48. Bari: Edipuglia, 2019.

De Ste Croix, G. E. M. "Ancient Greek and Roman Maritime Loans." In *Debits, Credits, Finance and Profits*, edited by H. C. Edey and B. S. Yamey, 41–59. London: Sweet & Maxwell, 1974.

De Villa, V. *Le 'usurae ex pacto' nel diritto romano*. Rome: Foro italiano, 1937.

Dimopoulou, Athina A. "'Ἄκυρον Ἔστω: Legal Invalidity in Greek Inscriptions." In *Symposion 2013: Vorträge zur griechischen und hellenistischen Rechtsgeschichte (Cambridge MA, 26.-29. August 2013)*, edited by M. Gagarin and A. Lanni, 249–76. Vienna: VÖAW, 2014.

Donatuti, G. "Di un punto controverso in materia di stipulazione penale." *SDHI* 1 (1935): 299–306.

Duncan-Jones, R. *Structure and Scale in the Roman Economy*. Cambridge: Cambridge University Press, 1990.

Edgar, C. C. *Catalogue général des antiquités égyptiennes du Musée du Caire*. Cairo: Le Caire Impr. de l'Institut français d'archéologie orientale, 1925.

Elefante, A. "'Interpellatio' e 'mora.'" *Labeo* 6 (1960): 30–49.

Elefante, A. "La 'mora ex re' e l''interpellatio.'" In *Mnemeion S. Solazzi*, 397–431. Naples: Jovene, 1964.

Emanuel, J. P. "Seafaring and Shipwreck Archaeology." In *The Oxford Handbook of the Phoenician and Punic Mediterranean*, edited by B. R. Doak and C. López-Ruiz, 423–33. Oxford: Oxford University Press, 2019.

Erxleben, E. "Die Rolle der Bevölkerungklassen im Aussenhandel Athens im 4. Jahrhundert v.u.Z." In *Hellenische Poleis: Krise, Wandlung, Wirkung*, edited by E. C. Welskopf, 1:460–520. Berlin: Akademie-Verlag, 1974.

Evers, K. G. *Worlds Apart Trading Together: The Organisation of Long-Distance Trade between Rome and India in Antiquity*. Oxford: Archaeopress, 2016.

Fargnoli, I. "Condictio aus Darlehen (mutuum)." In *Handbuch des Römischen Privatrechts*, edited by U. Babusiaux, C. Baldus, W. Ernst, F.-S. Meissel, J. Platschek, and T. Rüfner, 2:1906–11. Tübingen: Mohr Siebeck, 2023.

Fasolino, F. *Studi sulle usurae*. Salerno: Brunolibri, 2006.

Finkenauer, T. "Eid (iusiurandum)." In *Handbuch des Römischen Privatrechts*, edited by U. Babusiaux, C. Baldus, W. Ernst, F.-S. Meissel, J. Platschek, and T. Rüfner, 1:559–63. Tübingen: Mohr Siebeck, 2023.

Finley, M. I. *The Ancient Economy*. Berkeley: University of California Press, 1973.

Finley, M. I. *Studies in Land and Credit in Ancient Athens, 500–200 B.C.: The Horos Inscriptions*. New Brunswick, NJ: Rutgers University Press, 1952.

Fiori, R. "Contracts, Commerce and Roman Society." In *The Oxford Handbook of Roman Law and Society*, edited by P. J. du Plessis, C. Ando, and K. Tuori, 581–95. Oxford: Oxford University Press, 2016.

Fiori, R. "L'allocazione del rischio nei contratti relativi al trasporto." In *Diritto romano e economia: Due modi di pensare e organizzare il mondo (nei primi tre secoli dell'Impero)*, edited by E. Lo Cascio and D. Mantovani, 507–67. Pavia: Pavia University Press, 2018.

Fiori, R. "Rise and Fall of the Specificity of Contracts." In *Nova Ratione: Change of Paradigms in Roman Law*, edited by A. J. B. Sirks, 33–49. Wiesbaden: Harrassowitz Verlag, 2014.

Fischer-Bovet, C. *Army and Society in Ptolemaic Egypt*. Cambridge: Cambridge University Press, 2014.

Fraser, P. M. *Ptolemaic Alexandria*. Vol. 2. Oxford: Clarendon Press, 1972.

Frezza, P. "La clausola penale." In *Studi in memoria di Lorenzo Mossa, pubblicati per iniziativa della Facoltà di giurisprudenza dell'Università di Pisa*, 2:269–313. Padua: CEDAM, 1960.

Frier, B. W. *A Casebook on the Roman Law of Contracts*. Oxford: Oxford University Press, 2021.

Frier, B. W., trans. *The Codex of Justinian: A New Annotated Translation, with Parallel Latin and Greek Text*. Vol. 2. Cambridge: Cambridge University Press, 2016.

Frier, B. W. *The Rise of the Roman Jurists: Studies in Cicero's Pro Caecina*. Princeton: Princeton University Press, 1985.

Frunzio, M. "Il caso della Sfortunata navigazione di Callimaco: D.45.1.122.1 (SCAEV. 28 DIG.)." *SDHI* 83 (2017): 271–97.

Garland, R. *The Piraeus: From the Fifth to the First Century B.C.* Bristol: Bristol Classical Press, 1987.

Garner, R. *Law and Society in Classical Athens*. London: Croom Helm, 1987.

Garnsey, P. "Grain for Athens." *History of Political Thought* 6, nos. 1–2 (1985): 62–75.

Gaurier, D. *Le droit maritime romain*. Rennes: Presses Universitaires de Rennes, 2004.

Gernet, L. *Démosthène. Plaidoyers civils*. Vol. I, *Discours XXVII–XXXVIII*. Paris: Les Belles Lettres, 1954.

Gernet, L. "Sur la notion du jugement en droit grec." *Archives d'histoire du droit oriental* 1 (1937): 111–44.

Gibbins, D. "Shipwrecks and Hellenistic Trade." In *Hellenistic Economies*, edited by J. Davies and Z. H. Archibald, 273–312. London: Routledge, 2001.

Giuffrè, V. "'Faenus' e intraprese commerciali." *Seminarios complutenses de derecho romano* 7 (1995): 133–67.

Giuffrè, V. "Il prestito ad 'interessi marittimi' nel tardo impero." In *Atti dell'Accademia romanistica costantiniana: 12. Convegno internazionale in onore di Manlio Sargenti*, edited by G. Crifò and S. Giglio, 353–65. Naples: Edizioni scientifiche italiane, 1998.

Glück, C. F. von. *Ausführliche Erläuterung der Pandecten nach Hellfeld: Ein Commentar*. Vol. XXI. Erlangen: Johann Jacob Palm, 1820.

Gofas, D. "The Byzantine Law of Interest." In *The Economic History of Byzantium from the Seventh through to the Fifteenth Century*, edited by A. E. Laiou, 1095–1104. Washington, DC: Dumbarton Oaks, 2002.

Gofas, D. C. "Encore une fois sur la Tabula Pompeiana 13 (essai d'une interprétation nouvelle)." In *Symposion 1993: Vorträge zur griechischen und hellenistischen Rechtsgeschichte (Graz-Andritz, 12–16 September 1993)*, edited by G. Thür, 251–66. Cologne: Böhlau, 1994.

Gokel, J. M. *Sprachliche Indizien für inneres System bei Q. Cervidius Scaevola*. Berlin: Duncker & Humblot, 2014.

Gomme, A. W. *The Population of Athens in the Fifth and Fourth Centuries B.C.* Oxford: Blackwell, 1933.

Gradenwitz, O. "Schiedseid und Beweiseid im römischen Civilprozesse, Beitrag zur Erörterung der Eidesfrage von Dr. Gustav Demelius." *ZRG RA* 8 (1887): 269–78.

Gröschler, P. "Darlehensvalutierung und Darlehenszins in den Urkunden aus dem Archiv der Sulpizier." In *Festschrift für Rolf Knütel zum 70. Geburtstag*, edited by H. Altmeppen, I. Reichard, and M. J. Schermaier, 387–99. Heidelberg: C.F. Müller, 2009.

Gröschler, P. "Die Konzeption des Mutuum cum Stipulatione." *TvR* 74 (2006): 261–87.

Gröschler, P. *Die Tabellae-Urkunden aus den pompejanischen und herkulanensischen Urkundenfunden*. Berlin: Duncker & Humblot, 1997.

Gröschler, P. "Il 'mutuum cum stipulatione' e il problema degli interessi." In *Quaderni lupiensi di storia e diritto*, edited by F. Lamberti, 109–26. Lecce: Edizioni del Grifo, 2009.

Hadjidaki, E. "Underwater Excavations of a Late Fifth Century Merchant Ship at Alonnesos, Greece: The 1991–1993 Seasons." *Bulletin de Correspondance Hellénique* 2 (1996): 561–93.

Halbwachs, V. "Ipsae sibi negotia tractant: Zur Frau als Geschäftpartnerin im Spiegel römischrechtlicher Quellen." In *Règle et pratique du droit dans les réalités juridiques de l'antiquité*, edited by I. Piro, 349–63. Catanzaro: Rubbettino, 1999.

Hansen, M. H. "Two Notes on the Athenian Dikai Emporikai." In *Symposion 1979: Actes du IVᵉ Colloque International de Droit Grec et Hellénistique (Égine, 3–7 Septembre 1979)*, edited by P. Dimakis, 167–75. Cologne: Böhlau, 1983.

Harke, J. D. "Die interpellatio als Synonym für den Tatbestand des Schuldnerverzugs—Spuren der Rechtspraxis in den Digesten." In *Usus Antiquus Juris Romani: Antikes Recht in Lebenspraktischer Anwendung*, edited by W. Ernst and É. Jakab, 77–85. Berlin: Springer, 2005.

Harke, J. D. *Mora debitoris und mora creditoris im klassischen römischen Recht*. Berlin: Duncker & Humblot, 2005.

Harrauer, H., and P. J. Sijpesteijn. "Ein neues Dokument zu Roms Indienhandel. P. Vindob. G 40822." *Anzeiger der philosophisch-historischen Klasse / Österreichische Akademie der Wissenschaften* 122 (1985): 124–55.

Harris, E. M. "The Athenian View of an Athenian Trial." In *Use and Abuse of Law in the Athenian Courts*, edited by C. Carey, I. Giannadaki, and B. Griffith-Williams, 42–74. Leiden: Brill, 2018.

Harris, E. M. "How Strictly Did the Athenian Courts Apply the Law? The Role of 'Epieikeia.'" *BICS* 56 (2013): 27–48.

Harris, E. M. "Hypotheca in Roman Law and ὑποθήκη in Greek Law." In *Transferts culturels et droits dans le monde grec et hellénistique (Actes du colloque international,*

Reims, 14–17 mai 2008), edited by B. Legras, 433–41. Paris: Éditions de la Sorbonne, 2012.

Harris, E. M. "Law and Economy in Classical Athens: [Demosthenes], 'Against Dionysodorus.'" In *Athenian Law in Its Democratic Context*, edited by A. Lanni. Cambridge, MA: Harvard University Center for Hellenic Studies, 2003.

Harris, E. M. "The Meaning of the Legal Term Symbolaion, the Law about Dikai Emporikai and the Role of the Paragraphe Procedure." *Dike* 18 (2015): 7–36.

Harris, E. M. *The Rule of Law in Action in Democratic Athens*. Oxford: Oxford University Press, 2013.

Harris, R. "The Organization of India-to-Rome Trade: Loans and Agents in the Muziris Papyrus." In *Roman Law and Economics*, edited by G. Dari-Mattiacci and D. P. Kehoe, 1:163–96. Oxford: Oxford University Press, 2020.

Harris, W. V. "A Strange Fact about Shipboard Coin Hoards Throws Light on the Roman Empire's Financial System." *Athenaeum* 107 (2019): 150–55.

Harrison, A. R. W. *The Law of Athens*. Vol. 2, *Procedure*. Oxford: Clarendon Press, 1971.

Harvey, F. D. "The Maritime Loan in Eupolis' 'Marikas' (P. Oxy. 2741)." *ZPE* 23 (1976): 231–33.

Hasebroek, J. *Staat und Handel im antiken Griechenland*. Tübingen: Mohr Siebeck, 1928.

Hasebroek, J. *Trade and Politics in Ancient Greece*. Translated by L. M. Fraser and D. C. Macgregor. London: G. Bell & Sons, 1933.

Hauben, H. "'Ceux qui naviguent sur la mer extérieure' ('SB' III 7169)." *ZPE* 59 (1985): 135–36.

Haubner, D. *Studien zur lex Rhodia de iactu*. Munich: C.H. Beck, 2021.

Heichelheim, F. "Zu Pap. Berol. 5883 + 5853." *Aegyptus* 13, nos. 1–2 (1933): 187–92.

Hellwege, P., and G. Rossi. "Maritime Risk Management: Marine Insurance, General Average, Sea Loan." In *Maritime Risk Management: Essays on the History of Marine Insurance, General Average and Sea Loan*, edited by P. Hellwege and G. Rossi, 9–16. Berlin: Duncker & Humblot, 2021.

Hesnard, A., M.-B. Carre, M. Rival, B. Dangréaux, M. Thinon, M. Blaustein, A. Chéné, P. Foliot, and H. Bernard-Maugiron. "L'épave romaine Grand Ribaud D (Hyères, Var)." *Archaeonautica* 8 (1988): 5–180.

Hewitt, A. "Universal Justice and Epieikeia in Aristotle." *Polis* 25 (2008): 115–30.

Hopper, R. J. *Trade and Industry in Classical Greece*. London: Thames & Hudson, 1979.

Horden, P., and N. Purcell. *The Corrupting Sea: A Study of Mediterranean History*. Oxford: Blackwell, 2000.

Hunter, V. J. *Policing Athens: Social Control in the Attic Lawsuits, 420–320 B.C.* Princeton: Princeton University Press, 1994.

Huschke, Ph. E. "Das Schifflehen des Callimachus." *Zeitschrift für Civilrecht und Prozeß*, Neue Folge 10 (1853): 1–17.

Huschke, Ph. E. *Die Lehre des römischen Rechts vom Darlehn und den dazu gehörigen Materien: Eine civilistische Monographie*. Stuttgart: F. Enke, 1882.

Huvelin, P. *Études d'histoire du droit commercial romain (histoire externe-droit maritime)*. Paris: Recueil Sirey, 1929.

Ibbetson, D. *A Historical Introduction to the Law of Obligations*. Oxford: Oxford University Press, 2001.

Isager, S., and M. H. Hansen. *Aspects of Athenian Society in the Fourth Century B.C. A Historical Introduction to and Commentary on the Paragraphe-Speeches and the Speech Against Dionysodorus in the Corpus Demosthenicum (XXXII–XXXVIII and LVI)*. Translated by J. H. Rosenmeier. Odense: Odense University Press, 1975.

Jakab, É. "Chirographum in Theorie und Praxis." In *Römische Jurisprudenz—Dogmatik, Überlieferung, Rezeption. Festschrift für Detlef Liebs zum 75. Geburtstag*, edited by K. Muscheler, 275–92. Berlin: Duncker & Humblot, 2011.

Jakab, É. "Geld und Sport: Rezeption griechischer Topoi im römischen Recht?" *RIDA* 59 (2012): 93–125.

Jakab, É. "Loans and Securities: Tracing Maritime Trade in the Archive of the Sulpicii." In *Roman Law and Maritime Commerce*, edited by P. Candy and E. Mataix Ferrándiz, 137–70. Edinburgh: Edinburgh University Press, 2022.

Jakab, É. "Sponsoren und Athleten im römischen Recht: Das 'Ausbildungsdarlehen' der Athleten?" In *Sport und Recht in der Antike*, edited by K. Harter-Uibopou and T. Kruse, 249–73. Vienna: Holzhausen Verlag, 2014.

Jakab, É. "Vectura pro mutua: Überlegungen zu TP 13 und Ulp. D. 19, 2, 15, 61." *ZRG RA* 117 (2000): 244–73.

Jakab, É., and U. Manthe. "Recht in der römischen Antike." In *Rechtskulturen der Antike*, edited by U. Manthe, 239–309. Munich: C.H. Beck, 2003.

Jenks, S. "Capturing Opportunity, Financing Trade." In *The Routledge Handbook of Maritime Trade around Europe 1300–1600: Commercial Networks and Urban Autonomy*, edited by W. Blockmans, M. Krom, and J. Wubs-Mrozewicz, 36–56. London: Routledge, 2017.

Jhering, R. von. "Skizzen." *Jahrbücher für die Dogmatik des heutigen römischen und deutschen Privatrechts* 19 (1881): 1–23 (= "Skizzen." In *Gesammelte Aufsätze aus den Jahrbüchern für die Dogmatik des heutigen römischen und deutschen Privatrechts*, 3:211–32. Aalen: Scientia Verlag, 1969).

Johnston, D. "Breach of Contract." In *A History of Private Law in Scotland*, edited by K. Reid and R. Zimmermann, 2:175–94. Oxford: Oxford University Press, 2001.

Johnston, D. *Roman Law in Context*. 2nd ed. Cambridge: Cambridge University Press, 2022.

Jones, D. F. *The Bankers of Puteoli: Finance, Trade and Industry in the Roman World*. Stroud: Tempus, 2006.

Jouguet, P. "Dédicace grecque de Médamoud." *Le Bulletin de l'Institut français d'archéologie orientale* 31 (1931): 1–29.

Karlowa, O. *Römische Rechtsgeschichte*. Vol. 2. Leipzig: Veit, 1901.

Kaser, M. *Das römische Privatrecht*. Vol. 1. Munich: C.H. Beck, 1971.

Kaser, M. *Das römische Zivilprozessrecht*. 2nd ed., revised by K. Hackl. Munich: C.H. Beck, 1996.

Kaser, M. *Restituere als Prozeßgegenstand*. Berlin: C.H. Beck, 1932.

Kaser, M. "Stellvertretung und 'notwendige Entgeltlichkeit.'" *ZRG RA* 91 (1974): 146–204.

Klausberger, P. "Klagen aus Quasidelikten." In *Handbuch des Römischen Privatrechts*, edited by U. Babusiaux, C. Baldus, W. Ernst, F.-S. Meissel, J. Platschek, and T. Rüfner, 2:2647–60. Tübingen: Mohr Siebeck, 2023.

Kleinschmidt, H. *Das Foenus Nauticum und dessen Bedeutung im römischen Rechte*. Heidelberg: J. Hörning, 1878.

Klingenberg, G. "Formularprozess: Verhandlung apud iudicem." In *Handbuch des Römischen Privatrechts*, edited by U. Babusiaux, C. Baldus, W. Ernst, F.-S. Meissel, J. Platschek, and T. Rüfner, 1:413–75. Tübingen: Mohr Siebeck, 2023.

Klingmüller, F. "Fenus." In *Paulys Real-Encyclopädie der classischen Altertumswissenschaft*, edited by A. F. Pauly and G. Wissowa, 6.2:2187–2205. Stuttgart: J. B. Metzler, 1909.

Knütel, R. *Stipulatio poenae: Studien zur römischen Vertragsstrafe*. Cologne: Böhlau, 1976.

Korver, J. *De terminologie van het crediet-wezen in het Grieksch*. Amsterdam: Arno Press, 1934.

Krampe, C. "Der Seedarlehensstreit des Callimachus—D. 45,1,122,1 Scaevola 28 digestorum." In *Collatio iuris Romani: Études dédiées à Hans Ankum à l'occasion de son 65e anniversaire*, edited by R. Feenstra, A. S. Hartkamp, J. E. Spruit, P. J. Sijpesteijn, and L. C. Winkel, 207–22. Amsterdam: Gieben, 1995.

Krampe, C. "Fenus nauticum." In *Der neue Pauly: Enzyklopädie der Antike*, edited by H. Cancik, H. Schneider, and A. F. Pauly, 4:471–73. Stuttgart: J.B. Metzler, 1998.

Kränzlein, A. *Eigentum und Besitz im griechischen Recht des fünften und vierten Jahrhunderts v. Chr.* Berlin: Duncker & Humblot, 1963.

Kupiszewski, H. "Sul prestito marittimo nel diritto romano classico: Profili sostanziali e processuali." *Index* 3 (1972): 368–81.

Lambert, S. D. "Ten Notes on Attic Inscriptions." *ZPE* 135 (2001): 51–62.

Lanni, A. *Law and Justice in the Courts of Classical Athens*. Cambridge: Cambridge University Press, 2006.

Leão, D. F., and P. J. Rhodes. *The Laws of Solon: A New Edition with Introduction, Translation and Commentary*. London: I.B. Tauris, 2015.

Lenel, O. *Palingenesia iuris civilis*. 2 vols. Leipzig: Tauchnitz, 1889.

Lewis, D. M. "A Cargo of Slaves? Demosthenes 34.10." *Mariner's Mirror* 108, no. 2 (2022): 135–48.

Lewis, N. "The Meaning of Σὺν Ἡμιολίᾳ and Kindred Expressions in Loan Contracts." *TAPhA* 76 (1945): 126–39.

Ligt, L. de. "Law-Making and Economic Change during the Republic and Early Empire." In *Roman Law and Economics*, edited by G. Dari-Mattiacci and D. P. Kehoe, 1:85–108. Oxford: Oxford University Press, 2020.

Lipsius, J. H. *Das attische Recht und Rechtsverfahren*. Leipzig: O. R. Reisland, 1905.

Litewski, W. "Bemerkungen zum Römischen Seedarlehen." In *Studi in onore di Cesare Sanfilippo*, 4:381–97. Milan: Giuffrè, 1983.

Litewski, W. "'Non numerata pecunia' im klassischen römischen Recht." *SDHI* 60 (1994): 405–56.

Litewski, W. "Review of Castresana Herrero, A., *El préstamo marítimo griego y la pecunia traiecticia romana* (Salamanca: Ediciones Universidad de Salamanca, 1982)." *IVRA* 34 (1983): 116–21.

Litewski, W. "Römisches Seedarlehen." *IVRA* 24 (1973): 112–83.

Lloyd, G. E. R. *Polarity and Analogy: Two Types of Argumentation in Early Greek Thought*. Cambridge: Cambridge University Press, 1966.

Lohsse, S. "Vom Seedarlehen zur Versicherung in der mittelalterlichen Rechtswissenschaft." *ZRG RA* 133 (2016): 372–99.

López-Ruiz, C. *Phoenicians and the Making of the Mediterranean*. Cambridge, MA: Harvard University Press, 2021.

Lübtow, U. von. "Catos Seedarlehen." In *Festschrift für Erwin Seidl zum 70. Geburtstag*, edited by H. Hübner, E. Klingmüller, and A. Wacke, 103–17. Cologne: Hanstein, 1975.

Lübtow, U. von. "Das Seedarlehen des Callimachus." In *Festschrift für Max Kaser zum 70. Geburtstag*, edited by D. Medicus and H. H. Seiler, 329–49. Munich: C.H. Beck, 1976.

Luchetti, G. "Il prestito di denaro a interesse in età giustinianea." *Cultura giuridica e diritto vivente* 3 (2016).

MacCormack, G. "Periculum." *ZRG RA* 96 (1979): 129–72.

MacDowell, D. M. "The Athenian Penalty of Epobelia." In *Symposion 2007: Vorträge zur griechischen und hellenistischen Rechtsgeschichte (Durham, 2.-6. September 2007)*, edited by E. M. Harris and G. Thür, 87–94. Vienna: VÖAW, 2009.

MacDowell, D. M. *Demosthenes, Speeches 27–38*. Austin: University of Texas Press, 2004.

MacDowell, D. M. *Demosthenes the Orator*. Oxford: Oxford University Press, 2009.

MacDowell, D. M. *The Law in Classical Athens*. Ithaca: Cornell University Press, 1978.

Mantovani, D. *Le formule del processo privato romano: Per la didattica delle istituzioni di diritto romano*. Como: New Press, 1992.

Marek, C. *Die Inschriften von Kaunos*. Munich: C.H. Beck, 2006.

Marzano, A. "The Personal Infrastructure of Maritime Trade." In *Roman Law and Maritime Commerce*, edited by P. Candy and E. Mataix Ferrándiz, 57–76. Edinburgh: Edinburgh University Press, 2022.

Mataix Ferrándiz, E. *Shipwrecks, Legal Landscapes, and Mediterranean Paradigms: Gone under Sea*. Leiden: Brill, 2022.

Matthiass, B. *Das foenus nauticum und die geschichtliche entwicklung der bodmerei*. Würzburg: Druck der Thein'schen druckerei (Stürtz), 1881.

Metzger, E. "Cum Servo Agere." In *Inter cives necnon peregrinos: Essays in Honour of Boudewijn Sirks*, edited by J. Hallebeek, M. J. Schermaier, R. Fiori, E. Metzger, and J.-P. Coriat, 533–43. Göttingen: V&R Unipress, 2014.

Metzger, E. "Formularprozess: Verfahrenseinleitung." In *Handbuch des Römischen Privatrechts*, edited by U. Babusiaux, C. Baldus, W. Ernst, F.-S. Meissel, J. Platschek, and T. Rüfner, 1:350–71. Tübingen: Mohr Siebeck, 2023.

Metzger, E. *Litigation in Roman Law*. Oxford: Oxford University Press, 2005.

Metzger, E. *A New Outline of the Roman Civil Trial*. Oxford: Clarendon Press, 1997.

Metzger, E. "Republican Civil Procedure: Sanctioning Reluctant Defendants." In *The Oxford Handbook of Roman Law and Society*, edited by P. J. du Plessis, C. Ando, and K. Tuori, 245–56. Oxford: Oxford University Press, 2016.

Meyer, E. A. *Legitimacy and Law in the Roman World: Tabulae in Roman Belief and Practice*. Cambridge: Cambridge University Press, 2004.

Meyer, P. M. "Juristischer Papyrusbericht IV." *ZRG RA* 46 (1926): 305–49.

Meyer-Laurin, H. J. *Gesetz und Billigkeit im attischen Prozess*. Weimar: H. Böhlaus Nachfolger, 1965.

Meyer-Laurin, H. J. "Law and Equity in the Attic Trial." In *The Attic Orators*, edited by E. Carawan, translated by David Mirhady, 116–39. Oxford: Oxford University Press, 2007.

Meyer-Laurin, H. J. "Zur Entstehung und Bedeutung der καθάπερ ἐκ δίκης-Klausel in den griechischen Papyri Ägyptens." In *Symposion 1971: Vorträge zur griechischen und hellenistischen Rechtsgeschichte*, edited by H. J. Wolff, 189–204. Cologne: Böhlau, 1975.

Miglietta, M. *'Servius respondit': Studi intorno a metodo e interpretazione nella scuola giuridica serviana. Prolegomena I.* Trento: Universita degli Studi di Trento, 2010.

Miller, D. J. D., and P. Sarris, trans. *The Novels of Justinian: A Complete Annotated English Translation.* Vol. 2. Cambridge: Cambridge University Press, 2018.

Millett, P. *Lending and Borrowing in Ancient Athens.* Cambridge: Cambridge University Press, 1991.

Millett, P. "Maritime Loans and the Structure of Credit in Fourth-Century Athens." In *Trade in the Ancient Economy*, edited by P. Garnsey, K. Hopkins, and C. R. Whittaker, 36–52. London: Chatto & Windus, 1983.

Minaud, G. *Les gens de commerce et le droit à Rome.* Aix-en-Provence: Presses universitaires d'Aix-Marseille, 2011.

Mommsen, Th., ed. *Digesta Iustiniani Augusti.* 2 vols. Berlin: Weidmann, 1870.

Morelli, F. "Dal Mar Rosso ad Alessandria: Il 'verso' (ma anche il 'recto') del 'papiro di Muziris' (SB XVIII 13167)." *Tyche* 26 (2011): 199–233.

Moreno, A. *Feeding the Democracy: The Athenian Grain Supply in the Fifth and Fourth Centuries BC.* Oxford: Oxford University Press, 2007.

Mossé, C. "The 'World of the Emporium' in the Private Speeches of Demosthenes." In *Trade in the Ancient Economy*, edited by P. Garnsey, K. Hopkins, and C. R. Whittaker, 53–63. London: Chatto & Windus, 1983.

Noodt, G. *De foenore et usuris libri tres: In quibus multa juris civilis, aliorumque veterum scriptorum loca, aut illustrantur aut emendantur.* Lugdunum Batavorum: Fredericum Haaring, 1698.

Oppenheim, A. L. "The Seafaring Merchants of Ur." *Journal of the American Oriental Society* 74 (1954): 6–17.

Paley, F. A., and J. E. Sandys. *Select Private Orations of Demosthenes.* 2nd ed. Vol. 1. Cambridge: Cambridge University Press, 1886.

Paoli, U. E. *Studi di diritto attico.* Firenze: Bemporad & Figlio, 1930.

Paoli, U. E. *Studi sul processo attico.* Padova: A. Milani, 1933.

Paoli, U. E. "Zur Gerichtszeit der Δίκαι Ἐμπορικαί im Attischen Recht." *ZRG RA* 29 (1929): 473–77.

Pardessus, J.-M. *Collection de lois maritimes antérieures au XVIII siècle.* Vol. 1. Paris: Imprimerie Royale, 1828.

Parker, A. J. *Ancient Shipwrecks of the Mediterranean and the Roman Provinces.* Oxford: Tempus Reparatum, 1992.

Penrose, C. T. *Select Private Orations of Demosthenes.* Cambridge: Cambridge University Press, 1843.

Pestman, P. W. "Loans Bearing No Interest?" *JJP* 16–17 (1971): 7–29.

Phillips, D. *The Law of Ancient Athens.* Ann Arbor: University of Michigan Press, 2013.

Platschek, J. *Das Edikt de Pecunia Constituta: Die römische Erfüllungszusage und ihre Einbettung in den hellenistischen Kreditverkehr.* Munich: C.H. Beck, 2013.

Platschek, J. "Formularprozess: Verhandlung in iure." In *Handbuch des Römischen Privatrechts*, edited by U. Babusiaux, C. Baldus, W. Ernst, F.-S. Meissel, J. Platschek, and T. Rüfner, 1:372–412. Tübingen: Mohr Siebeck, 2023.

Pontoriero, I. *Il prestito marittimo in diritto romano*. Bologna: Bononia University Press, 2011.

Préaux, C. *L'économie royale des Lagides*. Brussels: Éditions de la Fondation Égyptologique Reine Élisabeth, 1939.

Pringsheim, F. *Der Kauf mit fremdem Geld: Studien über die Bedeutung der Preiszahlung für den Eigentumserwerb nach griechischem und römischem Recht*. Leipzig: Veit, 1916.

Pringsheim, F. *The Greek Law of Sale*. Weimar: H. Böhlaus Nachfolger, 1950.

Pulitanò, F. *De eo quod certo loco*. Milan: Giuffrè, 2009.

Purcell, N. "The Ancient Mediterranean: The View from the Customs House." In *Rethinking the Mediterranean: Papers from a Conference Organized by the Columbia University Center for the Ancient Mediterranean, September 21–22, 2001*, edited by W. V. Harris, 200–232. Oxford: Oxford University Press, 2005.

Purcell, N. "Taxing the Sea." In *The Sea in History—the Ancient World*, edited by P. Arnaud and P. de Souza, 319–34. Woodbridge, UK: Boydell & Brewer, 2017.

Purpura, G. "Review of Pontoriero, I., *Il prestito marittimo in diritto romano* (Bologna: Bonomia, 2011)." *IVRA* 62 (2014): 410–18.

Purpura, G. "Ricerche in tema di prestito marittimo." *AUPA* 39 (1987): 187–336. (= "Ricerche in tema di prestito marittimo." In *Studi romanistici in tema di diritto commerciale marittimo*, 91–240. Soveria Mannelli: Rubbettino, 1996).

Purpura, G. "Roman Documentation concerning Shipping in Bulk." In *Roman Law and Maritime Commerce*, edited by P. Candy and E. Mataix Ferrándiz, 109–36. Edinburgh: Edinburgh University Press, 2022.

Quinn, J. C. *In Search of the Phoenicians*. Princeton: Princeton University Press, 2018.

Rathbone, D. W. "The Financing of Maritime Commerce in the Roman Empire I–II AD." In *Credito e moneta nel mondo romano: Atti degli Incontri capresi di storia dell'economia antica (Capri 12–14 ottobre 2000)*, edited by E. Lo Cascio, 197–229. Bari: Edipuglia, 2003.

Rathbone, D. W. "Maritime Loans." In *The Oxford Classical Dictionary*, 4th ed., edited by S. Hornblower, A. Spawforth, and E. Eidinow. Oxford: Oxford University Press, 2012.

Rathbone, D. W. "Merchant Networks in the Greek World: The Impact of Rome." *Mediterranean Historical Review* 22, no. 2 (2007): 309–20.

Rathbone, D. W. "The 'Muziris' Papyrus (SB XVIII 13167): Financing Roman Trade with India." *Bulletin de la Société archéologique d'Alexandrie* 46 (2000): 39–50.

Ray, D. *Development Economics*. Princeton: Princeton University Press, 1998.

Reed, C. M. *Maritime Traders in the Ancient Greek World*. Cambridge: Cambridge University Press, 2003.

Reinoso Barbero, F. "El foenus nauticum de Calímaco." In *Scritti in onore di Arnaldo Biscardi*, edited by F. Pastori, 5:297–310. Milan: Istituto Editoriale Cisalpino, La Goliardica, 1984.

Rennie, W., ed. *Demosthenis Orationes*. Vol. 2, pt. 2, *Orationes XXVII–XL*. Oxford: Clarendon Press, 1921.

Rescher, N. *Cosmos and Logos: Studies in Greek Philosophy*. Frankfurt: Ontos Verlag, 2005.

Riccobono, S., Jr. "Profilo storico della dottrina della mora nel diritto romano." *AUPA* 29 (1962): 105–471.
Riccobono, S. "Stipulatio ed instrumentum nel Diritto giustinianeo." *ZRG RA* 43 (1922): 262–397. (= *Corso di diritto romano: Stipulationes, contractus, pacta.* Milan: Giuffrè, 1935).
Rice, C. "Mercantile Specialization and Trading Communities: Economic Strategies in Roman Maritime Trade." In *Urban Craftsmen and Traders in the Roman World*, edited by A. I. Wilson and M. Flohr, 97–114. Oxford: Oxford University Press, 2016.
Richardson, M. E. J. *Hammurabi's Laws: Text, Translation and Glossary.* London: Bloomsbury, 2004.
Riggsby, A. M. "For Whom the Clock Drips." *Arethusa* 42, no. 3 (2009): 271–78.
Robert, J. *Receptae iuris Civilis lectionis, libri II.* Helmstadt: Lucius, 1586.
Robert, L. *Études épigraphiques et philologiques.* Paris: Champion, 1938.
Robertis, F. M. de. "Sulla cronologia degli scritti giuristi classici." *Rivista italiana per le scienze giuridiche*, n.s. 15 (1940): 205–26. (= *Scritti varii di diritto romano (articoli da riviste e miscelanee). II: Storia del diritto. Diritto pubblico. Epigrafia giuridica*, 143–66. Bari: Cacucci, 1987).
Röhle, R. "Zum Beispiel D. 22,2,6." *SDHI* 45 (1979): 549–68.
Rostovtzeff, M. I. "Foreign Commerce of Ptolemaic Egypt." *Journal of Economic and Business History* 4, no. 4 (1932): 728–69.
Rotondi, G. "Natura contractus." *BIDR* 24 (1911): 1–115. (= "Natura contractus." In *Scritti giuridici.* Vol. 2, 159–267. Milan: Ulrico Hoepli, 1922).
Rougé, J. "Le Philogélôs et la navigation." *Journal des Savants* 1–2 (1987): 3–12.
Rougé, J. "Prêt et société maritimes dans le monde romain." In *The Seaborne Commerce of Ancient Rome: Studies in Archaeology and History*, edited by J. H. D'Arms and E. C. Kopff, 291–303. Rome: American Academy in Rome, 1980.
Rougé, J. *Recherches sur l'organisation du commerce maritime en Méditerranée sous l'Empire romain.* Paris: S.E.V.P.E.N., 1966.
Rovira Guardiola, R. "El Archivo Sulpicio y los tituli picti β: Circulación de comerciantes en el Mediterráneo." In *Acta XII congressus internationalis epigraphiae graecae et latinae (Barcelona, 3–8 Septembris 2002)*, edited by M. Mayer i Olivé, G. Baratta, and A. Guzmán Almagro, 1263–68. Barcelona: Institut d'Estudis Catalans, 2007.
Sacconi, G. *La 'pluris petitio' nel processo formulare.* Milan: Giuffrè, 1977.
Samter, R. "Das Verhältnis zwischen Scaevolas Digesten und Responsen." *ZRG RA* 27 (1906): 151–210.
Sancinito, J. *The Reputation of the Roman Merchant.* Ann Arbor: University of Michigan Press, 2024.
Santoro, R. "Le due formule della Tabula Pompeiana 34." *AUPA* 38 (1985): 333–50.
Saprykin, S. "The Pontic Proxenies and the Sea Routes of the Ancient Greeks in the Euxine." *International Journal of Maritime History* 26, no. 2 (2014): 353–63.
Savigny, F. C. von. *System des heutigen Römischen Rechts.* 6 vols. Berlin: Veit, 1847.
Schaefer, A. *Demosthenes und seine Zeit.* Vol. III:2. Leipzig: Teubner, 1885.
Schanbacher, D. "Zu Ursprung und Entwicklung des römischen Pfandrechts." *ZRG RA* 123 (2006): 49–70.
Scheuble, S. "Bemerkungen zu den μισθοφόροι und τακτόμισθοι im ptolemäischen Ägypten." In ". . . *vor dem Papyrus sind alle gleich!" Papyrologische Beiträge zu Ehren*

von Bärbel Kramer (P. Kramer) = ArchPF, edited by R. Eberhard, 213–22. Berlin: De Gruyter, 2009.

Schiller, A. A. *Roman Law: Mechanisms of Development*. The Hague: De Gruyter, 1978.

Schmidlin, B. "Horoi, pithana und regulae—zum Einfluß der Rhetorik und Kialektik auf die juristische Regelbildung." In *Aufstieg und Niedergang der römischen Welt*, edited by H. Temporini and W. Haase, II:15:101–30. Berlin: De Gruyter, 1976.

Schulz, F. *History of Roman Legal Science*. Oxford: Oxford University Press, 1946.

Schulz, F. "Überlieferungsgeschichte der Responsa des Cervidius Scaevola." In *Symbolae Friburgenses in honorem Ottonis Lenel*. Leipzig: Tauchnitz, 1931.

Schuster, S. *Das Seedarlehen in den Gerichtsreden des Demosthenes: Mit einem Ausblick auf die weitere historische Entwicklung des Rechtsinstitutes; Dáneion nautikón, fenus nauticum und Bodmerei*. Berlin: Duncker & Humblot, 2005.

Schwarz, A. B. *Die öffentliche und private Urkunde im römischen Ägypten: Studien zum hellenistischen Privatrecht*. Leipzig: Sächsischen Akademie der Wissenschaften, 1920.

Schwarz, F. *Die Grundlage der Condictio im klassischen römischen Recht*. Münster: Böhlau, 1952.

Seidl, E. "Juristische Papyruskunde." *SDHI* 24 (1958): 397–450.

Seidl, E. "Review of Bieżuńska-Małowist, I., and H. Kupiszewski, *Symbolae Raphaeli Taubenschlag dedicatae*, 2 (Warsaw: Ossolineum, 1956–57)." *SDHI* 23 (1957): 358–62.

Shelton, J. C. "Two Contracts of Loan from the Michigan Papyrus Collection." *JJP* 18 (1974): 157–62.

Siber, H. "Interpellatio und Mora." *ZRG RA* 29 (1908): 47–113.

Sicari, A. *Pena convenzionale e responsabilità*. Bari: Cacucci, 2001.

Sickinger, J. "Literacy, Documents, and Archives in the Ancient Athenian Democracy." *American Archivist* 62, no. 2 (1999): 229–46.

Sidebotham, S. E. *Berenike and the Ancient Maritime Spice Route*. Los Angeles: University of California Press, 2011.

Sieveking, H. *Das Seedarlehen des Altertums*. Leipzig: Veit, 1893.

Sirks, A. J. B. "Chirographs in Roman Law: Constitutive or Evidential." *TvR* 91 (2023): 93–114.

Sirks, A. J. B. "Chirographs: Negotiable Instruments?" *ZRG RA* 133 (2016): 265–85.

Sirks, A. J. B. "The Food Distributions in Rome and Constantinople: Imperial Power and Continuity." In *Herrschaftsstrukturen und Herrschaftspraxis: Konzepte, Prinzipien und Strategien der Administration im römischen Kaiserreich*, edited by A. Kolb, 35–44. Berlin: Akademie Verlag, 2006.

Sirks, A. J. B. "Sailing in the Off-Season with Reduced Financial Risk." In *Speculum Iuris: Roman Law as a Reflection of Social and Economic Life in Antiquity*, edited by J.-J. Aubert and A. J. B. Sirks, 134–50. Ann Arbor: University of Michigan Press, 2002.

Souza, P. de. *Piracy in the Graeco-Roman World*. Cambridge: Cambridge University Press, 1999.

Steinwenter, A. *Die Streitbeendigung durch Urteil, Schiedsspruch und Vergleich nach griechischem Recht*. Munich: C.H. Beck, 1925.

Stolfi, E. "Prinzipat." In *Handbuch des Römischen Privatrechts*, edited by U. Babusiaux, C. Baldus, W. Ernst, F.-S. Meissel, J. Platschek, and T. Rüfner, 1:54–74. Tübingen: Mohr Siebeck, 2023.

Strauss, Julia. "Shipwrecks Database." 2013. oxrep.classics.ox.ac.uk/databases/shipwrecks_database/

Sundahl, M. J. "Secured Credit in Athens: Reopening the Debate." In *Symposion 2013: Vorträge zur griechischen und hellenistischen Rechtsgeschichte (Cambridge MA, 26.-29. August 2013)*, edited by M. Gagarin and A. Lanni, 223–38. Vienna: VÖAW, 2014.

Talamanca, M. *Dike ouk eisagogimos: Contributi allo studio del processo attico*. Edited by A. Maffi. Vienna: VÖAW, 2017.

Talamanca, M. "I clienti di Q. Cervidio Scevola." *BIDR* 42 (2000): 483–701.

Talamanca, M. "I 'Pithana' di Labeone e la logica stoica." *IVRA* 26 (1975): 1–40.

Talamanca, M. "Rec. di 'Festschrift für Erwin Seidl zum 70. Geburtstag.'" *BIDR* 82 (1979): 273–96.

Tanev, K. "The Real Securities in the Agreement on the 'traiecticia pecunia.'" *Orbis Iuris Romani* 4 (1998): 76–84.

Tanev, K. "Some Highlights on the Problem of 'Maritime Loans.'" In *Règle et pratique du droit dans les réalités juridiques de l'antiquité*, edited by I. Piro, 537–44. Soveria Mannelli: Rubbettino, 1999.

Tarwacka, A. *European Legal Culture through the Prism of Jokes: The Example of the Philogelos*. Wrocław: Europe of Nations and Freedom, 2018.

Tchernia, A. "Dreams of Wealth, Loans, and Seaborne Trade." In *The Romans and Trade*, translated by J. Grieve and E. Minchin, 131–39. Oxford: Oxford University Press, 2016.

Tchernia, A. "Landowners and Traders." In *The Romans and Trade*, translated by J. Grieve and E. Minchin, 10–37. Oxford: Oxford University Press, 2016.

Tchernia, A. "Le plebiscitum Claudianum." In *Vocabulaire et expression de l'économie dans le monde antique*, edited by J. Andreau and V. Chankowski, 253–78. Bordeaux: Ausonius, 2007.

Tchernia, A. *The Romans and Trade*. Translated by J. Grieve and E. Minchin. Oxford: Oxford University Press, 2016.

Tchernia, A. "Wine Exporting and the Exception of Gaul." In *The Romans and Trade*, translated by J. Grieve and E. Minchin, 277–96. Oxford: Oxford University Press, 2016.

Terpstra, T. T. *Trade in the Ancient Mediterranean: Private Order and Public Institutions*. Princeton: Princeton University Press, 2019.

Thomas, J. A. C. "Pithanon Labeonis a Paulo Epitomatorum Libri VIII." In *Daube Noster: Essays in Legal History for David Daube*, edited by A. Watson, 317–25. Edinburgh: Scottish Academic Press, 1974.

Thompson, W. E. "An Athenian Commercial Case: Demosthenes 34." *TvR* 48, no. 2 (1980): 137–50.

Thompson, W. E. "The Athenian Entrepreneur." *L'Antiquité Classique* 51 (1982): 53–85.

Thür, G. "Arnaldo Biscardi e il diritto greco: (riflessioni sul prestito marittimo SB VI 9571)." *Dike* 3 (2000): 177–86.

Thür, G. *Beweisführung vor den Schwurgerichtshöfen Athens: Die Proklesis zur Basanos*. Vienna: VÖAW, 1977.

Thür, G. "'Der Sturm' in der Rede gegen Zenothemis (Dem. 32)." In *Dike: Essays on Greek Law in Honor of Alberto Maffi*, edited by L. Gagliardi and L. Pepe, 315–31. Milan: Giuffrè Francis Lefebvre, 2019.

Thür, G. "Die Aestimationsabrede im Seefrachtvertrag: Diskussionsbeitrag zum Referat Dimitri C. Gofas." In *Symposion 1993: Vorträge zur griechischen und hellenistischen Rechtsgeschichte (Graz-Andritz, 12–16 September 1993)*, edited by G. Thür, 267–71. Vienna: Böhlau, 1994.

Thür, G. "Griechische Zivilverfahren." In *Handbuch zur Geschichte der Konfliktlösung in Europa*, edited by N. Grotkamp and A. Seelentag, 1: Konfliktlösung in der Antike, 207–18. Heidelberg: Springer, 2019.

Thür, G. "Hypotheken-Urkunde eines Seedarlehens für eine Reise nach Muziris und Apographe für die Tetarte in Alexandria: (zu P. Vindob. G. 40.822)." *Tyche* 2 (1987): 229–45.

Thür, G. "Kannte das altgriechische Recht die Eigentumsdiadikasie?" In *Symposion 1977: Vorträge zur griechischen und hellenistischen Rechtsgeschichte (Chantilly, 1.-4. June 1977)*, edited by J. E. Modrzejewski and D. Liebs, 55–69. Cologne: Böhlau, 1982.

Thür, G. "Law and Rhetoric in Commercial Shipwreck Cases: Isolating the Facts." In *Ιουλίαν Βελισσαροπούλου Ἐπαινέσαι: Studies in Ancient Greek and Roman Law*, edited by A. A. Dimopoulou, A. Helmis, and D. Karambelas, 289–97. Athens: ΕΛΛΗΝΙΚΗ ΕΠΙΓΡΑΦΙΚΗ ΕΤΑΙΡΕΙΑ, 2020.

Thür, G. "Ownership and Secured Credit in Athens: A Response to Mark J. Sundahl." In *Symposion 2013: Vorträge zur griechischen und hellenistischen Rechtsgeschichte (Cambridge MA, 26.-29. August 2013)*, edited by M. Gagarin and A. Lanni, 239–48. Vienna: VÖAW, 2014.

Thür, G. "The Phrase Καθάπερ Ἐκ Δίκης in Greek and Hellenistic Documents." In *Our Beloved Polites: Studies Presented to Peter J. Rhodes*, edited by D. F. Leão, D. Ferreira, N. Simões Rodrigues, and R. Morais, 191–206. Oxford: Archaeopress, 2022.

Thür, G. "The Principle of Fairness in Athenian Legal Procedure: Thoughts on the Echinos and Enklema." *Dike* 11 (2008): 51–73.

Thür, G. "Review of Michael Gagarin, Writing Greek Law (Cambridge, 2008)." *ZRG RA* 126 (2009): 482–94.

Thür, G. "Sachverfolgung und Diebstahl in den griechischen Poleis (Dem. 32, Lys. 23, IC IV 72 I, IPArk 32 u. 17)." In *Symposion 1999: Vorträge zur griechischen und hellenistischen Rechtsgeschichte (Pazo de Mariñán, La Coruña, 6.-9. September 1999)*, edited by G. Thür and F. J. Fernández Nieto, 57–96. Cologne: Böhlau, 2003.

Thür, G. "Zum Seedarlehen κατὰ Μουζεῖριν. P. Vindob. G 40822." *Tyche* 3 (1988): 229–33.

Todd, S. C. *The Shape of Athenian Law*. Oxford: Clarendon Press, 1993.

Townshend, J. R. "Lex Claudia." In *The Oxford Classical Dictionary*, 4th ed., edited by S. Hornblower, A. Spawforth, and E. Eidinow. Oxford: Oxford University Press, 2012.

Tuori, K. "The ius respondendi and the Freedom of Roman Jurisprudence." *RIDA* 51 (2004): 295–337.

Vacek, A. "Ugarit, Al Mina, and Coastal North Syria." In *A Companion to the Archaeology of Early Greece and the Mediterranean*, edited by A. Kotsonas and I. S. Lemos, 1163–84. Newark, NY: John Wiley & Sons, 2020.

Van den Bergh, G. C. J. J. *Die holländische elegante Schule: Ein Beitrag zur Geschichte von Humanismus und Rechtswissenschaft in den Niederlanden 1500–1800*. Frankfurt: Klostermann, 2002.

Van Oven, J. C. "Les actions issues de la stipulation." *TvR* 27, no. 4 (1959): 391–411.

Varvaro, M. "Stipulationsklage mit unbestimmten (actio ex stipulatu) und bestimmten Klageinhalt (condictio)." In *Handbuch des Römischen Privatrechts*, edited by U. Babusiaux, C. Baldus, W. Ernst, F.-S. Meissel, J. Platschek, and T. Rüfner, 2:1927–37. Tübingen: Mohr Siebeck, 2023.

Veenhof, K. R., and J. Eidem. *Mesopotamia: The Old Assyrian Period*. Göttingen: Vandenhoeck & Ruprecht, 2008.

Vélissaropoulos-Karakostas, J. *Λόγοι Ευθύνης. Ιστορική γένεση και σύγχρονη αμφισβήτηση των πηγών της ενοχικής δεσμεύσεως*. Athens: Ant. Sakkoulas, 1993.

Vélissaropoulos-Karakostas, J. *Les nauclères grecs: Recherches sur les institutions maritimes en Grèce et dans l'Orient hellénisé*. Geneva: Droz; Paris: Minard, 1980.

Verboven, K. "Capital Markets and Financial Entrepreneurs in the Roman World." In *Capital, Investment, and Innovation in the Roman World*, edited by P. Erdkamp, K. Verboven, and A. Zuiderhoek, 381–416. Oxford: Oxford University Press, 2020.

Verboven, K. *The Economy of Friends: Economic Aspects of Amicitia and Patronage in the Late Republic*. Brussels: Latomus, 2002.

Verboven, K. "The Sulpicii from Puteoli and Usury in the Early Roman Empire." *TvR* 71 (2003): 7–28.

Verhagen, H. L. E. "Chirographs in Classical Roman Law: Constitutive or Probative?" *RIDA* 65 (2018): 251–306.

Verhagen, H. L. E. *Security and Credit in Roman Law: The Historical Evolution of Pignus and Hypotheca*. Oxford: Oxford University Press, 2022.

Vinogradoff, P. *Outlines of Historical Jurisprudence*. Vol. II, *The Jurisprudence of the Greek City*. Oxford: Oxford University Press, 1922.

Voci, P. "La responsabilità del debitore da 'stipulatio poenae.'" In *Studi in onore di Edoardo Volterra*, edited by L. Aru and G. Astuti, 3:319–58. Milan: Giuffrè, 1971.

Wacke, A. "Athleten als Darlehensnehmer nach römischen Recht." *SDHI* 44 (1978): 439–52.

Wacke, A. "Das nach siegreich bestandenem Wettkampf zurückzuzahlende Athleten-Darlehen: Eine Entgegnung auf Éva Jakab." *RIDA* 64 (2017).

Watson, A. *Law Making in the Later Roman Republic*. Oxford: Oxford University Press, 1974.

Watson, A. *The Law of Obligations in the Later Roman Republic*. Oxford: Oxford University Press, 1965.

Wilcken, U. "Punt-Fahrten in der Ptolemäerzeit." *Zeitschrift für ägyptische Sprache und Altertumskunde* 60 (1925): 86–102.

Wilhelm, A. "Papyrus Tebtunis 33." *JRS* 27 (1937): 145–51.

Willems, C. "Formularprozess: Vollstreckung." In *Handbuch des Römischen Privatrechts*, edited by U. Babusiaux, C. Baldus, W. Ernst, F.-S. Meissel, J. Platschek, and T. Rüfner, 1:476–91. Tübingen: Mohr Siebeck, 2023.

Wilson, A. I. "Developments in Mediterranean Shipping and Maritime Trade from the Hellenistic Period to AD 1000." In *Maritime Archaeology and Ancient Trade in the Mediterranean*, edited by D. Robinson and A. I. Wilson, 33–59. Oxford: Oxford Centre for Maritime Archaeology, 2011.

Wilson, A. I. "Red Sea Trade and the State." In *Across the Ocean: Nine Essays on Indo-*

Mediterranean Trade, edited by F. De Romanis and M. Maiuro, 13–32. Leiden: Brill, 2015.

Wolf, J. G. "Aus dem neuen pompejanischen Urkundenfund: Der Seefrachtvertrag des Menelaos." *Freiburger Universitätsblätter* 65 (1979): 23–36.

Wolf, J. G. "Aus dem neuen pompejanischen Urkundenfund: Die 'naulotike' des Menelaos—Seedarlehen oder Seefrachtvertrag?" In *Iuris vincula: Studi in onore di Mario Talamanca*, 423–63. Naples: Jovene, 2001.

Wolf, J. G. *Neue Rechtsurkunden aus Pompeji: Tabulae Pompeianae Novae*. Darmstadt: WBG, 2010.

Wolff, H. J. "Demosthenes as Advocate: The Functions and Methods of Legal Consultants in Classical Athens." In *The Attic Orators*, edited by E. Carawan, translated by J. Miner, 91–115. Oxford: Oxford University Press, 2007.

Wolff, H. J. *Die attische Paragraphe: Ein Beitrag zum Problem der Auflockerung archaischer Prozessformen*. Weimar: Böhlau, 1966.

Wolff, H. J. "The Praxis-Provision in Papyrus Contracts." *TAPhA* 72 (1941): 418–38.

Wolff, H. J. "Some Observations on Praxis." In *Proceedings of the Twelfth International Congress of Papyrology (Ann Arbor, Michigan, 13–17 August 1968)*, edited by D. H. Samuel, 527–35. Toronto: Hackert, 1970.

Woodard, Roger D. *Greek Writing from Knossos to Homer: A Linguistic Interpretation of the Origin of the Greek Alphabet and the Continuity of Ancient Greek Literacy*. Oxford: Oxford University Press, 1997.

Woolmer, M. "The Athenian Mercantile Community: A Reappraisal of the Social, Political, and Legal Status of Inter-Regional Merchants during the Fourth Century." PhD diss., Cardiff University, 2008.

Woolmer, M. "Emporoi Kai Nauklēroi: Redefining Commercial Roles in Classical Greece." *JAH* 3, no. 2 (2015): 150–72.

Woolmer, M. *A Short History of the Phoenicians*. 2nd ed. London: Bloomsbury, 2021.

Wooten, C. W. "Cicero and Quintilian on the Style of Demosthenes." *Rhetorica: A Journal of the History of Rhetoric* 15, no. 2 (1997): 177–92.

Young, G. K. *Rome's Eastern Trade: International Commerce and Imperial Policy, 31 BC-AD 305*. London: Routledge, 2001.

Youtie, H. C. "Notes on Papyri." *TAPhA* 91 (1960): 239–71.

Zamora Manzano, J. L. "Algunas notas en relación a los antecedentes romanos del seguro marítimo como desviación de la 'pecunia traiecticia.'" *BIDR* 39 (1997): 671–83.

Žiha, N. "The Insurance Function of Roman Maritime Loan." In *Maritime Risk Management: Essays on the History of Marine Insurance, General Average and Sea Loan*, edited by P. Hellwege and G. Rossi, 35–60. Berlin: Duncker & Humblot, 2021.

Ziliotto, P. "Dolo e iniuria nella pro Tullio di Cicerone." *BIDR* (2017–18): 133–48.

Zimmermann, R. *The Law of Obligations: Roman Foundations of the Civilian Tradition*. Cape Town: Juta, 1990.

Index Locorum

Note: Italicized page numbers indicate substantive discussion of the passage.

Epigraphic Sources

Papyri

General Index

Note: Italicized page numbers indicate substantive discussion of the topic.

Printed and bound by CPI Group (UK) Ltd, Croydon, CR0 4YY

16/09/2026

14963487-0003